£35

D0302964

POLITICAL SOCIETY IN LANCASTRIAN ENGLAND

The Greater Gentry
of Nottinghamshire

SIMON PAYLING

CLARENDON PRESS · OXFORD
1991

Oxford University Press, Walton Street, Oxford OX2 6DP

Oxford New York Toronto
Delhi Bombay Calcutta Madras Karachi
Petaling Jaya Singapore Hong Kong Tokyo
Nairobi Dar es Salaam Cape Town
Melbourne Auckland
and associated companies in
Berlin Ibadan

Oxford is a trade mark of Oxford University Press

Published in the United States
by Oxford University Press, New York

© Simon Payling 1991

British Library Cataloguing in Publication Data
Payling, Simon
Political society in Lancastrian England: the greater
gentry of Nottinghamshire—(Oxford historical
monographs).
1. Nottinghamshire. Gentry, 1399–1485
305.5232094252
ISBN 0–19–820209–1

Library of Congress Cataloging in Publication Data
Payling, Simon.
Political society in Lancastrian England: the greater gentry of
Nottinghamshire / Simon Payling.
p. cm.—(Oxford historical monographs)
Includes bibliographical references and index.
1. Great Britain—Politics and government—1399–1485. 2. England—
Social conditions—Medieval period, 1066–1485. 3. Nottinghamshire
(England)—Politics and government. 4. Nottinghamshire (England)—
Social conditions. 5. Nottinghamshire (England)—Gentry.
I. Title. II. Series.
DA245.P39 1991 942.5′204′08621—dc20 90–40420
ISBN 0–19–820209–1

Typeset by Hope Services (Abingdon) Ltd.
Printed and bound in
Great Britain by Bookcraft Ltd.,
Midsomer Norton, Bath

To
MY PARENTS

PREFACE

THIS book is an addition to the rapidly expanding corpus of work on the gentry of late-medieval England and as such it follows earlier work in taking as its principal themes the role of the gentry in county government, their relations with the crown, the nobility, and each other, and their involvement in local disorder. It differs only in perspective. These themes are examined against the background neither of the gentry community as a whole nor of a handful of families chosen for archival reasons, but rather from the standpoint of the dozen or so wealthiest county families. These families formed an élite amongst the county gentry: an élite that gained in definition as the later medieval period progressed. The individual histories of the families that at any one time composed it demonstrate a significant tendency for the frequent failure of the landowning families in the male line (and the consequent transmission of their estates to other families), combined with the great profits available to the late-medieval careerist, most notably the lawyer, to bring about a concentration of wealth in the hands of fewer families. As this wealth became increasingly concentrated, county administration and representation became more exclusively the preserve of the greater shire gentry, and it was they, distinguished from the bulk of their gentry neighbours by their wealth, who were the natural recipients of royal and baronial patronage. This patronage in turn reinforced their pre-eminent position in local affairs.

This, at least, is the picture conveyed by a study of political society in Nottinghamshire during the Lancastrian period and documented in the pages that follow. It should not, however, be imagined that there is any such thing as a typical late-medieval English county, and the concentration of this work on the wealth and power of a devolving county élite may be inappropriate in the context of other counties. There are certainly some grounds for thinking that this is so. Lancastrian Nottinghamshire was a county with a low index of both church and baronial wealth, and this may have served to give the greater gentry as a class a prominence in the county that they did not enjoy in the country at large. On the other hand, Nottinghamshire was not the only county in which the gentry enjoyed landed pre-eminence. Indeed, in this the county was probably more typical than atypical of England as a whole. Moreover, there can be little doubt that the dynamics of the process by which the leading gentry became more clearly delineated from their lesser gentry neighbours were general. This work is offered in the hope that an emphasis on the wealth and political independence of the families that this process had pushed to the forefront of county affairs can contribute to a greater understanding of English political society.

If this hope is realized much will be due to the advice and encouragement I have received, first in compiling the thesis on which this book is based, and second in turning the thesis into a book. My two principal academic debts are to T. B. Pugh, who first introduced me to the fifteenth century and has since been a constant source of help and inspiration, and Dr G. L. Harriss, who supervised my thesis with kindness, perception, and patience. I have also benefited much from the comments of Dr M. H. Keen and my thesis examiners, Dr J. R. Maddicott and Professor R. A. Griffiths. That the thesis ever became a book is due to the generosity of Balliol College, which elected me to the junior research fellowship which bears the name of Sir Lewis Namier. My greatest debt is, however, to my parents, who have in the past made most things possible. It is to them that this book is dedicated.

CONTENTS

LIST OF FIGURES

LIST OF TABLES

ABBREVIATIONS

(for full details see Select Bibliography)

BIHR	*Bulletin of the Institute of Historical Research*
BL	British Library
CAD	*Descriptive Catalogue of Ancient Deeds*
C. Ch. R.	*Calendar of Charter Rolls*
CCR	*Calendar of Close Rolls*
CFR	*Calendar of Fine Rolls*
Cal. Inq. Misc.	*Calendar of Inquisitions Miscellaneous*
CIPM	*Calendar of Inquisitions Post Mortem*
CPR	*Calendar of Patent Rolls*
CP	*Complete Peerage*
DKR	*Deputy Keeper's Report*
EHR	*English Historical Review*
FA	*Inquisitions and Assessments Relating to Feudal Aids*
HMC	Historical Manuscripts Commission
NMS	*Nottingham Medieval Studies*
Notts. IPM	*Abstracts of the Inquisitions Post Mortem Relating to Nottingham-shire*
Notts. Visit.	*The Visitations of the County of Nottingham in the Years 1569 and 1614*
NRO	Nottinghamshire Record Office
NUL	Nottingham University Library
Payling	S. J. Payling, 'Political Society in Lancastrian Nottinghamshire' D.Phil. thesis (Oxford, 1987)
PC	*Plumpton Correspondence*
PPC	*Proceedings and Ordinances of the Privy Council of England*
PRO	Public Record Office
RP	*Rotuli Parliamentorum*
Somerville	R. Somerville, *History of the Duchy of Lancaster, i. 1265–1603*
SR	*Statutes of the Realm*
TE	*Testamenta Eboracensia*
Thoroton	R. Thoroton, *The Antiquities of Nottinghamshire*
TRHS	*Transactions of the Royal Historical Society*
TSRS	Thoroton Society Record Series
TTS	*Transactions of the Thoroton Society*
VCH	Victoria County History
Wright	S. M. Wright, *The Derbyshire Gentry in the Fifteenth Century*

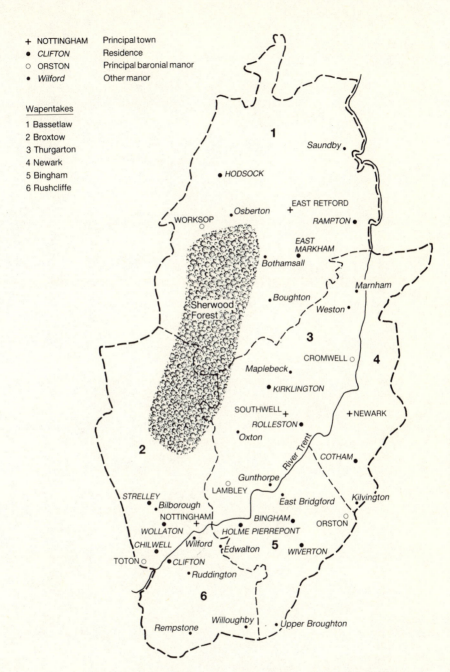

1

Saundby ●

● HODSOCK

EAST RETFORD
+
Osberton ● RAMPTON ●

WORKSOP ○

EAST
MARKHAM

● *Bothamsall*

Marnham ●

● *Boughton*

Sherwood
Forest

Weston ●

3

CROMWELL ○ **4**

Maplebeck ●

● KIRKLINGTON

SOUTHWELL + + NEWARK

ROLLESTON ●

Oxton ●

COTHAM ●

River Trent

2

Gunthorpe ●

LAMBLEY ○

Kilvington ●

STRELLEY
● *Bilborough*

East Bridgford ●

NOTTINGHAM ●

BINGHAM ●

ORSTON ○

WOLLATON

† *Edwalton*

HOLME PIERREPONT

CHILWELL *Wilford*

5 *WIVERTON* ●

TOTON ○ ● *CLIFTON*

● *Ruddington*

6

Rempstone ●

Willoughby ● *Upper Broughton*

Fig. 1. Residences of the leading Nottinghamshire families with their principal manors

I

THE BALANCE OF PROPERTY

In a society where the preponderant source of wealth is land, there is an obvious and direct relationship between political power and the ownership of real property. The immediacy of this relationship was first given open expression by James Harrington in his *Oceana* of 1656: 'As is the proportion of balance of Dominion or Property in Land, such is the nature of the Empire.'[1] It is seventeenth-century historians who have followed this theme most assiduously. Changes in the 'balance of property' lie at the heart of their protracted controversy over 'the rise of the gentry' provoked by Professor R. H. Tawney's famous article of 1941.[2] This controversy illustrates very clearly not only the difficulties, both qualitative and quantitative, inherent in measuring this balance and its change over time, but also the central importance of such measurement to the understanding of political society. The aim of what follows is to discuss what can be discovered about the balance of property between the baronage and the gentry in England, and more particularly in Nottinghamshire, during the first part of the fifteenth century. The conclusion that emerges suggests a need to revise the emphasis on the power of the baronage found in the work of those seventeenth-century writers such as Sir Walter Raleigh, who saw the late-medieval period as a golden age of baronial power,[3] and those modern historians whose emphasis on the political influence of the baronage has detracted from that of the gentry.

For the late-medievalist, any temptation to overstress the power of the baronage should long since have been dispelled by the figures Professor H. L. Gray abstracted from the comprehensive taxation returns of 1436. He calculated that there was a body of 183 non-baronial landholders, whom he dubbed the 'greater knights', whose share of the nation's

---

[1] H. F. Russell Smith, *Harrington and his Oceana* (Cambridge, 1914), 23.
[2] R. H. Tawney, 'The Rise of the Gentry, 1558–1640', *Economic History Review* 11 (1941), 1–38. The controversy is discussed in J. H. Hexter, 'Storm over the Gentry', in *Reappraisals in History* (London, 1961), 117–62.
[3] For Raleigh's views: ibid. 155–6.

wealth was only slightly inferior to that of the baronage. In percentage
terms, these 'greater knights', defined as landholders with an annual
income in excess of £100, possessed 19 per cent of the lay income from
land and annuities taxable in 1436 as against the 23 per cent of the
baronage (see Table 1.1).[4] This led him to conclude that the traditional
picture of a society dominated by the peerage was mistaken. In his view
the wealth and numbers of these 'greater knights' and the lesser gentry
beneath them gave the house of commons, in which they were
represented, an 'assurance of independence'.[5]

TABLE 1.1. *Income tax returns, 1436*

	Number	Total Income (£)	% of Whole	Average Income
Lay barons	51	45,000*	23.0	£882
Greater knights (more than £100)	183	38,000	19.4	£208
Lesser knights (£40–£100 p.a.)	750	45,200	23.0	£60
Esquires (£20–£39 p.a.)	1,200	29,400	15.0	£24 10s.
£10–£19 p.a.	1,600	19,200	19.6	£7 13s. 4d.
£5–£9 p.a.	3,400	19,200		
TOTAL	7,184	196,000	100.00	£27 6s.

* £39,708 from lands with at least £4,947 in annuities.

Despite the fact that this conclusion had a profound effect on the
work of the most distinguished of late-medievalists, K. B. McFarlane,[6]
it has never enjoyed general acceptance. In large part this is due to T. B.
Pugh's attack on the validity of Gray's statistics. He has shown that the
subsidy returns underestimated baronial wealth, while at the same time
exaggerating, in relative if not absolute terms, the wealth of the gentry:
not only were the incomes of baronial dowagers who had married into
the gentry assessed with the gentry, but, much more significantly, the
life annuities paid by the barons to the gentry, estimated by Pugh at a

[4] H. L. Gray, 'Incomes from Land in England in 1436', *EHR* 49 (1934), 630. The
percentages are my own calculations from Gray's figures.
[5] Ibid. 631.
[6] K. B. McFarlane, *The Nobility of Later Medieval England* (Oxford, 1973), p. xxii.

total of £7,000 per annum, were allowed to the barons as tax-free reprises and credited to the gentry as income.[7]

Too much weight has been attached to these necessary reservations. They are not enough to undermine Gray's basic conclusion that, in the England of 1436, the 'gentry' as a whole, very loosely defined as all lay, non-baronial landowners with an income of £5 per annum or more from freehold property, held a significantly greater percentage of the nation's wealth than their magnate superiors. In his figures, 77 per cent of all lay taxable income, in the hands of those with £5 per annum or more, was in the hands of the gentry as against only 23 per cent in those of the barons, a difference of such magnitude as to allow a considerable margin of error in the validity of the assumptions on which these calculations are based. Even if the 'gentry' are confined to those with £20 per annum or more, the minimum required income for a sheriff and later a justice of the peace,[8] and allowance is made for the transference of £7,000 from magnates to gentry in life annuities, their corporate wealth still exceeds that of the baronage, by more than two to one.

It is worth asking whether other fifteenth-century subsidy returns could not be exploited in a similar way, on a country- if not a nation-wide scale, to strengthen Gray's conclusions. The subsidy returns of 1451 seem at first to be the most promising area of enquiry for they are, theoretically at least, even more comprehensive than those of 1436, extending down to all lay landholders with £2 per annum in freehold or copyhold lands (or £3 per annum in the case of fees and wages). Yet the partial survival of particulars of account for individual counties means that few magnate assessments are available, and this, together with the extensive tax evasion that quite clearly took place (in 1436 the total assessable income of the whole country was £194,655; in 1451 it was only £157,605 despite the much greater comprehensiveness of the latter tax), renders these returns of limited value for such a purpose.[9] More useful are the 1412 returns, although these can only be used on county by county basis since landholders were assessed separately on their lands in each county rather than on their total landed wealth as they were in 1436 and 1451. A complete analysis is not possible because many of

[7] T. B. Pugh and C. D. Ross, 'The English Baronage and the Income Tax of 1436', *BIHR* 26 (1953), 1–28; T. B. Pugh, 'The Magnates, Knights and Gentry', in S. B. Chrimes, C. D. Ross, and R. A. Griffiths (eds.), *Fifteenth-Century England, 1399–1509* (Manchester, 1972), 97–101.

[8] For income qualifications for office, see below, p. 110.

[9] For the 1451 tax: R. Virgoe, 'The Parliamentary Subsidy of 1450', *BIHR* 55 (1982), 125–37.

the county returns are missing; yet, for those nineteen counties for which complete returns do survive, the 1412 assessments give an excellent insight into the social structure of the higher reaches of county society (the tax threshold being as high as £20 per annum) and a splendid opportunity to look at the comparative extent of the land-holdings of the barons and the more substantial gentry.[10] It is surprising that only McFarlane has used them in any considered way in print. He was able to demonstrate from them how wealthy were various west country knights, most notably Sir Humphrey Stafford (d. 1413) of Hooke in Dorset, and this led him to question the political dependence of such men on their baronial superiors.[11]

A detailed analysis of the Nottinghamshire returns proves similarly revealing for it shows that a small group of the leading resident non-baronial landholders not only held a far greater proportion of the taxable lay wealth of the county than did the baronage, but were, on average, individually wealthier within the county. Only William, Lord Roos of Belvoir, assessed at £80 per annum, had sufficient lands in the county to rival the greatest Nottinghamshire knights, headed by Sir Thomas Chaworth, assessed at £92 per annum, in wealth within the county. Moreover, below this élite of greater knights, there was a larger body of lesser knights and distrainees (that is, non-knights with an income of £40 per annum or more, sufficient to make them liable to distraint of knighthood), whose corporate wealth rivalled that of the greater knights and exceeded that of the baronage (see Table 1.2). Overall, the baronage accounted for only 17.5 per cent of the county's taxable lay wealth compared with 54.2 per cent for the resident county gentry. The validity of these statistics depends very much on the relative, if not absolute, accuracy of the returns. Since the basic taxable unit was an income of £20 per annum, 6s. 8d. being payable on each multiple and nothing on fractions of that sum, there was a marked tendency for the subsidy commissioners, not only in Nottinghamshire but also in other counties, to round income assessments to a multiple of £20. But the effect of the

---

[10] The surviving county returns are published in *FA*, vi. 391–551, with the exception of Notts. (Appendix 1) and Rutland (E179/387/21). Other extant returns not to be found in *FA* are those for London (published in *Archaeological Journal*, 44 (1887), 56–82) and Coventry (E179/192/41). For the granting of the tax: *RP*, iii. 648–9. For the commissions for its collection, issued on 2 Jan. 1412: *CPR, 1408–13*, 378–81. For the full text of this commission: *FA*, vi. 391–2.

[11] K. B. McFarlane, 'Parliament and "Bastard Feudalism" ', *TRHS* 26 (1944), 65–79. See also M. J. Barber, 'Surrey and Sussex at the Opening of the Fifteenth Century, Based on the Land Tax Assessments of 1412', B. Litt. thesis (Oxford, 1949).

TABLE 1.2. *Nottinghamshire subsidy returns, 1412*

	No. of assessments	Total wealth (£)	Average per assessment (£)	Landed taxable wealth (%)*
Magnates	18	503	27.9	17.5
Greater knights	11	607	55.2	21.2
Lesser knights/ distrainees	26	593	22.8	20.7 } 54.2
Lesser gentry	24	353 6s. 8d.	14.7	12.3
Royal annuities and farms	7	170 13s. 4d.	24.4	—
Unidentified/ illegible	3	34	—	—
Non-resident, non-baronial landholders	38	810 13s. 4d.	21.3	28.3
TOTAL	127	3,071 13s. 4d.		

Note: See Appendix 1 for the figures on which this table is based and the principles on which the assessees have been divided between the categories of 'greater knights', 'lesser knights/distrainees', and 'lesser gentry'.

* i.e. percentage of total less 'unidentified/illegible' and 'annuities'.

apparent rounding down (or possibly rounding up, though given the nature of taxation returns this seems unlikely) of assessments should be felt more or less equally on the total assessed wealth of the barons, greater knights, and others. Nor is it likely that the selective inclusion of some of those with less than £20 per annum in the county has much of a distorting effect. It appears that such landholders were only included if the commissioners knew them to hold lands in other counties, and hence their inclusion would be expected to exaggerate the relative wealth of the non-resident landholders, but an analysis of the returns shows that this effect was not very significant: assessments of under £20 per annum account for only £110 13s. 6d. of the £810 13s. 4d. assessed as in the hands of non-residents and this is more than counterbalanced by the £166 13s. 4d. they add to the wealth of the lesser gentry. The most impressive fact about the return is that it is extremely difficult to identify from other sources Nottinghamshire landowners worth £20 per annum or more in 1412 who escaped assessment. If there were a few they came from the class of lesser gentry and hence their possible omission (and it is unlikely that their total assessment was very great) can have no effect on the argument about the dominance of the gentry over the barons in county landholding. As far as baronial landholders are concerned, the only one to escape assessment was Joan (d. 1419), countess of Hereford, on her one-third of the manor of Arnold in Sherwood, worth no more than a few pounds.[12]

But what of the accuracy of the rounded assessments? Are we to assume that the only distortion in the individual assessments is this tendency to round down? This is a difficult question to answer with any certainty. Valuations in inquisitions *post mortem* are notoriously unreliable and of limited value for the sake of comparison. It can only be said that where a comparison can be made, the 1412 assessments are generally higher than the corresponding inquisition valuations. For example, on her death in 1435, Joan, Lady Beauchamp's soke of Oswaldbeck was valued at only 10 marks per annum[13] and yet she was assessed at £30 per annum in 1412; and Sir Geoffrey Scrope's manor of South Muskham and Carlton was valued at only £5 per annum on his death in 1418[14] compared with a 1412 assessment of £20 per annum. Occasionally, however, we can compare assessments with valuations drawn from contemporary *valors* or accounts, and this gives a much better idea of their accuracy. In 1412 Sir Roger Swillington and Sir John Eynesford were assessed between them at £83 on their manors of Bunny, Gonalston and Widmerpool, valued together at £70 11s. 8d. in a *valor* of 1429/30 when all three manors were in the hands of Ralph, Lord Cromwell;[15] while Sir William Bourchier was assessed at £40 on the manor of Kneesall valued at only £24 13s. 4d. in a contemporary *valor*.[16] A more extended comparison is that between the assessment of William, Lord Roos, at £80 and the accounts of William Heton from the period when the Roos estates were in royal hands after the death of William's son and heir, John, Lord Roos, in 1421. During the accounting year of 1422–3, the Roos manors of Orston, Eakring, Sutton-on-Trent, and Warsop

---

[12] Below, p. 221 n.3. Barber concluded from her analysis of the returns for the south-eastern counties that the commissioners made no 'flagrant omissions of persons or property': Barber, 'Surrey and Sussex', 17–18.

[13] *Notts. IPM, 1350–1436*, 200–1.   [14] Ibid. 163–4.

[15] For this *valor*: HMC, *Report on the Manuscripts of Lord De L'Isle and Dudley*, i (1925), 207–8.

[16] DL41/4/18 (this is a *valor* of the two purparties of the de Bohun inheritance: C. Rawcliffe, *The Staffords, Earls of Stafford and Dukes of Buckingham, 1394–1521* (Cambridge, 1978), 14 n. 18).

yielded a clear profit of just over £65, to which must be added, to give the
estate its full value, the £10 of annual rent paid to Geoffrey Paynell out
of the manor of Warsop and the value of the eight bovates of land in
Eakring assigned to John's widow, Margery, in dower. This gives a total
of just over £79.[17] These few comparisons at least give grounds for hope
that the 1412 assessments are reasonably accurate,[18] and can serve the
purpose for which they have been employed in Table 1.2.

Furthermore, the results set out in Table 1.2 gain some independent
confirmation from the returns of the holders of knights' fees made in
1428.[19] In March 1428 parliament voted a tax of 6s. 8d. per knight's
fee,[20] with no proportion of a knight's fee smaller than a quarter to be
taxed (i.e. £5 in 1412 terms), with an exemption for the church's tithable
possessions.[21] The Nottinghamshire returns, based like those for other
counties on the feudal aid returns of 1346, give a total of some 158 fees,
inclusive of the exempt fees, and these returns can be analysed wapentake
by wapentake under the same categories as those of 1412 (see Table
1.3). They show that, taking the county as a whole, of the knights' fees,
the church held 16 per cent, the nobility 13 per cent, the resident gentry
53 per cent, the non-resident, non-baronial landholders 17 per cent,
while the duchy of Lancaster (in the hands of the crown) retained 1 per
cent in its own hands. Such an analysis is less satisfactory than one based
on assessed income because a knight's fee can be assigned no exact
value, and yet it is true, as a general statement, that the wealthier the man
the greater would be the number of knights' fees he held.[22] It is hence
not without significance that the 1428 returns underline the fact that the
balance of property in Nottinghamshire lay very much in the favour of
the gentry; more particularly they confirm what the 1412 assessments so
clearly demonstrated, namely that, within this large class of gentry,
there was a small group of a dozen or so knightly families that were
distinguished by their wealth. As a body they possessed a greater
proportion of the county's wealth than the baronage: in 1412 they held
21.2 per cent of the taxable wealth of the county compared with the
baronage's 17.5 per cent, and in 1428 23 per cent of the knights' fees in
lay hands compared with the 15 per cent of the baronage.

---

[17] SC6/1121/13; *Notts. IPM, 1350–1436*, 171.

[18] For a similar analysis for the south-east: Barber, 'Surrey and Sussex', 9–11.

[19] For the Notts. returns: *FA*, iv. 125–39.

[20] In theoretical, if not practical, terms the same rate as the 1412 tax, since each knight's
fee had a notional nominal value of £20.   [21] *RP*, iv. 318.

[22] Cf. S. Painter, *Studies in the History of the English Feudal Barony* (Baltimore, 1943),
171.

TABLE 1.3. *Percentage of knights' fees in the hands of the church, nobility, and gentry, 1428*

	Rushcliffe	Bingham	Newark	Broxtow	Thurgarton and Lythe	Bassetlaw	Whole County
Fees (no.)	13	34	7	26	44	34	158
Religious houses (%)	5	27	14	17	20	6	16
Nobility (%)	3	12	0	14	14	20	13
Greater knights (%)	13	13	10	22	27	16	19
Lesser knights/ distrainees (%)	9	7	36	19	24	26	19
Lesser gentry (%)	18	13	24	25	9	15	15
Non-resident, noh-baronial landholders (%)	52	28	16	3	6	13	17
Duchy (%)	0	0	0	0	0	4	1

Note: Although they are included amongst the 26 Broxtow fees, I have excluded from the calculations the 8½ fees in Kirkby-in-Ashfield said to be in the king's hands by virtue of the minority of the daughters and heiresses of Sir Philip Darcy (d. 1418). The assessment of Kirkby at 8½ fees had been made by the commissioners purely in conformity to the returns of 1346, when Richard Willoughby, John, Lord Darcy, and John, Lord Grey of Codnor, had been returned as holding 10 fees in Bradmore, Barton, and Kirkby. They had complained that they each held by the service of only ½ fee: Bloom, pp. 148–9. In 1428 Willoughby was assessed at 1 fee in Bradmore and Grey at ½ fee in Barton; since Kirkby was in the hands of the crown it was easy for the commissioners to return the remaining 8½ fees under that place: *FA*, iv. 131.

Source: *FA*, iv. 125–39.

It should not be imagined, however, that this balance of property, particularly over such a comparatively small area as a single county, was static and unchanging even over a short period of time. The quantity of land in baronial hands was the most volatile largely due to the acquisitions made by Ralph (d. 1456), third Lord Cromwell. His gains were made chiefly at the expense of the non-resident gentry: in 1429 he inherited the manors of Widmerpool, Gonalston, and Bunny from the Belers heiress, Margaret, manors that had been in the hands of her husband, Sir John Gra of South Ingleby in Lincolnshire, in 1428, and in those of her father, Sir Roger Swillington and Sir Roger's step-father, Sir John Eynesford, in 1412; while, in 1441, he acquired a moiety of the manor of East Bridgford from his wife Margaret's childless cousin, Sir Robert Deincourt, who had held it in both 1412 and 1428.[23] Another who increased his estates at the expense of the non-resident gentry was

[23] Below, pp. 96–7.

Humphrey, earl of Stafford and afterwards first duke of Buckingham, who in 1438 inherited from his mother, Anne, countess of Stafford, the manor of Kneesall, which had been in the hands of Sir William Bourchier (d. 1420) in 1412. Five years earlier, in Michaelmas 1433, he had disseised his rival claimant for the Basset of Drayton inheritance, Sir Ralph Shirley (d. *c.*1443), of the manors of Colston Basset and Ratcliffe-on-Soar, a disseisin that proved to be permanent.[24] In the same year Henry (d. 1444), Lord Grey of Codnor, acquired the valuable manor of Dunham by his marriage to one of the two daughters and coheiresses of Sir Henry Percy (d. 1432) of Atholl, a manor which had been held by Elizabeth, widow of Sir John Scrope, in 1412.[25] Consequently, by the time of Grey's death in 1444, the quantity of land in baronial hands had significantly increased.

Yet it was not only the baronage who increased their share of the county's lands in the period before 1456; the small group of greater gentry families also made some important gains. Sir Hugh Willoughby (d. 1448) acquired the manor of Gunthorpe and Lowdham on his marriage to one of the Freville coheiresses in 1418; Sir Gervase Clifton (d. 1453) inherited the valuable north Nottinghamshire manor of Hodsock on the death of his step-father, Ralph Makerell, in 1436; Sir Thomas Rempston (d. 1458) acquired the Bekering manors of Tuxford and Laxton on the death of his father-in-law, Thomas Bekering, in 1425, and his mother, Margaret (d. 1454), widow of Sir Thomas Rempston (d. 1406), purchased the Sherwood forest manor of Arnold; finally, Sir John Zouche gained the manor of Kirklington in the right of his wife, Margaret Burgh, a manor he held in 1412 but on which he appears not to have been assessed.[26] Other estates changed hands within this group of greater gentry families; after Simon Leek's death without a son in *c.*1434 the bulk of the estates of the Leeks of Cotham passed to the Willoughbys and the Markhams, and, on the death of Margaret Burgh in 1451, her Nottinghamshire estates passed, albeit briefly, to the Rempstons and the Chaworths.[27]

These changes, the product of a pattern of inheritance which reflected the accidents of birth and death, meant that, by 1456, both the barons

---

[24] E. P. Shirley, *Stemmata Shirleiana* (London, 1873), 43, 388; Leicestershire Record Office, 26D53/64, 65.

[25] Below, p. 92.

[26] For these acquisitions: below, pp. 30, 35, 43, 47. For Margaret Rempston's purchase of the manor of Arnold: *CPR, 1436–41*, 551; Thoroton, ii. 233. Zouche, as one of the 4 assessors of the 1412 tax in Notts., appears to have under-assessed himself at only £25 p.a.: *CPR, 1408–13*, 379.   [27] Below, pp. 50, 239, 243

and the leading gentry enjoyed a greater share of the county's landed wealth than they had in 1412, and the balance of property between them was maintained. And yet, with Cromwell's death in January 1456, this balance was tipped further in favour of the greater gentry. The large Nottinghamshire estate he had built up between 1429 and 1441 was gradually dismembered. Although it remained for some time in the hands of his feoffees and executors, headed by William Waynflete (d. 1486), bishop of Winchester, a valuable portion of it was sold off in the 1460s for the fulfilment of his will: the manor of Bunny and other lands were purchased by Sir Richard Illingworth, chief baron of the exchequer;[28] the manors of Gonalston and Widmerpool, by Sir Henry Pierpoint (d. 1499); while a moiety of the manor of East Bridgford was eventually to pass to Magdalen College, Oxford. The rest of the inheritance was divided between Cromwell's two nieces: Maud (d. 1497), successively the wife of Robert (d. 1452), Lord Willoughby of Eresby, Thomas Nevill (d. 1460), second son of Richard (d. 1460), earl of Salisbury, and Sir Gervase Clifton (d. 1471) of Brabourne in Kent; and Joan (d. 1481), first the wife of Humphrey Bourchier (d. 1471), summoned to parliament as Lord Cromwell from 1461 to 1470, and then of Sir Robert Radcliffe (d. 1496) of Hunstanton in Norfolk.[29]

The dispersal of this estate, which was at its greatest extent for only fifteen years from 1441 to 1456, reminds us that the hegemony of a great magnate family within county politics was often a very short-lived phenomenon, an individual family being highly susceptible to extinction in the male line or temporary, and perhaps even permanent, eclipse through frequent minorities and long-lived dowagers (as in the case of the Roos family), or political miscalculation and incompetence. On the other hand, the small group of leading county families, distinguished from their fellow gentry by their wealth and often by their antiquity, had a much more continuous corporate existence, their number making them, as a body, less susceptible to such misfortunes. Although individual families died out and others joined the ranks of the leading families, through marriage, service in the law, or otherwise, their corporate existence and prominence in county affairs was a constant factor. Moreover, as a general rule, the longer a family survived the wealthier it became, generally as a result of marriage;[30] the Chaworths, Willoughbys, and Markhams rose to great wealth through a series of successful

[28] Below, p. 145.
[29] *CP*, iii. 533 n. b, 554; xii. pt. 2, 665–6. Joan died on 12 Mar. 1481, not 10 Mar. 1490, the date given in *CP*, iii. 554: HMC, *De L'Isle*, i. 227.   [30] Below, p. 64.

marriages in the fourteenth and fifteenth centuries, and the survival of such families often resulted in promotion to the peerage, particularly during the inflation of honours that took place under James I and Charles I.[31] An earlier example would be that of the Cromwells themselves; in the early fourteenth century they were to be accounted amongst the greater Nottinghamshire knights, of no greater wealth or status than their Strelley, Pierpoint, Clifton, and Chaworth neighbours, but, on account of the marriage of Ralph Cromwell (d. 1398) to the wealthy Bernak heiress in about 1360, the family were summoned to parliament in 1375.[32] In short, the history of the various leading landholding families in Nottinghamshire emphasizes the wealth and continuity of the greater shire gentry. It would indeed be surprising if this wealth was not directly translated into political influence and thence to a certain degree of political independence from their magnate superiors.

It remains to enquire how typical of fifteenth-century England as a whole was the balance of property that prevailed in Lancastrian Nottinghamshire. An analysis similar to that undertaken for Nottinghamshire for those other counties for which complete returns survive provides an answer. It would be a complex matter to categorize the gentry of these other counties in the same way as has been done for Nottinghamshire[33] since any such categorization would depend upon evidence taken from sources beyond the 1412 returns themselves; nor is such a categorization necessary because the more extensive tax returns of 1436 provide an easier way of comparing gentry wealth county by county.[34] But a knowledge of the composition of the much less numerous peerage, complete enough to identify land belonging to baronial families but temporarily out of their hands through dower, wardship, or forfeiture, makes it possible to calculate the extent of baronial wealth in other counties.[35] Table 1.4 tabulates the results of such an analysis, dividing

---

[31] i.e. in 1628 George Chaworth of Wiverton and Annesley was created Viscount Chaworth of Armagh, and in the same year his neighbour, Robert Pierpoint of Holme Pierrepont, created Viscount Newark in 1627, was promoted to the earldom of Kingston-upon-Hull.

[32] *CP*, iii. 551-2. [33] See Appendix 1. [34] Below, p. 17.

[35] In Table 1.4 lands held in wardship have been assigned to the family that held them in fee. Some returns specify such land but others do not, and in these cases I may have failed to identify some of the lands held in ward. The income of those gentry who had married the dowered widows of peers (there were 9 of these in 1412: *CP*, iv. 63-4; v. 199; viii. 52-3; ix. 605; xi. 503, 504, 542; xii. pt. 1, 181; xii. pt. 2, 733-4) have been assigned to their respective baronial families where it is obvious that the income was derived from the wife's estates.

TABLE 1.4. *Taxable wealth in baronial hands, 1412* (%)

	Greater baronage	Lesser baronage	Total
Rutland	48.6	5.2	53.8
Sussex	22.2	17.9	40.1
Huntingdonshire	17.8	19.4	37.2
Essex	16.7	14.5	31.2
Berkshire	15.6	13.4	29.0
Kesteven (Lincolnshire)	13.4	14.5	27.9
Hertfordshire	19.9	8.0	27.9
Hampshire	18.6	9.2	27.8
Bedfordshire	4.1	19.9	24.0
Somerset	11.5	11.1	22.6
Devon	16.6	3.6	20.2
Wiltshire	11.8	8.1	19.9
Dorset	11.3	8.6	19.9
Cambridgeshire	9.8	8.2	18.0
Nottinghamshire	2.7	14.8	**17.5**
Derbyshire	7.2	9.4	16.6
Middlesex	8.3	6.0	14.3
Surrey	6.1	7.0	13.1
Kent	7.2	5.7	12.9
AVERAGE	13.3	10.7	24.0

Note: Clerical assessments have been excluded from all calculations.

baronial wealth between the greater and lesser baronial families (i.e. between the earldoms and dukedoms on the one hand and the baronies on the other).[36] This wealth is expressed as a percentage of the total lay tax assessment of the county exclusive of the taxable income of the wife and sons of Henry IV (who, for these purposes, are not accounted amongst the greater baronage) and income derived from royal annuities that were limited to term of life.

Although the uneven quality of the returns may distort the percentages, they may be used as a rough comparative guide, showing quite strikingly the wide variation in baronial wealth from county to county. In Rutland, dominated territorially by the great lordship of Oakham (in 1412 in the

[36] The sons of baronial families have been given the status of their fathers for the purpose of these categories.

hands of Edward (d. 1415), duke of York, but soon to pass to the Staffords),[37] and, to a lesser extent, in Sussex, where both the FitzAlan, earls of Arundel and the Mowbray, dukes of Norfolk had extensive estates, the baronial landed interest was predominant. At the other end of the scale were the south-eastern counties of Kent and Surrey, where the estates of the lay baronage accounted for little more than 10 per cent of the taxable wealth. Nottinghamshire had more in common with these two counties than it did with the magnate-dominated counties of Rutland and Sussex: only 16.6 per cent of its taxable wealth was in baronial hands against the average for all the counties of 24 per cent. Nor was the distribution of wealth within the county's baronage typical. Whilst in most counties this wealth was fairly evenly distributed between the classes of greater and lesser barons, in Nottinghamshire the landed interest of the lesser baronage far outweighed that of the greater, which had a lower percentage of the taxable wealth than in any other county for which figures are available. However, the relatively high percentage of wealth in the hands of the lesser barons did not mean, at least in 1412, that any one lesser baronial family was dominant, unlike, for example, in Bedfordshire, where the Greys of Ruthin were comfortably the wealthiest family. In the Nottinghamshire of 1412 this wealth was fairly evenly distributed between the families of Roos, Talbot, Cromwell, and Grey of Codnor, all of whom were equalled or exceeded in wealth by the greater resident gentry (this position changed temporarily during the career of Ralph, third Lord Cromwell). This comparative paucity of baronial estates and the fairly even distribution of estates amongst a group of lesser baronial families was significant in determining the nature of political society in the county. But it was not the only factor. Equally important, in Nottinghamshire as elsewhere, was the distribution of non-baronial wealth. The question arises of whether, in those counties in which the landed interest of the baronage was small, this wealth was sufficiently uneven in distribution to allow for the existence of individual county élites of gentry capable of assuming the political leadership of the shire.

The tax returns of 1436 can be used to provide answers to this question (the later returns of 1451 are less suitable because of the extent to which tax was evaded nationwide), for they give an insight into the structure of freeholding society unmatched before the subsidy returns of 1524/7, and allow the assessed incomes of the various classes of

[37] VCH, *Rutland*, ii (1935), 12.

gentry society to be compared. Although it is probable that they underestimate both the number of those liable to tax (that is those with a freehold income of £5 per annum or more), and the incomes of those taxed, such underassessment was probably general and affected all counties. The returns can thus be used, like those of 1412, for comparative purposes.

TABLE 1.5. *Nottinghamshire tax assessments, 1436*

Income £ p.a.	Number of Assessments	Total Income	
		£ p.a.	%
200+	2	520	13.8
100–199	8	1,012	26.8
40–99	15	880	23.3
20–39	22	585	15.5
10–19	37	452	12.0
5–9	59	332	8.8
TOTAL	143	3,781	

As can be seen from Table 1.5, the Nottinghamshire returns confirm the familiar picture of freeholding society as a broadly-based pyramid with, not unexpectedly, an increasing number of taxpayers to be found as one moves down the income scale.[38] What is both surprising and significant is the very high concentration of wealth in the hands of the small group of resident landholders assessed at £100 per annum or more. Their ten assessments account for as much as 40.6 per cent of the county's taxable wealth. This percentage should be compared with that for the rank of society immediately below this élite, namely those assessed at between £40 and £99 per annum, whose fifteen assessments account for only 23.3 per cent of the county's wealth. Clearly any such classification of gentry society based on the evidence of one set of tax returns alone is rough and ready, taking no account of families temporarily eclipsed by minority or impoverished by dower settlements. However, corresponding figures drawn from the more sophisticated

[38] Wright, p. 4; R. B. Smith, *Land and Politics in the England of Henry VIII* (1970), 97–8; A. J. Pollard, 'The Richmondshire Community of Gentry during the Wars of the Roses' in C. D. Ross (ed.), *Patronage, Pedigree and Power in Later Medieval England* (Gloucester, 1979), 44–5.

classification of Nottinghamshire society set out in Appendices 1 and 5 produce very similar results. Nine of the thirteen families identified as the élite of the county in this classification are represented in the tax returns of 1436[39] and their twelve assessments (allowing for dowagers and heirs apparent with incomes in their own right) account for 42.1 per cent of the taxable wealth of the county. Twenty-one of the twenty-eight families identified as the second rank of society are represented, and their twenty-four assessments account for 27.1 per cent.

In view of the fact that the 1412 returns indicate that the landed wealth of this second rank of county society was only slightly inferior to that of the élite, the significantly greater wealth of the élite reflected in the tax returns is at first surprising. The reason for this discrepancy is not, however, hard to find: whereas the assessments of 1412 included only lands within the county, those of 1436 included all freehold lands in England. Since the wealthier a family the more likely it was to hold lands in other counties, the effect of this inclusion was to increase the assessments of the county élite compared with those of those below them on the social scale. All thirteen families who composed the élite of Lancastrian Nottinghamshire held lands in fee in other counties: the Chaworths in as many as ten others; the Zouches in eight; the Willoughbys and Rempstons in five; the Stanhopes in four; the Babingtons and Pierpoints in three; and the Cressys, Leeks of Cotham, Nevills of Rolleston, Strelleys, Cliftons, and Markhams in two others.[40] In contrast, the twenty-eight families immediately below them had much less widespread lands: only two, the Leeks of Langford and the Bekerings of Laxton, held lands in three other counties, a further three in two others, sixteen in only one other, and seven in none other.[41] It should also be said that the proportion of the county's freehold wealth in the hands of the first and second ranks of county society is exaggerated by the omission of assessments of the value of baronial and non-resident gentry families' lands in the county. In short, it should not be imagined

[39] Sir Henry Pierpoint apparently escaped assessment, while Sir Robert Markham was assessed at £120 p.a. in London: Gray, 'Incomes from Land', 636. The Leeks of Cotham had failed in the male line by this date.

[40] In total these families held lands in 17 other counties: 9 of them in Lincs., 8 in Derby., 7 in Yorks., 4 in Leics. and War., 2 in Northants., Herts., and Wilts., and 1 in Herefords., Hunts., Oxon., Bucks., Cambs., Beds., Suffolk, Hants, and Kent. Dr M. C. Carpenter, in her study of Warwickshire, has noted the 'clear relationship . . . between status and distribution of estates over England as a whole': 'Political Society in Warwickshire, c.1401–72', Ph.D. thesis (Cambridge, 1976), 25.

[41] In total, these 28 families held lands in 9 other counties: 7 in Lincs., 5 in Yorks., Derby. and Leics., 2 in War., and 1 in Norfolk, Worcs., Northants., and Hunts.

that as much as 42.1 per cent of the county's lay freehold property, in the hands of those with a landed income of £5 per annum or more, was possessed by nine leading county families in 1436, or that as much as 27.1 per cent was in the hands of twenty-one families of the second rank: the returns of 1412 and 1428 suggest a figure of nearer 20 per cent in each case. Nevertheless, making due allowance for these qualifications, there can be no doubt that gentry society in Lancastrian Nottinghamshire, at least in terms of income, was dominated by a mere handful of families that not only held a greater share of the lay wealth of the county than the baronage, but were distinguished from their immediate social inferiors, and the great mass of the lesser gentry, by a wealth derived from both lands within the county itself and significant estates in neighbouring shires.[42]

A contemporary reflection of the pre-eminence of these families is to be found in the heraldic decoration which once adorned the windows of the great hall of the archbishop of York's palace at Southwell, rebuilt by John Kemp, archbishop of York from 1425 to 1452.[43] On the windows of the east side were to be found the arms of the families of Chaworth, Pierpoint, Stanhope, Clifton, and Markham; and on the west side, those of Babington, Strelley, Willoughby, Mering, Nevill, Zouche, and Sutton.[44] In short, of the twelve families identifiable as the county élite from the taxation returns, only the Leeks of Cotham (whose failure in the main male line predates the windows)[45] and the Rempstons went unrepresented, while the two other gentry families represented, the Suttons and the Merings, were amongst the wealthiest of those families immediately below the élite.[46]

Was this phenomenon of a small gentry élite unique to Nottinghamshire? The evidence of a similar analysis of the 1436 returns, for the other counties for which they survive, is equivocal. The élite of Nottinghamshire society appears both larger and more clearly defined than that of other counties. Only in Huntingdonshire and Northumberland was a higher percentage of taxable wealth in the hands of those with

---

[42] A similarly well-defined gentry élite is readily identifiable in early 16th-c. Notts.: A. Cameron, 'Some Social Consequences of the Dissolution of the Monasteries in Nottinghamshire', *TTS* 79 (1975), 53.

[43] N. Summers, *A Prospect of Southwell* (London, 1974), 54.

[44] Bodleian Library, MS Rawlinson B396, pp. 26–30.

[45] The quartering of the arms of Strelley with Kemp dates the windows to after 1443: below, p. 58.

[46] For the Suttons: below, pp. 74–5. For the Merings: A. Cameron, 'Meering and the Meryng Family', *TTS* 77 (1973), 41–52.

TABLE 1.6. *Distribution of gentry wealth, 1436*

	£100+ (average £167)		£40–£99 (average £57.4)		Total	
	Number of Assessments	% of Total Wealth	Number of Assessments	% of Total Wealth	Number of Assessments	Taxable Wealth (£)
Huntingdonshire	2	43.7	3	22.8	32	648
Northumberland	2	42.6	4	27.4	35	1,314
Nottinghamshire	10	40.5	15	23.3	143	3,781
Essex	14	38.6	22	17.5	356	7,397
Worcestershire	5	36.8	22	18.2	127	2,494
Middlesex	3	34.3	7	36.1	37	1,261
Hertfordshire	5	34.0	10	24.8	116	2,476
Derbyshire	4	33.7	8	20.9	106	2,276
Cambridgeshire	4	33.5	7	20.5	101	1,982
Warwickshire	7	32.0	12	19.3	168	3,457
Leicestershire	6	29.4	9	19.1	121	2,480
Hampshire	4	25.5	19	40.4	138	2,531
Lincolnshire	9	19.6	32	24.7	370	6,226
Cumberland	2	18.8	7	36.2	55	1,163
Westmorland	nil	nil	6	47.2	53	942
TOTAL/AVERAGE:	77	31.8	169	24.0	1,958	40,428

Note: The relevant returns amongst the subsidy rolls are: E179/240/268 (Hunts. and Cambs.); 359/29 (Northumb.); 240/266 (Notts. and Derby.); 240/67 (Essex and Herts.); 200/68 (Worcs.); 238/90 (London and Middx.); 192/59 (War. and Leics.); 173/92 (Hants); 136/198 (Lincs.); 90/26 (Cumberland); 195/32 (Westmorland).

£100 per annum or more, and not much significance can be attached to these figures: Huntingdonshire was a small county with very few gentry worth £40 per annum or more, while the higher percentage recorded for Northumberland can be almost solely attributed to the great wealth of Sir Robert Umfraville (d. 1437) of Harbottle, who was assessed at £400. On the other hand, it can hardly be said that the phenomenon of a gentry élite was unique to Nottinghamshire. Both Essex and Worcestershire present a very similar picture, and it is quite clear from studies of gentry society in other counties that there was a general and considerable disparity in wealth between a small class of knights (a class which, at least in so far as the continued support of the rank of knighthood was concerned, diminished as the Lancastrian period progressed) and a more numerous class of esquires beneath them.[47] This division is very clearly reflected in an overall analysis of the surviving county returns: the average income of the seventy-seven non-baronial landholders

[47] Wright, p. 7; Carpenter, 'Political Society', 35.

assessed at £100 per annum or more was nearly three times that of the 169 with annual incomes between £40 and £99.[48] Nor were these wealthy gentry confined to those counties in which baronial interest was small. Essex, a county with very valuable baronial estates, had a gentry élite wealthier than that found in any other county for which 1436 returns survive. The most important point about Nottinghamshire, however, is that it combined a wealthy and well-defined élite with a low index of baronial land which, for most of the Lancastrian period, was evenly distributed between several lesser baronial families. In such circumstances it is not surprising that the political leadership of the county should have rested in the hands of the greater gentry. It is their history and role in county affairs that form the principal theme of the following chapters.

[48] Cf. Table 1.1.

2

THE COMPOSITION OF THE COUNTY ÉLITE

THE families identifiable as the élite of Lancastrian Nottinghamshire can be divided into three principal categories.[1] The first and largest reflects society at its most static and is composed of what might be termed the county's ancient aristocracy: families whose extensive local estates had long ensured them a place at the forefront of the local community. The second is composed of families similarly long-established in the county but only recently risen into the ranks of the élite. These families are generally characterized by a great leap forward in status over one or two generations: their rise was most frequently due to the highly successful career of one of their members in the law or some more direct form of royal service, a success which opened the way for a succeeding head of the family to marry profitably. Less common was the family who, without obvious recourse to what Dr M. J. Bennett has termed 'careerism',[2] steadily accumulated estates through marriage. The third and smallest category is composed of imports into the county: families who, through marriages to wealthy Nottinghamshire heiresses, suddenly found themselves amongst the leading families of the county. Such families were rare since these heiresses tended to marry within the county but Lancastrian Nottinghamshire provides two examples. One was the younger son of a baronial house who, because the estates his family had settled on him were so scattered, made his home at the *caput honoris* of his wife's inheritance; the other, the scion of a successful mercantile family whose establishment in the county was the result of the wealth which enabled them to purchase a valuable wardship and marriage, and the good fortune which transformed the ward (in her issue) into a more substantial heiress than could have been anticipated at the time of the purchase.

---

[1] The families discussed below are covered in greater detail in Payling, pp. 40–92. Their family trees are to be found in Appendix 4.

[2] M. J. Bennett, *Community, Class and Careerism: Cheshire and Lancashire Society in the Age of Sir Gawain and the Green Knight* (Cambridge, 1983); id., 'Careerism in Late Medieval England', in J. Rosenthal and C. Richmond (eds.), *People, Politics and Community in the Later Middle Ages* (Gloucester, 1987), 19–39.

The first category, composed of six families, is the most homogeneous. With the exception of the greatest of them, the Chaworths of Wiverton, their histories prior to the Lancastrian period have an important feature in common: although each had accumulated substantial estates by the end of the thirteenth century, principally through marriage, they failed to add significantly to them during the century that followed.

Two of these families were ancient enough to have taken their names from their ancient patrimonies. The Strelleys had been established at Strelley and nearby Chilwell since at least the time of Henry I.[3] In the thirteenth century they added substantially to these estates through a series of marriages, the most notable of which was that of Sir Robert Strelley (d. 1302) to Elizabeth, daughter and heiress of William Vavasour of Shipley in Derbyshire. She brought with her lands ideally situated to supplement those the Strelleys already held: the manor of Shipley, lying just across the border from Strelley, and that of Bilborough, immediately adjacent to the Strelley residence.[4] These thirteenth-century acquisitions left the family with an unusually compact estate, their only outlying lands being at Ferrybridge and Friston near Pontefract in the West Riding,[5] but this remained the full extent of their lands right down to their failure in the main male line in the first years of the sixteenth century. Their neighbours, the Cliftons, almost certainly had as long an association with the county,[6] but did not reach a position of prominence until the second half of the thirteenth century. The real founder of the family's fortunes was Sir Gervase Clifton (d. 1323). Sometime before 1280 he was enfeoffed in fee by Sir Gerard de Rodes of Langar of the manors of Clifton and Wilford, both lying just to the south of Nottingham, and he added to these the manor of Upper Broughton in the far south-east of the county[7] acquired from the Sulny family. It was not until the first part of the fifteenth century that this estate, wholly confined to the county, was further extended.

---

[3] W. Farrer, *Honors and Knights' Fees* (London and Manchester, 1923–5), i. 178.

[4] Ibid. 179; Thoroton, ii. 219; *Early Yorkshire Charters*, ed. C. T. Clay, 10 vols. (Wakefield, 1935–65), v. 169 n. 4; *CIPM*, iv. no. 99.

[5] These lands were in the hands of the Strelleys by 1290, probably acquired as a result of the Vavasour marriage: *CAD*, vi, C4789.

[6] *Notts. Visit.*, 16; A. C. Wood, 'Notes on the Early History of the Clifton Family', *TTS* 37 (1933), 24–6; Thoroton, i. 103.

[7] Farrer, *Honors*, i. 236–8; Thoroton, i. 103, 141. Upper Broughton continued in the Clifton family until the 17th c. when Sir Gervase Clifton (d. 1676), second baronet, was persuaded to sell it, which, according to Thoroton, 'he oft repented himself of, being so long in his Family, and he not necessitated, as he hath several Times told me himself'.

Another family resident near Nottingham, the Pierpoints, present a similar picture of stagnation. They came originally from Pierrepont, near Grandcourt in Picardy, and settled at Hurstpierpoint in Sussex soon after the Conquest;[8] but it was not until the marriage, in the second half of the thirteenth century, of Sir Henry Pierpoint (steward of the castle of Knaresborough which belonged to Edmund of Almaine (d. 1300), earl of Cornwall) to Annora, daughter and eventual heiress of Sir Michael Manvers (d. 1255) of Holme Pierrepont, that a branch of the family became major Nottinghamshire landholders.[9] In addition to the valuable manor of Holme (subsequently known as Holme Pierrepont), she brought to Sir Henry the south Yorkshire manor of Anston,[10] and the couple also made several purchases: from Sir Ralph Salvayn, the manor of Holbeck Woodhouse in north-west Nottinghamshire; from Sir Richard Weston, the manor of Weston near Tuxford; and from Sir Robert Tibetot, the manor of Sneinton near Nottingham.[11] They made further acquisitions at Ashover in Derbyshire and Langford near Newark.[12] Their son, Sir Robert (d. 1334), a notable soldier and keeper of Newark Castle, added a manor at Rolleston, also near Newark, granted to him by his father-in-law, Sir John Heriz (d. 1299), in free marriage.[13] Thereafter, it was not until c.1469, when Sir Henry Pierpoint (d. 1499) finally acquired the manors of Gonalston, Widmerpool, and Tibshelf, once of Sir John Heriz and over which Sir Henry's grandfather, Sir Henry (d. 1452), had been in dispute with Ralph (d. 1456), Lord Cromwell, that any significant addition was made to the very considerable estates the family held at the end of the thirteenth century,[14] and it was not until the marriage in 1601 of Robert Pierpoint (1584–1643),

---

[8] L. C. Loyd, *The Origins of Some Anglo-Norman Families*, Harleian Society, 103 (1951), 78; W. S. Ellis, 'Descent of the Manor of Hurst-Pierpoint, and of its Lords', *Sussex Archaeological Collections* 11 (1859), 50–3.

[9] Thoroton, i. 175, 178; C. Moor, *Knights of Edward I*, Harleian Society, 5 vols., 80–4 (1929–32), iv. 50. Before this marriage the Pierpoints appear to have held Notts. lands at Kirkby-in-Ashfield: BL, MS Loan 29/60, fo. 213; Thoroton, i. 178.

[10] J. Hunter, *South Yorkshire* (London, 1828–31), i. 305.

[11] BL, MS Loan 29/60, fos. 51, 103^v, 111; CP25(1)/183/15/72.

[12] BL, MS Loan 29/60, fo. 229; CP25(1)/184/26/25. The Langford lands had been acquired by 1316: *FA*, iv. 104.

[13] BL, MS Loan 29/60, fo. 174.

[14] The full extent of the estates of Sir Robert (d. 1334) is revealed in a series of fines by which he settled lands on his son, Sir Henry (d.v.p.), at the time of his son's marriage in 1317, and by which he later attempted to disinherit this son's issue in favour of his 14 children by Cecily Annesley: below, p. 72. A complete list of the Pierpoints' early 15th-c. estates is to be found in C1/39/35.

later first earl of Kingston-upon-Hull, that the family again married an heiress.[15]

These three families, all with their principal residences in the immediate environs of Nottingham and estates largely confined to Nottinghamshire, show English society at its most conservative. After initial successes, their failure to marry heiresses may have been the result of a cautious concern not to overstretch themselves by acquiring far-flung estates: as Dr M. C. Carpenter has pointed out, 'heiresses were delightful in theory, in practice they could mean an unmanageable estate and impossibly widespread political responsibilities'.[16] There is some slight evidence to suggest that this was the attitude of the Strelley family. The son and heir of Sir Robert Strelley (d. 1302), another Sir Robert (d. 1350), married a minor heiress, Constance, one of the three grand-daughters and coheiresses of Thomas of Pontop, but instead of holding on to the lands she brought him at West Matfen in Northumberland, he sold them in 1335 to her half-brother, Sir William Fenton of Edlingham.[17] With this exception, the fourteenth-century heads of these three families tended to marry into other Nottinghamshire knightly families. Indeed, on at least two occasions they inter-married: the long-lived Sir Gervase Clifton (d. 1389) married, as his first wife, Margaret (d. 1340), daughter of Sir Robert Pierpoint (d. 1334), while Sir Nicholas Strelley (d. 1430) married Elizabeth, daughter of Sir Edmund Pierpoint (d. 1370).[18] They drew other brides from the Nottinghamshire families of Heriz of Gonalston, Annesley of Annesley, Nevill of Rolleston, Hercy of Grove, and Monboucher of Gamston. This insularity in marriage was both a reflection and a cause of their lack of lands in other counties.

The histories of two other families of the first category of the élite of Lancastrian Nottinghamshire, the Nevills of Rolleston and the Cressys of Hodsock, present slightly different features. Both held important estates outside the county and were less exclusively connected with Nottinghamshire. The Nevills had acquired the manors of Rolleston near Newark, Pickhill in north Yorkshire, and Rigsby in south Lindsey by the end of the twelfth century, all held of the honor of Richmond

---

[15] For the first earl's marriage: *CP*, vii. 304; VCH, *Huntingdon*, iii (1974), 192. For the 16th-c. family pedigree: Thoroton, i. 176.

[16] M. C. Carpenter, 'The Fifteenth-Century English Gentry and their Estates', in M. C. E. Jones (ed.), *Gentry and Lesser Nobility of Late Medieval Europe* (Gloucester, 1986), 40.

[17] *CFR, 1327–37*, 93, 108, 125; Northumberland County History Committee, *A History of Northumberland* (Newcastle etc., 1893–1940), xii. 274.

[18] Thoroton, i. 104; ii. 220.

and all apparently acquired by marriage.[19] Early members of the family
were prominent men who played on the national rather than the local
stage: Jollan de Nevill (d. 1207) was an exchequer clerk who may have
been the compiler of the early part of the 'Testa de Nevill', and his son,
another Jollan, was a superior justice at Westminster from 1241 to
1245.[20] King John granted Shorne in Kent to the first Jollan but the
family abandoned their interest in c.1246,[21] and thereafter settled down
to a prominent role in the local affairs of Yorkshire and, more particularly,
of Nottinghamshire. The fourteenth century saw some slight expansion
in their north Yorkshire estates, chiefly through the marriage of Sir
William Nevill (d. c.1420) to the heiress of the Fencotes family.[22]

The greater breadth of the family's interests, compared with those of
the Strelleys, Cliftons, and Pierponts, is reflected in an earlier marriage
which should have added substantially to their estates, for Sir William's
mother was Cecily, the daughter and, in her issue, the heiress of Sir
Ranulph Blanchminster, who died in 1348 seised of the Scilly Isles, a
substantial estate in north-east Cornwall, and the Yorkshire manor of
Wighill near Tadcaster.[23] In 1377 the last remaining male heir of the
Blanchminsters, Sir Ranulph's younger son, Guy (d. 1404), rector of
Lansallos in Cornwall, settled his valuable Cornish lands on his niece,
Emma, and her husband, the notorious Sir Robert Tresilian (ex. 1388),
CJKB, and their male issue, with remainder to his nephew and second
coheir, Sir William Nevill and Sir William's male issue. Unfortunately
for the Nevills, this fine was subsequently disregarded; the Blanch-
minster estates passing to Emma's issue by her second husband, John
Colshull.[24] Their failure to oppose successfully the weaker claim of the

[19] VCH, *North Riding*, i (1914), 379; W. O. Massingberd, 'Lincolnshire Nevill Families', *The Genealogist* 27 (1910), 2; Thoroton, iii. 102; *The Book of Fees*, 2 vols. in 3 (1920–31), i. 287. In 1307 they had a grant of free warren in their demesne lands in the three manors together with a market and fair at Pickhill: *C. Ch. R., 1300–26*, 106.
[20] *Dictionary of National Biography*, xiv. 269–70; E. Foss, *A Biographical Dictionary of the Judges of England, 1066–1870* (London, 1870), 474–5.
[21] E. Hasted, *The History and Topographical Survey of Kent*, 12 vols. (Canterbury, 1797–1801), iii. 444.
[22] This marriage brought him the manor of Little Fencote in Kirkby Fleetham: VCH, *North Riding*, i. 322. Sometime before 1340 Sir William's father, Sir Thomas, acquired the manor of Watlass in Thornton Watlass from Simon de Stutvill and, in 1340, he exchanged it for the nearby manor of Yarnwick in Kirklington with Sir Geoffrey Scrope, CJKB: ibid. 345, 376. For the full extent of the family's north Yorks. estates see the inquisition taken on the death of Thomas Nevill in 1503: *CIPM, Henry VII*, ii, no. 862.
[23] *CIPM*, ix, no. 108. In 1376 Guy Blanchminster, clerk, sold the reversion of Wighill to Sir Brian Stapleton (d. 1394) of Carlton near Snaith: H. E. Chetwynd-Stapleton, *The Stapletons of Yorkshire* (London etc., 1897), 130.
[24] *Records of Blanchminster's Charity*, ed. R. W. Goulding (Louth etc., 1898), 18a,

Colshulls illustrates the difficulties inherent in making good title to estates in counties remote from a claimant's principle area of influence.

While the Nevills had an important landed interest in north Yorkshire, through which they nearly became major landholders in Cornwall, the Cressys of Hodsock held extensive Lincolnshire estates. Probably originally from Cressy near Bellencombre in the Pays de Caux and of the same family as the Cressys of Blythborough in Suffolk and Rotting-dean in Sussex, who failed in the male line in 1263,[25] they became established at Hodsock in north Nottinghamshire during the reign of Henry II (they also held lands at West Melton in south Yorkshire).[26] In *c.*1240 they added very considerably to these estates through the marriage of Roger Cressy (d. *c.*1245) to Sibyl (d. 1282), daughter and sole heiress of John de Braytoft, who brought the family scattered but valuable Lincolnshire manors at Claypole, Bratoft, and Risegate.[27] It was at the most valuable of these, Risegate near Surfleet in Holland, that the main line of the family settled in the first part of the fourteenth century. Their move was occasioned by the life interest that a younger son, Sir Edmund Cressy, enjoyed in Hodsock from 1317, on the unexpected death without issue of his elder brother Hugh, until his own death in 1347.[28] Both Sir Edmund's great nephew, Sir Hugh Cressy (d. 1347), and Sir Hugh's son, Sir John (d. 1383), willed burial in the parish church of Surfleet,[29] although it is probable that by the latter's death Hodsock had once more become the centre of the inheritance, for Sir John was much more active in local government in Nottinghamshire than in Lincolnshire.

It is unfortunate that the surnames of the wives of the fourteenth-century heads of the Cressy family are unknown, but what is known of the marriages of their daughters suggests that the family's connections

---

23*a*–25*a*. By a fine of 1440 the lands were resettled on Colshull's grandson by Emma, Sir John Colshull (d. 1484), and his male issue, with successive remainders to his sister, Joan, and her issue, and thence to Thomas Nevill and his heirs male, but none of these lands ever came to the Nevills, although they unsuccessfully sued for them in 1438 and 1548: ibid. 32*a*–33*a*; CP40/710, rot. 137; G. F. Farnham, *Leicestershire Medieval Pedigrees* (Leicester, 1925), 35.

[25] Loyd, *Anglo-Norman Families*, 35; I. J. Sanders, *English Baronies* (Oxford, 1960), 16.
[26] *The Cartulary of Blyth Priory*, ed. R. T. Timson, 2 vols., TSRS, 27–28 (1973), i, p. xxxvii; *CP*, iii. 528; Hunter, *South Yorkshire*, i. 364.
[27] W. O. Massingberd, 'Some Lords of a Manor in Bratoft', *Lincolnshire Notes and Queries* 7 (1902–3), 118; *CP*, iii. 528.
[28] Ibid., 529 n. *c*.
[29] Lincolnshire Archives Office, Bishop's Register VII, fos. 218[d]–219; XII, fo. 262. A brief abstract of Sir Hugh's lengthy and generous will is given in J. Raine, *The History and Antiquities of the Parish of Blyth* (Westminster, 1860), 135–6.

were fairly widespread. One of the daughters of Sir Hugh Cressy, Katherine (d. 1400), married Sir William Erghum (d. *c.*1403) of Argam in the East Riding, while her sister, Elizabeth (d. 1404), married another Yorkshireman, William Vavasour (d. 1369) of Hazlewood in the West Riding.[30] Sir John's daughters, however, married into Nottinghamshire families, one into the Cliftons and the other into the Markhams, and this probably reflects the return of the family to Hodsock and their consequent concern to re-establish links with their erstwhile neighbours. On the other hand, their brother Hugh (d. 1408) married further afield. His wife was Margaret, daughter of Sir William Skipwith, JCB, of Skipwith in north Yorkshire and South Ormsby in Lincolnshire, not far from the Cressy manor of Bratoft.[31] Nevertheless, while this marriage and those of Hugh's aunts demonstrate that the family had wider connections than the more insular families of Strelley, Clifton, and Pierpoint, they were no more successful in or desirous of finding heiresses to marry. In common with the other ancient Nottinghamshire families they made no significant additions to their estates during the fourteenth century.

The exception to this rule was the Chaworth family, who, already substantial landholders by the end of the thirteenth century and perhaps even then the greatest gentry family with estates in Nottinghamshire, were able to expand their patrimony and thus become not only one of the richest families in the county but also one of the wealthiest gentry families in England. Indeed, there can be few better examples of a family that rose to local pre-eminence through a series of profitable marriages concluded over a period of several centuries.

They originally came from Sourches near Le Mans in Maine, and it is probable that one Bouchard de Cadurcis was with the Conquerer at Hastings. But it was the line descended from Bouchard's brother Hugh which settled in England.[32] The marriage of Patrick de Cadurcis (d. 1133) to Maud, one of the daughters of Ernulf de Hesding (d. *c.*1091), brought the Gloucestershire honor of Kempsford to the family, and,

[30] *CPR, 1399–1401*, 411; *CP*, xii, pt. 2, 236.
[31] This marriage did not prove a happy one. It was dissolved shortly before 20 June 1399 on the grounds of Hugh's impotence, and Margaret then married Hugh's first cousin, Sir Henry Vavasour (d. 1413): Borthwick Institute, Archbishop's Register 16, fos. 24^d–25.
[32] *Calendar of Documents Preserved in France, Illustrative of the History of Great Britain and Ireland*, i, *918–1206*, ed. J. H. Round (London, 1899), p. xlviii; L. Chaworth Musters, 'Some Account of the Family called in Latin Cadurcis, in French Chaources, and in English Chaworth', *TTS* 7 (1903), 121.

over a century later, their great-great-grandson, another Patrick (d. 1258), acquired the Welsh marcher lordship of Kidwelly by his marriage to Hawise, the daughter and heiress of Thomas de Lounders.[33] The senior line of the family ended in Maud (d. *c.*1322), the granddaughter of Patrick and Hawise, who, having been made a ward of Edward I's brother, Edmund, earl of Lancaster, in 1291, was married to Edmund's second son, Henry 'Tortcol' (*c.*1281–1345), shortly before March 1297.[34]

However, much earlier, in *c.*1160, a younger branch of the family had become established in the east midlands through the marriage of Robert, probably a younger son of the first Patrick, to the heiress of the Walchervilles of Marnham in east Nottinghamshire and Wadworth in south-east Yorkshire.[35] Their grandson William was to make an even better match: his marriage to Alice, the sister and coheiress of Thomas de Alfreton of Norton, brought the family the Derbyshire manors of Alfreton and Norton and the Nottinghamshire manors of Edwalton and Osberton.[36] In September 1257 Thomas, the eldest son of William and Alice, was granted free warren in his demesne lands in these four manors and in those of Marnham, Wadworth, and Medbourne (Leicestershire), the last of which had been acquired by William before 1235, together with a weekly market and yearly fair at Marnham.[37] Thomas's son, another Thomas (d. 1315), was summoned to the parliament of March 1299,[38] but this summons had no sequel, and it is perhaps more than a coincidence that it should have occurred soon after the marriage of his cousin Maud to the king's nephew, Henry 'Tortcol'.

The family's fortunes took another major step forward in the following century, again as a result of a highly profitable marriage. Sir William Chaworth (b. 1352)[39] married Alice, the sole heiress of both her father,

---

[33] Sanders, *English Baronies*, 125.

[34] *CPR, 1281–92*, 464; *CP*, vii. 400. Through this marriage Sir Thomas Chaworth (d. 1459) of Wiverton was a ninth cousin once removed of Henry IV. The pride the later Chaworths took in this royal connection is reflected in the very detailed pedigree they submitted at the herald's visitation of 1569: *Notts. Visit.*, 123–8.

[35] Thoroton, iii. 184; *The Red Book of the Exchequer*, ed. H. H. Hall, Rolls Series, 3 vols. (1896), i. 344.

[36] S. Glover, *The History of the County of Derby*, ed. T. Noble (Derby, 1829), ii. 10–11; Thoroton, i. 122; iii. 184–5, 402.

[37] *C. Ch. R., 1226–57*, 472–3. For the grant in 1272 of a weekly market and yearly fair at Alfreton: ibid. 400. For Medbourne: G. F. Farnham and A. Hamilton Thompson, 'The Manor and Advowson of Medbourne', *Transactions of the Leicestershire Archaeological Society*, 13 (1923–4), 95.

[38] *CP*, iii. 153.

[39] *CIPM*, xiii, no. 15; *CCR, 1369–74*, 506.

Sir John Caltoft (d. 1353)[40] of South Thoresby in Lincolnshire, and her maternal uncle, Sir John Brett of Wiverton in Nottinghamshire. This marriage probably occurred shortly after the childless death in October 1374 of Alice's first husband and former guardian, Sir Thomas Hethe of Tottenham in Middlesex, who had been granted Alice's wardship and marriage by Queen Philippa of Hainault.[41] She brought at once to her new Chaworth husband the Caltoft lands, namely a moiety of the manors of East Bridgford in south Nottinghamshire and Saxby in north Leicestershire, and the manors of South Thoresby and West Allington, with lands at Toynton in Lincolnshire.[42] Additionally, on the death of her uncle, Sir John Brett, in c.1385,[43] she brought the manor of Wiverton, with parcels of land in several surrounding south Nottinghamshire vills, lands at Williamthorpe, Calow, Inkersall, and Woolley in Brackenfield in north Derbyshire, at Easenhall in Monks Kirby in Warwickshire, and at Timberland in Lincolnshire.[44]

The acquisition of these estates caused the focus of the Chaworth's inheritance to move some thirty miles north from the Leicestershire manor of Medbourne, where the Chaworths appear to have resided through much of the fourteenth century,[45] to Wiverton in south Nottinghamshire, where they now had a compact estate centred on the manors of Wiverton, East Bridgford, and Edwalton. But, while their interests became increasingly centred in Nottinghamshire, the career of Sir Thomas Chaworth, who came into an unencumbered inheritance on the deaths of his parents, Sir William and Alice, in December 1398 and early 1400 respectively, saw the extension of the family estates yet farther afield. His first wife, Nicola, whom he married in c.1395, and who was the daughter of Sir Gerard Braybrooke (d. 1429),[46] was not an heiress, but it was the connections of her family that enabled him, after

---

[40] *CIPM*, x, no. 71; *CCR, 1349–54*, 560.
[41] *CIPM*, xiv, no. 34; *CPR, 1354–8*, 258.
[42] *CPR, 1292–1301*, 222; *CIPM*, vi, no. 82; ibid., *Henry VII*, iii, no. 370.
[43] The last reference to him alive is May 1385: *CPR, 1381–5*, 523.
[44] *CCR, 1364–8*, 313–14; *1377–81*, 295–6; *CIPM, Henry VII*, ii, no. 370.
[45] They built a manor house there in the late 13th or early 14th c.: N. Pevsner, *Leicestershire and Rutland*, The Buildings of England (1984), 314. Sir Thomas Chaworth (d. c.1347) was summoned to represent Leics. in the parliament of September 1337, and his son, Sir Thomas (d. 1370), represented that county in the parliament of May 1360.
[46] *TE*, i. 220 n., Thoroton, i. 198, and *Notts. Visit.*, 126, have Nicola as the daughter of Sir Gerard's brother, Sir Reginald (d. 1405), while V. J. Watney, *The Wallop Family and their Ancestry* (Oxford, 1928), i. 194, has her as Gerard's daughter. Watney must be correct since, if Nicola had been a daughter of Sir Reginald, her daughter by Sir Thomas, Elizabeth Scrope, would eventually have been one of the coheirs to the barony of Cobham: *CP*, iii. 345–6.

her death in 1411,[47] to marry one of the eventual coheiresses of the Aylesburys of Milton Keynes.[48]

The Aylesburys had been as successful as the Chaworths in the marriage market, having in the space of two generations married the heiresses of the wealthy families of Keynes of Milton Keynes in Buckinghamshire and Basset of Weldon in Northamptonshire.[49] By the early fifteenth century they were one of the more substantial English knightly families. And yet, when the marriage between Sir Thomas Chaworth and Isabel, the daughter of Sir Thomas Aylesbury, took place in 1415,[50] there was little reason to imagine that Isabel would ever come into any part of her family's considerable landed fortune; not only did she have a brother John Aylesbury, but John himself had a young son, Hugh. Fate, however, intervened. The deaths of Sir Thomas Aylesbury in September 1418, John Aylesbury in May 1422 and Hugh in October 1423, led to the partition of the Aylesbury estates between Isabel and her younger sister, Eleanor, the wife of Sir Humphrey Stafford (d. 1450) of Grafton in Worcestershire.[51] Isabel's moiety was an extremely scattered estate consisting of the Hertfordshire manors of Albury, Triscott in Tring, and Wilstone in Tring, the Oxfordshire manor of Rousham, the Wiltshire manor of Zeals Aylesbury, and the Buckinghamshire manor of Drayton Beauchamp, all of which had been settled on Chaworth, Hampden, and other feoffees by Sir Thomas Aylesbury in May 1416, plus a moiety of the Northamptonshire manor of Blatherwycke, and the advowson of the Leicestershire priory of Launde.[52] In addition, on the

---

[47] Chaworth Musters, 'Some Account', 127.

[48] In May 1416 Edmund Hampden (d. 1420), an esquire in the household of Sir Gerard's uncle, Robert Braybrooke (d. 1404), bishop of London, and a kinsman and close associate of both the Aylesbury and Braybrooke families, acted with Sir Thomas Chaworth and Sir Thomas Aylesbury in a conveyance connected with Chaworth's marriage to Aylesbury's daughter: L. H. Butler, 'Robert Braybrooke, Bishop of London (1381–1404), and his Kinsmen', D.Phil. thesis (Oxford, 1952), 366–74; *CCR, 1409–13*, 191, 284; C138/33/35; *CFR, 1413–22*, 256. It is Hampden's involvement in this and subsequent conveyances that so strongly suggests that it was Chaworth's connections with the Braybrookes that led to the Aylesbury marriage.

[49] G. Baker, *The History and Antiquities of the County of Northampton* (London, 1822–41), i. 355–6; *CP*, ii. 12–13.

[50] By a fine of Ascension 1415 (given and recorded in the following Trinity) the Notts. manor of Marnham, and lands in Medbourne and Burton Overy in Leics. were settled on Chaworth and Isabel in jointure: CP25(1)/291/63/29. On 21 June in the same year Chaworth made a feoffment of all his lands to Sir Thomas Aylesbury, Sir Ralph Shirley, and others: R. White, *The Dukery Records* (Worksop, 1904), 295, 322, 389–90.

[51] *CFR, 1422–30*, 71–2.

[52] C138/33/35; C44/24/20; *CAD*, iii, C3721; VCH, *Buckinghamshire*, iv (1927), 284, 304.

death of Margaret, the widow of John Aylesbury, in 1429, Isabel inherited moieties of the Northamptonshire manors of Weston-by-Welland and Ashley;[53] on the death of Katherine, the widow of Sir Thomas Aylesbury, in 1436, a moiety of the Northamptonshire manor of Pytchley and 5 marks of annual rent from mills at Newport Pagnell in Buckinghamshire;[54] and finally, on the death of a distant Aylesbury kinsman, John Cressy, in 1453, moieties of the Northamptonshire manor of Dodford and the Warwickshire manor of Oxhill.[55] This far-flung estate, which came to the Chaworths rather by accident than design and which, given the difficulties inherent in its administration, they might not have chosen to acquire, explains why Sir Thomas was assessed at as much as £320 per annum for the income tax of 1436, an income far in excess of that of the other ancient Nottinghamshire families.

It was, in part, the wide-ranging connections of the Chaworths that allowed them to continue into the fifteenth century their tradition of marrying for land: in contrast, the main lines of the other ancient Nottinghamshire families of Strelley and Pierpoint, who were much less widely connected, found heiresses in neither the fourteenth nor fifteenth centuries. But the Chaworths were not the only one of these ancient families to advance themselves through marriage in the fifteenth century. The Cliftons and the Nevills, after more than a century in which they had failed to add significantly to their estates, did so too. In the early 1380s John Clifton, heir-apparent of his grandfather, Sir Gervase Clifton (d. 1389), married as his second wife, Katherine, one of the daughters of Sir John Cressy of Hodsock.[56] When this marriage took place, Katherine was not her father's heiress since she had a surviving brother, Hugh, who succeeded their father as a minor in 1383 and had livery of the Cressy inheritance on coming of age in 1396.[57] But five years later, in 1401, Hugh levied a fine of this considerable inheritance: he settled the remainder of one moiety on Katherine, Sir John Clifton, and their issue, and the remainder of the other on Sir John Markham.

[53] C139/40/55; *CFR, 1422–30*, 274.

[54] C139/82/50; *CFR, 1430–7*, 306; J. Bridges, *The History and Antiquities of North-amptonshire* (London, 1791), ii. 124.

[55] C139/150/39; 163/7; *CFR, 1452–61*, 205–6. He only made good his claim after prolonged litigation: CP40/778, rot. 131; C1/24/51.

[56] For a fragment of the marriage agreement dated *c.*1382: NUL, Cl. D 621. On 27 March 1383 Sir John Cressy entered into an £80 recognizance with Sir Gervase Clifton, presumably in connection with this marriage: *CCR, 1381–5*, 296.

[57] *CIPM*, xv, nos. 965–6; *CCR, 1392–6*, 28–9; *CFR, 1391–9*, 198.

JCB and his issue by Katherine's deceased sister, Elizabeth.[58] This was a recognition on Hugh's part that his sisters would be left as his coheiresses (for he had recently been divorced from his wife, Margaret Skipwith, on the grounds of his impotence)[59] and this is what happened on his death in September 1408.[60] Unfortunately for the immediate prospects of the Cliftons, Sir John had been killed fighting for Lancaster at the battle of Shrewsbury on 21 July 1403, and his widow, Katherine, had taken a second husband, the Derbyshire esquire Ralph Makerell. On her death, Ralph was to enjoy courtesy (a husband's common law entitlement to a life interest in his deceased wife's estates provided living issue had been born between them) in her moiety of the Cressy inheritance, the Nottinghamshire manor of Hodsock, the Lincolnshire manor of Claypole, and moieties of the south Yorkshire manor of Melton and the Lincolnshire manor of Exton, until January 1436[61] when these manors finally came to Katherine's son by Sir John, Sir Gervase Clifton (d. 1453). The acquisition of these valuable lands made Sir Gervase, according to the tax assessments of 1436, the third richest man in the county, with an annual income of £193 per annum, and, for the first time, gave the Cliftons estates outside the county. It also occasioned their move thirty miles to the north from their ancient seat at Clifton to that of the Cressys at Hodsock.

Marriage brought about a more dramatic territorial realignment in the case of the Nevills. In *c.*1450 William, the son and heir of Thomas Nevill, married Katherine, one of the four daughters and heiresses of Thomas Palmer of Holt in south Leicestershire.[62] On Palmer's death in 1475, William made his home at Holt and did not return to reside at Rolleston after his father's death in 1482. Thereafter, Holt became the centre of the senior branch's interests.[63] The mid-sixteenth century saw the dismemberment of their ancient estates: Rolleston, Pickhill, Rigsby, Little Fencote, and Yarnwick were all sold by Sir Thomas Nevill, who died intestate and without a male heir in 1571.[64]

---

[58] *CPR, 1399–1401*, 411; CP25(1)/290/59/24.

[59] Above, p. 25 n.31.   [60] C137/67/30.   [61] C139/74/21.

[62] On 16 Jan. 1450 Palmer granted his south Leics. manor of Lubenham to William, Katherine, and their lawful issue, while on 26 Jan. Thomas Nevill settled his Lincs. manor of Rigsby in the same way: Leicestershire Record Office, Peake MTD 54, 55.

[63] Both William Nevill (d. 1497) and his son, Thomas (d. 1503), were buried in the south Lincs. priory church of Launde: G. F. Farnham and A. Hamilton Thompson, 'The Manor, House and Chapel of Holt', *Transactions of the Leicestershire Archaeological Society* 13 (1923–4), 218.

[64] VCH, *North Riding*, i. 322, 376, 379; Thoroton, iii. 103. For the interesting settlement made by Sir Thomas in 1564, when he had given up hope of a son, 'to advance

These Clifton and Nevill marriages to heiresses, together with the profitable series of marriages made by the Chaworths, cannot disguise the fact that the main lines of those families long established amongst the principal county families only infrequently extended their estates through marriage or otherwise. When they did so it usually resulted in a substantial addition, and the cumulative effect of such marriages was to promote an accumulation of estates in the hands of fewer families. But they did not monopolize the local marriage market in heiresses, and this ensured that the élite of the county remained permeable. Their failure to add consistently to their own estates left others with the opportunity to add to theirs. Thus it was possible for lesser, more ambitious families to rise up the social scale to rival and even surpass the ancient families in wealth. The principal method by which this came about in Nottinghamshire, as elsewhere, was service in the law.

The fourteenth century was the great age for the social promotion of judicial families with those of Scrope of Bolton, Scrope of Masham, Cobham, Bourchier and others achieving promotion to the parliamentary peerage, and the law remained one of the principal means of advancement throughout the later middle ages.[65] In the first instance the rise of judicial families was fuelled by the purchase of land since judges were in a uniquely advantageous position to exploit the local land market. First, the excess capital provided by judicial salaries and other legal fees both provided the necessary cash for outright purchases and enabled judges to extend mortgages to the financially embarrassed who might later prove unable to redeem their property.[66] Second, the legal training and position of a judge gave him the skill and connections to defend his purchases against rival claimants who so often made life difficult for the purchasers of land in late-medieval England.

In the fifteenth century, judicial salaries were high: the long-established basic salaries of 60 marks for chief justices and 40 marks for puisne justices were supplemented by substantial increments of 180 marks, 140 marks, and 110 marks for the chief justices of king's bench and

with his living such as shall be of his blood and seed first, and after some other of his stock and kinsfolk, and to preserve the premises in the name of the Nevills for that it has been an ancient and old house and name': Farnham and Thompson, 'Holt', 221–3.

[65] M. Bloom, 'The Careers of Sir Richard II de Willoughby and Sir Richard III de Willoughby, Chief Justice of the King's Bench (1338–1340), and the Rise of the Willoughbys of Nottinghamshire', D.Phil. thesis (Oxford, 1985), 7–14; McFarlane, *The Nobility*, 12–13.

[66] For the methods, both legal and illegal, of Edward II's justices in the acquisition of land: D. J. M. Higgins, 'Judges in Government and Society under Edward II', D.Phi' thesis (Oxford, 1986), 227–30.

common pleas and puisne justices respectively.[67] These high increments
are partially to be accounted as compensation for fees which, from the
late 1380s, were no longer paid to justices by lay and ecclesiastical
magnates.[68] The loss of these fees probably meant that the most
profitable years of a successful lawyer's career were those he spent
before promotion to the bench as a serjeant-at-law. This was certainly
the opinion of Sir John Fortescue, CJKB, who, in his *De Laudibus Legum
Anglie*, written between 1467 and 1471, claimed that no 'advocate in the
whole world . . . enriches himself by reason of his office as much as the
serjeant'. The potential profits of the office are reflected in the high cost
of the ceremony involved in taking up the order, a sum Fortescue
reckoned at £266 13s. 4d., equivalent to the annual landed income of a
very wealthy knight.[69] Indeed, so remunerative was the office that some
were reluctant to accept promotion to the bench. In 1441 the Lincolnshire lawyer William Ayscogh complained that his promotion to the
common bench after only two years as a serjeant had cost him 'all his
Wynnings that he sholde have hade in the . . . office of serjeant and alle
the fees that he had in England weere and be cessed and expired fro hym
to his grete empoverysshyng for they weere the grete substance of his
lyvelode'.[70] However, there is no evidence that such reluctance was
general. Ayscogh may have been more dependent than his fellows on the
greater profits open to the serjeant for he was, according to his own
testimony, the poorest of the royal justices. Most serjeants, after a few
very profitable years in the office, could well afford to accept promotion.

The effects of these judicial profits were felt in the localities and had a
significant impact on the higher reaches of gentry society. The example
of Nottinghamshire well illustrates how significant this impact could be:

[67] These salaries were handsomely supplemented by a share of court fees (which may
have been worth as much as £50 p.a. to each justice), an annuity of £20 for acting as a
justice of assize and *ad hoc* payments for other specific services: G. O. Sayles, *Select Cases in
the Court of King's Bench under Richard II, Henry IV and Henry V*, Selden Society, 88 (1971),
p. xv; E. W. Ives, *The Common Lawyers of Pre-Reformation England* (Cambridge, 1983),
323.
[68] J. R. Maddicott, 'Law and Lordship: Royal Justices as Retainers in Thirteenth- and
Fourteenth-Century England', *Past and Present*, Suppl. 4 (1978), 80.
[69] Sir J. Fortescue, *De Laudibus Legum Anglie*, ed. S. B. Chrimes (Cambridge, 1942),
123, 125. For John Gower, writing in about 1380, the gold rings proffered by the aspiring
serjeants at the ceremony signified that they would be taking gold back again in greater
abundance for the rest of their lives: J. H. Baker, *The Order of Serjeants at Law*, Selden
Society Supplementary Series, 5 (1984), 35. For an account of the ceremony: Ives, *The
Common Lawyers*, 64–5.
[70] S. Lysons, 'Copies of Three Remarkable Petitions to King Henry the Sixth',
Archaeologia 16 (1812), 3.

three of the leading families of Lancastrian Nottinghamshire owed their prominence in the first instance to the successful legal career of one of their members. The Willoughbys of Wollaton, the best documented of all late-medieval Nottinghamshire families, were the most famous of these. The extent if not the method of their meteoric rise during the thirteenth and fourteenth centuries is without parallel in the history of medieval Nottinghamshire. They traced their origins back to Ralph Bugge (d. *c*.1250) of Nottingham, a highly successful wool merchant, who purchased piecemeal a coherent manorial estate in the south Nottinghamshire vill of Willoughby-on-the-Wolds.[71] He settled this estate on his younger son Richard while his elder son Ralph took over his commercial interests and later purchased the manor of Bingham, establishing a knightly family which took its name from that vill and failed in the male line at the end of the fourteenth century.[72] The younger son Richard (d. 1290/3) established a much more successful and enduring family. He made further purchases in Willoughby, like his elder brother taking his name from the vill in which he resided, and extending his landed interests into several surrounding vills.[73] But it was his son, another Richard, who accelerated the family's advance into the ranks of the more substantial county gentry. A pleader in the court of common pleas from 1301, he rose to the office of chief justice of the bench in Ireland in 1323.[74] This success, although modest compared with that later achieved by his son, enabled him to extend the family's estates far beyond Willoughby and its immediate neighbourhood, chiefly, and in a manner typical of judicial families in this period, at the expense of an insolvent knightly family, in his case, that of Morteyn, lords of Dunsby in Lincolnshire, Wollaton in Nottinghamshire, and Risley in Derbyshire. In 1310 his son, Richard, was married to Sir Roger Morteyn's daughter Isabel, and thereafter the Willoughbys acquired a large part of the Morteyn patrimony from both Sir Roger and Sir Roger's son, Sir William.[75]

The story of the career of this younger Sir Richard, who followed his father into the law, is well known. His kidnap by the criminal bands of Folville and Coterel in January 1332 and his dismissal from the office of chief justice of the king's bench in July 1340 for allegedly selling the laws 'as if they had been oxen or cattle', were the most notable incidents in a

[71] Bloom, 'The Willoughbys', 7–14.
[72] *CPR, 1258–66*, 536; Thoroton, i. 272–3.
[73] Bloom, 'The Willoughbys', 14–20.   [74] Ibid. 50–64.
[75] Ibid. 27–38.

noteworthy career.[76] What is less well known is the remarkable volume of purchases he made on the land market: through purchase alone he increased the landed income of his family from about £140 per annum on the death of his father in 1325 to more than £500 per annum on his own death in 1362,[77] in the process making the Willoughbys comfortably the wealthiest non-baronial family with lands in the county.

Through factors largely beyond Sir Richard's ability to control or anticipate, this lone pre-eminence was, at least for the immediate future, to be short lived. After his death the family went into a half-century of decline, the substantial landed provisions he made for his younger sons; the further fragmentation of the estates between these younger sons on the childless death of his son and heir, another Sir Richard, in 1369; and the illegal conveyances made by his second son Hugh (d. 1406), a clerk (who unexpectedly came into the bulk of the inheritance in 1369), to secure an hereditary estate for his issue by his concubine, Joan Spencer, at the expense of Hugh's younger half-brother, Sir Edmund, combined cumulatively to greatly diminish the estate inherited by the next Hugh, grandson of Sir Edmund and great-grandson and eventual heir of Sir Richard (d. 1362), in the early fifteenth century.[78] Nevertheless, this estate was still a substantial one, quite adequate to ensure this Hugh a place amongst the leading Nottinghamshire knights. It comprised the south Nottinghamshire manors of Wollaton, Willoughby-on-the-Wolds (with a sub-manor called 'Nowers fee'), Bradmore, Sutton Passeys, and Car Colston, together with parcels of land scattered through various vills, mostly in the south of the county, the north Leicestershire manors of Cossington, Hamilton, and Wymeswold (the first two of which his grandfather, Sir Edmund, had acquired by his marriage to the Somerville heiress), the south Lincolnshire manors of Dunsby and Wigtoft, and 10 marks of annual rent from the Derbyshire manor of Elvaston.

He was soon to add substantially to these estates by marriage and hence dramatically to reverse the family's recent decline. This raises a second important consideration about the rise of families which were judicial in origin. As Dr D. J. M. Higgins has remarked in his study of the judges of Edward II, their acquisition of land through marriage was

---

[76] Bloom, 'The Willoughbys', 129–34, 183; Maddicott, 'Law and Lordship', 43.

[77] Bloom, 'The Willoughbys', 109, 281.

[78] Ibid., ch. 6. Through the conveyances of Hugh, the clerk, the main line of the family lost the Derbys. manors of Risley and Mapperley, and the Notts. manor of Cossall: ibid. 356.

modest. Their wives were generally from families of local influence belonging to a somewhat higher level of the gentle class than that of the judges' own families,[79] but they were rarely heiresses. A judge was more likely to find a substantial widow, and this was certainly the case with Chief Justice Willoughby, who married as his second wife, Joan, the widow of the wealthy Northumberland knight, Sir Bertram Monboucher (d. 1332), and, as his third, Elizabeth, the widow of Richard Champer-nowne of Modbury in Devon.[80] But, although judges themselves only infrequently married heiresses, the advance in social status that their careers brought to their families often enabled their descendants to marry with advantage, and it was marriage rather than continued service in the law that enabled the social advance of the family to continue. It is in this context that Hugh's marriage to Margaret (d. 1493), one of the three daughters and eventual coheiresses of Sir Baldwin Freville (d. 1400) of Tamworth in Staffordshire is to be seen.[81] She brought to the Willoughbys a scattered but valuable estate consisting of the manors of Middleton, Whitnash, and Wykes in Warwickshire, the manor of Gunthorpe and Lowdham in Nottinghamshire and the manors of Mowne, Ferne, and Broadfield in Herefordshire.[82] By the time of the tax assessments of 1436 these lands had made Sir Hugh (a knight by 17 November 1429) the richest of the Nottinghamshire knights save only Sir Thomas Chaworth (although it should be noted that the great estate he enjoyed was likely to be only very temporarily united in the hands of the Willoughbys since his heir-apparent, Richard, was his son by his first marriage and hence had no claim to the Freville lands).

A better illustration of the part played by marriage in the rise of judicial families is provided by the two other such families that formed part of the élite of Lancastrian Nottinghamshire: the Babingtons and the Markhams. Their histories have much in common. Both families enjoyed early prominence followed by a lengthy period of obscurity during the fourteenth century and a sudden emergence into the ranks of the county aristocracy during the early fifteenth century.

[79] Higgins, 'Judges in Government', 182.

[80] Bloom, 'The Willoughbys', 102–5, 245–7. Joan was the heiress of the Northumber-land family of Charron but it was the issue of her first Monboucher husband that were the heirs to the Charron estates.

[81] Margaret was Hugh's second wife. His first, Isabel, daughter of Thomas Foljambe (d. 1433) of Walton, had died on 29 Dec. 1417: *TTS* 6 (1902), 51. He lost no time in finding a new wife for he had married Margaret by 23 May 1418: NUL, Mi. D 1103. He probably did so very soon after she became an heiress on the death of her brother, Baldwin, which occurred on 3 Apr. 1418: C138/35/47.

[82] CP25(1)/292/68/170; NUL, Mi. D 4764; *CIPM, Henry VII*, i. nos. 865–7.

The Babingtons, originally from Bavington in Northumberland, had held lands in Nottinghamshire since the second half of the thirteenth century when Sir Hugh Babington (d. 1296) held a manor at Rolleston near Newark and served as under-sheriff in the county to the archbishop of York in 1271.[83] Little is known of the family in the fourteenth century. They seem to have largely abandoned their Northumberland interests by the middle of that century,[84] and towards its end their focus of interest appears to have shifted from Cambridgeshire, where they held the manor of Woodbury in Gamlingay, to Nottinghamshire, where, in addition to Rolleston, they had acquired the Purchace estate in East Bridgford.[85] John Babington married a Cambridgeshire bride, but served as a tax collector in Nottinghamshire in 1382, was styled as 'of Rolleston' in a mainprise of 1386, and was buried in the church at East Bridgford.[86] The marriage of his son and heir, William, to the heiress of the Martels of Chilwell, increased their landholdings in the county for, through her, they inherited the manors of Chilwell and Ruddington, both near Nottingham.[87] But the real foundation of the family's fortunes lay not in this marriage but in William's spectacularly successful legal career. His rise was meteoric: in 1413, when in his late thirties,[88] he was employed as an apprentice-at-law by the duchy of Lancaster; in January of the following year he was appointed the king's attorney in the court of common pleas; by Easter 1418 he had reluctantly taken up the degree of serjeant-at-law; in November 1419 he became chief baron of the exchequer; in June 1420 he was promoted to a seat on the common bench; and, in May 1423, he became chief justice of that court, serving in that capacity until his retirement in February 1436.[89] He was quick to exploit his success in the furtherance of his family. The influence he exerted through his judicial office and legal expertise enabled his

---

[83] Moor, *Knights of Edward I*, i. 30: G.T.C., 'Inedited Additions to the Pedigree of Babington', *The Topographer and Genealogist*, 1 (1846), 138–9.

[84] G.T.C., 'The Pedigree of the Family of Babington of Dethick and Kingston', *Collectanea Topographica et Genealogica*, 8 (1843), 316; id., 'Inedited Additions', 136.

[85] VCH, *Cambridgeshire*, v (1973), 73; Thoroton, i. 296; A. du Boulay Hill, *East Bridgford* (London, 1932), 43.

[86] *CFR, 1377–83*, 337; *CCR, 1385–9*, 144; G.T.C., 'The Pedigree', 317. According to Thoroton's transcription from John Babington's now lost tomb, John died in 1409, but a John Babington appears as lord of Gamlingay in 1412 and a John Babington of East Bridgford is named on a jury panel for the wapentake of Bingham in June 1414: Thoroton, i. 298; *FA*, vi. 408; KB9/204/2/11.

[87] Thoroton, i. 126–71; ii. 181.

[88] He acted as a mainpernor in chancery as early as 1395: *CCR, 1392–6*, 404.

[89] Somerville, p. 424; *CPR, 1413–16*, 150; *1416–22*, 253, 295; *1422–9*, 87; *CCR, 1413–19*, 216; *RP*, iv. 107; Foss, *A Biographical Dictionary*, 32.

younger brothers and sons to attract a remarkable series of wealthy brides. His brother Norman (d. 1434) married Margaret Nesfield, a servant or distant relative of Elizabeth Arundel (d. 1425), widow of Thomas Mowbray (d. 1399), duke of Norfolk,[90] and one of the three FitzAlan coheiresses; a marriage which, on Margaret's death in 1451, brought a third of the FitzAlan manor of Woolston in Chigwell in Essex, together with other lands in Essex and Shropshire, to the retired chief justice.[91] Much more important was the marriage of another brother, Thomas (d. 1466), to Isabel, one of the two daughters and coheiresses of Robert Dethick of Dethick near Matlock in Derbyshire, through which Thomas acquired the Derbyshire manors of Dethick and Litchurch and established a family that was to be very prominent during the sixteenth century.[92] Of William's sons, John married Maud (d. 1426), the granddaughter of Eleanor, heiress of the barony of St Amand, by Sir Gerard Braybrooke (d. 1429) and hence one of the three coheiresses of that barony on the death of her father, Gerard Braybrooke, in 1422, but both John and Maud died young and childless.[93] Another son, Robert (d. 1464), married Elizabeth, the daughter and heiress of Ralph Williamscote of Kiddington in Oxfordshire, establishing a branch of the family in that county,[94] while William, the eventual heir of Chief Justice Babington, married a minor Lincolnshire heiress, Elizabeth, the daughter of John Gibthorpe of Thorpe-by-Wainfleet.[95]

This extraordinary series of marriages greatly increased the landed wealth of the Babington family as a whole, but more significant for the main branch were the chief justice's land purchases, which exploited

[90] P. Morant, *The History and Antiquities of the County of Essex*, 2 vols. (London, 1768), i. 168; C139/142/18.

[91] At the time of the marriage William settled his East Bridgford lands on the couple, while the duchess, by a fine of 1425, settled a third of the manor of Woolston and a third of two-thirds of the manor of Margaretting in Essex, together with a third of the manor of Kemberton and woodland at Wellington in Salop, on the couple and the heirs of Norman: G.T.C., 'The Pedigree', 320; *Feet of Fines for Essex, 1423–1547*, ed. P. H. Reaney and M. Fitch (Colchester, 1964), 6; VCH, *Essex*, iv (1956), 31. These Essex and Salop lands were valued at only £5 6s. 8d. in Norman's inquisition *post mortem* of 1434: C139/62/12. His widow, Margaret (d. 1451), styled as of East Bridgford, was assessed at an income of £7 p.a. in 1451: E179/159/84.

[92] This marriage had taken place by Nov. 1431 when these manors were settled on Thomas and Isabel and their issue, with remainder to Isabel's right heirs: *Derbyshire Feet of Fines, 1323–1546*, ed. H. J. H. Garratt, Derbyshire Record Society 11 (1985), no. 1079. The Catholic conspirator, Sir Anthony Babington (ex. 1546), was a direct descendant of this marriage in the male line: Thoroton, i. 22.

[94] VCH, *Oxfordshire*, vi (1959), 270; G.T.C., 'Inedited Additions', 266–79.

[95] G.T.C., 'The Pedigree', 319; J. C. Wedgwood, *History of Parliament, 1439–1509* (HMSO, 1936–8), i. *Biographies*, 373.

both the surplus cash of the lawyer and the contacts he made as an executor and feoffee, roles for which he was much in demand amongst not only his fellow Nottinghamshire landowners but also the much wider circle of contacts he made as a justice. One of his most substantial purchases was made in this way for it was as an executor of the will of Sir Gerard Braybrooke that he bought the Braybrooke manor of Clifton in Bedfordshire,[96] a contact which no doubt also explains the marriage of his son, John, to the St Amand heiress. Not surprisingly, however, most of his purchases were made nearer home in Nottinghamshire and, to a greater extent, in Derbyshire. In 1417 he purchased a quarter of the Nottinghamshire manor of Oxton from the heir general of the Strelleys of Woodborough; in the same year, he purchased a moiety of the manor of Blackwall, near Alfreton in Derbyshire, from John Trussebut; four years later, in 1421, he purchased the other moiety of the same manor, together with moieties of the adjacent manors of South Normanton and Pinxton, from one of the coheiresses of the Solney family; and, in 1420, he purchased the reversion of the 'Berford' moiety of the manor of Measham in the far south of Derbyshire (now in Leicestershire) having probably already acquired the Dabridgecourt moiety of the same manor.[97] While these purchases are insignificant compared with those made more than half a century earlier by Chief Justice Willoughby, they still marked a significant advance for the family. These purchased estates were valued in his inquisition *post mortem* at as much as £49 per annum compared with a total valuation for all his estates of only £59 per annum.[98] It seems probable that the other lands listed, with the exception of 'Babyngton maner' in Rolleston, were also purchased. Significantly, the manors of Chilwell and Ruddington, the inheritance of his wife, the lands at East Bridgford, and the Cambridgeshire manor of Woodbury in Gamlingay, which he had inherited from his father, were omitted, and it would seem that the chief justice had made them over to his son and heir-apparent, William, some time before his own death at an advanced age in October 1454.[99] The tax returns of 1436 and 1451 certainly suggest that this was so: in 1436 he was assessed as the fourth richest man in the county at £160 per annum but by 1451 his assessment had

[96] VCH, *Bedfordshire*, ii (1908), 276. The manor was valued at £8 13s. 4d. at Sir William's death in 1454: C139/157/23.

[97] CP25(1)/186/38/4; *Derbyshire Fines*, nos. 1052, 1057; *CCR, 1413–19*, 444; J. C. Cox, *Notes on the Churches of Derbyshire* (Chesterfield, 1875–9), i. 283; *Descriptive Catalogue of Derbyshire Charters*, ed. I. H. Jeayes (London, 1906), no. 1873.

[98] C139/157/23.

[99] For his will, dated 3 Oct. 1454: Borthwick Institute, Prob. Reg. 2, fos. 301ᵛ–302.

fallen to £40 per annum while that of his son, William, had risen from £37 to £100 per annum.[100]

A similar combination of land acquisition by marriage and purchase is to be found in the case of the Markhams. William Camden (d. 1623) in his *Britannia* of 1586 noted that this family were 'very famous heretofore both for antiquity and valour',[101] but it is by their success in the law and on the marriage market that they were most distinguished in the fifteenth century. Traditionally the family pedigree is traced back to Sir Alexander Markham (said to have been castellan of Nottingham Castle in the late twelfth century), whose son, William, married Cecilia, sister and in her issue, coheiress of Henry Lexington (d. 1258), bishop of Lincoln.[102] The Lexington estates did not remain in the family for long since William's grandson, Sir Robert Markham, died in 1289 leaving three daughters as his coheiresses (from these daughters descended the important Nottinghamshire families of Longviliers, Stanhope, Bekering, and Mering).[103] It is very probable that the fourteenth-century family established at East Markham was a younger branch of this Lexington line, perhaps descended from a younger brother of Sir Robert (d. 1289), but their early history is very obscure.[104] John Markham (d. 1329) and his son, Robert, are said to have both served as king's serjeants and to have married heiresses of the families of Bothamsall and Caunton,[105] but it is not until the time of Robert's son, Sir John Markham, that the obscurity surrounding the family lifts. It was as a result of his highly successful legal career that the family was elevated to the first rank of the Nottinghamshire aristocracy. A Nottingham justice of the peace from March 1382 and a serjeant-at-law by January 1383, he was retained by Henry, earl of Derby, in 1392–3, served as chief justice at Lancaster in 1394, and was promoted to the common bench on 7 July 1396, where he served until Hilary 1408.[106] The profits of office enabled him to

[100] E179/240/266; 159/84; Appendix 2.
[101] 'Markhams of Markham, Cotham, and afterwards of Becca', *The Herald and Genealogist*, ed. J. G. Nichols, 7 (1873), 320.
[102] *Notts. Visit.*, 23; 'The Visitation of Lincolnshire, 1562–4', *The Genealogist*, ed. G. W. Marshall, 4 (1880), 249; C. R. Markham, *Markham Memorials* (London, 1913), i. 6. For a scholarly account of the family's early history: *Rufford Charters*, ed. C. J. Holdsworth, TSRS (1972–81), i, pp. xcix–cii.
[103] *Notts. IPM, 1242–1321*, 33–6; Thoroton, iii. 220.
[104] *Rufford Charters*, i, p. cii; Thoroton, iii. 230.
[105] *Notts. IPM, 1321–50*, 32; *CCR, 1343–6*, 334; Markham, *Markham Memorials*, 8–9; Thoroton, iii. 228. Neither is mentioned in Baker, *Serjeants at Law*.
[106] *CPR, 1381–5*, 139; Baker, *Serjeants at Law*, 158; Somerville, pp. 386, 468; G. O. Sayles, *Select Cases in the Court of King's Bench under Edward III*, Selden Society, 82 (1965), p. lxxix.

speculate on the property market and he purchased the north Notting-hamshire manors of Bothamsall and Upton *iuxta* Headon, both lying only a few miles from East Markham.[107] But it was his two marriages that did most to increase the wealth of the family. His first wife, Elizabeth, was the sister and, in her issue, the coheiress of her brother, Hugh Cressy (d. 1408) of Hodsock. In the partition of the considerable Cressy inheritance made in April 1409 Sir John and his heirs by Elizabeth were assigned the valuable south Lincolnshire manor of Risegate, another Lincolnshire manor at Bratoft near Skegness, and a moiety of the south Yorkshire manor of Melton.[108] His second marriage led to a further acquisition of estates. After the death of Nicholas Burdon of Maplebeck, fighting for Lancaster at the battle of Shrewsbury on 21 July 1403, Sir John married Nicholas's widow, Milicent (d. 1419), the daughter of Sir John's neighbour, Thomas Bekering (d. 1388), and it was as a result of this marriage that Robert, his eldest son by his first wife, married Milicent's step-daughter, Elizabeth, the sole heiress of the Burdon estates.[109] This brought to the Markhams the north Nottinghamshire manors of Maplebeck and Boughton[110] to the south and south-west of East Markham, and left them, along with their neighbours the Stanhopes of Rampton, the dominant landholders in the north-east of the county.

Their wealth was further extended by the marriage of Robert's half-brother, John, some time before May 1436, to one of the four daughters and coheiresses of Simon Leek of Cotham, which brought John the Lincolnshire manor of Sedgebrook and the Leicestershire manor of Swannington.[111] This marriage also supplemented the wealth of the main line for it led to the marriage in about March 1445 of his young nephew Robert to Joan Daubeney, the sole heiress of her mother, Mary (d. 1443), another of the Leek coheiresses.[112] These two Leek marriages meant that by the second half of the fifteenth century two very substantial Markham families had taken root, one established at East Markham and

[107] CP25(1)/186/36/66; 69; 70 (all fines of 1395). He purchased Bothamsall from Sir Ralph Bracebridge of Kingsbury, War., the heir of the Lincs. family of Boselingthorp: L. A. S. Butler, 'An Unrecorded Brass at Bothamsall Church', *TTS* 67 (1963), 25–7.
[108] NUL, Cl. D 674; below, pp. 204–5. In the Lincs. inquisition taken on Sir John's death, Risegate and Bratoft were valued together at £53 6s. 8d. C137/78/30.
[109] For the Burdon family: *Rufford Charters*, i, pp. lxxxiv–lxxxvii.
[110] In 1428–9 the total rent charge of Boughton, Maplebeck, and lands in nearby vills was £29 7s. 10d.: NUL, Ne. M 146.
[111] G. F. Farnham, *Leicestershire Medieval Village Notes* (1929–33), iv. 200.
[112] *CP*, iv. 100–1 n. g; *TE*, ii. 113. She brought the Leek residence of Cotham to the senior line of the Markhams and they had made it their home by the end of the century: Thoroton, i. 343.

Cotham, and the other just over the Lincolnshire border at Sedgebrook. This latter junior line was doubly indebted to the law for its advance since its founder, John, as the younger son of Justice Markham, had followed his father into the law and proved even more successful, rising to the office of chief justice of the king's bench (1461–9).[113] There could be no better example than the Markhams of a family who converted success in the law to success on the marriage market.

The history of late-medieval Nottinghamshire leaves no doubt of the importance of the law as a means, and probably the principal means, of social advancement: the Pastons, Catesbys, Yelvertons, and others are eloquent testimony that this phenomenon was not confined to Nottinghamshire.[114] There seems little reason to look further for an explanation of the success of judicial families than the wealth provided by legal fees and salaries and the fact that judges, unlike merchants, who also enjoyed considerable financial resources, could easily convert their wealth into social progress because they were themselves usually gentle in origin. For Fortescue, however, the explanation was much less prosaic. For him, the judges, of which he was one, enjoyed a divine benediction. In his view their race was 'so perpetuated by grace that scarcely any of [the judges] die without issue, which is like a great and as it were an appropriate benediction of God'. He continued that he thought it 'no less a divine gift that more leaders and magnates of the realm, who have made themselves rich, illustrious and noble by their own prudence and industry, arise from the issues of judges than from any other estate of men in the realm'.[115] Such a supernatural explanation for a readily observable phenomenon has little to recommend it to the modern historian; it is sufficient to note that the profound effect of judicial profits on the social structure of late-medieval England was as obvious to contemporaries as it is to the modern student.

The law was not, however, the only method by which families rose into the ranks of the shire élite. Other forms of more direct royal service could be equally remunerative. For gentry families this was particularly true in the years immediately after the Lancastrian usurpation of 1399. When Henry IV made himself king, the baronial affinity of Lancaster, with access to the patronage of the duke of Lancaster, was transformed into the royal affinity of England, with access to the much greater

---

[113] For his career: Foss, *A Biographical Dictionary*, 435–6.

[114] See Bennett's comments on Lancs. and Ches.: Bennett, *Community, Class and Careerism*, 200–3.

[115] Fortescue, *De Laudibus*, 129, 131.

patronage of the king: a king, moreover, who had a particular reason to reward his servants for the loyal service that had put him on the throne. Such families as the Pelhams and the Norburys saw rapid social promotion as a result of their service to Henry IV,[116] and Nottinghamshire provides an equally striking example in the family of Rempston.

The Rempstons were an ancient family: they had been established at the south-east Nottinghamshire vill of Rempstone from before the time of Henry III.[117] But the early generations of the family were middling gentry who failed to advance themselves either through marriage or otherwise, and it was not until the spectacularly successful career of Sir Thomas Rempston (d. 1406) that the family were elevated to the first rank of the county aristocracy. His lengthy service to Henry Bolingbroke, both before and after Henry became king, brought him commensurate rewards and saw him extend the estates of the family very considerably.[118] His major acquisition was the reversion of the valuable south Nottinghamshire manor of Bingham,[119] together with the nearby manor of Clipston *iuxta* Plumtree, both of which had long been in the hands of the Bingham family. On the death of the indebted and intestate Sir Richard Bingham in 1387,[120] and that of his young grandson and heir, Robert, soon afterwards,[121] his feoffees, in a somewhat unusual arrangement (which worked to the disadvantage of either the collateral heirs of the Bingham family,[122] or John of Gaunt, to whom the manor of Bingham should have escheated in default of such collaterals) had granted the reversion of these manors to Richard II.[123] After his deposition, by a fine levied in November 1399, Richard, styled as late king of England, passed the reversion to Rempston and his heirs, saving the life interests

---

[116] For the impact of the Lancastrian usurpation on local society: Barber, 'Surrey and Sussex', 213–46; id., 'John Norbury (*c.*1350–1414): An Esquire of Henry IV', *EHR* 68 (1953), 66–76; T. John, 'Sir Thomas Erpingham, East Anglian Society and the Dynastic Revolution of 1399', *Norfolk Archaeology*, 35 (1970–3), 96–108; N. E. Saul, *Scenes from Provincial Life: Knightly Families in Sussex, 1280–1400* (Oxford, 1986), 70–2.

[117] Thoroton, i. 60.   [118] For his career: below, pp. 121–2.

[119] A partially legible extent of this manor is to be found in the inquisition *post mortem* of Sir Richard Bingham in 1387: *Notts. IPM, 1350–1436*, 103–4. It is clear that it was a very valuable one, for Joan Paveley, who held it in 1412, was assessed at as much as £66 p.a., apparently on the manor alone, in the tax returns of that year: Appendix 1.

[120] *CCR, 1381–5*, 306, 426; *CPR, 1388–92*, 283.

[121] Robert was still alive in May 1390 when his marriage was granted to Sir Gerard Braybrooke (d. 1429) and Isabel, the widow of William Bingham: *CPR, 1388–92*, 248. But he was dead by October 1393: ibid., *1391–6*, 320.

[122] The pedigree of the family is uncertain but the Binghams of Car Colston appear to have been a junior branch: below, p. 179.

[123] *CPR, 1391–6*, 320.

of Joan, widow of Sir Richard Bingham, in Bingham, and Isabel, widow of Sir Richard's son, William, in Clipston, together with that of Sir William Arundel (d. 1400) and Agnes, his wife, to whom Richard had granted the reversion of Bingham in 1393.[124] This grant was clearly a reward for Rempston's part in Richard's overthrow: the fine no doubt being levied at the instigation of the new king, although, ironically, Rempston never gained possession of Bingham for Joan survived him.[125] This direct mark of royal favour was very far from marking the limit of his landed acquisitions: by 1405 he had acquired the Northamptonshire manors of Etton and Northborough (valued together at 46 marks in 1412); at an unknown date, the Derbyshire manor of Hopwell; and, in 1405, the south Lincolnshire manor of Brant Broughton (valued at £40 in 1412); all apparently by purchase.[126] The excess cash which allowed him such activity on the land market came from the profits of office and patronage. At his untimely death (he was drowned in the Thames on 31 October 1406 when still at the height of his career), these profits from Henry IV's largesse had laid the basis for the future landed prominence of the family. Their enhanced status is reflected in the marriage of his son and heir, another Sir Thomas, to Alice, the daughter and heiress of Thomas Bekering by Isabel, one of the two sisters and coheiresses of Sir John Loudham (d. 1390) of Lowdham. On Bekering's death in 1425, Alice inherited the manor of Beckering in Holton in Lincolnshire, the Huntingdonshire manor of Catworth, a moiety of the Warwickshire manor of Farnborough, and Nottinghamshire manors in Tuxford and Laxton,[127] and, in 1451, after a long wait for the death of her uncle's widow, Margaret Zouche, two further Nottinghamshire manors at Lowdham and Bilsthorpe.[128]

In most cases the profits of the successful career of one of its members was a necessary preliminary to a family's gaining access to those

[124] CP25(1)/186/37/10.

[125] She died in *c.*1413: Bridges, *Northamptonshire*, i. 313; Watney, *The Wallop Family*, iii. 612. Rempston did, however, gain the advowson of Bingham church since this was in King Richard's hands when the fine was levied, and it was in the chancel of that church that he was buried: *TE*, ii. 224 n. In Michaelmas term 1400 he had unsuccessfully sued Joan for Bingham and Isabel for Clipston: CP40/559, rot. 510[d].

[126] Bridges, *Northamptonshire*, ii. 510; *FA*, i. 262, 302; vi. 481, 500; C1/31/158; *CCR*, *1405–9*, 68, 72–3, 75–6.

[127] These lands were extended at £24 10*s.* 5*d.* p.a. in Bekering's inquisition *post mortem*, and they were almost certainly worth a good deal more: C139/23/25.

[128] *CFR, 1445–52*, 218–19. She had, however, gained an immediate third share of the Derbyshire manors of Walton, Brimington, and Whittington, all near Chesterfield: *FA*, i. 290, 292.

heiresses who came on to the marriage market. The Leeks of Cotham appear to have been an exception to this rule, their rise to the forefront of Nottinghamshire society being based on a series of profitable marriages over a number of generations. They were an ancient knightly family, established at West Leake in the south-east corner of the county since the time of King John,[129] but, in the thirteenth century, far inferior to the Strelleys, Cliftons, Pierpoints, Chaworths, and Nevills in status. It was not until the mid-fourteenth century and the marriage of Sir Simon Leek (d. *c*.1382) to Margaret, the daughter and heiress of Sir John Vaux (d. 1349) of Cotham near Newark, that the family made any progress up the social scale.[130] Sir Simon added to the lands his wife brought him by acquiring the manor of Kilvington near Cotham from the financially embarrassed Nottinghamshire knight, Sir Richard Bingham.[131] Thereafter, the family's rise was swift. Their landed position in the area south of Newark was further strengthened by the marriage of Sir Simon's younger son, William, to Avicia, the heiress of John Stockton of Screveton, a marriage which had taken place before 1384 and had brought to William the manor of Kirkton Hall in Screveton, together with lands in Lincoln, Coventry, Kirby Bellars, and Long Clawson (the last two in north Leicestershire).[132] Sir Simon's son and heir, Sir John (d. *c*.1413), also married an heiress, although his was a less attractive match. According to the 1562 visitation of Lincolnshire, his wife was one of the two daughters and coheiresses of Thomas Towers of Somerby-by-Gainsborough, but it is difficult to discover what lands she brought with her.[133] Of much greater significance were the marriages of Sir John's two sons, Simon and John. The elder, Simon, married in

[129] Thoroton, i. 48; *CIPM*, vi, no. 507; *Notts. IPM, 1321–50*, 4–5.

[130] *CFR, 1347–56*, 171; *TE*, i. 29; *Calendar of Entries in the Papal Registers Relating to Great Britain and Ireland: Papal Letters, 1198–1492*, 14 vols. in 15 (HMSO, 1893–1960), iii. 456. Margaret brought to the Leeks the manor of Cotham and lands over the Lincs. border at Westborough, Dry Doddington, Stubton, and Thorp: Thoroton, i. 341–3; CP40/701, rot. 340.

[131] Thoroton, i. 320.

[132] Ibid. 248–9. William's son and heir, William, was assessed (on his Notts. lands alone) at £40 p.a. in 1412, and his grandson, Ralph (on his lands in all counties) at as much as £72 p.a. in 1436.

[133] 'The Visitation of Lincolnshire, 1562–4', 49. The other coheiress married a Lincs. man, Walter Topcliffe. The Towers family held lands at Cabourn, Hamby in Alford, Welton, Somerby-by-Gainsborough, and Sutterby in Lincs. By 1428 the Cabourn, Somerby, and Sutterby lands were in the hands of the Topcliffe family: *FA*, iii. 259, 261, 282, 284, 346, 354, 366. The Welton and Hamby lands were said to be held by the heirs of Thomas Towers, but there is no record of these lands ever being held by the Leeks of Cotham or their descendants: ibid. 257, 291.

*c.*1405, Joan, the daughter and heiress of the Leicestershire knight, Sir John Talbot of Swannington; in addition to the manor of Swannington, she brought him the Lincolnshire manor of Sedgebrook, which lay just across the border from Cotham.[134] The younger, John, made an even better match. Before September 1403, he married Alice, one of the two daughters and coheiresses of John Grey of Sandiacre,[135] who was a considerable landholder: in addition to the south Derbyshire manors of Sandiacre and Kirk Hallom, he held the manor of Sutton Scarsdale in the north of the same county, Nottinghamshire manors at Hickling and Langford, the Leicestershire manor of Harston, and the manors of Crown East and Ridge Hall in St John in Bedwardine in Worcestershire (an inheritance valued in excess of £110 per annum in the tax returns of 1412).[136] Although the dower and jointure interests of his widow, Emma, who died in December 1434,[137] meant that the two coheiresses were kept out of a significant part of these lands for over thirty years, the childless death of the twice-widowed elder coheiress, Isabel, in March 1436,[138] ensured that the whole Grey inheritance was ultimately reunited in the hands of John Leek,[139] from whom the seventeenth-century earls of Scarsdale descended in a direct male line.

In the space of only three generations and in little over half a century the Leeks had married five heiresses, four of them substantial ones, bringing them lands in five counties and establishing not just one but three wealthy families. Consequently, even after the senior line, established at Cotham, failed in the male line in the early 1430s, the two junior branches of Screveton and Sutton Scarsdale remained.[140] This

---

[134] J. Nichols, *The History and Antiquities of the County of Leicester* (London, 1795–1815), iii. 1123; Farnham, *Leicestershire Medieval Village Notes*, iv. 199–200. By a fine of Hilary 1405, Sir John settled the manor of Kilvington on Simon and Joan and their issue: CP25(1)/186/37/16.

[135] John Grey was not a direct male descendant of the ancient family of Grey of Sandiacre, a junior branch of the Greys of Codnor. He was the son and heir of Alice, daughter and heiress of William Grey of Sandiacre, by one Edward Hillary, but, since his mother was such a great heiress, he took her name rather than that of his father: Thoroton, i. 143; Nichols, *County of Leicester*, ii. 214. He died in Sept. 1403: C137/34/1.

[136] This excludes the Leics. and Worcs. lands, a moiety of which was valued at £7 18*s*. 10*d*. in an inquisition *post mortem* of 1436: C139/76/17.

[137] C139/61/29.

[138] C139/74/17; *CFR, 1430–7*, 291; *CCR, 1435–41*, 23. In the tax returns of 1436 she had been assessed at £46 p.a., and John Leek at £40 p.a.: Appendix 2.

[139] It appears that John also held the ancient lands of the Leeks in south-west Notts. for they were in the hands of his grandson, another John, on the latter's death in 1505: *CIPM, Henry VII*, iii, nos. 30, 1020.

[140] The Screveton branch failed in the male line towards the end of the century but the Sutton Leeks survived until 1736: Thoroton, i. 249–50; *CP*, xi. 519.

series of marriages was without parallel in late-medieval Nottinghamshire and emphasizes, if any emphasis were needed, the central importance
of marriage as a means of social advancement.

The two other leading families of Lancastrian Nottinghamshire were
quite different in character from the eleven already discussed for their
connection with the county was very recent in origin. Imports from
outside the county into the upper reaches of local society were a
comparatively rare phenomenon. The histories of the families of Zouche
and Stanhope illustrate two of the limited number of ways such imports
could become established in the county.

Sir John Zouche was a younger son of William (d. 1396), third Lord
Zouche of Harringworth, and one for whom more than generous
provision was made. In 1392 he was granted jointly with his wife
Margaret in fee tail the reversion, on the death of his paternal uncle
Thomas, of the Zouche manors of Aveley in Assington in Suffolk,
Ightham, and Eynsford in Kent, 'Ing's Place' in Wheathampstead in
Hertfordshire, King's Worthy in Hampshire, and 'le Conyngar' in
Amesbury in Wiltshire.[141] Consequently, on Thomas's death in October
1404, he came into a substantial estate valued at more than £63 in the tax
assessments of 1412.[142] This, together with the £20 per annum he had
been granted out of the Zouche's Derbyshire manor of Ilkeston,[143]
ensured that he would have an income commensurate with his position
as the scion of a minor noble house. Yet so scattered and fragmented
were these estates that they gave him no obvious place in county society,
hence it was on those lands brought to him by his wife, Margaret, that he
eventually settled. She was the widow of the Nottinghamshire knight,
Sir John Loudham (d. 1390) of Lowdham, and one of the daughters and
eventual coheiresses of Sir John Burgh (d. 1393) of Burrough Green in
Cambridgeshire and Walton in Yorkshire.[144] At the time of her marriage
to John Zouche, she held the Nottinghamshire manors of Lowdham and
Bilsthorpe, and the Lincolnshire manors of Winterton and Marton, all

---

[141] CP25(1)/289/56/246.

[142] *FA*, vi. 455, 477, 535. This valuation does not include the manors of Wheathampstead and Aveley, valued together at £9 p.a. in Thomas's inquisition *post mortem*: C137/
47/17. For Thomas, MP for Beds., Nov. 1390: A. E. Goodman, 'The Parliamentary
Representation of Bedfordshire and Buckinghamshire, 1377–1422', B. Litt. thesis,
(Oxford, 1964), 259.

[143] *FA*, vi. 415.

[144] For the Burghs: W. M. Palmer, 'A History of the Parish of Borough Green',
Cambridge Antiquarian Society Publications, 54 (1939), 3–17; J. W. Walker, 'The Burghs of
Cambridgeshire and Yorkshire and the Watertons of Lincolnshire and Yorkshire',
Yorkshire Archaeological Journal 30 (1930–1), 311–48.

of which her first husband, Sir John Loudham, had settled on her before their marriage, together with a third of the Derbyshire manor of Walton in dower.[145] On the death of her half-brother, Thomas Burgh, in *c.*1401, she brought to her Zouche husband an even more valuable estate: the manor of Kirklington in central Nottinghamshire, and the manors of Bolton-upon-Dearne and Wildthorpe with lands at nearby Barnburgh in south Yorkshire.[146] The couple settled at Kirklington, a manor held of the archbishopric of York's lordship of Southwell, and had the marriage produced male issue the Zouches of Kirklington would have become one of the foremost Nottinghamshire families.

This is exactly what did happen to their fellow imports, the Stanhopes. Their history is in many ways the most interesting of those of the leading families of Lancastrian Nottinghamshire. They were unique amongst them in having a comparatively recent mercantile origin, although it appears that the Newcastle and Berwick merchants from whom the Nottinghamshire Stanhopes traced their descent were themselves a junior branch of a gentry family, long established at Stanhope in Weardale (Co. Durham), which died out in the male line in 1352.[147] Richard Stanhope (d. 1379)[148] was a wealthy wool merchant, who served twice as mayor of both Berwick-on-Tweed and Newcastle-on-Tyne and twice represented the latter in parliament.[149] His wealth enabled him to purchase the wardship and marriage of Elizabeth, the daughter and heiress of Stephen Malovell of Rampton in north Nottinghamshire, from Sir Roger Beauchamp, who had the same by grant of Queen Philippa, in April 1353.[150] At this date no one could have anticipated how substantial an heiress Elizabeth would, in her issue,

---

[145] *CFR, 1445–52*, 218–19; C139/141/12. Her generous jointure worked to the disadvantage of the families of Foljambe, Bekering, and Rempston, who were the heirs of the Loudhams.

[146] The couple were in possession of Kirklington by Sept. 1401: NRO, Foljambe DD FJ 6/2/1.

[147] 'Durham Records', *DKR* 45 (1884), app. i, p. 259.

[148] The visitation pedigree of 1569 gives, as the father of this Richard, another Richard, '*qui habuit amplissima possessiones in partibus borialibus Regni Angliae*', while Richard the son is styled 'Lord of Elswick' near Newcastle: *Notts. Visit.*, 5. These statements were probably designed to disguise the mercantile origin of the family. There is no reliable contemporary evidence to support them.

[149] *CCR, 1349–54*, 173, 318, 595; *1354–60*, 305–6; C. H. Hunter Blair, 'The Mayors and Lord Mayors of Newcastle upon Tyne', *Archaeologia Aeliana*, 4th series, 18 (1940), 7, 8; id., 'Members of Parliament for Newcastle upon Tyne', ibid. 14 (1937), 25; 'Durham Records', app. i, p. 262.

[150] *CPR, 1340–3*, 271–2; *CCR, 1349–54*, 595–7. For the Malovells: Revd H. Chadwick, 'The History of the Manor of Rampton in Nottinghamshire', *TTS* 24 (1920), 4–12.

become. He married her to his son, John, before July 1364 when the manor of Rampton was settled on John and Elizabeth and their issue, with successive remainders to Elizabeth's issue, Richard Stanhope for life, and the right heirs of Elizabeth.[151] John was quick to establish himself amongst the county gentry: in 1374–5 he served as escheator, and, in the second half of the 1370s, as a Nottinghamshire JP.[152] He also increased his landed estate by an advantageous second marriage to another midlands heiress, Elizabeth, the daughter of Thomas Cuyly and the heiress of her cousin, Sir Roger Cuyly (d. 1359) of Ansty in Warwickshire, in c.1377.[153] She brought to him the manor of Ansty, the Derbyshire manor of Brizlincote in Bretby, the Leicestershire manor of Radcliffe Cuyly and a Nottinghamshire manor in Oxton, and, by a fine levied in 1380, the year of his death, he was able to secure these lands for his issue by his first wife.[154] His eldest son, John, who was in 1379–80 contracted to marry Elizabeth, the sister of the Nottinghamshire knight, Sir Edmund Pierpoint,[155] either failed to outlive him or died before coming of age, since, late in the reign of Richard II, it was his younger son, Richard, who inherited the Malovell and Cuyly estates.[156]

It was early in Richard's career that the family was elevated to the first rank of Nottinghamshire society; a promotion that owed much to good fortune, for a series of childless deaths in the knightly family of Longviliers of Tuxford, which made his mother in her issue heiress of this ancient family, left him as their heir to an important estate in the north of the county. His great-grandmother, Elizabeth, the wife of Robert Malovell of Rampton, was the daughter of Sir Thomas Longviliers (d. 1349).[157] The deaths of her two young nephews in 1369 had left her niece, Agnes, as the sole heiress of Longviliers, and Agnes brought these lands to her second husband, Sir Reynold Everingham, the second son of Adam (d. 1388), Lord Everingham of Laxton. In 1387 her inheritance was settled by fine: a moiety of the sub-manor of Egmanton, a quarter of the neighbouring manor of Laxton and a third of the manor of Tuxford were jointly settled on Agnes and Sir Reynold and their issue

---

[151] CP25(1)/185/33/396.

[152] *CFR, 1369–77*, 269, 301; *CPR, 1367–70*, 66–7; *1374–7*, 136, 491; *1377–81*, 44; *CCR, 1374–7*, 187.

[153] *Derbyshire Fines*, no. 930.

[154] In 1404 Roger Deincourt, the son of Sir Roger Cuyly's widow, claimed that this fine was a forgery: *RP*, iii. 588. Two years later, in 1406, he exchanged his claim to the manor of Ansty for Sir Richard Stanhope's royal annuity of 40 marks: *CCR, 1405–9*, 231; *CPR, 1405–8*, 277. This dispute is discussed in Payling, p. 85.

[155] Thoroton, iii. 244.

[156] Richard was of age by Oct. 1398: *CPR, 1396–9*, 392.

with successive remainders to the male heirs of Reynold's body and the right heirs of Agnes, while several hundred acres of land in Haughton, Ollerton, and elsewhere in north Nottinghamshire were settled on Agnes and Sir Reynold and their issue, with remainder to Agnes's right heirs.[158] This settlement was made to the potential disinheritance of the young Stanhope should Sir Reynold have male issue by a second wife, in the event of Agnes dying without issue. Indeed, this is very nearly what happened. On Agnes's death, Sir Reynold married Joan, a sister of Sir Gerard Braybrooke (d. 1429),[159] and, after his death on 2 August 1398, she bore him a son, Edmund.[160] But the luck of the Stanhopes held. This infant survived for only a few months, and on 12 November 1398 the escheator of Nottinghamshire and Derbyshire was ordered to deliver the Longvilers lands to Richard.[161] Together with the Malovell manor of Rampton, these lands formed a compact and valuable estate in a part of the county[162] where the only resident greater gentry family was the Markhams of East Markham.

The social promotion of certain families within the county and the import of others such as the Stanhopes into it demonstrate the consistently changing composition of the shire élite. Stability was impossible to achieve in face of the frequent failure of families in the main male line, and it was this propensity to failure that was the principal engine of a social change narrowly defined in terms of the rise and fall of landed families. Without it, rising families, armed with fortunes made in the law courts or elsewhere, would not have found heiresses to marry and would have been entirely dependent on a sluggish land market for the estates required to increase their wealth and status.

---

[157] For what follows: C. T. Clay, 'The Family of Longvillers', *Yorkshire Archaeological Journal* 42 (1967–70), 42, 50; *CP*, v. 192n. *c*.

[158] CP25 (1)/186/35/37; 38; *CFR, 1391–9*, 286–7.

[159] On Sir Reynold's death, Joan (d. *c*.1437) married Sir William Thirning (d. 1413), CJCB. On 30 Sept. she was to be assigned dower in Tuxford, Egmanton, and Laxton by virtue of her late husband's joint estate: *CCR, 1399–1402*, 25–6. Some dispute over these dower rights probably underlay the mutual recognizances entered into by Joan and Richard Stanhope in 1419: *CCR, 1413–19*, 527.

[160] *Notts. IPM, 1350–1436*, 135–6.

[161] *CFR, 1391–9*, 286–7. Edmund, born after 19 Aug. 1398, died on 1 or 2 Oct. following: *CP*, v. 192 n. *c*.

[162] The lands listed ibid. do not represent the whole of the Longvilers inheritance that eventually came to Stanhope through Malovell, for they exclude the small manors of Skegby and Markham Clinton: Thoroton, iii. 190, 228; CP40/681, rot. 138^d. The detailed extent taken in 1361 on the death of Sir John Longviliers gives the true value of

During the Lancastrian period, four of the thirteen families identifiable as the Nottinghamshire élite failed in the main male line. Inevitably their failure led to a major reordering within the ranks of the élite and, although this reordering would have been greater if the four families involved had not left as many as eleven coheiresses between them,[163] an analysis of the transfers of property it occasioned reveals a tendency for the county élite to contract in size over time. This tendency was the product of a significant degree of intermarriage between leading county families when heiresses were involved, with the result that one consequence of family failure was to add to the wealth of families already established among the élite. Hugh Cressy's death in 1408 increased the wealth of the Cliftons; that of Simon Leek in *c.*1434 briefly brought new lands to the Willoughbys and substantially increased the wealth of the Markhams,[164] whose advance into the county élite had previously been accelerated by a marriage to one of the Cressy heiresses; while that of Sir John Zouche in *c.*1445 both supplemented the wealth of the main line of the Chaworths and endowed a junior branch of the same family (although this was soon undone by the failure of both these Chaworth lines).[165] It is not surprising that this should have been so.[166] The leading county families were ideally placed to marry the heiresses of other local families and had an obvious incentive for doing so in the acquisition of estates likely to 'dovetail politically and economically' with their own.[167] The resulting contraction of the élite was the continuation of an ongoing process more fully discussed in the following chapter, and was exactly analogous to the process by which ancient peerage titles became concentrated in the hands of fewer families as the late-medieval period progressed.[168]

this inheritance (in excess of £50 p.a.) and demonstrates the inaccuracy of the inquisition *post mortem* taken on Sir Richard Stanhope's death in 1436: *Notts. IPM, 1350–1436*, 45–9; C139/74/28. Stanhope's Nottinghamshire lands were assessed at £60 p.a. in 1412.

[163] For these heiresses see the family trees of Cressy, Leek, Zouche, and Rempston in Appendix 4.

[164] Below, pp. 52–3.   [165] Below, p. 53.

[166] Cf. Wright, p. 42 for the implied view that the more substantial the heiress, the greater, and hence wider, would be the competition for her hand.

[167] Carpenter, 'The Fifteenth-Century English Gentry', 39.

[168] For the consolidation of baronial estates and titles: G. A. Holmes, *The Estates of the Higher Nobility in Fourteenth-Century England* (Cambridge, 1957), 8–9, 40; McFarlane, *The Nobility*, 59, 152–3; and Sir John Fortescue's contemporary comment in *The Governance of England*, ed. C. Plummer (Oxford, 1885), 130. It is interesting to note that, as late as the Restoration, Sir William Temple proposed that, in order to check the declining number of barons and gentry, heiresses should be allowed to marry only younger sons: Russell Smith, *Harrington and his Oceana*, 133.

While, however, the enhancement of the wealth and prestige of well-established families was perhaps the principal effect of family failure, it was not the only one. Another was the promotion of lesser families who owed their ability to marry above themselves to success in the law. The marriage of Sir John Markham (d. 1409), JCB, to one of the Cressy heiresses marked the entry of the Markhams into the county élite (although it should be noted that her brother and any issue he might have had stood between her and the Cressy inheritance at the time the marriage was contracted).[169] Later, Richard, the son and heir of Sir Richard Bingham (d. 1476), JKB, married Margaret, the youngest of the three daughters and coheiresses of Sir Thomas Rempston (d. 1458), and, if he had had issue by her, the Binghams too would have joined the ranks of the élite.[170] It is a striking coincidence, but probably no more, that both the Markhams and the Binghams were junior branches of families who had in earlier centuries been numbered amongst the leading Nottinghamshire landholders.

The third and final effect of family failure was to take lands out of the hands of county families into those of families of equivalent rank from other, usually neighbouring, shires. In the case of heiresses such out-of-county marriages were rare but the close connections that often existed between the leading families of neighbouring shires ensured that they were not unknown. Sometime before 28 May 1449, Elizabeth, Sir Thomas Rempston's eldest daughter, married the lawyer John Cheyne, son and heir-apparent of Laurence Cheyne of Fen Ditton in Cambridgeshire,[171] while in 1451 her sister Isabel married Sir Brian Stapleton of Carlton near Snaith in Yorkshire.[172] Both these marriages are readily explicable in terms of existing kinship networks. Stapleton was the brother-in-law of Rempston's nephew (of the half-blood) and feoffee, Sir William Plumpton of Plumpton in Yorkshire and Kinoulton in Nottinghamshire, and had served with Rempston in France in the household of John, duke of Bedford,[173] while John Cheyne's grandmother, Katherine Pabenham, was the mother of Isabel, wife of another

[169] Above, p. 40.
[170] By 2 Aug. 1476 Margaret was dead without issue: *Notts. IPM, 1437–85*, 78.
[171] *CPR, 1446–52*, 258–9. For the careers of Laurence and John Cheyne: Wedgwood, *Biographies*, 181–2, 183.
[172] Chetwynd-Stapleton, *The Stapletons*, 146.
[173] For his career: ibid. 145–9; A. Gooder, *The Parliamentary Representation of the County of York, 1258–1832*, Yorkshire Archaeological Society Record Series (1936–8), i. 192–3. He and Rempston were both feoffees for Plumpton under a feoffment of 1439: *PC*, pp. lii–liii. For Plumpton as a feoffee of Rempston: *CPR, 1446–52*, 258–9; C1/21/9a.

of Rempston's feoffees, Sir Thomas Chaworth.[174] These marriages demonstrate that the kinship networks amongst the leading gentry formed a framework for social relations wider than the county, and even, on occasion, wider than the region. This worked against, but was not sufficient to negate, the tendency for lands to concentrate in the hands of those resident county families who survived in the male line. The result of the marriages of the two Rempston heiresses was to transfer not only the ancient Rempston lands but also those of the old Nottingham-shire families of Bekering, Bingham, and Loudham to non-resident families. Two factors, however, prevented this passage of lands from leading Nottinghamshire families to non-residents reducing significantly the land available to the resident élite. First, and most obviously, marriages that brought about such transfers of property were counter-balanced by marriages between resident families and the heiresses of non-resident families with lands in the county.[175] Second, there was a marked tendency for the lands so transferred to come back into the hands of leading resident families by either marriage or purchase. This is what happened in the case of the valuable manor of Bingham, which came to the Stapletons on the death of Sir Thomas Rempston in 1458 but was sold by them to Sir Thomas Stanhope (d. 1496) of Shelford towards the end of the sixteenth century.[176] A more immediate example occurs in the case of Mary, the senior of the four daughters and coheiresses of Simon Leek, and the only one of them to marry outside the county. In about April 1434, after the death of her father, she became the second wife of Sir Giles Daubeney, who had a residence at South Ingleby in Lincolnshire near the Leek estate at Saxilby but who was principally resident at South Petherton in Somerset.[177] In the division of the estates, she brought Daubeney the

[174] This family relationship later led John Cheyne to claim the Pabenham manor of Blatherwycke in Northants. against John Ormond, the heir general of the Chaworths: CP40/899, rot. 108[d]; 922, rot. 317. It may also be significant in explaining this marriage that Cheyne and Rempston were Hunts. neighbours: Rempston held Catworth and Cheyne had nearby Great Gidding, which was put into the hands of feoffees headed by Chaworth at the time of the marriage: *CPR, 1446–52*, 258–9.

[175] Below, p. 66.

[176] Thoroton, i. 274.

[177] The approximate date of the marriage is established by a recognizance of 20 Apr. 1434 between Daubeney and two of Simon Leek's feoffees, Nicholas Wimbish, clerk, and John Pygot, esq., in which Daubeney undertook to settle his manor of South Ingleby on Mary for her life: *CCR, 1429–35*, 308. For his career: *CP*, iv. 100–1. For the Leek lands at Saxilby: *FA*, iii. 358.

principal Leek manor of Cotham,[178] but this did not long remain out of the hands of the county élite. The marriage of her young daughter and heiress Joan to Robert Markham brought it to the senior branch of the Markhams, who later made their residence there.[179]

It is quite clear that the marriage patterns of the heiresses of leading county families tended to reinforce the landed pre-eminence of families already established in the county. As we have seen, only occasionally and in unusual circumstances such as the Stanhope purchase of the wardship of the Malovell heiress and the unexpected transformation of the issue of this ward into the heirs of the Longviliers inheritance, did a new family come to be established through marriage alone amongst the county élite. Indeed, such accidental factors must often have been the explanation for the transfer of lands from a leading county family into the hands of an inferior family from either inside or outside the county. A later example involves the inheritance of the Zouches of Kirklington, the coheiresses of which both married into the Chaworths. After the death of Sir William Chaworth in 1467, his wife Elizabeth, the senior of the two coheiresses, married far below herself to a member of the lesser gentry, John, the son and heir of Robert Dunham of Darlton in north Nottinghamshire.[180] At the time of this marriage there can have been little prospect of her issue by Dunham becoming heirs to any part of the extensive Zouche inheritance. However, capricious fate intervened. The premature deaths without issue of Elizabeth's son by Sir William Chaworth and of her nephew, the only son and heir of her sister Margaret by John Chaworth, in 1483 and 1485 respectively, left her son by Dunham as Zouche's sole heir.[181] Thus, suddenly and fortuitously, the Dunhams were elevated from the minor gentry into the ranks of the leading Nottinghamshire families. Such accidents were too infrequent to have much impact on a pattern of property transfer through marriage

[178] On 1 June 1439 Simon Leek's feoffees headed by Thomas Rempston appointed attorneys to deliver seisin of the manor of Cotham with lands in neighbouring Hawton to Mary and her issue, with remainders in fee and in order of seniority to her three sisters: NRO, Portland, DDP 8/3. She and Daubeney must have enjoyed the lands earlier for Daubeney was appointed one of the Nottinghamshire subsidy assessors of 1436 and was assessed at £99 p.a. in the county: *CFR, 1430–7*, 261; E179/240/266.

[179] Above, p. 40. The fact that the remainders had been settled in order of seniority meant that Robert Markham also inherited the manor of Stoke *iuxta* Newark and other neighbouring estates on the death without issue of Richard Willoughby, the husband of the youngest coheiress, Anne, in 1471: *Notts. IPM, 1485–1546*, 20–1.

[180] Robert was assessed at as little as £8 p.a. in the tax returns of 1436: E179/240/266.

[181] *Notts. IPM, 1485–1546*, 28–9.

which tended to concentrate lands in the hands of fewer families, but they should be borne in mind in any discussion of the rise and fall of families. The higher the concentration of land became over time, the greater were the potential effects of such accidents, a fact nowhere better illustrated than in the rise of the present premier dukes of England, the FitzAlan Howards of Norfolk.[182]

While the leading county families were all prone to permanent eclipse through the failure of male heirs, individual heads of these families were subject to temporary impoverishment through minorities and the survival of a dowager or, worse still, dowagers. There is no doubt that amongst tenants-in-chief (documented in the inquisitions *post mortem*) minorities were extremely common. In his survey of 107 male landholders who died during the reigns of the first two Lancastrian kings, Professor J. T. Rosenthal has shown that as many as fifty-nine (55 per cent) were succeeded by an under-age heir: the situation was even worse in the case of those succeeded by a son, for forty-three (64 per cent) of sixty-seven of these sons were minors.[183] It is thus striking that the Nottinghamshire élite seem to have been singularly unaffected by the inconvenience of minorities. Of the twenty-one heads of élite families who died during the Lancastrian period, only four (19 per cent) were succeeded by minors. This happy situation did not prevail amongst other Nottinghamshire landholders: of the sixty heirs of fifty-one male landholders, a mixture of lesser county gentry who happened to be tenants-in-chief and knightly families from other counties who held Nottinghamshire lands, twenty-six (43 per cent) were minors.[184] Clearly the leading Nottinghamshire families were particularly fortunate in respect of minorities and it is consequently difficult to make any remarks about the effect of minorities on these families. The only county family to be significantly affected were the Markhams, who account for two of the four minorities that these families suffered during the Lancastrian

---

[182] McFarlane, *The Nobility*, 155.

[183] J. T. Rosenthal, 'Heirs' Ages and Family Succession in Yorkshire, 1399–1422', *Yorkshire Archaeological Journal* 56 (1984), 88. It should be noted that Rosenthal has mistakenly taken 21 instead of 14 as the age of female majority, although it is an error which does very little to undermine the validity of his figures.

[184] These figures are abstracted from *Notts. IPM, 1350–1436*, 136–204; *1437–85*, 1–56. To avoid overlap with Rosenthal's figures I have excluded the peerage since many of the peers who held lands in Notts. also held lands in Yorks. Nor have I followed his practice of counting only the senior coheir when coheirs were involved but I have, like him, excluded the inquisitions of women, who left a higher proportion of heirs of age since their appearance amongst the inquisitions generally depended on them having survived their husbands.

period.[185] Robert Markham was a minor from 1410 to 1420, and his son, another Robert, from 1446 to *c.*1456.[186] This explained the obscurity of the family for much of the period and may also have underlined the importance of the Stanhopes, who were the only family of equivalent rank in the north-east of the county.

It was not only their rarity that reduced the threat of minorities to these families during the Lancastrian period. The practice of enfeoffment-to-use meant that the worst consequences of minorities, like the wasting of the estate by an unscrupulous royal farmer, could generally be avoided. While, under chapter 6 of the statute of Marlborough (1267), the crown had a remedy against a tenant-in-chief who enfeoffed his lands with the clear intention of depriving the king of his feudal rights, such collusion was difficult to prove, and it was not until the early Tudor period that a concerted effort was made to restrain the abuse of uses.[187] It was through uses that the Markhams evaded royal wardship twice in less than forty years. Their task was made easier by the fact that they did not hold directly of the crown by knight service: their Nottinghamshire and Yorkshire lands were held of the duchy of Lancaster honors of Tickhill and Castle Donington, while their Lincolnshire manors of Risegate and Bratoft were held of the king in socage.[188] This meant that the crown had no right of prerogative wardship and the Markhams were free to enfeoff their lands without royal licence.[189] Both Sir John Markham and his son Sir Robert took advantage of this freedom. When inquisitions *post mortem* were taken after Sir Robert's death in October 1446 it was returned that he held no lands in demesne or in service of the king nor of any other, and that his son and heir was 11 and more.[190] Clearly he had made an enfeoffment of his entire estate in anticipation of his son's minority and it is unfortunate for our purposes that the

---

[185] The other two occurred in the families of Rempston and Clifton. Thomas Rempston, who succeeded his father in 1406, must have been a minor because his parents did not marry until after the death of his mother's first husband in 1388, while Gervase Clifton was said to be 'fourteen and more' in the inquisition taken on the death of his father in 1403: E152/389/6.

[186] C137/78/30; *Notts. IPM, 1437–85*, 26.

[187] This is a large subject, the best short discussion of which is *The Reports of Sir John Spelman*, ed. J. H. Baker, 2 vols., Selden Society, 93, 94 (1976–7), ii. 192–203.

[188] *Notts. IPM, 1485–1546*, 20–1; *CIPM, Henry VII*, iii, no. 551; C137/78/30. In 1508 the manor of Risegate was returned as held in chief by knight service, a reflection of Henry VII's successful efforts to extend his feudal rights: *CIPM, Henry VII*, iii, no. 452.

[189] For the exemption of lands held of the crown in socage or *ut de honore* from prerogative wardship: *Prerogativa Regis*, ed. S. E. Thorne (New Haven, 1949), pp. xiv, xvii; *Spelman*, ed. Baker, i. 176.

[190] C139/128/31.

inquisition jurors did not return the details of this feoffment. More is known of the conveyance made by Sir John Markham when faced with a similar situation. According to an inquisition *post mortem* taken in Lincolnshire he had, on Christmas Eve 1409, conveyed his manors of Risegate and Bratoft to Henry (d. 1425), Lord FitzHugh, Robert (d. 1452), Lord Willoughby of Eresby, Sir John Leek, Simon Leek, and a chaplain, Robert Bothamsall.[191] The fact that no similar inquisition was taken in Nottinghamshire, although a writ of *diem clausit extremum* was rather belatedly issued for the county,[192] implies that he also conveyed his Nottinghamshire lands to these feoffees, and it was presumably they who took the profits until the heir came of age in *c*.1421. Sir John Clifton, who was killed at the battle of Shrewsbury in July 1403, leaving a son and heir of only 14, seems to have employed the same tactics as the two Markhams for his inquisition *post mortem* returns that he held no lands. It was the combination of the good fortune of leaving very few under-age heirs, and the foresight to make suitable provision when a minority threatened, that enabled the élite of Lancastrian Nottinghamshire to avoid the evils of minorities. The fact that such provision could so readily be made was due in part to the privileged position of most leading Nottinghamshire landholders as tenants of the crown *ut de honore* rather than *ut de corona*.

Of much more serious concern to these landowners was the problem of dowagers. Here the interests of the heir were not so easy to protect for three important factors worked against him. The first was the frequency with which wives survived their husbands: of the twenty-one heads of families of the Nottinghamshire élite who died during the Lancastrian period, as many as fourteen definitely left a widow,[193] while only one is known to have died a widower.[194] The second was the long life expectancy of these widows. In the eight Nottinghamshire cases in which the dates of death of the husband and his widow are known, the average period by which the widow survived her husband was nearly twenty years. This was, in part, due to an understandable but, from the heir's point of view,

[191] C137/78/30. On 7 Mar. 1410, by virtue of the findings of this inquisition, the escheator of Lincs. was ordered to meddle no further in these manors: *CCR, 1409–13*, 28.

[192] Writs for Lincs. and Yorks. were issued on 4 Jan. 1410 but, for some unknown reason, the Notts. writ was delayed until the following 24 June: *CFR, 1405–13*, 160. Only in Lincs. was the writ acted upon.

[193] I have included amongst these 14, Hugh Cressy (d. 1408), who was survived by Margaret Skipwith (d. 1415), the wife he had divorced: above, p. 25 n. 31. The divorce extinguished her dower rights.

[194] Sir Thomas Chaworth's second wife Isabel predeceased him by 11 weeks: BL, Add. MS 5832. The status of the remaining 6 is uncertain but the fact that there is no evidence of their wives' survival suggests they died widowers.

regrettable, habit of widowers: they tended to marry young women after the deaths of their first wives. Five of the fourteen heads of families who were definitely survived by a widow were survived by second wives. Of these by far the most striking case is that of Sir Hugh Willoughby, whose second wife, the heiress Margaret Freville, was not only some twenty years his junior but also, most unfortunately for the prospects of both his and her heirs, survived Sir Hugh by nearly half a century.[195] It is hard to avoid the cynical conclusion that a landowner with the advancement of his future son and heir most at heart would be well advised to marry first, for money, an heiress to bring him land and sons, and second, for love, an older woman who was unlikely to compromise his heir by surviving him (or, it might be added, bearing him a second family to provide for).

The third factor working against the interest of the heir was the practice of settling estates in jointure at the time of marriage. It was this that posed the gravest threat to the heir's prospects because, while dower was limited to a third of the family estate, there was no limit to the proportion of the estate that could be settled in jointure. As a general rule, the wealthier the bride, the greater the proportion of the family estate needed to secure her. In McFarlane's view it was jointure that ensured 'the peculiar prominence of dowagers in late-medieval England', and there can be no doubt that its effect on individual noble families was often profound.[196] The picture with respect to the gentry is less clear. Dr Wright, in her study of the fifteenth-century Derbyshire gentry, has argued that, in general, only a small portion of a family's patrimony was settled in jointure, contrasting this with the nobility, who were much more generous to their wives.[197] This view has not found acceptance with Dr Carpenter: her Warwickshire gentry were not only generous but also profligate in their jointure settlements, especially when the wealth or political connections of the bride made her particularly attractive.[198] The Nottinghamshire evidence is ambivalent but would tend to warn against both too much emphasis on the deleterious effects of jointure and the dangers of generalization from the experience of the gentry of a particular county at a particular time.

It is possible, as Carpenter has suggested, that the dispute which arose between the Willoughby heir, Richard, and his step-mother,

---

[195] Born in *c*.1402, she died in 1493: *CCR, 1419–22*, 48; *CIPM, Henry VII*, i, no. 865.
[196] McFarlane, *The Nobility*, 65; R. E. Archer, 'Rich Old Ladies: The Problem of Late Medieval Dowagers', in A. J. Pollard (ed.), *Property and Politics: Essays in Later Medieval History* (Gloucester, 1984), 15–35.
[197] Wright, pp. 32–3.
[198] Carpenter, 'The Fifteenth-Century English Gentry', 41–2.

Margaret Freville, on the death of Sir Hugh in 1448 was a dispute over what Richard saw as the unjustifiably generous jointure settlement Sir Hugh had made in order to secure Margaret's hand.[199] More probably, however, it arose because Sir Hugh made a generous settlement in Margaret's favour long after the marriage, by choice rather than compulsion, so that she might make suitable provision for the very large family she had borne him.[200] In general, Nottinghamshire jointure settlements were highly circumspect. When in *c.*1405 Simon Leek married Joan, the heiress of Sir John Talbot of Swannington in Leicestershire, the only Leek manor settled jointly on the couple was that of Kilvington, while when William Chaworth married Elizabeth, granddaughter and coheiress-apparent of Sir John Zouche, her jointure was set at just 40 marks per annum, a small sum compared with the total value of the great Chaworth inheritance.[201] Sir Thomas Chaworth had not been much more generous to William's mother, Isabel Aylesbury: in 1415 he had settled on her the Nottinghamshire manor of Marnham with a Leicestershire estate in Medbourne and Burton Overy.[202] No doubt he would have had to be much more open-handed if at the time of her marriage she had been the great heiress she was subsequently to become. Sir Robert Strelley (d. 1488) was similarly cautious: in 1443 when he married, as his second wife, the well-connected Isabel, a niece of John Kemp, cardinal-archbishop of York, he settled on her in jointure only the small manor of Oxton.[203] Yet more striking is the fact that Sir Richard Stanhope, on his marriage in 1411 to Maud, daughter of Ralph (d. 1416), Lord Cromwell, appears to have made no settlement in her favour. When she died in 1454 she was returned as seised only of her common-law dower.[204]

Moreover, the leading families of the county could also benefit both directly and indirectly from jointures. A clear case of direct gain is Sir John Zouche's marriage to Margaret Burgh. Her first husband, Sir John Loudham, settled the bulk of his inheritance, including his *caput honoris* of Lowdham, on her for life at a time when only a young half-brother stood between her and a third part of the very substantial Burgh inheritance. He died without issue in 1390 and Margaret took most of his estates to her second husband, Sir John Zouche. Her longevity

---

[199] Carpenter, 'The Fifteenth-Century English Gentry', 59 n. 13.
[200] Below, pp. 72–3, 208.
[201] CP25(1)/186/37/16; Payling, p. 71 (quoting BL, Add. Ch. 20542).
[202] Above, p. 28 n. 50.   [203] *CAD*, iii. C3415.
[204] *Notts. IPM, 1437–85*, 43.

kept the Loudham coheirs, Sir John Loudham's two sisters and their descendants, out of the Loudham estates for over sixty years.[205] Although Nottinghamshire evidence is lacking, there must also have been a much more indirect gain in the form of the jointures that lesser families anxious to marry above themselves were prepared to settle on the daughters of these leading families.[206] All in all, it seems fair to conclude that these families were not as vulnerable as lesser ones to the damaging effects of jointure since the greater a family the less pressure there was upon it to make itself an attractive family for a father to marry his daughter into (the same argument could be made in respect of the higher nobility).

This is not to say that these families never suffered the penalties of excessive jointure settlements but that during the Lancastrian period they escaped lightly. Parallel examples of the sort of jointure settlement Carpenter found so common in fifteenth-century Warwickshire can be found amongst the leading Nottinghamshire families in the later fifteenth century. Robert Willoughby (d. 1474) and Sir Gervase Clifton (d. 1491), both of whom married into the wealthy Griffith family of Wichnor in Staffordshire and Burton Agnes in Yorkshire, settled the *caput honoris* of their inheritances on their wives and in each case their sons and heirs suffered as a result.[207] These cases serve only to highlight the general good fortune of the leading families of Lancastrian Nottinghamshire in respect of jointure. There was, however, one very important exception: the story of the career of the most famous of the county's fifteenth-century gentry, Sir Thomas Rempston (d. 1458), illustrates the very wide repercussions that a combination of generous jointure and the long survival of a widow could have on the prospects of an heir.

Although there is no direct evidence of the settlement Sir Thomas Rempston (d. 1406) made in favour of his wife Margaret, the sister of his friend, Sir John Leek, and widow of Sir Godfrey Foljambe (d. 1388) of Hassop in Derbyshire, subsequent tax returns show it to have been a generous one. In 1412 she was assessed at as much as £170 13s. 4d., and

---

[205] Below, p. 239.

[206] The marriage of William Leek (d. 1458) to Katherine, daughter of Sir Thomas Chaworth, gives some hint of this, William settled his entire paternal inheritance on her in jointure: *Notts. IPM, 1437–85*, 49–50. This did not, however, amount to as generous a settlement as it first appears since the principal wealth of his family lay in the Grey of Sandiacre inheritance, which remained in the hands of his mother until her death in 1459.

[207] For Willoughby: A. Cameron, 'Sir Henry Willoughby of Wollaton', *NMS*, 74 (1970), 15; C1/51/230–5; Carpenter, 'The Fifteenth-Century English Gentry', 42. For Clifton: *CIPM, Henry VII*, iii, no. 1036.

this must have represented the entire Rempston estate.[208] Sir Thomas II was probably still just a minor at this time but even when he obtained his majority soon afterwards (he represented Nottinghamshire in the parliament of May 1413) he came into very little of his paternal inheritance. According to the subsidy returns of 1428, only the manor of Rempstone and the purchased lands in Northamptonshire had descended to him,[209] while the valuable manor of Bingham, which his father had held in reversion, fell to his already wealthy mother.[210] In 1436 he was assessed at only £60 (making him the poorest of the Nottinghamshire knights) compared with his mother's £106.[211] Moreover a significant part of this £60 came not from his paternal inheritance but rather from those lands brought to him by his wife, Alice Bekering.[212]

The fact that he held so much of his inheritance only in reversion, and his mother's obstinate refusal to die, were probably the principal factors in determining his career: between 1415 and 1450 he spent little time in England, making for himself instead a career as one of the foremost commanders of the English armies in France.[213] Since it was probably poverty that drove him into this career, it is unfortunate that his lengthy military service should have turned out to be a stark illustration of the potential profitlessness of such service in the last phase of the Hundred Years' War. Whilst it brought him posthumous fame, it also brought him a heavy ransom that came near to ruining him. On 18 June 1429, at the disastrous English defeat at Patay, he was captured by the notorious Tanguy du Châtel who, ten years earlier, had been the assassin of John the Fearless. Châtel demanded the huge ransom of 18,000 *écus d'or* (about £3,000).[214] Hardly surprisingly, this sum was not immediately

---

[208] Appendix 1; *FA*, vi. 413, 481, 500. The dower she held from her first marriage was of little value: *CIPM*, xvi, nos. 688–9; C139/152/7.

[209] *FA*, iv. 47, 136.

[210] Ibid. 133. The ownership of Bingham was later to come into dispute. By an award dated between Nov. 1448 and Jan. 1450, Sir Thomas was to take the revenues of the manor, paying to Dame Margaret an annuity of £10, while her life estate in other unspecified lands was confirmed: C1/21/9c; below, p. 203. Up to this date it seems that feoffees had held Bingham to her use: C1/21/9b (cf. C1/29/498).

[211] Appendix 2.   [212] Above, p. 43.

[213] For his career in France: *Dictionary of National Biography*, xvi. 896; C. Brown, *Lives of Nottinghamshire Worthies* (Nottingham, 1881), 63–9; *English Suits before the Parlement of Paris, 1420–1436*, ed. C. T. Allmand and C. A. J. Armstrong, Camden Society, 4th series, 26 (1982), 302–3.

[214] For the subsequent ransom negotiations: *CCR, 1429–35*, 228–9; *Catalogue des Rolles Gascons, Normans et Francois*, ed. T. Carte, 2 vols. (Paris and London, 1743), ii. 277, 279, 282, 288; *PPC*, iv. 164–5, 278–9; *CPR, 1429–36*, 270; 'Calendar of French Rolls', *DKR* 48 (1887), 299, 300; *RP*, iv. 488–9.

forthcoming. Negotiations were long and tortuous, giving Sir Thomas every reason to suspect that certain parties at home were doing less than their utmost to secure his release. According to his own testimony, he languished 'in harde and streyte prison welnere be the space of vij yere', eventually being released late in 1435.[215] Only half the original ransom demanded was paid, the rest being commuted in return for the release from English captivity of the long-held French esquire, William Botiller, one of the hostages for the payments due under the 1412 treaty to Buzançais; but this sum was still sufficient to have a dire effect on Sir Thomas's fragile finances. Even though the crown granted him, on 30 June 1436, 1,000 marks towards its payment, the refusal of the exchequer officials to deliver the cash led him to present a petition in the parliament of January 1437 complaining of 'the grete losse that he has borne in making chevishaus of money' for the payment of the ransom,[216] and this (together with another ransom he appears to have paid in the 1440s) explains why, by 1451 his tax assessment had dropped from its 1436 figure of £60 per annum to just £20 per annum.

His lengthy and expensive captivity did nothing to deter him from further military adventures in France. His mother's continued survival meant that he had little to go back to in England. From 1437 to an unknown date he served as lieutenant of Calais and from 1440 to 1442 as seneschal of Gascony. But this second period of service proved just as profitless as the first. When Saint-Sever fell to the French in July 1442 he was captured and again endured a lengthy captivity. It is not clear when he was released or what ransom he had to pay. He was still a prisoner in March 1445 when the wealthy London merchant, Sir William Estfeld, bequeathed the sum of £10 'ad financium suam si vixerit'[217] and he was not definitely back in England until 13 January 1449 when he attested a Nottinghamshire election.[218] In the following year the final collapse of the English position in France entailed the loss of his French lordships of Gacé and Bellencombre.[219]

---

[215] He was presumably free by the morrow of All Souls 1435 when he acted in a fine for Sir John Zouche: CP25(1)/292/68/177.

[216] E404/52/411; SC8/137/6844. He asked as a remedy assignment of the 1,000 marks on the issue of the duchy of Cornwall.

[217] Lambeth Palace, Reg. Stafford, fo. 141.

[218] C219/15/6/71. On 20 Mar. 1449 he was appointed to the Notts. bench for the first time. This suggests that his return to England was recent and that it is probably to be dated to after the issue of the previous peace commission for the county on 6 July 1448: *CPR, 1446–52*, 593.

[219] *Letters and Papers Illustrative of the Wars of the English in France*, ed. J. Stevenson, Rolls Series (1861–4), II, pt. ii, 622, 623.

It is the final irony of his career that within a few years of returning from his second period of service in France he became the substantial landed knight that, with better luck, he would have been from early in the century. The death of Margaret Zouche in May 1451 brought him a moiety of the Loudham lands that were part of his wife's inheritance,[220] while, much more significantly, the long awaited death of his elderly mother on 21 April 1454 finally enabled him to enter the valuable estates from which she had kept him for so long.[221] He had only a few years to enjoy this new-found and very considerable wealth: he died on 15 October 1459[222] leaving three daughters as his coheiresses, between whom his great inheritance, so recently and so briefly united, was partitioned.

Rempston's misfortunes do not, however, detract from the general conclusion that the leading families of Lancastrian Nottinghamshire were fortunate and probably, in comparison with the baronage and leading gentry of other counties, remarkably so in generally avoiding the worst effects of dowagers and minors. It may have been this good fortune as much as the high concentration of the county's landed wealth in their hands that underpinned their political pre-eminence during the Lancastrian period; a pre-eminence that was *prima facie* greater than that enjoyed by similar groups of families in other counties.

---

[220] *Notts. IPM, 1437–85*, 33; *CFR, 1445–52*, 218–19.

[221] Her inquisition *post mortem* lists only her Foljambe dower lands and the Notts. manor of Arnold: C139/152/7. But her 1451 tax assessment of £120 shows that she was still enjoying the profits of most of the Rempston inheritance to the end of her life. Seisin was vested in the hands of feoffees.

[222] C139/171/14. No mention is made in his inquisition *post mortem* of his paternal inheritance which was in the hands of a large group of feoffees headed by Sir Thomas Chaworth: C1/21/9a. The surviving feoffees retained seisin until at least as late as 1476: *Notts. IPM, 1437–85*, 77.

3

THE COUNTY ÉLITE: DEVELOPMENT
AND KINSHIP

THE tendency, observable during the Lancastrian period and noted in the previous chapter, for the landed élite of the county to contract over time can be more convincingly demonstrated by examining the leading Nottinghamshire families over a longer period. Such an examination illustrates a significant change in the anatomy of county society during the late-medieval period: the families that formed the social élite of the county in the early fifteenth century were, in general, individually wealthier and corporately less numerous than their early-fourteenth-century predecessors. This contrast is starkly demonstrated by an analysis of the landed élite of the county in the second quarter of the fourteenth century. By combining the returns of the great council summons of May 1324 and the Roxburgh campaign summonses of a decade later[1] with the manorial histories in Thoroton's *Nottinghamshire* it is possible to arrive at an accurate estimate of the number of knightly families resident in the county in the period 1324–35. Making a deduction for those knights returned under Nottinghamshire in 1324 and 1334–5 who had their principal residences elsewhere (readily established from Moor's *Knights of Edward I* and the index to Palgrave's *Parliamentary Writs*), and allowance for the small number of resident knights who escaped return,[2] one is left with a preliminary estimate of thirty-three such families. To these must be added those families that had recently supported knighthood but, due to the recent death of the head of the family, did not do so at the time of the summonses. Into this category come the families of Barry of Teversal, Burdon, Compton, Furneaux, Husy, Leek, Loudham, Mering, Rempston, Saundby, Sutton and Vaux. This increases the number of resident knightly families to

---

[1] *Parliamentary Writs*, ed. F. Palgrave, Record Commission (1827–34), II. ii. 650–1; C47/2/25/4 and 5; *Rotuli Scotiae*, Record Commission, 2 vols. (1814–19), i. 313.
[2] There appear to be 3 of these: Sir Richard Willoughby (d. 1325); Sir Richard Whatton (d. *c*.1336) of Whatton; and Sir Reginald Aslockton (d. *c*.1328) of Aslockton: Thoroton, i. 261; ii. 210; H. Lawrence and T. E. Routh, 'Military Effigies in Nottinghamshire before the Black Death', *TTS* 28 (1924), 133–4.

forty-five, with twenty-two actual knights resident in 1324. These families were by no means of equal status: both the Everinghams and Chaworths, lords of several manors in neighbouring counties, were wealthy enough to receive personal writs of summons to parliament,[3] while families such as the Saundbys and Aslocktons were lords of only single eponymous manors.[4] Nevertheless, together these families, distinguished by knighthood from the mass of freeholders, represent the leading landowners then resident in the county.

Their subsequent histories demonstrate two things: first, those families fortunate enough to survive in the male line often increased their estates by marriage to those (from both inside and outside the county) not so fortunate; second, those families which survived in the male line but failed to increase their estates had, except in the cases of the very wealthy like the Pierpoints and the Strelleys, abandoned knighthood by the early fifteenth century and descended into the developing county squirearchy. The increasing wealth of the successful families is clearly apparent: the Chaworths had, by the second decade of the fifteenth century, acquired extensive estates spread over several neighbouring counties from the heiresses of the families of Brett, Caltoft, and Aylesbury; by the sixth decade of the same century the Rempstons had acquired the Nottinghamshire estates of the Binghams, Bekerings, and Loudhams; the senior branch of the Leeks had added the estates of the families of Saundby and Vaux to their own before they themselves failed in the male line in the early 1430s; and the Cliftons acquired a moiety of the extensive estates of the Cressys of Hodsock in 1436. Two knightly families who did not figure amongst those of mid-fourteenth-century Nottinghamshire made substantial gains: the Markhams of East Markham acquired the other moiety of the Cressy estates and later a large share of the Leek of Cotham lands, while the Stanhopes united in their hands the Nottinghamshire estates of the Malovells of Rampton and the Longviliers of Tuxford. All but two of these acquisitions came about as the result of marriage and this was undoubtedly and predictably the major factor in the growing wealth of those families identifiable as the county élite of the early fifteenth century, but it is not to be seen in

---

[3] *CP*, iii. 153; v. 187, 190.

[4] This picture corresponds well with Astill's description of knightly society in Leics. For the later period 1350–99 he identified between 45 and 50 knightly families with their main interests in Leics. 2 of these, the Belers of Kirby Bellars and the Bassets of Sapcote, being particularly distinguished by their wealth, but as many as 34 had their Leics. interests confined to just one or two villages: G. G. Astill, 'The Medieval Gentry: A Study in Leicestershire Society, 1350–1399', Ph.D. thesis (Birmingham, 1977), 6–7.

isolation. As we have seen, the profits of the legal profession and the rewards of royal service both allowed a family to increase its estates by purchase and provided a preliminary to success in the marriage market. The Willoughbys, Markhams, and Babingtons, all of whom provided royal justices in the fourteenth and fifteenth centuries, first employed the profits of office to purchase estates and in later generations found heiresses to marry. The Rempstons did the same with the generous patronage of Henry IV. Another, although a much less certain, means of advancement was trade. It was the profits of the Flanders wool trade that enabled the Newcastle merchant, Richard Stanhope (d. 1379), to demonstrate the very direct connection between a lucrative career and the extension of a family's estate through marriage, for he used his wealth to purchase the marriage of the Malovell of Rampton heiress for his son. It is these avenues of social advancement, particularly the law, which enabled families in the later middle ages to accumulate extensive estates in a comparatively short time and hence join at the forefront of county society more ancient and conservative families who owed their prominence to valuable estates long maintained in continuous male lines.

This new-found ability of ambitious families rapidly to expand their estates, together with the tendency for some ancient families like, most notably, the Chaworths, to marry heiresses, meant that the lands in the hands of the knightly families of the early fourteenth century progressively became concentrated in the hands of fewer and fewer county families. The question of how far this concentration can be seen as a general phenomenon amongst the English knightly class as a whole (rather than simply the product of the particular and statistically unique pattern of marriage, careerism, and family extinction in Nottinghamshire) is complex; a complexity resulting from the fact that the major single factor in bringing about this concentration, the frequent failure of families in the male line, could in certain circumstances, as we have seen, bring about the opposite. If county heiresses frequently married into families with no previous landed interest in the county and which did not thereafter move to the heiresses' Nottinghamshire estates; if such heiresses consistently married men far beneath them in social status; or if the estates of families failing in the male line were repeatedly fragmented between heiresses rather than passing intact to a single heiress, the pattern of accumulation would have been much less pronounced or even reversed. Such eventualities certainly occurred but their effect was more than counterbalanced by marriages made within the knightly aristocracy of the county: for example, those of Chaworth to

Brett of Wiverton and Annesley of Annesley; Leek to Vaux of Cotham and Grey of Langford; Rempston to Bekering of Laxton and Loudham of Lowdham; and Markham and Clifton to Cressy of Hodsock.[5] Furthermore, as noted in the previous chapter, just as estates passed away from the county aristocracy as heiresses married outside the county, so the county aristocracy was able to augment its wealth through marriage to heiresses from neighbouring counties. The wealthier a family became, the more likely it was to attract such an heiress; the marriage of Willoughby to Freville is an outstanding Nottinghamshire example (the marriage of Chaworth to Aylesbury might also be cited but it should be noted that the Aylesbury bride was neither an heiress nor was expected to become one at the time of the marriage).

The principal determining factor in the accumulation of estates in the hands of fewer families was the rate of family extinction: a very low rate would ensure a low rate of accumulation liable to be negated by occasional marriages to non-resident families or the fragmentation of a few estates; conversely, a very high rate would make accumulation impossible, as so few families would retain their estates for more than a generation or two. This raises two questions: what was the extinction rate in Nottinghamshire, a county in which estate accumulation demonstrably occurred, and can this rate be used as a basis for generalization, or are rates of extinction so prone to the influence of accidental factors as to render meaningless any generalization over time and place? Of the forty-five knightly families resident in Nottinghamshire in 1325, thirteen had failed in the male line by 1400, a further eighteen failed during the fifteenth century, eight during the sixteenth century, and three more during the seventeenth century. Of the three families that remained in 1700, two failed before 1800, and the last, the Cliftons of Clifton and Hodsock, in 1869.[6] A comparison of these figures with those of the late K. B. McFarlane for the baronage (admittedly a much larger sample of 357), reveals that the knightly families of Nottinghamshire had a much higher survival rate than their national baronial superiors. For the two centuries between 1300 and 1500, McFarlane calculated that, on average, a baronial house had no better than a 75 per

---

[5] Of the 11 heiresses of families of the county élite that came on to the marriage market from the 1380s to 1461 (i.e. the coheiresses of the families of Cressy of Hodsock, Leek of Cotham, Rempston, and Zouche), 8 married inside the county, 6 of them into other families of the county élite: Appendix 4.

[6] Appendix 3. In determining these dates I have employed the same rules as K. B. McFarlane, *The Nobility of Later Medieval England* (Oxford, 1973), 172–3.

cent probability of surviving in the male line in any twenty-five year period (roughly equivalent to a generation) and that this probability did not vary much over time, reaching a peak of about 76.5 per cent in the period 1325–49 and a trough of about 64.5 per cent in the period 1400–24.[7] By contrast, amongst the Nottinghamshire knightly families between 1325 and 1400, there was, despite the visitations of the plague, as high a probability as 89.2 per cent of a family surviving in the male line in any twenty-five-year period, and, between 1400 and 1500, a probability of 81.3 per cent. How far are these figures typical for the knightly class as a whole? Of the fifty-three Leicestershire knightly families of 1325 listed by Dr G. G. Astill, thirty-four survived in 1400, and ten in 1500, giving a twenty-five-year survival rate of 86.2 per cent between 1325 and 1400, but of only 73.6 per cent from 1400 to 1500.[8] These varying rates warn against generalization, especially when such comparatively small samples are involved. Nevertheless, the demonstrable estate accumulation that was occurring within both the English baronage and the knightly families of Nottinghamshire suggests that a twenty-five-year survival rate of between about 70 per cent and 90 per cent would result in a steady increase in the size of the estates of a proportion of those families that survived in the male line.

The very considerable effect of such survival rates on the turnover of landed property between families can be statistically demonstrated by a comparison between the 1346 returns of the holders of knights' fees and those of 1428. This shows that in Nottinghamshire in a period of approximately three generations no less than 64.6 per cent of the knights' fees in lay hands passed from the possession of one family to

---

[7] Ibid. 146–7, 173–6.

[8] These figures are extracted from Astill, 'Leicestershire Society', Fig. 1. A similar table in Wright's *The Derbyshire Gentry* suggests a 25-year survival rate of over 90%: Wright, Appendix 1. Arnold calculated a rate of 85.4% for the West Riding gentry: C. E. Arnold, 'A Political Study of the West Riding of Yorkshire, 1437–1509', Ph.D. thesis (Manchester, 1984), 42. An analysis of Dr A. Grant's figures for the Scottish nobility reveals marked variations in survival rate over rank and time; during the 14th c. a ducal or comital family had only a 66.1% probability of surviving any 25-year period compared with 77.1% in the 15th c., while the barons and lords of parliament fared much better, with a rate of 83.3% in the 14th c. and 93.2% in the next: 'Extinction of Direct Male Lines among Scottish Noble Families in the Fourteenth and Fifteenth Centuries', in K. J. Stringer (ed.), *Essays on the Nobility of Medieval Scotland* (1985), 212, 215. Perroy's figures for noble *lignages* in Forez in south-central France are another point of comparison, giving a rate of 82.5% in the 14th c. and 81.9% in the next, despite rules of inheritance that gave preference to male cadets over daughters of the main line: E. Perroy, 'Social Mobility among the French Noblesse in the Later Middle Ages', *Past and Present* 21 (April 1962), 31.

another at least once.[9] This percentage was not, of course, a constant
over the county as a whole for there were substantial regional variations.
In the wapentake of Broxtow as few as 30.1 per cent of the knights' fees
changed hands while, in the largest of the county's wapentakes, that of
Bassetlaw, the figure was as high as 79.5 per cent.[10] This latter
percentage illustrates even more starkly than the extinction rates the
volatility of land ownership. It was this flow of lands from family to family
over the generations, variable over time and place but always appreciable,
balanced by the presence of a handful of very long-lived families, that
allowed estates to accumulate in the hands of fewer families.

Two other factors affecting estate accumulation are worthy of mention:
one was the practice of entailing estates in the male line, and the other,
the making of landed provision for younger sons. The first clearly had
consequences for both the transmission of estates from family to family
through heiresses and the ability of a family to perpetuate its estates in
the male line. For Derbyshire Dr Wright has found evidence that the
growing popularity of tail male, allied with a related preference for male
heirs, particularly younger brothers, at the expense of daughters, even
in the absence of such an entail, meant that heiresses became increasingly
scarce from *c.*1430.[11] This was not the case amongst the leading
Nottinghamshire families.[12] Nor perhaps more generally, to judge from
Sir John Habakkuk's remark of a later period that when a landowner was
'free to consult his own affections the property was likely to go to his
daughter'.[13] Since they held little land in tail male,[14] most landholders in
Lancastrian Nottinghamshire enjoyed this freedom and used it in
favour of their daughters (it is worth noting that daughters were
additionally protected by earlier settlements of the family property in tail
general since such entails could not lawfully be converted into tail male).
In the cases of the two most important families that failed in the direct
male line during the Lancastrian period, the Leeks of Cotham and
Rempstons of Bingham, the cadet heir male was totally excluded. The

---

[9] This percentage and the percentages that follow are drawn from an analysis of the
returns printed in *FA*, iv. 111–24, 125–39.

[10] The percentages of knights' fees changing hands in the county's other four wapentakes are as follows: Thurgarton 75.7%, Rushcliffe 68.3%, Bingham 54.3%, and Newark
43.4%.

[11] Wright, pp. 35–8, 42–4.

[12] Nor in the West Riding: Arnold, 'West Riding', 42.

[13] J. Habakkuk, 'The Rise and Fall of English Landed Families, 1600–1800', *TRHS*,
5th ser., 29 (1979), 190.

[14] This is demonstrated by inquisitions *post mortem* and feet of fines. Tail male was
similarly rare in late 14th-c. Leicestershire: Astill, 'Leicestershire Society', 68.

great inheritance of the Leeks passed in its entirety to Simon Leek's four daughters, even though Simon had a surviving younger brother, John Leek of Sandiacre in Derbyshire, and the Rempston lands passed to the three daughters of Sir Thomas Rempston in preference to his younger brother, Robert Rempston (d. 1476) of Scarrington. It may be that John Leek was excluded because he was already well provided for through his marriage to the Grey of Sandiacre heiress, while Robert Rempston was elderly and childless, and yet it is significant that no part of the estates of either family had previously been entailed in the male line. Later in the century the heir male fared better: on the childless death of Thomas Chaworth, the grandson of Sir Thomas Chaworth (d. 1459), in 1483, the bulk of his inheritance, including the Aylesbury lands of his grandmother, and the important Chaworth manors of Alfreton, Marnham, and Medbourne, settled in tail general in the fourteenth century, passed to his sister, Joan Ormond (d. 1507), and thence to her three daughters and coheiresses, but the Nottinghamshire manor of Wiverton, the family's principal residence, and nearby Edwalton, which had been in the family since the early thirteenth century, eventually passed to the issue of Thomas's uncle, George Chaworth of Annesley.[15] A parallel example is to be found early in the following century, when another of the ancient Nottinghamshire families, the Strelleys of Strelley, failed in the direct male line. The deaths of John Strelley of Strelley in January 1501 and of his young son and heir, another John, shortly afterwards, were the prelude to a dispute between his four daughters and the heir male, his nephew, Sir Nicholas Strelley (d. 1560). Ultimately the manors of Strelley and Oxton, which had been settled in tail male in 1435 and 1443 respectively, came to Sir Nicholas, while the remaining lands were divided between the coheiresses.[16] As the century

---

[15] *CIPM, Henry VII*, i, no. 3; iii, nos. 368, 370, 392, 487, 1009, 1167; Thoroton, i. 199; iii. 186; *Notts. IPM, 1485–1546*, 124–7. For the failed attempt by the heirs male to claim that the Leicestershire manor of Medbourne was also held in tail male: C141/1/13. If the provisions of Sir Thomas Chaworth's will had been implemented, the entire Chaworth estate (excluding the Aylesbury lands brought to him by his wife) would have passed to the heirs male but the earlier settlements in tail general prevented their implementation for a substantial part of the estate: Borthwick Institute, Archbishop's Register 20, fos. 274^d–277^d (this will is printed with several important omissions in *TE*, ii. 220–9).

[16] For the settlement of Strelley and Oxton in tail male and the October 1535 partition between the coheiresses: *Notts. IPM, 1437–85*, 6–7; *CAD*, iii, C3415; Thoroton, ii. 220–1. Oxton was assigned to the Ayscoghs but was claimed by Sir Nicholas. George (d. 1538), earl of Shrewsbury, and others, acted as arbiters: *Letters and Papers, Foreign and Domestic, of the Reign of Henry VIII, Addenda* (1929–32), no. 1515. Even though the common voice of the county was that Oxton should go to the heir male, it appears that Sir Nicholas had to pay the Ayscoghs £220 in compensation: ibid., no. 1471.

progressed the prospects of the heir male improved yet further, reflecting in part the increasing proportion of land held in tail male. By the mid-sixteenth century a rough and variable balance of interest had been reached between heirs male and general; the latter could now expect to inherit about a third of the family property.[17]

However, before the late fifteenth century there is little indication that either tail male, or settlements made in favour of a brother or other collateral before death, had any significant impact on conventional common-law inheritance patterns in Nottinghamshire. Moreover, even if estates held in tail male had predominated over those held in tail general or fee simple, heiresses, although fewer, would still have carried lands from family to family as lineages met with complete extinction in the male line: as McFarlane has observed, 'Tail male might stave off the day all feared; it could not prevent it from ever coming.'[18]

Besides the division of estates between coheiresses or between heir general and heir male, another potential factor in bringing about the disintegration of large accumulated estates was the landed provision made for younger sons. Amongst the leading Nottinghamshire families such settlements were not uncommon; indeed, it was only the most substantial families that could afford them. If made during the lifetime of the father this was often at the time of the younger son's marriage but, increasingly frequently, as it became possible to devise land *post mortem* through uses, it occurred when the father drew up his will. Nevertheless, since these settlements usually involved only relatively minor parcels of purchased or recently inherited land, they did not significantly affect the prospects of the eldest son and heir.[19] In 1411, for example, Sir Nicholas Strelley (d. 1430) settled the lesser of his two manors in Oxton, recently acquired from the Stanhopes, on his younger son, John, and John's wife, Joan, the only child and heiress-apparent of Thomas Hunte (d. 1428) of Linby, in tail general, probably at the time of their marriage.[20] At about the same time Sir Richard Stanhope settled three small manors in north Nottinghamshire on his younger sons, Thomas (d. 1462) and James (d. 1456), for their lives:[21] temporary alienations probably made to help

[17] J. P. Cooper, 'Patterns of Inheritance and Settlement by Great Landowners from the Fifteenth to the Eighteenth Centuries' in J. Goody *et al.* (eds.), *Family and Inheritance: Rural Society in Western Europe, 1200–1800* (Cambridge, 1976), 210.

[18] McFarlane, *The Nobility*, 145.

[19] For a similar conclusion: Wright, pp. 31, 46–8. For a useful general discussion of provision for younger children: Cooper, 'Patterns of Inheritance', 212–33.

[20] E13/130, rot. 24.

[21] As early as 1410 Sir Richard had granted his Longviliers manors in Skegby and

these sons attract prosperous brides. In his will of January 1459, the immensely wealthy Sir Thomas Chaworth chose to provide for his two unmarried sons in a different way, granting one a cash portion of 300 marks and an annuity of £10 and the other a cash portion of 200 marks and an annuity of £5, the annuities to be enjoyed until they had reached the age of 28 or were married. To another son he willed an annuity of £5, but the only estates he alienated from his eldest son were his purchased lands in Cropwell Butler and his small and isolated Warwickshire manor of Easenhall, both of which were settled in tail male with reversion to the main line.[22] One reason for this apparent neglect of the wider interests of the family was that the leading county families were often able to make provision for their younger sons by marriage: an excellent illustration of wealth attracting wealth. Of the thirteen leading Nottinghamshire families, no fewer than seven were able to provide for at least one of their younger sons in this way during the Lancastrian period, the Chaworths and Babingtons being particularly successful in this respect.[23] Some of the families that originated from such marriages became extremely prominent. The Leeks of Sutton Scarsdale, discussed in the previous chapter, are one example; another is the Chaworths of Annesley. They descended from George Chaworth, the third son of Sir Thomas Chaworth (d. 1459) and his wife Alice, the daughter and sole heiress of John Annesley (d. 1437) of Annesley; after the failure of the senior Chaworth line in 1483 they inherited the manors of Wiverton and Edwalton; and, in a junior branch of their own, they became Viscount Chaworths of Armagh in 1628.[24] It is clear that, for the leading county families, marriage to an heiress was the best and cheapest prospect of founding a successful cadet line. With the exception of the Pierpoints of Langford and the Willoughbys of Risley (Derbyshire), all the cadet lines of these families had their origins in such marriages.

Those few instances in which provision for younger sons was anything more than a minimum were the product of affection for a second wife and her issue overcoming duty to the issue of a long-dead first wife.[25] It

South Muskham to Thomas for life at an annual rent of 20 marks, to be paid only during Sir Richard's life. Also, at an unknown date, he settled his Longviliers manor in South Cottam on James for life: NUL, Mellish D4/26; C139/74/28. Thomas and James were assessed at £27 12s. and £15 18s. respectively in the tax of 1451. Thomas's greater wealth is to be explained by the Leics. lands he held in the right of an unnamed wife: E13/141, rot. 34.

[22] Borthwick Institute, Arch. Reg. 20, fos. 275–275ᵈ.
[23] Below, p. 78.
[24] Thoroton, i. 199–200; *CP*, iii. 155–6.
[25] Cooper, 'Patterns of Inheritance', 215.

was fortunate for eldest sons that most husbands were spared this conflict and that, when they were not, earlier entails frequently restricted their freedom of action. In 1329 Sir Robert Pierpoint (d. 1334) attempted, in a settlement that can only be described as bizarre, to disinherit his young grandson from his first marriage in favour of his fourteen children by his second wife: the *caput honoris* of the inheritance, the manor of Holme Pierrepont, was settled by fine successively on these six sons and eight daughters in tail male, reserving Sir Robert's life interest with a notional rent of £200 per annum.[26] He would probably have tried to carry his grandson's disinheritance further had he not, a decade before, settled a substantial part of his inheritance in favour of the now deceased son of his first wife.[27] As it transpired, even the settlement of Holme Pierrepont was tortious for it broke an earlier entail of 1288–9, and the only long-term effect of his machinations was to establish the descendants of his second wife on an estate at Langford near Newark.[28] Late medieval Nottinghamshire provides no further instance of such flagrant disregard for the rights of the eldest son, but within the history of the Willoughby family are to be found two examples of provision for younger sons by later wives considerable enough to diminish the inheritance of the senior line very significantly. It was only because the accidents of birth and death conspired to make a well-endowed cadet line the senior line of the family that the wealth of the Willoughbys was not seriously dispersed. By his death in 1362 Sir Richard Willoughby, CJKB, had alienated about a sixth of his vast estate, most of which he himself had purchased, to Edmund, his only son by his second wife, Joan Charron, and half as much again to his younger sons by his first wife: settlements which reduced the income of his eldest son and heir, Sir Richard (d. 1369), to between 65 and 75 per cent of that enjoyed by the judge in his later years.[29] Early in the fifteenth century, however, the Willoughby inheritance was largely reunited in the hands of Edmund's issue, due to the failure of the judge's children by his first wife to produce a legitimate heir (although not before Edmund had alienated a valuable part of the lands settled on him, and his half-brother, Hugh the clerk, had carved out an estate in Derbyshire centred on Risley for the issue of his concubine).[30] By a codicil to his will of September 1443

---

[26] CP25(1)/184/26/26; BL, MS Loan 29/60, fo. 38[d].

[27] CP25(1)/285/30/148, 149.   [28] CP25(1)/184/26/25.

[29] M. Bloom, 'The Careers of Sir Richard II de Willoughby and Sir Richard III de Willoughby, Chief Justice of the King's Bench (1338–1340), and the Rise of the Willoughbys of Nottinghamshire', D.Phil. thesis (Oxford, 1985), 298–306.

[30] Ibid. 337–57.

Edmund's grandson, Sir Hugh, attempted once more to break up the integrity of the Willoughby inheritance by settling all his entailed lands on the issue of his second wife, the wealthy heiress Margaret Freville, at the expense of Richard, his eldest son by his first wife. A subsequent arbitration between Richard and Margaret overturned the more extreme provisions of this codicil, but still resulted in the alienation from the main line of the Lincolnshire manors of Dunsby and Wigtoft together with various parcels of land in Nottinghamshire. Fortunately, however, Richard's childless death in 1471 meant that this alienation proved only temporary.[31]

The Nottinghamshire evidence indicates that, at least as far as that county was concerned, neither the practice of settling estates in tail male nor landed provision for younger sons had any significant impact on the tendency for estates to accumulate in the hands of those families that survived in a direct male line through the late-medieval period. Nevertheless, from the point of view of the individual family, such accumulation was not inevitable: the limited supply of heiresses, together with the tendency for certain of the newer and more ambitious families to marry more than their fair share, ensured that this was so. Nor was the failure to marry heiresses confined to the lesser knightly families. Two of the leading knightly families of early fourteenth-century Nottinghamshire, the Pierpoints of Holme Pierrepont and the Strelleys of Strelley, failed to add to their estates by marriage during the fourteenth and fifteenth centuries. Even so these families were wealthy enough to maintain their place in county society and continue to support the distinguishing mark of knighthood. But what of those lesser knightly families that failed to find heiresses on the marriage market? To take, for example, the sixteen knightly families of the early fourteenth century that survived in a direct male line throughout the Lancastrian period and beyond; six (Chaworth, Willoughby, Clifton, Nevill, Strelley, and Pierpont), already wealthy in the early fourteenth century, and four of them yet wealthier a century later, are to be accounted amongst the county élite of Lancastrian Nottinghamshire, while the history of the remaining ten illustrates a gradual transformation occurring within the ranks of county society as the gap between the richest and the poorest of the knightly families widened.

Four of these ten families, the Hercys of Grove, the Suttons of Averham, the St Andrews of Gotham, and the Stauntons of Staunton-

---

[30] Below, pp. 208–11, 242.

in-the-Vale, were represented by knights of the middle rank in the early fourteenth century, each claiming distinguished ancestry. However, their failure to add to their estates by marriage as the fourteenth century progressed meant that they suffered a decline relative to those families above them in the social scale who did augment their estates by marriage; a decline reflected in an abandonment of knightly rank. The St Andrews abandoned the rank in 1360, the Stauntons in *c.*1389, the Suttons in 1397, and the Hercys in 1425. The latter two took up the rank again in the sixteenth century but the former two never did so despite surviving in the male line into the seventeenth century.[32] These families did not abandon knighthood because they had a clear income of less that £40 per annum, at which an esquire could be distrained to take up the rank.[33] All four were distrained for knighthood on several occasions during the fifteenth and early sixteenth centuries. Rather, their decline relative to both the surviving greater knightly families of the early fourteenth century who had added to their estates and the careerist families such as Markham and Babington, made it no longer appropriate for them to support the rank. The gulf that had opened up between them and the leading county families, who continued to support knighthood save for a general and temporary abandonment of the rank in the mid-fifteenth century,[34] is illustrated by the taxation returns of 1412, 1436 and 1451 (see Table 3.1). It was the existence of this gap which ensured that knighthood would increasingly become a mark of social distinction as it moved further along the road from its original solely military

[32] G. Baker, *The History and Antiquities of the County of Northampton*, 2 vols. (London, 1822–41), i. 160–1; Thoroton, i. 306; *Notts. Visit.*, 142–3; *TE*, i. 409. For further details of these families: Payling, pp. 119–20.

[33] There were distraints of knighthood in 1410–11 (*CCR, 1409–13*, 155, 182; E198/4/39); 1430 (*CCR, 1429–35*, 67; *PPC*, iv, 54; E372/275, Adhuc Item London); 1439 (E372/284, Item adhuc Res' London); 1457–8 (*CCR, 1454–61*, 205; E198/4/16; E370/2/22); 1465 (E198/4/37; E370/2/22); 1483 (*CCR, 1476–85*, no. 1035; the fines were probably never levied since this distraint was for the coronation of Edward V); 1500–1 (E198/4/19); 1503–4 (E198/4/20, 21); 1508 (E198/4/23); 1509 (E198/4/26, 27). The surviving returns are of varying comprehensiveness, the best are to be found enrolled on the pipe roll of 1438–9 where as many as 541 distrainees (paying fines totalling £1,760 10s.) are listed: E372/284, Item adhuc Res' London. The high yield of this distraint of 1439 suggests that distraint was already becoming the extra-parliamentary tax it was to be under Henry VII and Henry VIII: H. Leonard, 'Knights and Knighthood in Tudor England', Ph.D. thesis (London, 1970), 60–80.

[34] There were 12 resident knights in the county in 1412; only 5 by 1450; and none between the death of Sir Thomas Chaworth in Feb. 1459 and the knighting of Robert Strelley during 1460. This temporary decline may reflect the lack of foreign campaigns during the middle years of the century: Wright, pp. 8–9. By 1488 the number of knights had recovered to at least 7, all from the most substantial county families.

TABLE 3.1. *Tax assessments of surviving fourteenth-century knightly families*

	Tax (£)		
	1412*	1436	1451
Chaworth of Wiverton	92	320	199
Willoughby of Wollaton	80	200	40
Clifton of Clifton	60	193	100
Nevill of Rolleston	20	120	79 6s. 8d.
Strelley of Strelley	40	100	100 10s.
Pierpoint of Holme Pierrepont	80	—	53 6s. 8d.
Mering of Meering	22	61	42
Sutton of Averham	20	34	47
Hercy of Grove	40	40	20
St Andrew of Gotham	—	33	20
Staunton of Staunton	53	30	15
Husy of Flintham	20	—	—
Compton of Hawton	20	—	—
Thorpe of Thorpe-by-Newark	20	—	—
Bevercotes of Bevercotes	20	8	8
Barry of Tollerton	20	12	7 6s. 8d.

* Nottinghamshire lands only.

purpose to the principally administrative role it was to assume in the sixteenth century.[35]

If such families as the Hercys of Grove and the Suttons of Averham came to abandon knighthood in the late fourteenth and early fifteenth centuries, obviously so too did those knightly families below them in social status. The Bevercotes of Bevercotes provided no more knights after the early fourteenth century,[36] the Thorpes of Thorpe-by-Newark and Comptons of Hawton lost the rank in the middle of the same

[35] For the importance of knighthood as a mark of social distinction in the second half of the 16th c.: Leonard, 'Knights and Knighthood', 116–18, 298.
[36] The last knight of the family was Sir John Bevercotes, a verderer of Sherwood Forest in 1327: CCR, 1327–30, 180. Established at Bevercotes since the reign of King John, the family failed to make any significant additions to its estates right up to its extinction in the late 16th c.: Thoroton, iii. 355–7. In the inquisition taken on the death, in 1513, of William Bevercotes, styled as a mere gentleman, his estates were valued at as little as 22 marks: Notts. IPM, 1485–1546, 77–8.

century,[37] and the Barrys of Tollerton and the Husys of Flintham early
in the next. None of them ever took up the rank again, nor were they
wealthy enough to be distrained.[38] The decline from knighthood of such
families had consequences for social organization and nomenclature.
First, and most obviously, it led to a dramatic decline in the number of
knights. According to the calculations of the late N. H. Denholm-
Young, made largely on the basis of the Parliamentary Rolls of Arms of
*c.*1310, there were about 1,250 knights, inclusive of the earls and
barons, in early fourteenth-century England.[39] By the 1430s, however,
this number had fallen to some 300 only, inclusive of a parliamentary
peerage of about fifty, although there remained more than a thousand
men in England with an income sufficient to make them liable to
distraint.[40] Second, it was an important factor in the development of
greater stratification within the ranks of the county landholders: a
stratification which paralleled that taking place within the baronage
during the same period, and reflected the increasingly clear demarcation
between the baronage and the rest of armigerous society.[41] As Dr N. E.
Saul has observed, there was no stratification below the rank of knight in
1300, but by 1400 an armigerous county squirearchy had emerged, soon
to be followed by the rank of gentleman, which came to designate the
lowest rung of gentle society.[42] The arms of esquires first appear on

[37] The last knights of these two families, Sir William Thorpe and Sir Robert Compton,
witnessed a deed for their neighbour, Sir Geoffrey Staunton, in 1361: HMC, *Various
Collections*, vii (1914), 370.
[38] Other families that did not survive the Lancastrian period had abandoned knighthood before their extinction: the Annesleys of Annesley in 1410, the Bekerings of Tuxford
in 1389, the Monbouchers of Gamston in 1384 and the Jorces of Burton Joyce in *c.*1340:
CFR, 1405–13, 160; *CIPM*, xvi, nos. 516–18; *Notts. IPM, 1350–1436*, 95–6; Thoroton,
iii. 20.
[39] N. H. Denholm-Young, 'Feudal Society in the Thirteenth Century: The Knights',
in *Collected Papers on Medieval Subjects* (Oxford, 1946), 61. This figure may itself reflect a
decline from a total of up to about 2,000 in the first half of the 13th c.: J. Quick, 'The
Number and Distribution of Knights in Thirteenth Century England: The Evidence of
the Grand Assize Lists', in P. R. Coss and S. D. Lloyd (eds.), *Thirteenth Century England: 1*
(1986), 119.
[40] J. C. Wedgwood, *History of Parliament, 1439–1509* (HMSO, 1936–8), ii. *Register*,
p. lxxxvii; H. L. Gray, 'Incomes from Land in England in 1436', *English Historical Review*
49 (1934), 630. For the steady increase in the number of knights during the first half of the
16th c. to about 540 in 1550, and its subsequent decline to about 330 in 1600: Leonard,
'Knights and Knighthood', 102 (Leonard's figures are exclusive of peers). The declining
number of knights in 14th- and 15th-c. England was paralleled in France: P. Contamine,
'Points de vue sur le chevalerie en France á la fin du Moyen Age', *Francia* 4 (1976), 259–
62.   [41] McFarlane, *The Nobility*, 122–6.
[42] N. E. Saul, *Knights and Esquires: The Gloucestershire Gentry in the Fourteenth Century*
(Oxford, 1981), 16–18.

rolls of arms in *c.*1370, and Denholm-Young has seen in this the culmination of the 'remarkable rise of the squirearchy' by which men from below the rank of knight assumed not only a prominent role in local government and parliamentary representation but also assumed the knightly privilege of bearing heraldic arms.[43] Yet it seems that this 'remarkable rise' had as much to do with the relative decline of many armigerous knightly families from knighthood as a rise from below occasioned by greater opportunities for social advancement that prevailed in the wake of the Black Death. Third, the prestige attached to the knightly rank was greatly enhanced; the wealthier families continued to support a rank which their social inferiors had abandoned. In short, by the second quarter of the fifteenth century, knighthood was well on its way to becoming what it was in the sixteenth century, a particular mark of social distinction confined to a small group of the wealthiest county landowners.

The small group of county families at the head of Nottinghamshire society in Lancastrian England was distinguished from the rest of gentry society not only by its wealth and a continuing tradition of knighthood, but also by the nature and extent of its social relationships. This is to be seen particularly in the most important of all such relationships, that of marriage. The pattern of the marriages of this élite group of families markedly differed even from that of those families immediately below them in the social scale. Between 1399 and 1461 as many as ten of the twenty-six known marriages contracted by senior members (heads or heirs apparent) of these families involved heiresses (although not all of these were heiresses of heiresses-apparent at the time of marriage),[44] compared with only one out of fifteen for senior members of the second rank of county society, the 'lesser knightage and greater squirearchy'.[45] Moreover, since the greater families tended to marry into other families of an equivalent social rank from inside or outside the county, when heiresses were involved they were generally heiresses to substantial

[43] N. H. Denholm-Young, *The County Gentry in the Fourteenth Century* (Oxford, 1969), 4.

[44] For these 26 marriages: Appendix 4.

[45] For the wives of the second rank of county society: Payling, pp. 76, 86; Thoroton, i. 18, 39, 249, 308; ii. 253; iii. 109, 189, 232, 263; *Notts. Visit.*, 13, 143; Hunter, *South Yorkshire*, i. 251; Borthwick Institute, Prob. Reg. 2, fos. 216ᵛ–217. I have excluded those marriages by which a family from outside the county became established amongst this rank of Notts. society: i.e. Thomas Curson of Kedleston, Derby., to the heiress of Bulcote; Richard Wentworth of North Elmsall, Yorks., to the heiress of Everton; and Ralph Makerell of Breaston, Derby., to Katherine, daughter and coheiress of Sir John Cressy of Hodsock and widow of Sir John Clifton.

estates. The result was that the social gap separating those families that had already risen to wealth and prominence, whether through earlier marriages, the profits of the law or the rewards of royal service, from the second rank of county society was maintained and widened. Nor was it only the senior members of the leading families that married heiresses, so also did their younger sons: during the Lancastrian period no fewer than ten heiresses are known to have married junior members of these families, and even though these heiresses were in general only minor ones, not to be compared in wealth with those who married into the senior lines of these families, it is notable that these younger sons should have been so much more successful in this respect than the senior members of the second rank.[46] Indeed, it is not improbable that this success was achieved at their expense; the large number of heiresses, both greater and lesser, marrying into the greater families creating a dearth of heiresses for those lesser families that did not have access to the profits of law or service. In counties which were particularly insular in their marriage patterns a high degree of endogamy produced a situation uniquely favourable to marriages between the younger sons of wealthy families and local heiresses resulting in a profusion of cadet branches of the greater families amongst the lesser gentry.[47] In Nottinghamshire this process did not go so far, but several families, later to rise to prominence within the county or in the surrounding counties, originated as a result of such marriages contracted during the Lancastrian period: the Chaworths of Annesley and the Leeks of Sutton Scarsdale, both elevated to the peerage in the seventeenth century, the Markhams of Sedgebrook, seventeenth-century baronets, the Babingtons of Dethick, and the Nevills of Ragnall and Grove are examples, all of which long survived the senior branches of the families from which they sprang.[48]

[46] For these heiresses: above, pp. 37, 40, 45, 53, 70, 71. In addition, Nicholas Willoughby, younger son of Sir Hugh Willoughby by Isabel Foljambe, married the heiress of Rand in Lincs.: C1/41/233. And William Nevill, a younger brother of Thomas Nevill (d. 1482) of Rolleston, married a minor north Notts. heiress, Joan, widow of John de Taukirslay, who brought him small parcels of land in South Leverton, Laneham, and Rampton: CP40/598, rot. 26ᵈ. Her family is uncertain but it is said in the pedigrees to be Barker: E. R. Nevill, 'Nevill of Rolleston, Grove and Thorney', *The Genealogist* NS 33 (1917). I have not included the marriage of Sir Gervase Clifton (d. 1471), illegitimate half-brother of Sir Robert Clifton (d. 1478) to Isabel, widow of William Scot (d. 1432) of Brabourne in Kent, nor that of Thomas Stanhope to a Leics. widow or heiress: Payling, p. 90; above, pp. 70–1 n. 21.
[47] R. A. Houlbrooke, *The English Family, 1450–1700* (London and New York, 1984), 51; C. Haigh, *Reformation and Resistance in Tudor Lancashire* (Cambridge, 1975), 89.
[48] *CP*, iii, 155–6; xi, 516–19; C. R. Markham, *Markham Memorials* (London, 1913), i. 121–62; above, p. 37. For the Nevills of Ragnall and Grove, descended from William

With the increasing frequency of settlements in tail male towards the end of the fifteenth century, their survival meant that they might eventually, as in the case of the Chaworths of Annesley, inherit the main estates of the family on the failure of the senior line, and this, as Dr P. W. Fleming has observed in his study of fifteenth-century Kent, where the phenomenon of scions of established families was more pronounced, encouraged 'titular stability' since the risks of extinction in the male line were shared between several branches of the same family.[49]

Two reasons for the success of these families in the search for heiresses are clear. First, and most obviously, their greater wealth meant that they could expand greater resources on marriage, whether in terms of jointure, landed provision for younger sons, or cash (although the want of formal marriage agreements for Nottinghamshire precludes the giving of any comparative figures).[50] As Sir John Habakkuk has remarked for a later period, 'landed heiresses were generally obtained in marriage by the landowners who could afford the best terms'.[51] Second, their wealth and the wider distribution of their estates was reflected in extensive social and political connections denied to lesser families, enabling them to cast their nets more widely in the search for suitable wives. Of the twenty-six identified wives of the senior members of the county élite, only twelve came from Nottinghamshire itself, a further eight came from the surrounding counties of Derbyshire (three), Yorkshire (two), Leicestershire (two) and Lincolnshire (one), three came from Lancashire, one from Staffordshire, and two from much farther afield, namely Kent and Buckinghamshire (within this group the heiresses were similarly distributed: five from Nottinghamshire, two from Leicestershire, and one each from Buckinghamshire, Staffordshire, and Lincolnshire). Younger sons tended to marry within narrower confines: of the ten heiresses to whom they were married, six came from Nottinghamshire and one each from Lincolnshire, Derbyshire, Bedfordshire, and Oxfordshire, the latter two marriages coming about as a result of Sir William Babington's exceptionally wide connections as a

Nevill of South Leverton: Payling, p. 80; *Notts. Visit.*, 64–5. The general success of these junior branches of the gentry contrasts with the general failure of similar branches of the baronage to become established: McFarlane, *The Nobility*, 78.

[49] P. W. Fleming, 'The Character and Private Concerns of the Gentry of Kent, 1422–1509', Ph.D. thesis (Swansea, 1985), 147.

[50] For a comparison between jointures given by leading families and those given by lesser gentry: Arnold, 'West Riding', 101; Wright, pp. 207–8.

[51] Habakkuk, 'Rise and Fall', 193.

royal justice.[52] There is little doubt that the superior wealth and rank of these families made their younger sons attractive spouses for minor local landholders with heiresses to marry off, such as, for example, the lawyer Thomas Hunte (d. 1428) of Linby, who married his only daughter and heiress-apparent to John (d. 1421), a younger son of his wealthy neighbour, Sir Nicholas Strelley of Strelley.

The large number of heiresses from both inside and outside the county who married into the leading Nottinghamshire families would tend to cast doubt on Dr Carpenter's suggestion that the prime consideration in the contracting of marriages, even for those of male heirs, was political, and that some families consciously avoided heiresses.[53] And yet it is worth noting that those Nottinghamshire families most avid in their search for heiresses were those newly risen to the ranks of the county élite. Longer established families tended to be more circumspect, at least in the case of eldest sons. In the case of younger sons, however, the search for an heiress was imperative even for the most conservative of families, and this meant that few families chose wives for their sons for reasons of politics alone, leaving all thoughts of property aside. It was rather to their non-inheriting daughters that they looked to broaden their political horizons: this was one reason, aside from parental love, why they were prepared to lavish substantial marriage portions upon such daughters.[54] The pattern of the marriages of these daughters reflects the importance attached to ties with leading landholders in other counties, particularly, of course, in counties in which the families themselves held estates: of the twenty-two such marriages recorded, only nine took place within the county, while a further seven drew husbands from the neighbouring counties of Yorkshire (four), Derby-

[52] The only younger son for whom the identity of the wife is known and who did not marry an heiress is Norman Babington: above, p. 37. This does not, of course, mean that nearly all the younger sons of leading families married heiresses but simply that the evidence generally fails where they did not.

[53] M. C. Carpenter, 'The Fifteenth-Century English Gentry and their Estates', in M. C. E. Jones (ed.), Gentry and Lesser Nobility of Late Medieval Europe (Gloucester, 1986), 38–42.

[54] Few figures are available for Notts. In his will of 1443 Sir Hugh Willoughby bequeathed 200 marks, above a considerable quantity of plate, to each of his four unmarried daughters: NUL, Mi. F6. One of these daughters, Eleanor, received twice that sum when she married John Shirley (d. 1486), son and heir-apparent of Ralph Shirley (d. 1466): NUL, Mi. D 4768. In his will of 1403 Sir Thomas Rempston left only 100 marks to the marriage of his daughter: Borthwick Institute, Arch. Reg. 5A, fo. 334. For the portions given by leading families in other counties: Wright, pp. 45, 207, 210; Arnold, 'West Riding', 99–101. Fleming, 'Gentry of Kent', 211. For a wider perspective: Cooper, 'Patterns of Inheritance', 306–12.

shire (two), and Lincolnshire (one), and the remaining six from further afield (two from Lancashire, two from Hertfordshire, one from War- wickshire, and one from Worcestershire).[55] The marriage of Isabel, the eldest daughter of Sir Hugh Willoughby by Margaret Freville, is a well-documented example of this desire to establish connections with landowners from the vicinity of the family's outlying estates. In 1429 Sir Hugh purchased the marriage and wardship of Philip, son and heir of Sir Philip Boteler (d. 1420) of Woodhall in Watton (Hertfordshire), from the executors of Sir John Cokayn (d. 1429), JCB, of Bury Hatley (Bedfordshire), uncle of Sir John Cokayn (d. 1438) of Ashbourne (Derbyshire). Since 1412 this branch of the Boteler family had held lands at Middleton in Warwickshire, the chief part of which had come to Sir Hugh through his marriage to Margaret, and it is hence clear why he should have wished to purchase this marriage for Isabel.[56] Before his death in 1448 he had further strengthened his connections in the immediate vicinity of Middleton by the marriage of another daughter, Joyce, to Richard Bracebridge of nearby Kingsbury.[57]

However, it was not only lands in other counties that could provide the motivation and opportunity for a leading family to extend the range of its social connections beyond the county boundaries. Take, for example, the Stanhopes: three members of this family married into families from Lancashire, a county in which they held no lands. These marriages resulted from the connections the family established in that county through the pre-1399 marriage of Sir Richard Stanhope to Elizabeth, daughter of Sir Ralph Staveley of Stayley (Cheshire), steward of the household of Henry, earl of Derby, connections which were later reinforced by Sir Richard's grandson John's service in the royal house- hold in the 1440s and 1450s. In 1403 Agnes Stanhope, a daughter of this marriage, was married to Staveley's stepson and ward, Henry Trafford (d. 1408) of Trafford (Lancashire);[58] in 1427 John Stanhope married Elizabeth, a daughter of Sir Thomas Talbot of Bashall in Bowland (Lancashire) and stepson of Sir John Assheton (d. 1428) of Ashton-upon-Lyne, nephew of the groom's grandmother, Elizabeth

---

[55] These marriages are listed in Appendix 4 and with references in Payling, pp. 285–6.
[56] NUL, Mi. D 4791, 4792; *CFR, 1422–30*, 281–2; VCH, *Warwickshire*, iv (1947), 157; C137/90/16.
[57] HMC, *Middleton* (1911), 507.
[58] *Calendar of Entries in the Papal Registers Relating to Great Britain and Ireland: Papal Letters, 1198–1492*, 14 vols. in 15 (HMSO, 1893–1960), v. 529; VCH, *Lancashire*, iv (1911), 332 n. 44; J. S. Roskell, *The Knights of the Shire for the County Palatine of Lancaster, 1377–1460*, Chetham Society, NS 96 (1937), 108, 110.

Staveley;[59] and, sometime before 1443, Katherine Stanhope, Agnes's sister, married, as her second husband, another Lancashire man, John Tunstall of Tunstall, uncle of one of Henry VI's squires of the body, Richard Tunstall (later king's carver and one of Henry VI's foeffees).[60] This last marriage may have been made through the royal household for Katherine's nephew, John, was also a household esquire.[61] John's second marriage is probably to be explained in the same way for it may have been as early as 1460 that he married Katherine, widow of Sir Ralph Radclyffe (d. 1460) of Smithills (Lancashire) and sister of Sir Richard Molineux of Sefton (Lancashire), who had been killed fighting for Lancaster at the battle of Blore Heath in the previous year.[62] The Stanhopes were not the only Nottinghamshire family in the latter years of Lancastrian rule to exploit their household connections in the search for spouses: Joyce, daughter of Robert Strelley of Strelley, a household esquire during the 1450s,[63] married Humphrey Salway of Stanford-on-Teme (Worcestershire), marshal of the court,[64] while William Babington, another household esquire, married the heiress of the Lincolnshire yeomen of the crown, John Gibthorpe.[65] Other marriages came about through the connections of the leading families with local magnates,[66] and this was another factor in broadening the connections of these families.

In very marked contrast, the families below them in the social scale very rarely married outside the county. Amongst the senior members of the second rank of county society, who would have had the greatest opportunity of all the gentry below the élite to form connections with families from other shires: of their fifteen known brides, eleven came from within the county, three from the neighbouring counties of Derbyshire (two) and Yorkshire (one), and one from Lancashire.[67] There seems little reason to doubt that lesser families, with estates not only confined to the county but also, in most cases, to a single manor, were even more constrained in their choice of marriage partners,

[59] Thoroton, iii. 245; Roskell, *Knights of the Shire*, 115.
[60] CP40/730, rot. 263; J. C. Wedgwood, *History of Parliament, 1439–1509* (HMSO, 1936–8), i. *Biographies*, 881–2.
[61] For John Stanhope as a household esquire: below, p. 148.
[62] *The Visitation of the County Palatine of Lancaster, 1664–5*, ed. F. R. Raines, 2 vols., Chetham Society, 84–5 (1872), ii. 205; VCH, *Lancashire*, v (1911), 13.
[63] For Strelley as a household esquire: below, p. 148.
[64] J. Burke, *A Genealogical and Heraldic History of the Commoners of Great Britain and Ireland*, 4 vols. (1833–8), i. 152; VCH, *Worcestershire*, iv (1924), 344; *PPC*, vi. 224.
[65] Above, p. 37. For Babington as a household esquire: below, p. 148.
[66] Below, pp. 101–2; Payling, pp. 46, 89–90.   [67] Above, p. 77 n. 45.

generally marrying within the immediate sphere of their estates, although lack of reliable pedigrees makes this difficult to demonstrate. Even in the seventeenth century it appears that 'small parish gentry . . . were narrowly locked into their county by their relative poverty and the restricted nature of their education, property-holding, marriages, and aspirations for office':[68] this restriction was probably even more strongly felt in the fifteenth century.[69]

The breadth of the social connections of the leading families meant that the degree of inter-marriage between them, although not entirely negligible, was not high. If no heiress was involved it was uncommon for a senior member of a leading Nottinghamshire family to marry into another. Of the twenty-six marriages known, only four came into this category. Two involved the Stanhopes, who, in the early years of Lancastrian rule, were new to the county and perhaps anxious to establish links with the existing county élite: in the first few years of the century Richard, son and heir-apparent of Sir Richard Stanhope, married Elizabeth, daughter of Sir John Markham, JCB, of East Markham, the greatest landholder in the north-east of the county, the area in which the Stanhope's estates lay; and, shortly after 1408, Sir Richard's daughter, Agnes, married Robert Strelley, son and heir-apparent of the south Nottinghamshire knight, Sir Nicholas Strelley.[70] The limitations of the surviving evidence, in particular the fact that the identity of the wives of those younger sons who failed to marry heiresses is so rarely known, may underestimate the extent of the marital connections between the leading families, but the high percentage of the known marriages of non-inheriting daughters which took place outside the county suggests that any such underestimate is not significant.

If these families did not depend upon each other for marriage partners, was there nonetheless a high degree of collective dependence in those conveyances of property so essential to the late-medieval landowner? This dependence was certainly not negligible. It would be tedious to cite all the examples of members of this small group of families acting together in such conveyances. A few examples will suffice to show the extent of this dependence. In 1417, when William Babington (d. 1454) purchased a quarter of the Nottinghamshire manor of Oxton, he employed as his feoffees Sir Thomas Chaworth, Sir John Zouche, and Sir Thomas Rempston;[71] in 1423 Sir Thomas Chaworth

---

[68] J. C. F. Stone and L. Stone, *An Open Élite? England 1540–1880* (Oxford, 1984), 37.
[69] Wright, p. 57.   [70] Thoroton, iii. 245.
[71] CP25(1)/186/38/4.

conveyed his considerable estates to a group of twelve feoffees including Sir Thomas Rempston, William Babington, and Simon Leek of Cotham;[72] in 1449 Sir Thomas Rempston, when his daughter, Elizabeth, married John Cheyne, conveyed his manor of Bingham to *inter alia* Sir Thomas Chaworth, Sir William Babington, John Markham, JKB, and Richard Willoughby;[73] and, in 1457, the feoffees for the performance of Richard Willoughby's will included William Chaworth, William Babington (d. 1474), and Robert Clifton in a deed witnessed by Sir Thomas Chaworth, Sir Thomas Rempston, and Robert Strelley.[74] The most outstanding example, however, is the agreement drawn up in June 1437 for the marriage of Elizabeth Zouche and William Chaworth which involved as feoffees for one side or the other six heads and one heir-apparent of the eleven leading county families (the Cressys of Hodsock and the Leeks of Cotham had failed in the male line by this date): in addition to Sir Thomas Chaworth, the bridegroom's father, and Sir John Zouche, the bride's grandfather, Sir Thomas Rempston, Sir William Babington, Sir Robert Markham, Thomas Nevill of Rolleston, and Richard Willoughby were involved.[75]

Nevertheless, despite an obvious degree of interdependence amongst these families, a natural result of ties of neighbourhood and collective involvement in the government of the county, the extensiveness of their out-of-county estates and the widespread kinship networks they consequently developed sometimes led them to employ in their transactions prominent gentry from other counties, over and above the lay and ecclesiastical magnates occasionally employed.[76] Sir John Zouche's feoffees, at the time of the marriage settlement of June 1437, although they included several of his prominent Nottinghamshire neighbours, also included others with their main landed interests in south Yorkshire: Sir William Harington (d. 1440) of Brierley, Sir Robert Roos (d. 1451) of Ingmanthorpe, one of the king's carvers, Thomas Wombwell (d. 1451) of Wombwell, William FitzWilliam of Sprotborough, Nicholas Fitz-William of Adwick-upon-Dearne, and Thomas Wentworth of Doncaster.

---

[72] CP25(1)/291/65/18. See also the feoffment made by Sir Thomas Chaworth in November 1425, witnessed by Sir John Zouche and Sir Henry Pierpoint: *CCR, 1422–9*, 315.
[73] Several prominent Cambridgeshire associates of the Cheynes were also involved in this feoffment: C1/21/9a.
[74] NUL, Mi. D 4770.   [75] BL, Add. Ch. 20542.
[76] For Thomas Langley, bishop of Durham, and Ralph, Lord Cromwell as feoffees of Sir Thomas Chaworth: Payling, p. 71. For John, Lord Beaumont, and William, Lord Lovell, as feoffees of Sir John Zouche: CP25(1)/292/68/177.

All of these men held lands in the neighbourhood of one of the enfeoffed manors, that of Bolton-upon-Dearne, and this, with the connections of Wombwell and Nicholas FitzWilliam with Zouche's wife, Margaret, daughter and coheiress of Sir John Burgh of Burrough Green (Cambridgeshire) and Walton (Yorkshire),[77] explains why these men were employed. More striking is the case of Sir Hugh Willoughby whose marriage to one of the Freville coheiresses in 1418 led him to employ his wife's kinsmen to the virtual exclusion of his Nottinghamshire peers. On 24 March 1435, by a deed dated at his manor of Wollaton, he conveyed this manor, in preparation for its joint settlement on himself and his wife, to: his wife's brothers-in-law, Thomas Ferrers (d. 1459), second son of William (d. 1445), Lord Ferrers of Groby (Leicestershire), and Sir Roger Aston (d. 1447) of Haywood (Staffordshire), constable of the Tower of London; his wife's nephew, Robert Aston; his own son-in-law, Philip Botelar of Woodhall in Watton (Hertfordshire) and Norbury (Staffordshire); and Sir Ralph Botelar of Sudeley (Gloucestershire), chief butler of England and, as a distant cousin of the Frevilles, coheir with them to the de Montfort lands.[78] Although this deed and several others made at about the same date was witnessed by his Nottinghamshire neighbours, Sir Thomas Chaworth, Sir William Babington, Sir Gervase Clifton, and Sir Robert Strelley, no Nottinghamshire man, with the exception of the wealthy Nottingham merchant, Richard Samon, was included amongst the feoffees either in this conveyance or in the others made during the same year.[79] However, such transactions, dominated by men from outside the county, were the exception. Most transactions involved only a small circle of men drawn from inside the county, with local lawyers prominent, and, for the most intimate of these transactions, the executing of wills, it was rare to look much beyond the context of the immediate family and friends.[80] For example, the executors of the 1398 will of Sir William Chaworth were his wife, Alice, his son, Thomas, his confessor, Henry de Neuton, and his neighbour and frequent associate, Sir John Leek of Cotham, while, in 1453, Sir Gervase Clifton contented himself with appointing his wife, Isabel, as his sole executrix.[81] In short, the emphasis in the majority of

---

[77] They were amongst the supervisors of her 1449 will: *TE*, ii. 154.

[78] For this deed: NUL, Mi. D 1611. For the husbands of the other Freville coheiresses: *CP*, v. 357 n. *a*.; J. C. Wedgwood, 'Staffordshire Parliamentary History, 1213–1603', *William Salt Archaeological Society* (1917), 205.

[79] For the other conveyances: NUL, Mi. D 1108, 4755.

[80] Wright, pp. 53–4.

[81] Borthwick Institute, Arch. Reg. 16, fo. 134; *TE*, ii. 170.

conveyances of the leading gentry was on kin, local lawyers and a narrow circle of county neighbours.

Nevertheless, it is clear that the county élite of Lancastrian Notting-hamshire was neither inward looking nor closely related. Its kinship networks, like its lands, extended beyond the county boundaries, and these ties of kinship may have mattered more than those of neighbour-hood. It is difficult to discern any sense of community in its marriages and conveyances beyond that minimum degree of interaction guaranteed by proximity. Nor does it seem likely that any real sense of county existed amongst the lower reaches of the county gentry. For lesser landholders the scope of their social horizons probably extended no further than the immediate vicinity of their narrowly-confined estates.[82] To find any sense of a community of the shire, aware of its own identity, rights and privileges, one has to look to office-holding and administration. The leading gentry co-operated in county government, only rarely taking up office in counties where they held lands peripheral to their main estates, while the county court, particularly in its function as the electoral body of the knights of the shire, served to some extent to focus gentry loyalties on the county.

---

[82] Similar conclusions about the 'county community' have been reached for the neighbouring counties of Derbyshire and Leicestershire: Wright, pp. 58–9; Astill, 'Lei-cestershire Society', 127, 129. Cf. M. J. Bennett, 'A County Community: Social Cohesion amongst the Cheshire Gentry, 1400–1425', *Northern History* 8 (1973), 24–44. For a discussion of a coherent community narrower than the county: A. J. Pollard, 'The Richmondshire Community of Gentry during the Wars of the Roses', in C. D. Ross (ed.), *Patronage, Pedigree and Power in Later Medieval England* (Gloucester, 1979).

4
THE BARONAGE AND BASTARD FEUDALISM

I⊤ is a common assumption of much writing on the political history of fifteenth-century England that the horizontal bonds of neighbourhood and community which bound the gentry together were subordinate to the vertical and stronger bonds of lordship and bastard feudalism. The most powerful assertion of this view is found in the work of Dr M. C. Carpenter. She has argued that in fifteenth-century Warwickshire the influence of the baronial affinity was all pervasive; the connection of the able Richard Beauchamp (d. 1439), earl of Warwick, dominated the social relations of even the most substantial gentry, who found feoffees and marriage partners within its framework, and provided the major unifying force amongst the county gentry. In such circumstances it followed that 'only the unimportant would be without a lord' and it was 'almost impossible to thrive outside the reigning affinity'.[1] She has found support in the work of Dr M. Cherry on late fourteenth-century Devon: there Edward Courtenay (d. 1419), earl of Devon, had a 'striking degree of control over local affairs' and his affinity 'was the dominant feature of political life in the county'.[2]

Other studies, however, have been very different in emphasis. Dr N. E. Saul, in his study of fourteenth-century Gloucestershire, has concluded that there was a significant body of gentry unconnected with any magnate, a conclusion he has supported by citing the frequent denunciations of maintenance by the parliamentary commons,[3] going so far as to interpret the statute of 1390 against livery and maintenance as 'a

[1] M. C. Carpenter, 'Political Society in Warwickshire, c.1401–72', Ph.D. thesis (Cambridge, 1976), 66. See also: id., 'The Beauchamp Affinity: A Study of Bastard Feudalism at Work', EHR 95 (1980), 514–32.

[2] M. Cherry, 'The Courtenay Earls of Devon: The Formation and Disintegration of a Late Medieval Aristocratic Affinity', Southern History 1 (1979), 75, 79.

[3] N. E. Saul, Knights and Esquires: The Gloucestershire Gentry in the Fourteenth Century (Oxford, 1981), 97–8, 102–3. He suggests that at most two-thirds of the knights and esquires of Glos. were retained by magnates. Even this appears to be an over-estimate: J. M. W. Bean, review of Saul's Gloucestershire, Speculum 58 (1983), 536.

measure of the influence in parliament and in the shires of men who lived outside the embrace of "bastard feudalism" '.[4] In a further study of east Sussex during the same period he has concluded that the society of that region 'does not give the impression of a local society organised in or around a magnate affinity'.[5] Dr S. M. Wright has also played down the role of 'bastard feudalism' in local affairs: she has remarked on the 'essentially transient and extraneous nature of the retinue', and for her the affinity was only one 'element', and by no means the most important 'in the composite pattern of gentry relationships'. She has concluded that the infrastructure of county society 'existed independently of any retinue and function without a magnate'.[6]

In large part this very marked difference of opinion over a question so basic to any understanding of late-medieval political society reflects both the distribution of the residences of the greater baronage and differences in the balance of property between barons and gentry in the counties concerned: Gloucestershire and Derbyshire were without substantial baronial estates (with the partial exception in the case of the former of the Berkeley estates), while both Warwickshire and Devon had a great lord with his *caput honoris* in the county. Nottinghamshire fits very much into the former category. On the one hand, a low level of baronial wealth, which for most of the period was fairly evenly distributed amongst a group of lesser baronial families, ensured that the affinity would never be in the ascendant. On the other, the concentration of non-baronial wealth in the hands of an élite of gentry families made the leading gentry the natural leaders of county society.[7] The principal aim of this chapter is to examine the nature of the relationship between this élite and those baronial families with lands in the county, and so to add quantitative to the qualitative evidence presented earlier in support of the view that counties dominated by the baronage, such as early fifteenth-century Warwickshire, were the exception rather than the rule in late-medieval England.

Of the fourteen baronial families assessed as holding land in Nottinghamshire in 1412, none had their principal residence there, but three,

---

[4] Saul, *Gloucestershire*, 105. See also: S. K. Walker, 'John of Gaunt and His Retainers, 1361–1399', D.Phil. thesis (Oxford, 1986), 260. Cf. M. C. Carpenter, 'Law, Justice and Landowners in Late Medieval England', *Law and History Review* 1 (1983), 206–7.

[5] N. E. Saul, *Scenes from Provincial Life: Knightly Families in Sussex, 1280–1400* (Oxford, 1986), 56.

[6] Wright, pp. 65–6.

[7] Above, pp. 13–18.

the Greys of Codnor, the Roos of Belvoir, and the Cromwells of Tattershall, lived near enough the county boundaries to warrant their taking more than a cursory interest in the county's affairs. The Greys of Codnor had long resided at their castle of Codnor in south-east Derbyshire, twelve miles from Nottingham and very close to their principal Nottinghamshire manor at Toton. The Roos family had more recently moved close to the county: towards the end of the fourteenth century William (d. 1414), Lord Roos, made his principal residence at Belvoir, at the meeting of the counties of Nottinghamshire, Leicestershire, and Lincolnshire and lying only a few miles from his ancient Nottinghamshire demesne manor of Orston. The Cromwells had probably had their principal residence at their central Nottinghamshire manor of Lambley until the 1360s when, as a result of the marriage of Ralph Cromwell (d. 1398) to the wealthy Bernak heiress, they moved to Tattershall in neighbouring Lincolnshire, thirty-seven miles to the east of Lambley. Nevertheless, Lambley continued to be of special importance to the family. Ralph (d. 1416), second Lord Cromwell, appears to have resided there because of the life interest of his mother, Maud Bernak, in the Bernak estates,[8] while he, his wife, Joan Gray (d. 1434), his father Ralph (d. 1398), first Lord Cromwell, and Maud Bernak (d. 1419) were all buried in the parish church there.[9] Moreover, from the mid-1440s, the third lord had a major residence near the Nottinghamshire border: his magnificent new manor-house at South Wingfield in Derbyshire lay only fifteen miles to the north-west of Nottingham.[10] A fourth baronial family, the Talbots, earls of Shrewsbury, were to become very important in Nottinghamshire politics during the following century. It is worth noting here only that the origins of their interest in the north midlands

[8] For deeds of the second lord attested at Lambley: Sheffield Central Library, CD 393, 396 (both 1398); CD 402 (1408); CD 406 (1412). In a bond of 1411 he is styled 'lord of Lambley': CD 403. For the Cromwells' manor house there: C. Weir, 'The Site of the Cromwells' Mediaeval Manor House at Lambley, Nottinghamshire', *TTS* 85 (1981), 75–7.

[9] The third lord made provision for the rebuilding of the parish church in the 1454 codicil to his will of 1451, although he himself was to be buried in his new collegiate church at Tattershall: R. Marks, 'The Re-Building of Lambley Church, Nottinghamshire, in the Fifteenth Century', *TTS* 87 (1983), 87–9. It seems that he had spent much of his early life at Lambley for in indictments of June 1414 he is styled as 'of Lambley' and he attested a deed there in Jan. 1412: KB9/204/2/6; Sheffield City Library, CD 405. Later he undertook some additional building work at the manor: A. Emery, 'Ralph, Lord Cromwell's Manor at Wingfield (1439–*c*.1450): Its Construction, Design and Influence', *Archaeological Journal* 142 (1985), 329.

[10] For a detailed discussion of this manor-house, 'the most important baronial residence' surviving from the mid-15th. c.: ibid. 282–332.

lay in their marriage in *c.*1407 to the Furnival heiress which brought them the south Yorkshire town of Sheffield with its appurtenant estates, including the north Nottinghamshire manor of Worksop.

Although the Nottinghamshire landholdings of these four baronial families were far outweighed by those of the leading resident gentry families, their histories, particularly those of the Cromwells and Greys, are important to an understanding of the county's politics during the Lancastrian period.

Grey of Codnor

The Greys of Codnor were a minor baronial family. When first summoned to parliament in 1299, Henry (d. 1308), first Lord Grey of Codnor, was seised of extremely scattered properties. Although he had a compact estate centred on the castle of Codnor and including the nearby Derbyshire manors of Heanor and Denby and the neighbouring Nottinghamshire manors of Toton, Eastwood, and Radcliffe-on-Trent (to which they added the manor of Barton-in-Fabis in the early 1330s), with other midland manors at Stoke in High Peak, Evington in Leicestershire, and Newbottle in Northamptonshire, their most valuable lands lay in south-east England, with the Kentish manors of Hoo St Warburgh and Aylesford, the Essex manor of Grays Thurrock, and Hampshire manors at Tunworth and Upton Grey.[11] It was not until the time of Richard, the fourth lord, that there was a significant expansion in these states. His marriage to Elizabeth, one of the two daughters and coheiresses of Ralph, first and last Lord Basset of Sapcote, took place before Basset's death in July 1378, when Elizabeth was only 5 and Richard not much older.[12] It was eventually to bring Richard something more than a moiety of the Sapcote barony. Until her death on 12 October 1412 much of this barony remained in the hands of Basset's widow, Alice, in jointure and dower,[13] but on her death, because of a favourable settlement made in favour of her and her issue by Basset, her

[11] For the Grey estates on the death of the first lord in 1308: *CIPM*, v, no. 116. For the manor of Barton-in-Fabis: CP25(1)/185/27/88 and 94.

[12] *CIPM*, xv, no. 83; *CP*, vi. 127.

[13] *FA*, vi, pp. 479, 500; *CIPM*, xv, nos. 83–91; *CFR, 1405–13*, 254–7. Very little of the Basset inheritance had remained to be divided between the coheiresses in 1378: ibid., *1377–83*, 117, 165.

only daughter, Elizabeth, came into a substantial estate concentrated in Lincolnshire.[14]

Richard also furthered his fortunes by making a highly successful career in the service of the first two Lancastrian kings: he was a royal councillor, king's chamberlain from 1405, a frequent royal ambassador, and the holder of many military offices who saw extensive service in Scotland, Wales, and France.[15] He was well rewarded by Henry IV. He enjoyed the keepership of certain lands in royal hands, most notably various Welsh marcher lordships during the minority of Edmund (d. 1425), earl of March, and, in November 1409, his earlier royal annuity of 100 marks was increased to as much as 400 marks, 'until he be provided by the king with lands and rents to that value' (this was never done).[16] His local influence in Nottinghamshire and Derbyshire was augmented by the grant to him in June 1405 of the custody of the royal castle of Horston, and, much more importantly, by his appointment in November 1406 as constable of Nottingham Castle and steward of Sherwood Forest in succession to Sir Thomas Rempston (d. 1406).[17] Such royal bounty, together with the acquisition of the Sapcote lands in 1412, promised to raise the Greys of Codnor from the ranks of the minor baronage, a fact which makes the subsequent decline of the family after the fourth lord's death in August 1418 all the more striking.

One reason for this decline is clear: the survival of the fourth lord's widow, Elizabeth Basset. He had enjoyed the benefits of the major part of her inheritance only during the last six years of his life; his sons were to suffer from her survival for a further thirty-three years. Down to her death in 1451, she enjoyed not only her part of the Sapcote barony but also the Grey manors of Barton-in-Fabis, Newbottle, Upton Grey, and Tunworth, with parcels of Codnor and Grays Thurrock.[18] Even worse for the long-term prospects of the family was her decision to pass a substantial part of her Sapcote inheritance, comprising the manors of Cheal, Metheringham, and Benefield, not to her grandson and heir,

[14] In addition to a moiety of the Bassets' properties at Castle Bytham in south Lincolnshire and Sapcote in Leicestershire, she inherited the Lincolnshire manors of Cheal in Holland and Metheringham, the Derbyshire manor of Langwith Basset, and the Northamptonshire manor of Benefield, all of which had been jointly settled on her parents and their issue: ibid., *1405–13*, 254–7.

[15] For his career: *Dictionary of National Biography*, viii. 642–3; *CP*, vi. 127–9; A. Rogers, 'The Royal Household of Henry IV', Ph.D. thesis (Nottingham, 1966), 733; C. Given-Wilson, *The Royal Household and the King's Affinity: Service, Politics and Finance in England, 1360–1413* (New Haven and London, 1986), 194.

[16] *CPR, 1401–5*, 483; *1405–8*, 145, 293; *1408–13*, 146.

[17] Ibid., *1405–8*, 20, 260; *1408–13*, 370.

[18] C139/116/35; 144/34.

Henry (d. 1496), the seventh lord, but to her favourite daughter, Elizabeth (d. 1460), and her issue by John Zouche of Bulwick, younger son of William (d. 1415), Lord Zouche of Harringworth.[19] However, the marriage of Henry (d. 1444), the sixth lord, to Margaret, one of the two daughters and coheiresses of Sir Henry Percy of Atholl,[20] partly compensated him for the loss of his mother's Sapcote and dower lands. On the death of her father in October 1432 Margaret brought to Grey the north Nottinghamshire manor of Dunham with lesser manors at Ponteland and Mitford in Northumberland.[21] Dunham was an extremely rich manor, valued at over £67 per annum on Percy's death, and this partly explains why Grey was assessed at as much as £403 per annum in 1436, despite the fact that so much of his inheritance was in the hands of his mother, Elizabeth Basset, who was markedly under-assessed at £91 per annum.[22]

The later history of the Greys of Codnor during the Lancastrian period can be briefly summarized. Henry, the sixth lord, died on 17 July 1444, having been obliged to make over to his local rival, Ralph, Lord Cromwell, the valuable manors of Hoo and Toton (with the small manor of Stoke), together valued at just over £135 per annum in a 1450s *valor*,[23] and he left a son and heir, another Henry, of only 9 years old. The wardship of those Grey lands not in Cromwell's hands was granted to John (d. 1460), Viscount Beaumont, until Henry, the seventh lord, came of age in *c.*1456.[24] First summoned to the Coventry parliament of November 1459, the seventh lord was with Queen Margaret at the battle of St Albans in February 1461 and at the battle of Towton in the

---

[19] *CCR, 1441–7*, 314–17, 467–70; C139/144/34; J. Bridges, *The History and Antiquities of Northamptonshire* (London, 1791), ii. 397. The manor of South Witham appears to have passed to the seventh lord with the rest of the Sapcote inheritance: *Testamenta Vetusta*, ed. N. H. Nicolas (London, 1826), ii. 412.

[20] Percy was a grandson of Henry (d. 1408), the first earl of Northumberland. For a brief account of his career: C. D. Ross, 'The Yorkshire Baronage, 1399–1435', D.Phil. thesis (Oxford, 1950), 87–8.

[21] She married Grey before Jan. 1433 when she was said to be over 17, and died seised of these lands in 1464: C139/58/37; C140/14/30.

[22] In 1431/2 her Sapcote lands, excluding the Lincs. manor of Metheringham (assigned to one John Warner) but including £20 from the sale of wood at Cheadle (Staffs.), had yielded her a clear income of £76 12s. 10d.: NUL, Mi. M137/6. To this must be added the value of those Grey lands she held in dower and jointure, considerably underassessed at £37 13s. 4d. in her inquisition *post mortem* of 1451: C139/144/34.

[23] Below, p. 198.

[24] Beaumont held this wardship from July 1444 but it was officially granted to him only after Elizabeth Basset's death in 1451: C139/116/35/11; *CPR, 1446–52*, 519. Margaret took the Atholl lands to her second husband, Sir Richard Vere, younger son of John, earl of Oxford (ex. 1462).

following month but, unlike his neighbour, Thomas (ex. 1464), ninth Lord Roos, did not subsequently remain committed to the Lancastrian cause.[25]

Roos of Helmsley and Belvoir

Although much wealthier than the Greys of Codnor (the Roos barony was worth something over £1,000 per annum),[26] the Roos family, after the death of William, sixth Lord Roos, in September 1414, played a less active role in Nottinghamshire politics than did the Greys. First summoned to parliament in 1299, their main estates lay in Yorkshire, centred on the castle and lordship of Helmsley in the North Riding, with residences also at Seaton Ross and Turnhall in the East Riding.[27] By the end of the fourteenth century, however, partly as a result of the considerable jointure interests of Beatrice Stafford (d. 1415), widow of Thomas (d. 1384), fourth Lord Roos, their east midland estates had become of equal importance and William, the sixth lord, chose as his chief residence the castle of Belvoir in north Leicestershire.[28] Although his mother Beatrice's jointure interests were considerable enough to have crippled William financially (Belvoir being one of the few Roos estates in which she did not hold jointure),[29] a comparison of their respective inquisitions *post mortem* shows that she demised back to him a significant portion of her jointure estates, including the castle of Helmsley itself.[30] In Nottinghamshire, where she held jointure in three of the four Roos manors, namely Orston, Warsop, and Sutton-on-Trent (the fourth being Eakring),[31] she had granted Warsop and Sutton

---

[25] *CP*, vi. 131; C. F. Richmond, 'The Nobility and the Wars of the Roses, 1459–61', *NMS* 21 (1977), 75.

[26] T. B. Pugh and C. D. Ross, 'The English Baronage and the Income Tax of 1436', *BIHR* 26 (1953), 24.

[27] For their Yorkshire estates: *CIPM*, xvi, no. 49; *Inquisitions Post Mortem Relating to Yorkshire, of the Reigns of Henry IV and Henry V*, ed. W. Paley Baildon and J. W. Clay, Yorkshire Archaeological Society Record Series 59 (1918), 102–4, 107–9.

[28] Ross, 'The Yorkshire Baronage', 101–4.

[29] For her jointure: *CIPM*, xvi, nos. 32–52; Pugh and Ross, 'The English Baronage', 23–4.

[30] *Yorks. IPM*, 142–3, 174–7.

[31] Thomas (d.1384), the fourth lord, had granted the manor of Eakring to John of Gaunt's servant, Robert Morton (d. 1396) of Bawtry, and Joan, Robert's wife, for term of their lives. It had passed into William's hands by 1 Nov. 1398, when he made a further feoffment of it: C138/14/144/11.

to her son, John, fifth Lord Roos, William's elder brother, and his heirs, and, after John's death in 1393, she demised her remaining manor, that of Orston, to William for life.[32] As a result, William's lands in the county were, in the tax returns of 1412, amongst the five richest lay estates there. Since his main Nottinghamshire manor of Orston lay only a few miles from the castle of Belvoir and his north Leicestershire estates, it is not surprising that he should have played a prominent part in the county's affairs down to his death in September 1414. Moreover, he, like Richard (d. 1418), Lord Grey of Codnor, made a successful career at court, serving as Lord Treasurer of England from September 1402 to December 1404, and being granted a life annuity of 100 marks at the end of his term of office.[33]

After William's death, however, the Roos family played an ever-diminishing role in the county's affairs; its declining influence being a consequence of short-lived lords and long-lived dowagers. His widow, Margaret Arundel, survived until July 1438. His son and heir, John, was killed at the battle of Baugé in March 1421, leaving a widow, Margery Despenser, who survived until April 1478. John was succeeded by a brother, Thomas, who died in France in August 1430, soon after attaining his majority but not before he had married Eleanor Beauchamp, who survived until March 1467. Thomas left an infant son, another Thomas, thus condemning the barony to a lengthy minority.[34] Even though this minority ended prematurely in March 1446, when the young Thomas had special livery of his much depleted, dower-ridden inheritance at the age of 18, the family was unable to regain its political influence and suffered a further setback when Thomas was attainted by the Yorkists in November 1461, having fled to Scotland with the defeated Lancastrians. He was executed in May 1464 after the battle of Hedgeley Moor, and the family had to wait until the accession of Henry VII for the reversal of his attainder.[35]

[32] *Notts. IPM, 1350–1436,* 97–8, 128–9, 155; C138/14/144/8–11; *CCR, 1413–19,* 164; 'An Annual Account Roll of the Manors of Scarrington, Car-Colston, Screveton and Orston, 1413–1414', ed. L. V. D. Owen, in *A Miscellany of Nottinghamshire Records,* ed. T. M. Blagg, TSRS 11 (1945), 170–5.

[33] For his career: Ross, 'The Yorkshire Baronage', 111–25. He did not benefit from royal patronage to the same extent as did Richard, Lord Grey of Codnor.

[34] Ibid. 104–11, 126–39; Pugh and Ross, 'The English Baronage', 23–5. John (d. 1443), Lord Tiptoft, the younger Thomas's guardian, did not play any traceable part in Notts. affairs by virtue of the Roos lands. Indeed, on 11 May 1434, the keeping of the valuable manor of Orston was granted to Sir Thomas Chaworth: *CFR, 1430–7,* 199–200.

[35] For these misfortunes and others that followed: *CP,* xi. 105–7; J. Leland, *Itinerary,* ed. L. Toulmin Smith (1906–8), i. 97–8.

It is ironic that, while the leading gentry families escaped lightly from the deleterious consequences of minorities and dowagers, the baronial houses of Roos and Grey should have suffered so badly from them. The resulting decline of the Roos family after 1414 and the weakness of the Greys of Codnor from 1418 left Nottinghamshire as a county without a significant lay magnate interest until Ralph, Lord Cromwell, began to extend his lands in the county from the late 1420s. It would be obtuse not to see his rise to power in county politics as a product in part of the declining status of these two longer-established baronial houses.

Cromwell of Tattershall

The Cromwells could trace their descent back in a direct male line to an Englishman, Haldane, who held Cromwell and Lambley in central Nottinghamshire at the time of Domesday, and were for centuries a prominent knightly family both in that county and Derbyshire, where they held West Hallam.[36] Up to the fifteenth century their most distinguished member was a younger son, John Cromwell, steward of the household of Edward II, who was summoned to parliament as a baron from 1308 until his death in 1335.[37] The foundations of the prominence of the fifteenth-century baronial family, descended from John's elder brother, Ralph (d. 1299), can be discerned in two fourteenth-century marriages: that of Ralph Cromwell (d. 1356) to Avice, daughter and, in her issue, heiress of Edward II's notorious chief baron of the exchequer, Sir Roger Belers (d. 1326); and that of their son, another Ralph, to Maud, daughter and eventual heiress of Sir John Bernak (d. 1346) of Tattershall, by Joan, one of the two daughters and co-heiresses of John (d. 1335), Lord Marmion. This second marriage brought an immediate and considerable expansion in the family's estates. On the death of her brother William Bernak in December 1360, Maud brought to Cromwell, *inter alia*, the manors of Tattershall, Tumby, and Candlesby in Lincolnshire and the manors of Old Bukenham,

[36] VCH, *Nottinghamshire*, i (1906), 234; *Curia Regis Rolls of the Reign of Henry III*, x (HMSO, 1949), 148; *CP*, iii. 551. In Feb. 1453 Cromwell revealed his pride in his ancestry, declaring that his ancestors, 'berynge the same name aswell before the conquest . . . as at all tymes sith', had been true liegemen: *CPR, 1452–61*, 95.
[37] C. Moor, *Knights of Edward I*, Publications of the Harleian Society (1929–32), i. 255–6; *CP*, iii. 553.

Hethersett, Besthorpe, and Wymondham in Norfolk.[38] These properties were extremely valuable: in a *valor* of 1429/30 the total clear annual value of Maud's inheritance was in excess of £400.[39] Such a large addition to the wealth of the family explains Ralph's summons as a baron to the parliament of April 1376. On his death in August 1398 Maud's survival ensured that their son Ralph (d. 1416), second Lord Cromwell, was amongst the poorer baronage, having only his relatively meagre paternal inheritance: the Nottinghamshire manors of Cromwell, Lambley, Basford, Bleasby, and Hucknall Torkard with the Derbyshire manor of West Hallam. However, Maud's death in April 1419 was the prelude to the remarkable career of her grandson, Ralph, third Lord Cromwell, Lord Treasurer of England from 1433 to 1443. Partly by inheritance and partly by purchase, he expanded his meagre paternal inheritance of six manors into a landed estate worth some £2,000 per annum by his death in January 1456.[40] The lands he inherited from his grandmother Maud in 1419 and his third cousin, the Belers heiress Margaret Gra, in October 1429, together with the lands brought to him by his wife Margaret, one of the two coheiresses of the baronies of Deincourt and Grey of Rotherfield, account for about half of this increase, but the rest was the result of an extraordinary series of purchases, mostly made in Lincolnshire and Rutland during his treasurership.[41]

The expansion of his Nottinghamshire inheritance is particularly significant for the study of Nottinghamshire politics; an expansion which came about almost entirely through inheritance rather than purchase. In 1423, from his marriage to Margaret, one of the two sisters and coheiresses of William (d. 1422), Lord Deincourt he gained a moiety of the south Nottinghamshire manor of Granby. Six years later, in 1429, on the death of Margaret, wife of the Lincolnshire knight, Sir John Gra, he reaped the benefits of the marriage of his great-grandfather, Ralph Cromwell (d. 1356), to Avice Belers nearly a century before, inheriting the south Nottinghamshire manors of Gonalston, Widmerpool, and Bunny, valued together at over £70 per annum in a *valor* of 1429/30.[42]

[38] *CIPM*, x, no. 630; *CFR, 1356–68*, 151; C138/42/72.
[39] HMC, *Report on the Manuscripts of Lord De L'Isle and Dudley*, i (1925), 207–8.
[40] A *valor* from late in his career but of uncertain date gives his lands a total value of £2,263 p.a., but some of this income was derived from land held by royal grant. It is striking to note that of this clear income no less than £1,322 19*s*. 10*d*. was spent on new building (exclusive of £359 4*s*. 2*d*. allowed for repairs and deducted from the gross income): SC11/822, mem. 10.
[41] R. L. Friedrichs, 'The Career and Influence of Ralph, Lord Cromwell, 1393–1456', Ph.D. thesis (Columbia, 1974), 176 ff.
[42] Above, p. 6.

On the childless death of his cousin, Sir Robert Cromwell, in June 1441, he inherited a third of the north Nottinghamshire manors of Markham Clinton and Tuxford, and, in November of the same year, on the childless death of his wife's cousin, Sir Robert Deincourt, these lands were supplemented by a yearly rent of 10 marks from Tuxford and, more important, a moiety of the south Nottinghamshire manor of East Bridgford.[43] In addition, some time before 1444–5, he purchased from the Swillington heir, John Hopton, scattered parcels of land in the south Nottinghamshire vills of East and West Leake, Stanton-on-the Wolds, Sutton Bonington, and Hickling.[44] In 1453, on the death of his cousin Anne, one of the two daughters and coheiresses of Thomas (d. 1408), Lord Bardolf, he also acquired the manor of 'Everyngham fee' in Shelford.[45]

Another acquisition owed nothing to either inheritance or purchase but was rather an expression of his great influence in local and national affairs. In August 1441 Henry, sixth Lord Grey of Codnor, was obliged to convey his manor of Toton near Nottingham, valued at as much as £46 per annum, to feoffees nominated by Cromwell, and Cromwell himself appears to have enjoyed the profits down to his death in January 1456, when his executors restored it to Grey's son and heir, Henry (d. 1496), seventh Lord Grey of Codnor.[46] Cromwell's extensive Nottinghamshire estates, concentrated in the Trent valley and far southwest of the county, yielded him a landed income of more than £300 per annum (including Toton) from the late 1440s until his death, an income from the county far greater than that of even the wealthiest county knights.[47] Furthermore, his influence in the county was considerably supplemented by royal grants. In February 1433 he was granted the keeping of the royal manors of Mansfield, Linby, and Clipstone, and, in June 1434, he became constable of Nottingham Castle and steward of Sherwood Forest, offices previously held by Sir Thomas Rempston (d. 1406) and Richard (d. 1418), Lord Grey of Codnor.[48] In February 1445 these two very important offices were granted to him in fee.[49] His influence in the county from the early 1440s was also augmented by his

[43] *Notts. IPM, 1437–85*, 15–17.

[44] C. Richmond, *John Hopton* (Cambridge, 1981), 25.

[45] Magdalen College, Misc. 356(2); *Notts. IPM, 1437–85*, 74.

[46] *Notts. IPM, 1437–85*, 19–21; Magdalen College, Misc. 357; below, p. 198.

[47] For the valuation of his Notts. estates: SC11/822, mem. 1; HMC, *De L'Isle*, i. 207–8; Magdalen College, Misc. 356(1); 185/11 (a *valor* of Cromwell's lands dividing them between his coheirs).

[48] *CFR, 1430–7*, 136–7, 205; *CPR, 1436–41*, 19.   [49] *CPR, 1441–6*, 325.

close political alliance with the Talbots, who held the valuable north Nottinghamshire manor of Worksop, and were the only other magnate house with a significant landed interest in the county.

Talbot

The manor of Worksop came to the Talbot family by virtue of the marriage (before 12 March 1407) of John (*c*.1384–1453), Lord Talbot, later the Talbot earl of Shrewsbury, to Maud, only daughter of Thomas Nevill (d. 1407), by Joan (d. 1395), daughter and heiress of William Furnival (d. 1383), Lord Furnival.[50] The manor was part of a much larger and compact estate centred on the nearby south Yorkshire manor and town of Sheffield and including several manors in north Derbyshire.[51] If John had not inherited the extensive Welsh march estates of the Talbots in December 1421, on the death of his niece, Ankaret, the only child of his elder brother, Gilbert (d. 1418), fifth Lord Talbot, it is probable that he would have played an important part in the affairs of the north-east midlands. Indeed, during the career of John's great-grandson George (d. 1538), fourth earl of Shrewsbury, it was this area rather than Shropshire that became the Talbot's main centre of interest.[52] The beginnings of this shift of interest are to be discerned in the career of John (d. 1460), the second earl. For the first earl the family's midland estates were peripheral, and in 1435/6 he settled the manor of Worksop on John, his eldest son and heir-apparent. It was this John who expanded the family estate in the midlands by the purchase of several north Derbyshire manors.[53] He drew up his will at Sheffield Castle on 6 September 1446 and, on his death at the battle of Northampton on 10 July 1460, was buried with his Furnival mother at Worksop Priory. After his death two of his daughters married into the two greatest knightly families of Nottinghamshire and Derbyshire: in *c*.1466 Margaret married Thomas Chaworth (d. 1483), son and heir-apparent of Sir William Chaworth (d. 1467) of Wiverton, and, at about the same time, Anne

[50] *CP*, v. 591. Thomasine, widow of William, held the manor of Worksop in dower until her death on 20 July 1409: C137/71/25.

[51] Ross, 'The Yorkshire Baronage', 59–60.

[52] G. W. Bernard, *The Power of the Early Tudor Nobility: A Study of the Fourth and Fifth Earls of Shrewsbury* (Brighton etc., 1985), 139 ff.

[53] A. J. Pollard, 'The Family of Talbot, Lords Talbot and Earls of Shrewsbury in the Fifteenth Century', Ph.D. thesis (Bristol, 1968), 34, 65; Wright, p. 74.

married Henry Vernon (d. 1515), son and heir-apparent of Sir William Vernon (d. 1467) of Haddon.[54] This second marriage was to lead John (d. 1473), the third earl, into involvement in the violent dispute between the Vernons and Henry (d. 1496), seventh Lord Grey of Codnor, in 1467–8.[55]

Derbyshire was more central to the interests of the Talbots than was Nottinghamshire. It was not until after the death of his friend, Ralph, Lord Cromwell, in January 1456 that the second earl played any significant part in the affairs of the latter county.[56] He then used his position as a justice of the peace to protect the interests of Cromwell's executors and feoffees, of which he was one, in the manors of Gonalston, Widmerpool, and Bunny.[57] The relationship between the two men had undoubtedly been a close one: in 1441 Talbot acted for Cromwell in a fine concerning the Northamptonshire manor of Collyweston; in September 1446, on the eve of his departure to take up the office of chancellor of Ireland, Talbot appointed Cromwell as the sole supervisor of his will; Cromwell was one of those who supported Talbot against the attempt by his step-mother, Margaret Beauchamp, countess of Shrewsbury, to partition his inheritance on the death of the first earl in 1453; in 1452 Talbot was named as Cromwell's senior lay feoffee; in July 1455 it was to Talbot that Cromwell fled for protection when accused by Richard, earl of Warwick, of instigating the first battle of St Albans; and on 4 January 1456 at South Wingfield Talbot was present at Cromwell's deathbed.[58] He was later to extend his landed interest in Derbyshire through the purchase of the manors of South Wingfield, with its fine new manor house, and Crich, from Cromwell's executors.[59] It is this friendship with Cromwell that is the most important fact about the second earl's career for the study of Nottinghamshire politics.

What was the nature of the relationship between these baronial families (and those with a lesser stake in the county) and the leading Nottinghamshire gentry? In view of the landed pre-eminence of the latter within the county and their more continuous concern with the county's affairs

[54] NRO, Foljambe DD FJ 4/27/5; Wright, p. 233.   [55] Ibid. 139.
[56] For his possible involvement in the Notts. elections of Oct. 1449 and June 1455: below, p. 166.
[57] S. J. Payling, 'Inheritance and Local Politics in the Later Middle Ages: The Case of Ralph, Lord Cromwell, and the Heriz Inheritance', *NMS* 30 (1986), 88–9.
[58] CP25(1)/179/95/103; *TE*, ii. 253; Pollard, 'The Family of Talbot', 58, 71; *CPR, 1452–61*, 199–200; *The Paston Letters*, ed. J. Gairdner (London, 1904), iii. 44; C1/26/76.
[59] Payling, 'Inheritance and Local Politics', 87.

it would be surprising if this relationship was one of subservience on their part. Indeed, a survey of their connections with local barons strongly suggests that the gentry élite not only saw themselves as the leaders of political society but were recognized as such by both the crown and their social superiors amongst the baronage: a fact reflected in the patronage they attracted.

Those barons with only a peripheral interest in the county looked to them to oversee the administration of their local estates.[60] For example, on 24 April 1443, William (d. 1462), Lord Zouche of Harringworth, who held the west Nottinghamshire castle and manor of Greasley, appointed Robert Strelley of nearby Strelley, as the chief steward of his Nottinghamshire and Derbyshire estates.[61] Similarly, in the following year, on 3 June 1444 Edward Nevill (d. 1476), summoned as Lord Bergavenny from 1450, and who held the Nottinghamshire soke of Oswaldbeck in the right of his wife, Elizabeth Beauchamp (d. 1448),[62] appointed Strelley as his steward at Oswaldbeck.[63] Even lords with a much more considerable estate in the county looked to the same families. On 15 July 1454 William Bothe (d. 1464), archbishop of York, appointed William Chaworth, son and heir apparent of the very wealthy Sir Thomas Chaworth, as the steward of the archiepiscopal lordship of Southwell,[64] an office previously held by Sir John Zouche, the grandfather of William Chaworth's wife, during the archbishopric of Henry Bowet (1407–23).[65] Such connections, probably merely formal, served as both a recognition and a reinforcement of these leading gentry families' traditional prominence in the county.[66]

Other connections, less formal but probably closer in personal terms, underline this baronial dependence on the greater gentry. William, Lord Roos, after he had moved south from Helmsley to Belvoir, cultivated his influence in the south of the county in the early years of the fifteenth century through his companion in the service of Henry IV, the influential Sir Thomas Rempston, and Rempston's close associates, the Leeks of Cotham, who resided just to the north of Roos's

[60] Wright, pp. 61, 63.
[61] *CAD*, vi, C5735. Strelley held his nearby Derbys. manor of Shipley of Zouche's manor of Ilkeston: C139/48/28.
[62] *CP*, i. 27–30.; *Notts. IPM, 1350–1436*, 200–1.
[63] BL, Harley Charters 112B.50. For later connections between Bergavenny and Strelley: *CAD*, iii, A4689; vi, C4791.
[64] Borthwick Institute, Arch. Reg. 20, fo. 166ᵛ.
[65] Below, p. 193.
[66] Wright, p. 63.

manor of Orston.[67] Rempston was godfather to Roos's second son, Thomas (d. 1430), later eighth Lord Roos, born at Belvoir on 26 September 1406,[68] while Simon Leek, the son and heir-apparent of Sir John Leek of Cotham, was a member of his household and later an executor of his will.[69] With the support of the leading county families in such demand amongst the local nobility, it is not surprising that the wealthiest of the county's knights, Sir Thomas Chaworth, should have been in particularly great demand. Such was his standing that he frequently acted as a feoffee for his baronial neighbours: in 1418 he was one of the seven feoffees for the execution of the will of Richard, Lord Grey of Codnor;[70] in April 1430 he, with his Nottinghamshire neighbour and associate, Sir William Babington, CJCB, were amongst those to whom Thomas, Lord Roos, committed various estates in Sussex and elsewhere before accompanying the young Henry VI to France;[71] and in May 1445 he, and other leading Nottinghamshire men, were feoffees for William, Lord Zouche, in the castle of Greasley.[72] His status is brought even more sharply into focus by the marriage of his eldest daughter, Elizabeth, to John Scrope, a younger brother of the ill-fated Henry, Lord Scrope of Masham, executed in August 1415 for his part in the Southampton plot. It is uncertain when this marriage took place but it had certainly done so by 24 August 1418.[73] John was not at this date the heir to the Scrope of Masham barony, but he became so on the death of his brother, Stephen Scrope, archdeacon of Richmond, on the following 5 September.[74] Since both Stephen and the other of John's elder brothers, Geoffrey (who had died on the previous 10 April) were childless, it is probable, assuming the marriage to have taken place after Henry Scrope's execution, that John (or at least his issue by his

---

[67] For Sir Thomas Rempston's career and his connections with the Leeks: below, pp. 121–3. Sir Thomas's younger brother, William, had been connected with the Roos family from at least 1380: *CCR, 1377–81*, 347; *1381–5*, 219, 488; *CIPM*, xvi, no. 43.

[68] *RP*, iv. 319–20.

[69] *The Register of Henry Chichele, Archbishop of Canterbury, 1414–1453*, ed. E. F. Jacob, 4 vols., Canterbury and York Society, 42, 45–7 (1937–47), ii. 25–6. For further details of Simon Leek's connection with William, Lord Roos: *CCR, 1405–9*, 477; *1413–19*, 257; *1435–41*, 421; *CPR, 1408–13*, 25; *Yorks. IPM*, p. 109. In Sept. 1419 he was a feoffee for William's son and heir John, Lord Roos (d. 1421): ibid. 177. His first cousin, William Leek of Screveton, was an annuitant of William, Lord Roos, in 1413–14: 'An Annual Account Roll', 173.

[70] C139/116/35.

[71] *CPR, 1429–36*, 62; *CCR, 1429–35*, 75, 77; C139/93/48. He was also amongst Roos's feoffees in Notts.: NUL, Mi. 6/170/91; D936.

[72] *Notts. IPM, 1437–85*, 63.   [73] *TE*, i. 388.

[74] Ross, 'The Yorkshire Baronage', 175–6. Cf. *Notts. IPM, 1350–1436*, 163–4.

Chaworth wife) could, when this marriage took place, have ultimately expected to come into this barony. Even though the barony was under an attainder at the time of the marriage and was not restored until 1425, it is significant that John should have seen Elizabeth Chaworth as a valuable match: when he eventually came into what was his he made a substantial jointure settlement in her favour.[75]

However, it is Sir Thomas's close connection with Ralph, Lord Cromwell, the magnate who exercised the greatest influence in the county during the Lancastrian period, that best reveals his importance. There is no doubt that Cromwell saw him as a vital ally, and it was a connection that worked to their mutual benefit. As early as 1423 Cromwell, then at the start of his career, is to be found amongst Sir Thomas's feoffees.[76] This early connection suggests that Cromwell, as one of Henry VI's minority councillors, was behind his appointment in July 1423 to the commission to negotiate with the Scottish ambassadors for the ransom of James I (1394–1437) of Scotland, a commission on which Cromwell also served, and his appointment, again in company with Cromwell, in the following November as one of the keepers of the temporalities of the archbishopric of York during the vacancy occasioned by the death of Henry Bowet.[77] He certainly benefited from Cromwell's patronage later in his career. His son, George, and his daughters, Margery and Joan, married wards of Cromwell,[78] and it is possible that it was Cromwell who secured for him the keeping of the Roos manor of Orston during the minority of Thomas (d. 1464), ninth Lord Roos, in May 1434, when Cromwell was Lord Treasurer.[79] In return for these marks of favour he performed various services for Cromwell: in addition to serving as one of Cromwell's feoffees in the disputed Heriz manors,[80] he was active in Cromwell's support in the

---

[75] At an unknown date he settled on her in jointure 7 manors valued at over £100 p.a. in inquisition *post mortem* values and hence probably worth considerably more: C140/21/41.

[76] CP25(1)/291/65/18.

[77] *Calendar of Documents Relating to Scotland, 1108–1509*, ed. J. Bain, 4 vols. (Edinburgh, 1881–8), iv, no. 929; *PPC*, iii. 121; *CFR, 1422–30*, 59.

[78] For George's marriage to the heiress, Alice Annesley: Payling, p. 46. Margery married John Benstede of Bennington (Herts.), whose wardship and marriage Cromwell obtained from the royal grantee Henry Radcliffe in 1442: *CFR, 1437–45*, 70; E404/59/283; *CPR, 1441–6*, 461; *1446–52*, 452. Chaworth paid an unspecified sum for the Benstede marriage: Magdalen College, Misc. 303. Joan married Thomas Goldsburgh of Goldsborough (Yorks.), a ward of Cromwell in 1438–9 in right of his Lincs. lordship of Blankney: HMC, *De L'Isle*, i. 226; *Notts. Visit.*, 127; C1/70/159.

[79] *CFR, 1422–30*, 199–200. This may, however, have been due to Chaworth's service as one of the feoffees of Thomas (d. 1430), Lord Roos: above, p. 101.

[80] Payling, 'Inheritance and Local Politics', 76.

latter's disputes with Sir Henry Pierpoint over these manors and later with Henry (d. 1444), Lord Grey of Codnor. In March 1435 he served with Cromwell on a commission of enquiry into concealments of the crown's feudal rights in Nottinghamshire which produced vexatious presentments against Pierpoint;[81] in July 1440 he was appointed to the commission of *oyer* and *terminer* obtained by Cromwell in his dispute with Grey; and in September 1441 he was one of the arbiters in this dispute, which produced a harsh award against Grey; and later, in April 1445, he witnessed Grey's mother's quitclaim of the valuable manors with which her son was forced to part as a consequence of his failure to abide by the terms of the award.[82]

The pattern of Chaworth's extensive connections amongst the baronage finds a local parallel in the career of Sir Richard Vernon (d. 1451) of Haddon in Derbyshire.[83] Just as he made use of Chaworth in Nottinghamshire, Cromwell employed the well-connected Vernon in Derbyshire: in April 1431 Vernon was amongst his feoffees in the Heriz manors;[84] in July 1440 he was commissioned on the *oyer* and *terminer* obtained against Grey;[85] and on New Year's Day 1448 he and Chaworth were with him at South Wingfield when he took Richard Willoughby's oath not to impede the execution of Sir Hugh Willoughby's will.[86] Later, in the 1460s, the pre-eminence of these two families of Chaworth and Vernon in their respective counties was recognized by the Talbots when two daughters of John (d. 1460), second earl of Shrewsbury, married the heirs apparent of the two families.[87] The existence of such exceptionally wealthy knightly families, parallel examples of which were to be found in most English counties, underlines McFarlane's point that fifteenth-century society cannot be divided into 'powerful barons on the one hand and humble commoners on the other, into leaders among the peers and led among the knights'.[88] Moreover, these families, although wealthier than their fellow leading gentry, were simply *primi inter pares*, they stood at the heads of their particular county élites, bearing the main

[81] Ibid. 79. Chaworth appears to have been hostile to Pierpoint for he headed the anti-Pierpoint grand jury before the Derbys. *oyer* and *terminer* commissioners of 1434: Wright, pp. 129–30.

[82] *CPR, 1436–41*, 450; *Notts. IPM*, 19; *CCR, 1441–7*, 351–2. For the full context of Cromwell's dispute with Grey: below, pp. 195–8.

[83] For Vernon's career: J. S. Roskell, 'Sir Richard Vernon of Haddon, Speaker in the Parliament of Leicester, 1426', *Derbyshire Archaeological Journal* 82 (1962), 43–53; Wright, *passim*, esp. pp. 66–73.

[84] Payling, 'Inheritance and Local Politics', 76.

[85] *CPR, 1436–41*, 450.   [86] Below, p. 209.   [87] Above, pp. 98–9.

[88] K. B. McFarlane, 'Parliament and "Bastard Feudalism"', *TRHS* 26 (1944), 69.

burden of county administration and representation with other leading families. Although, in Nottinghamshire, Cromwell employed Chaworth in the management of those local affairs in which he had an interest, he did not rely on him exclusively. He cultivated other allies amongst the leading families of the shire. His sister, Maud, was the wife of Sir Richard Stanhope, and early in his career the connection between the two men was close,[89] although perhaps of greater importance were his connections with the Babingtons of Chilwell. William Babington, the son and heir apparent of Sir William Babington, CJCB, was particularly close to Cromwell: in August 1441 he, along with such of Cromwell's intimates as William Stanlowe and John Leynton, acted as an agent from Cromwell in a feoffment made by Henry, Lord Grey of Codnor;[90] in 1453 he acted with Cromwell in the purchase of the Bardolf manor of Shelford;[91] and he was Cromwell's deputy in the constableship of Newark Castle.[92]

These connections, his estates in the county, which became progressively more extensive as his career progressed, and the national prominence he enjoyed through a large part of this career, explain why Cromwell was able to exert so much influence in the county: an influence most clearly manifested in his defeat of Sir Henry Pierpoint in the dispute over the Heriz manors, although this appears to have owed as much to legal ingenuity as local might; his destruction of the local influence of Henry, Lord Grey of Codnor; and the return of his servant, Richard Illingworth, to represent the county in four parliaments between February 1447 and July 1455.[93] And yet this influence depended on the goodwill of at least some of the leading men of the shire, men of independent local power. Had either Pierpoint or Grey enjoyed the support of their leading shire neighbours, or had there been eligible and willing candidates for parliament amongst the greater gentry of the county during the late 1440s and early 1450s, Cromwell's impact on the affairs of the county would have been much diminished. There can be

[89] This marriage took place in 1411: Thoroton, iii. 245; Sheffield City Library, CD403. The fact that it did so reflects the comparatively lowly status of the Cromwells before the brilliant career of the third lord. For Stanhope's early connections with him: below, p. 192; *CCR, 1422–9*, 135; *TE*, ii. 39–41. It was probably through his connection with Cromwell that Stanhope entered the service of Thomas, duke of Clarence, who sued him in the Easter term 1418 as his receiver: CP40/629, rot. 266. For the close connection between Clarence and Cromwell: Friedrichs, 'Cromwell', 10–12.
[90] C139/116/35/14, 15, 17; below, p. 198.   [91] *Notts. IPM, 1437–85*, 38.
[92] SC11/822 mem. 1. For Cromwell's other connections amongst the Notts. gentry: below, pp. 140–1, 146.
[93] For Illingworth's elections: below, pp. 144–7.

little doubt that if any magnates hoped to exercise a significant degree of
political power in the county he was obliged to cultivate the goodwill of
at least some of the local gentry, who were the natural governors of the
shire and as such dominated the major offices of shire administration
and representation.[94] These gentry were thus too substantial to depend
on baronial patrons for their place in shire politics and it was the
baronage who depended on them for influence in the county.

It would not be prudent to generalize about the extent to which this
high degree of greater gentry independence was typical of England as a
whole. Recent gentry studies have suggested that there was no such
thing as a typical English county, and Nottinghamshire certainly cannot
be regarded as one. Figures drawn from the taxation returns of 1412 and
1436 show it to have had both a lower than average percentage of
baronial land and a higher than average concentration of non-baronial
wealth in the hands of a few substantial gentry families. In some other
counties the position was very different. In late-fourteenth-century
Devon and early-fifteenth-century Warwickshire, in the shape of the
Courtenays and Beauchamps respectively, there was a territorially
dominant, long-established, baronial house, which could rely on its
local landed wealth and the traditional loyalties of the county gentry for
its authority. Indeed, it is impossible to deny that great magnate houses
could and did exercise a very high degree of influence over the affairs of
their localities through their affinities. What can be questioned, however
is the degree of subservience implied in the relationship between
baronage and gentry, especially the wealthier gentry, and the extent to
which the usages of 'bastard feudalism' pervaded English society as a
whole, as opposed to particular counties at particular times.[95] Not only
was the hegemony of a great magnate in county affairs often only a
temporary phenomenon compared with the much more continuous
corporate existence of a shire 'establishment' composed of the leading
shire gentry,[96] but simple mathematics demonstrates that, over the
county as a whole, a significant proportion, and perhaps even the
majority, of knights and esquires were not in receipt of fees from their
baronial superiors. The largest documented retinues of the fifteenth
century, the ninety-two indentured retainers of William (d. 1483), Lord
Hastings, and the eighty-four of Humphrey Stafford (d. 1460), duke of

[94] For the pattern of county office-holding: below, pp. 109–19.
[95] For some useful comments on what Richmond sees as the recent over-emphasis on
the power of the baronage: C. F. Richmond, 'After McFarlane', *History*, 68 (1983), 57–60.
[96] Above, p. 10.

Buckingham, were exceptional in size, and Buckingham's indentured retinue, the more typical of the two in terms of composition, included a large proportion of professional lawyers and administrators of lesser gentry status and menial household servants of non-gentry status.[97] Of his eighty-four annuitants of 1447/8 less than half were knights or esquires, although his ten knights and twenty-seven esquires of that year probably made his the greatest of all fifteenth-century retinues[98] (allowing for the fact that Hastings's affinity was largely an artificial creation based on royal patronage).[99] By contrast, the minor baronage had much less exalted affinities: a striking example is Reginald (d. 1450), Lord de la Warr, who, in 1436, numbered not one knight or esquire amongst his seventy-six annuitants.[100] More typical perhaps was the retinue of Henry, Lord Grey of Codnor, which, in the same year consisted of 18 life annuitants receiving fees totalling £54. One was a knight, the powerful Sir John Bertram of Bothal near Grey's Northumberland lands at Mitford, paid a token fee of 40s per annum probably to act in Grey's interest in that county, and three more were styled esquires, John Belasys of Belsay in the same county, Richard Neuport of Codnor, and John Curson of Kedleston, both in Derbyshire; the remainder, with the exception of four lawyers, Ralph de la Pole, later a justice of the king's bench, Peter Arderne, later a justice of the common pleas, John Bowes and Gerard Meynell, who all had loyalties to other lords besides Grey, were lesser men of sub-gentry status.[101]

The fact that the bulk of the parliamentary peerage of some 50 barons each retained only a few knights and esquires, with just a handful of earls

[97] For the size and composition of 15th-c. indentured retinues: G. L. Harriss, 'Introduction', in K. B. McFarlane, *England in the Fifteenth Century* (London, 1981), p. xi; Wright, p. 65; C. Rawcliffe, *The Staffords, Earls of Stafford and Dukes of Buckingham, 1394–1521* (Cambridge, 1978), 73–5; Pugh, 'The Magnates, Knights and Gentry', in S. B. Chrimes *et al.* (eds.), *Fifteenth-Century England, 1399–1509* (Manchester, 1972), 101–9; G. G. Astill, 'The Medieval Gentry: A Study in Leicestershire Society', Ph.D. thesis (Birmingham, 1977), 209–10; J. M. W. Bean, *From Lord to Patron: Lordship in Late Medieval England* (Manchester, 1989), 164–74. For the exceptional composition of Hastings's retinue, which contained no one below the rank of gentleman: W. H. Dunham jun., *Lord Hastings' Indentured Retainers, 1461–1483*, Transactions of the Connecticut Academy of Arts and Sciences 39 (1955), 28.

[98] Pugh, 'The Magnates', 105.

[99] Wright, pp. 78–82; I. D. Rowney, 'The Hastings Affinity in Staffordshire and the Honour of Tutbury', *BIHR* 57 (1984), 35–45.

[100] Pugh, 'The Magnates', 101.

[101] E163/7/31, pt. 1. For Bertram: J. S. Roskell, *The Commons in the Parliament of 1422* (Manchester, 1954), 151–2. For Meynell: Wright, pp. 98–9, 249. For de la Pole: Wright, pp. 84, 98–9; E. Foss, *A Bibliographical Dictionary of the Judges of England, 1066–1870* (London, 1870), 522. For Arderne: ibid. 16. For Bowes: below, p. 142.

and dukes retaining significant numbers, is to be seen in the context of Professor H. L. Gray's calculations from the tax returns of 1436: in his view there were in excess of 900 non-baronial landholders with an income of £40 per annum or more, and more than 2,100 with £20 per annum or more.[102] In these circumstances, there can be little doubt that a significant number of those with £40 per annum, and probably the majority of those with £20 per annum were without any formal baronial connection as manifest in the receipt of a life annuity, the most obvious outward expression of that form of social organization commonly called 'bastard feudalism'.[103] No doubt many of those without fees had informal connections with the baronage, belonging to that nebulous circle of well-wishers which surrounded the more substantial magnates,[104] and yet such connections must by their very nature have been tenuous, temporary, and *ad hoc*, allowing a good degree of independence to the well-wisher and implying no degree of dependence. Nor was a life indenture and an annuity any guarantee of exclusive loyalty.[105] The degree of subservience which prevailed in the connections of 'bastard feudalism' can thus be justly questioned. Dr S. K. Walker, in his excellent study of the greatest of all late-medieval affinities, that of John of Gaunt, has painted a stark picture of the nature of these connections. In his view, not only did the claims of family and locality outweigh the importance of the Lancastrian allegiance for most of Gaunt's retainers, but the county gentry, although happy enough to seek Gaunt's lordship, 'were equally prepared to forego, and, if necessary, to flout it'.[106] He concluded that, on the evidence of Gaunt's dealings with the gentry, 'the position of the magnates and their dependants at the local level seems at times beleaguered—one which was defended against the lawless depredations of the gentry only with difficulty' for the gentry were often only too ready to abuse the 'good lordship' of a magnate in pursuance of their own private disputes.[107] These conclusions must, as Dr Walker

---

[102] Above, p. 2.

[103] This conclusion finds support in Dr Walker's work on John of Gaunt. He has calculated that Gaunt's great affinity in Lancs. comprehended no more than a third of the county gentry: Walker, 'John of Gaunt', 158–61. He concluded that, 'even under the most favourable circumstances, "bastard feudalism" was never an all-embracing form of social organization': ibid. 194.

[104] For the structure of a baronial affinity: M. C. Carpenter, 'The Beauchamp Affinity; A Study of Bastard Feudalism at Work', *EHR* 95 (1980), 515–17.

[105] K. B. McFarlane, 'The Wars of the Roses', *Proceedings of the British Academy* 50 (1964), 109–12; Richmond, 'After McFarlane', 58.

[106] Walker, 'John of Gaunt', 264. For a particular example, see id., 'Lancaster *v.* Dallingridge: A Franchisal Dispute in Fourteenth-Century Sussex', *Sussex Archaeological Collections* 121 (1983), 87–94.   [107] Walker, 'John of Gaunt', 263.

points out, be qualified by the exceptional nature of this affinity: although Gaunt spent in excess of £3,000 per annum upon it,[108] a quite unprecedented sum, its widespread distribution, the fact that it was intended principally to meet the demands of military service and court ceremonial rather than local politics, and the lengthy absences abroad of its leader, meant that it lacked the cohesion of the much less expensive but more highly localized affinities of Courtenay and Beauchamp.[109] Nevertheless, the degree of influence that these two affinities were able to exercise in their respective localities was very much the exception: and even Beauchamp was dependent on political alliances with lesser Warwickshire magnates while the Courtenay dominance in Devon was under threat from William, Lord Bonville, from the 1440s and did not survive the house of Lancaster.[110] Much more typical must have been the situation that prevailed in Lancastrian Nottinghamshire where a wealthy, independent gentry establishment was the principal factor in shire politics: it was through them that baronial influence had to be exercised if it was to be exercised at all.

[108] Walker, 'John of Gaunt', 15. Compare this with the sum of nearly £600 spent by Humphrey, duke of Buckingham, in 1447–8, and the approx. £640 spent by Richard Beauchamp, earl of Warwick, in c.1431 on their affinities: Rawcliffe, *The Staffords*, 74; Carpenter, 'Political Society', 67–8.

[109] Walker, 'John of Gaunt', 254.

[110] Carpenter, 'The Beauchamp Affinity', 517–18; Cherry, 'The Courtenay Earls of Devon', 90–7.

5
OFFICE-HOLDING AND THE KING'S AFFINITY

THE analysis of the personnel of county office-holding is a laborious and often unrewarding process. It is difficult to make sense of an apparently random series of appointments and elections. Rarely is it possible to discover why a particular individual was appointed to a particular office at a particular time, still less what motivated him to either seek or shirk the responsibilities that office brought with it: motive has to be inferred. Nevertheless, despite these difficulties, certain basic questions about the personnel of local office are fairly easily answered. Earlier county studies have shown, and the Nottinghamshire evidence confirms, that there was a clear hierarchy of offices in terms of the social status of those who held them: at the top was the office of sheriff, closely followed by those of parliamentary knight of the shire and justice of the peace; below them came that of escheator, and thence down to the minor offices of coroner, undersheriff, and clerk of the peace.[1] Not surprisingly, the social status of the office-holders expressed the political importance of the offices they held: in the Lancastrian period the shrievalty remained the most important local office, despite the growing power of the commission of the peace.[2]

It is much more difficult to go further and determine any causality in appointment beyond this vague notion of status. There can be no doubt that on occasions appointments and elections were determined by the connection of the appointed or elected with a local magnate. On the other hand, it is equally clear that a magnate seeking to secure the appointment or election of his own nominee had to work within the county's existing social hierarchy.[3] Indeed, during the late fourteenth and early fifteenth centuries the parliamentary commons had secured

[1] Cf. M. C. Carpenter, 'Political Society in Warwickshire, c. 1401–72', Ph.D. thesis (Cambridge, 1976).
[2] Ibid. 39–41.
[3] Cf. 'If a man represented the shire in parliament it was almost certainly because he had a magnate's backing.': ibid. 53. 'Those appointed qualified for office by virtue first and foremost of their own resources.': Wright, 94.

the passing of statutes that greatly restricted the field from which potential officers could be drawn, ensuring that the wealthier shire gentry would monopolize the major local offices. In 1368 a statute laid down that escheators should have at least £20 per annum from land; in 1371 this qualification was extended to sheriffs, the income to be derived from land in the county of appointment; in 1413 a residence qualification was imposed on the parliamentary knights of the shire, with, in 1445–6, an income qualification equal to the level of distraint; and, in 1414, a further statute extended the residence qualification to justices of the peace, followed by another statute in 1439–40 adding an income qualification of £20 per annum from land.[4] If a magnate was to influence local appointments and elections, he had to draw substantial county gentry into his affinity. Some wealthy magnates did this so successfully that they were able to exercise a temporary dominance over appointments in a particular county or region. Outstanding examples are Edward Courtenay (d. 1419), earl of Devon, in the Devon of the last two decades of the fourteenth century, and Richard Beauchamp (d. 1439), earl of Warwick, in early fifteenth-century Warwickshire.[5] But an altogether more significant and less transient influence in determining local appointments and elections was membership of the greatest of all affinities, that of the king. It was in his service, at least during the first decades of Lancastrian rule, that the most substantial rewards were to be had, and it was hence into his service that the leading shire gentry were drawn.[6] In Nottinghamshire, appointments and elections to local office are to be seen in the context of the expansion of John of Gaunt's considerable Lancastrian affinity in the county into an even greater royal affinity in the years immediately following 1399 and the subsequent decline of that affinity during the reign of Henry VI.[7] However, royal or magnate connections allied with landed income sufficient to qualify for office were not the only criteria for appointment

[4] *RP*, ii. 296, 308; iv. 8, 51; v. 28, 116; *SR*, i. 388; ii. 170, 187, 309–10, 342; below, pp. 112, 167.

[5] M. Cherry, 'The Courtenay Earls of Devon: The Formation of Disintegration of a Late Medieval Aristocratic Affinity', *Southern History* 1 (1979), 75–6, 84–7, 91–2; Carpenter, 'Political Society', 48–9; G. L. Harriss, 'Introduction', in K. B. McFarlane, *England in the Fifteenth Century: Collected Essays* (London, 1981), pp. xv–xvi.

[6] C. D. Ross, 'The Yorkshire Baronage, 1399–1435', D.Phil. thesis (Oxford, 1950), 368–70.

[7] T. B. Pugh has seen the rise and decline of the Lancastrian affinity as a general phenomenon: 'The Magnates, Knights and Gentry', in S. B. Chrimes *et al.* (eds.), *Fifteenth-Century England, 1399–1509* (Manchester, 1972), 107–8. Cf. B. P. Wolffe, *Henry VI* (London, 1981), 99–101.

or election. It is quite clear that the frequency with which a county family held major office was directly related to its wealth. Dr S. M. Wright, in her study of the Derbyshire gentry, has shown that a social élite dominated the administration of the shire,[8] and the Nottinghamshire evidence strongly underlines her conclusion. These greater county families were, of course, more likely than their social inferiors to attract the patronage of the crown, but their dominance over local office rested first and foremost on their landed wealth: a wealth that gave them a right to office.

The extent to which the leading families dominated the major county offices is easily demonstrated. Between 1399 and 1461, twenty-seven Nottinghamshire men were appointed to the joint shrievalty of Nottinghamshire and Derbyshire, serving 41 terms between them.[9] Of these twenty-seven, seventeen, serving 23 terms in total, came from the thirteen families that formed the county élite; and a further eight, serving 14 terms, were drawn from the second rank of county society, the lesser knights and distrainees. Only one sheriff, John Hickling of Linby, heralded from the lesser squirearchy, and it is only the appointment of William Rigmayden, who served three times in the office between 1408 and 1417, that can certainly be said to have been entirely due to political connections independent of social considerations.[10] A similar analysis of county representation reveals the same picture.[11] The 78 parliamentary seats for which returns survive were filled by thirty-eight men: sixteen of these men came from the county élite and they sat on a total of 44 occasions between them; twelve came from the lesser knights and distrainees and took 18 seats; and only four, taking 7 seats, were from the lesser squirearchy. Of the remaining six, three, Sir Robert Plumpton, Sir William Plumpton, and Nicholas FitzWilliam, were drawn from prominent Yorkshire families with land in the county, while the election of the other three, Richard Illingworth, William Rigmayden, and John Kniveton, is to be explained solely in political terms.

[8] Wright, pp. 5, 94. For the same conclusion for the Yorkshire officers drawn from the West Riding: C. E. Arnold, 'A Political Study of the West Riding of Yorkshire, 1437–1509', Ph.D. thesis (Manchester, 1984), 70, 332.
[9] For appointments to this shrievalty: *CFR, 1399–1461, passim; List of Sheriffs for England and Wales*, Lists and Indexes, 9 (1898), 103. For the 4 surviving pricked lists (naming the 3 men from whom the sheriff for a particular year was chosen): C47/34/2/2–5. [10] For these figures: Appendix 5.
[11] For those elected to represent the county in parliament: *Return of the Name of Every Member*, Parliamentary Papers, 1878, vol. lxii (London, 1878), pt. i, 257–356; *CFR, 1437–45*, 140.

Dr N. E. Saul, in his excellent study of the Gloucestershire gentry, concluded that over the fourteenth century as a whole the county's representatives in parliament were drawn from both the greater and lesser gentry with the latter being preponderant in the 1330s, but that by the 1370s the shire representatives were usually knights or well-endowed esquires with several manors. As a consequence, he added, representation was falling into the hands of a smaller circle of men than in the earlier part of the century.[12] The Nottinghamshire evidence supports this hypothesis. There is certainly no late fourteenth-century parallel for the career of John de Oxenford, who represented the county in five parliaments during the 1330s, to four of which he returned himself as sheriff. As the son of an Oxford goldsmith whose only Nottinghamshire lands were the dower of his wife, his qualifications for such a prominent role in county affairs were slight.[13] By the 1370s Nottinghamshire's representatives in parliament were drawn from a much more restricted sphere, with the long-established families of Leek and Annesley particularly to the fore. This process of restriction continued into the fifteenth century as the dominance over shire representation of an increasingly well-defined social élite became more pronounced. This dominance, observable in Nottinghamshire as in other counties, was reflected in the statute of 1445–6, which laid down that henceforward shire representatives should be 'notable Knyghtes of the same Shires for the which they shall so be chosen; other ellys such notable Squiers, Gentilmen of birth, of the same Shires as be able to be Knyghtes; and no man to be it, that stondeth in the degree of Yoman and bynethe'.[14] In practice, these men had for some time enjoyed a virtual monopoly of the county seats, with the wealthier knights and distrainees being particularly prominent; the importance of this statute was that it gave statutory recognition to this monopoly, and, by so doing, theoretically excluded from parliament the lower ranks of the magnate affinities, men who owed their importance to a magnate connection alone as distinct from those who, by virtue of their position in landed society, attracted the patronage of a local lord.

The property qualification for shire representatives, fixed by this statute at the level of distraint, namely £40 per annum, theoretically

---

[12] N. E. Saul, *Knights and Esquires: The Gloucestershire Gentry in the Fourteenth Century* (Oxford, 1981), 120–1, 126. A conclusion supported by N. B. Lewis: 'Re-election to Parliament in the Reign of Richard II', *EHR* 48 (1933), 376.

[13] For Oxenford's remarkable career: J. R. Maddicott, 'The Birth and Setting of the Ballads of Robin Hood', *EHR* 93 (1978), 286–92.

[14] *RP*, v. 116; *SR*, ii. 342.

made them the greatest of local officers, requiring an income twice as great as that needed to qualify for the offices of sheriff, justice of the peace, or escheator.[15] In reality, however, it was the same men who served the county in parliament who acted as sheriffs and justices, the office of escheator being generally filled by men of lesser status. Only eight of the twenty-seven Nottinghamshire men who held the shrievalty during the Lancastrian period never represented the county in parliament and the same number were never appointed to the commission of the peace.[16] It was rare for the head of one of the thirteen leading families not to hold more than one of these offices: of the thirty men who headed these families between 1399 and 1461, as many as fourteen held all three during their careers; a further six held two of the three; and only eight held just one[17] (the two men who never held major office were Henry Pierpoint (d. 1457), who headed his family for only five years, and the obscure Sir Edmund Willoughby (d. 1414)). Those immediately below them in status, the twenty-six families of the lesser knightage and greater squirearchy, although qualified by income to hold major office, were much less prominent. Twelve of the thirteen leading families provided a justice of the peace during the Lancastrian period, ten a sheriff and ten a knight of the shire. Compare this with the twenty-six families below them: nine provided a justice of the peace, eight a sheriff, and 11 a knight of the shire, while only four heads of these families took all three offices (Sir Thomas Hercy, Sir William Mering, Ralph Makerell,[18] and John Wastnes). These statistics leave no room for doubt that it was a small group of families, distinguished from their fellow

---

[15] Above, p. 110.

[16] For the personnel of the commission of the peace: Payling, pp. 299–303.

[17] This figure includes Sir Robert Strelley, head of the Strelleys of Strelley from 1430 until his death in 1438, who never held office in Notts. but served as sheriff of Staffs. in 1434–5.

[18] Ralph Makerell of Hodsock (d. 1436): MP Notts. Nov. 1414, Dec. 1420, and Oct. 1427; sheriff Notts./Derbys. 1411–12, 1419–20, and May 1422 to Feb. 1423; JP Notts. Feb. 1422 to July 1423; escheator Notts./Derbys. 1416–17 and Jan. to Dec. 1426. I have assumed that all these offices were held by the same man, but this assumption may not be correct. There were two contemporary Ralph Makerells: Ralph the father, a member of the lesser Derbys. gentry, and Ralph the son, very wealthy as the result of his marriage to one of the Cressy coheiresses. It would be reasonable to suggest that it was the younger and wealthier Ralph who held all these offices and yet, in Nov. 1420, Ralph junior is said to have been returned to parliament by the sheriff, Ralph Makerell. There are two possibilities: either Ralph the father was sheriff in 1419–20, or the addition of junior was made by Ralph the son, as sheriff, to disguise the fact that he had illegally returned himself to parliament. In this context it may be significant that Ralph the son was involved in electoral malpractice in 1427: J. S. Roskell, *The Commons in the Parliament of 1422* (Manchester, 1954), 15–16.

gentry by their wealth and often also by their antiquity, who dominated the major offices of shire administration.

Not only was there a hierarchy of local office, with the dominance of the leading families the more pronounced the greater the office, but there was also something of *cursus honorem* in local government. At the beginning of this *cursus* was the office of parliamentary knight of the shire.[19] As many as twenty-seven of the thirty-eight men elected to represent Nottinghamshire during the Lancastrian period had no previous administrative experience in that county or any other when first elected. The apparent effect of a first election, however, was to bring the elected to the notice of the crown as a potential office-holder. While twenty-seven were without administrative experience when first returned, only eight were to end their careers without having served as sheriff, justice of the peace, or escheator.[20] Clearly recognition locally by electors frequently preceded, and by implication led to, direct government appointment to one or more of these offices. Sometimes this connection was very direct. Dr Saul noted no fewer than eleven Gloucestershire instances, mostly from the second half of the fourteenth century, in which a man was appointed to the shrievalty were soon after sitting in parliament, and suggested that parliamentary sessions provided the council and exchequer with an opportunity to become familiar with potential candidates for local office.[21] There can be little doubt that this was so. Indeed, it was not uncommon for a man to become sheriff while actually sitting in parliament. Between 1399 and 1461 a serving knight of the shire was pricked as sheriff on four of the fourteen occasions on which the appointment was made to the joint shrievalty of Nottingham-shire and Derbyshire when parliament was in session or prorogation: Sir Richard Stanhope during the parliament of October 1404; Sir Thomas Chaworth during that of 1423–4; Norman Babington during that of 1433; and Sir John Gresley during that of 1453–4. To these must be added those other occasions on which a sheriff was appointed soon after the dissolution of a parliament in which he had served: the most striking example being that of Sir John Clifton, who became sheriff four days after the dissolution of the parliament of 1402.[22] A similar pattern is

[19] R. Virgoe, 'The Parliament of 1449–50', Ph.D. thesis (London, 1964), 124.
[20] For those who served in the joint escheatorship of Notts. and Derbys.: *CFR, 1399–1461, passim; List of Escheators for England and Wales*, List and Index Society, 72 (1971), 110–12.   [21] Saul, *Gloucestershire*, 127–8.
[22] John Wastnes, MP for Notts. July 1455 to Mar. 1456, became sheriff in Nov. 1456; Nicholas Fitzherbert, MP for Derbys. Feb. to Mar. 1447, became sheriff in Nov. 1447; John Stanhope, MP for Notts. Mar. 1453 to Apr. 1454, became sheriff in Nov. 1454.

reflected in the returns for other counties. During the Coventry parliament of October 1404, thirteen sheriffs were appointed, five of whom, including Stanhope, were sitting shire knights, and, while this was a higher percentage than was normal, it was not uncommon for between a sixth and a quarter of the sheriffs to be appointed from the sitting shire knights if parliament happened to be in session or prorogation.[23]

It is less easy to see any direct correlation between parliamentary service and appointment to the bench, but there are a few examples of a shire knight either being first appointed or reappointed to the bench while serving in parliament: Sir Richard Stanhope first appeared on the bench on 12 November 1404, the day on which the parliament in which he was serving made a grant of taxation; his grandson, John Stanhope, was first appointed to the bench on 20 April 1454 at the end of his lengthy service in the Reading parliament of 1453–4; and, in December 1460, during the prorogation of the Yorkist parliament in which he was sitting, Sir Robert Strelley was reappointed to the bench after an absence of two years. Whether these men, appointed to the shrievalty or to the bench, actually sought their appointment, or whether it was simply their presence in parliament that prompted the government to appoint them is impossible to say with certainty but such evidence as there is would suggest the former. Knights of the shire sometimes took advantage of their return to parliament to secure grants of royal patronage,[24] and it is probable that a similar system applied to the appointment of local offices.

It is clear from the foregoing discussion that those appointed to the shrievalty or county bench were, in general, men of greater experience than those having their first experience of parliamentary service. Of the nineteen men who served the county both on the bench and in parliament, twelve had represented the county in parliament before their first appointment to the bench. Similarly, of the nineteen Nottinghamshire men who were both sheriff and knight of the shire for the county, twelve saw parliamentary service before becoming sheriff. But if

[23] During the Lancastrian period there were 13 parliaments, excluding the Coventry parliament of Oct. 1404, in session or prorogation at the time of the annual election of sheriffs. The highest proportion of county sheriffs chosen from sitting members was 7 out of 24 in the parliament of Oct. 1427; the lowest, 2 out of 24 in the parliament of Oct. 1435. Over the period as a whole, including the parliament of Oct. 1404, 54 out of 278 shrieval appointments involved sitting members (i.e. 4.66 per 24). These figures are abstracted from: *CFR, 1399–1461, passim*; *Return of the Name*, pt. i, 257–356.

[24] e.g. John Gaitford, Sir Thomas Chaworth, and Sir William Mering: below, pp. 123, 128, 148 n. 155.

election to parliament generally came before an appointment to the
other two offices, it is not possible to say whether the shrievalty or the
commission of the peace came first in a typical office-holder's career.
Nineteen of the twenty-seven Nottinghamshire men who served as
sheriff were also appointed to the bench: nine had been sheriff before
their first appearance on the commission of the peace, and nine had
become a justice of the peace before first becoming sheriff (it is not clear
into which category Sir John Zouche comes for it is not known when he
was commissioned as a justice).[25] What is noteworthy, however, is that,
whichever came first, the two very often came close together. There are
several examples: Sir Richard Stanhope was first appointed sheriff on
22 October 1404 and, despite the fact that as a serving sheriff he was
disqualified,[26] he first became a justice of the peace in the following
November; Sir William Mering became a justice of the peace in July
1432 and was appointed sheriff in the following November (an appointment that occasioned his removal from the bench); Robert Strelley was
appointed to the bench in February 1444 and became sheriff for the first
time in November 1445 (no new commission of the peace was enrolled
during his shrievalty); Richard Willoughby became a justice of the peace
in July 1448 and sheriff in December 1449 (as with Strelley no new
peace commission was enrolled); Robert Clifton ended his first term as
sheriff on 8 November 1451 to find his first employment on the county
bench three days later; and John Stanhope was first appointed a justice
in April 1454, seven months before becoming sheriff for the first time
(he appears on the peace commission of 4 December 1455 despite the
fact that he was still sheriff). For all seven of these men, these
appointments marked the beginnings of extremely active careers in
county administration. They had much else in common: each was at the
head of a substantial county family (or else the heir with a very
immediate prospect of inheriting); four of them had previously served
the county in parliament, and the other three were later to do so; and,
with the possible exception of Sir Richard Stanhope, each was at least
30 years of age. Such was the typical biography of a holder of major
office in Lancastrian Nottinghamshire.

---

[25] He was paid for sitting as a JP on 6 days between 30 Sept. 1427 and 5 Oct. 1431 and
yet he does not appear on any of the enrolled commissions: E372/275, rot. 36ᵈ; 277, rot.
29.
[26] For sheriffs and their position with regard to their service on the bench: *Proceedings
Before the Justices of the Peace in the Fourteenth and Fifteenth Centuries*, ed. B. H. Putnam,
Ames Foundation (London, 1938), pp. lxxx–lxxxi.

It remains to ask whether this general picture of office-holding varied over time. For example, were those appointed to office in the reign of Henry IV different in type from those who served during the majority of his grandson? Since men were most frequently introduced into local government through an election to parliament, it is parliamentary representation that most closely measures changes in the pattern of office-holding, and one would expect any such changes to be reflected in the relative administrative experience of those returned. Although twenty-seven of the thirty-eight men returned for the county had had no previous experience when first elected, this is not to say that experienced men were not frequently returned. Since many knights of the shire represented the county on several occasions, it is clear that, even if they had not held major county office (that is, sheriff, justice of the peace, or escheator) when first returned, on subsequent elections they would probably have done so. Of the 78 known parliamentary seats for which the name of the knight of the shire is known, only 38 saw a man returned who had not held any of these offices in Nottinghamshire or elsewhere. In the early part of the Lancastrian period it was common for such men to be elected together. Before and including the parliament of October 1419 this happened on nine occasions but thereafter only twice. Consequently, as many as 22 of the 28 parliamentary seats of October 1419 and before were filled by men with no local government experience, and only 16 of the 50 thereafter. It is also interesting to note that, of the eight men who represented the county in parliament but never held any other office there or elsewhere, seven were returned in or before October 1419. It would be unwise to draw any conclusions from these rather striking statistics without examining the social status, careers, and connections of the individuals returned but, taken together with statistics relating to re-election and the election of parliamentary novices, some preliminary observations regarding the changing pattern of office-holding over time may be made from them. Table 5.1 shows the percentage of seats in each Lancastrian reign taken by parliamentary novices (that is, those who had never served in parliament before), by local government novices (that is, those who had never held a major county office), by novices to both parliament and local government, and by men who were returned to parliament only once.

The figures given in Table 5.1 are as complete as they can be in view of the fact that the names of those returned to the parliaments of January 1410, February 1413, November 1415, and October 1416 are unknown, but it is probable that any inaccuracies occasioned by these *lacunae*

TABLE 5.1. *Office-holding* (%)

Temp.	Parliamentary novices	Local government novices	Novices of both	Men returned only once
Henry IV	75	75	63	62
Henry V	39	61	33	25
Henry VI (minority)	25	25	10	33
Henry VI (majority)	46	42	25	47
OVERALL	45	49	38	58

cancel themselves out. The only figure to be seriously distorted by the failure of evidence is that for the percentage of men, returned during the majority of Henry VI, who served only once in parliament during their careers; this is certainly too high for it is probable that some of them were returned to the parliaments of November 1461, April 1463, and November 1470, for which returns do not survive.

The most impressive fact about the Table is the high percentage recorded in all four categories for the reign of Henry IV. An examination of the personnel of local administration during the 1380s and 1390s shows why this was so, for the first three categories at least. The Lancastrian revolution of 1399 brought about a considerable change in the personnel of the office-holders in the county, and this was reflected in the parliamentary returns. Thereafter, parliamentary representation and, to a rather lesser extent, local office-holding in general became concentrated in the hands of those men who had begun their careers in the first decade of the century, most notably Sir Richard Stanhope (d. 1436), Sir Thomas Chaworth (d. 1459), and Sir John Zouche (d. 1445), who together represented the county on as many as 21 occasions between September 1402 and February 1445 (36.2 per cent of the seats during this period). Increased continuity in county representation was the result, with fewer novices being returned and a greater overlap between the major local offices and that of knight of the shire. A peak of stability was reached during the minority of Henry VI when only 10 per cent of those returned were novices to both parliament and major local office. In the 1440s and 1450s, however, a new generation of office-holders arose to replace the old, the members of which had either died or were too old to make the journey to parliament. These decades saw the beginnings of the lengthy and active careers of John Stanhope (d. 1493), Robert Clifton (d. 1478), and Robert Strelley (d. 1488). Not a single man elected to represent the county in February 1445 and before ever served in parliament again. Nevertheless, demographic factors alone cannot entirely explain changing patterns in local office-holding. It is quite clear that the high percentage of men elected during the reign of Henry IV who served only once was due partly to the electoral influence of Sir Thomas Rempston, and the similarly higher percentage recorded during the majority of Henry VI, in part to be accounted for by the failure of returns in the following reign, was also in part due to the electoral influence of Ralph, Lord Cromwell, and the crown. The rest of this chapter is concerned to document the changing influences at work on appointments and elections to office during the Lancastrian period, and, in particular, the relationship between these officers and the crown.

Henry IV

A brief glance at the major office-holders (that is sheriffs and justices of the peace) and parliamentary representatives of Nottinghamshire during the reigns of Richard II and Henry IV confirms that the Lancastrian revolution of 1399 brought about a considerable change in personnel. Of the twenty-nine men who held major office or represented the shire in parliament between 1399 and 1413, only seven had done so before 1399.[27] Such a transformation is at first sight surprising, for not only was Nottinghamshire a county in which Lancastrian influence was strong before 1399, with several members of John of Gaunt's affinity holding office there, but, in the country as a whole, there was a significant degree of continuity between the retinues of both kings since Henry IV retained many leading county office-holders formerly retained by Richard II.[28] There is certainly no evidence that a body of men who had been prominent in local affairs under Richard II was systematically excluded under his successor. In Derbyshire, for example, a county in

[27] I have excluded from this analysis the barons and non-county lawyers who were appointed to the bench.
[28] C. Given-Wilson, *The Royal Household and the King's Affinity* (New Haven and London, 1986), 232–3.

which Gaunt's influence had admittedly been very strong, as many as fifteen of the twenty-eight men who held office under Henry IV had done so before 1399. Why then did the Lancastrian revolution bring about such a major change in Nottinghamshire? The answer lies partly in accidental factors, for many of those who had held office in the last decade or Richard II's reign were either dead or elderly by 1399, and partly in a considerable expansion of Lancastrian influence in the county, which brought to the fore new and younger men. Under Richard II several Lancastrian retainers had held major office in the shire: under Henry IV a Lancastrian connection became almost a *sine qua non* for those who aspired to such office. Nevertheless, it would be mistaken to see in this the rise of a narrow clique of Lancastrian retainers excluding a former body of office-holders. Under both Richard II and Henry IV the pattern of office-holding very largely reflected the social structure of the county; the great majority of the important offices falling to leading county families. The much closer relationship that existed between the county officers and the crown under Henry IV is to be explained by the expansion of the pre-1399 Lancastrian affinity into a much larger (and very expensive) royal affinity. A similar process occurred in Derbyshire but there its impact on the personnel of office was less, partly because the existing Lancastrian affinity left less room for expansion and partly because of a higher survival rate amongst those who had held office under Richard II.

While in Nottinghamshire the duchy of Lancaster did not hold extensive estates in demesne as it did in Derbyshire (its demesne holdings being confined to a few manors in the north-east of the county, principally Wheatley and Gringley),[29] the duke, principally through his honor of Tickhill, was a very considerable overlord, particularly in the northern part of the county.[30] Few of the leading county families were unconnected to him by tenure. The Chaworths, Markhams, Hercys, Cressys (and later the Cliftons), Stanhopes, Husys, and Willoughbys, were tenants of the honor of Tickhill to a greater or lesser degree, while the Chaworths, Burdons (and later the Markhams), Cliftons, Rempstons, and St Andrews held manors of the honors of either Tutbury or Leicester.[31] It is this Lancastrian interest in the county which explains why Gaunt and Bolingbroke drew several of their retinue from the

[29] For the duchy's demesne lands in Nottinghamshire: SC6/545/8669.
[30] All information regarding tenure is taken from the Nottinghamshire inquisitions *post mortem* published by the Thoroton Society.
[31] For details: Payling, pp. 151–2.

county and consequently why Lancastrian retainers were so conspicuous amongst local office-holders during Richard II's reign. The most notable of these was Sir Thomas Rempston. He had been in the service of Bolingbroke since at least February 1389,[32] and had accompanied him on his Prussian expedition of July 1390 to April 1391 in the honourable position of standard-bearer.[33] His prominence in local administration during the 1390s was a product of this personal connection rather than of his wealth. Indeed, so close were his ties with the heir of Lancaster that he was one of that select band who followed Bolingbroke into exile in October 1398 and accompanied him on his victorious return in the following June.[34] This loyal service brought its just reward. On 31 August 1399 he was appointed constable of the Tower of London for life, an office that carried with it the handsome fee of £100 per annum;[35] on the following 15 October he became steward of the royal household,[36] and a month later, on 10 November, he was granted the keeping of the extensive midland estates formerly held by Thomas Mowbray (d. 1399), duke of Norfolk.[37] In addition, by October 1401, he enjoyed annuities of 40 marks from the duchy fee farm of Gunthorpe and Lowdham and £20 from the lordship of Higham Ferrers.[38] His local influence was further augmented by the addition of the reversion of the valuable south Nottinghamshire manor of Bingham to his own meagre estates, and the grant of the offices of constable of Nottingham Castle and steward of Sherwood Forest, offices that carried with them the

---

[32] *CPR, 1388–92*, 7.

[33] *Expeditions to Prussia and the Holy Land Made by Henry, Earl of Derby*, ed. L. Toulmin Smith, Camden Society, NS 52 (1894), 106, 131. Early in this expedition both he and his fellow Notts. knight, Sir John Clifton of Clifton, were captured and imprisoned by Vladislaw II, king of Poland. They were not released until Mar. 1391 when Gaunt wrote to the Polish king requesting their immediate release: *The Diplomatic Correspondence of Richard II*, ed. E. Perroy, Camden Society, 3rd Series, 48 (1933), 218.

[34] *Historia Vitae et Regni Ricardi Secundi*, ed. G. B. Stow (Pennsylvania, 1977), 153: *RP*, iii. 553.

[35] *CPR, 1396–9*, 593; *1399–1401*, 264; *1405–8*, 281; DL42/15, pt. 1, fo. 97.

[36] He held this office until 20 Feb. 1401, when he was replaced by Thomas Percy, earl of Worcester, as part of the baronial and commons' reaction to Henry IV's reliance on lesser men: A. Rogers, 'The Royal Household of Henry IV', Ph.D. thesis (Nottingham, 1966), 678; id., 'The Political Crisis of 1401', *NMS* 12 (1968), 85–96.

[37] *CFR, 1399–1405*, 24, 32; *CPR, 1401–5*, 107. He was also steward of the honor of Leicester from Michaelmas 1399 at a fee of £20 p.a. On 13 July 1401 he was reappointed to this office with the additional office of steward of Castle Donington: Somerville, p. 563; DL42/15, pt. 1, fo. 35.

[38] Ibid., pt. 1, fo. 97; DL28/27/5 (an account of annuities charged on the duchy *temp.* Henry IV which dates from before Oct. 1401).

additional fee of 40 marks.[39] Even though he did not benefit from Henry IV's patronage to the same extent as his fellow household servants, Sir John Pelham and John Norbury,[40] the Lancastrian revolution made him a wealthy man.

Until his death in October 1406, Sir Thomas was one of the new king's most intimate associates, frequently serving on diplomatic missions, and accompanying Henry's chosen queen, Joan of Navarre, from Brittany early in 1403.[41] It was through him that the crown made appointments to local office, influenced county elections, and dispensed patronage in Nottinghamshire. During the early years of the reign most of those who held major office there were his connections. His wife's numerous Leek kinsmen were the chief beneficiaries. His wife, Margaret, was a sister of Sir John Leek of Cotham,[42] and the relationship between him and his wife's family was a close one. When in November 1399 he was granted the keeping of the Mowbray's midland lands, Sir John Leek acted as one of his sureties; in 1401 Sir John's nephew, William, acted with him in the purchase of an estate near Nottingham; in the same year both Sir John and William served on a commission to investigate his complaints about the infringement of his milling rights as constable of Nottingham Castle; Sir John was the senior feoffee for the implementation of his will of 13 May 1403; and, in November 1405, Sir John, William, and Sir John's eldest son, Simon, acted with him in the purchase of the Lincolnshire manor of Brant Broughton.[43] There can be little doubt that it was this connection that explained Sir John Leek's appointment to the shrievalty of Nottinghamshire and Derbyshire on 27 August 1399, the election of William Leek to the parliament of the following October,

[39] *CPR, 1399–1401*, 353. He was appointed to these offices on 4 Aug. 1400 but had effectively held them from July 1399: E101/42/27 (where he authorized the expenditure of John Kniveton, lieutenant of the constable of Nottingham Castle, from 20 July 1399).

[40] For Pelham: Saul, *Scenes from Provincial Life* (Oxford, 1986), 70–2. For Norbury: M. Barber, 'John Norbury (*c.*1350–1414): An Esquire of Henry IV', *EHR* 68 (1953), 66–76.

[41] On 25 Oct. 1402 he left London for Brittany with a retinue of 3 knights, 28 esquires, and 60 archers, for whom he claimed wages until the following 4 Feb.: E364/41, mem. 2ᵈ. For accounts of his diplomatic activity and career: *Dictionary of National Biography*, xvi. 895; Rogers, 'The Royal Household', 774–5; N. H. Nicolas, *The Scrope and Grosvenor Controversy* (London, 1832), ii. 199–200.

[42] She was the widow of Sir Godfrey Foljambe of Hassop, the grandson of another Sir Godfrey Foljambe (d. 1376), Gaunt's chief steward. He died in Sept. 1388 soon after coming of age. The custody and marriage of his year-old daughter and heiress by Margaret was granted to Sir John Leek: *CIPM*, xvi, nos. 685–9; *CPR, 1388–92*, 192; *CFR, 1383–91*, 324. Godfrey himself had been a ward of the Leeks: ibid., *1377–83*, 317, 356.

[43] *CFR, 1399–1405*, 26; CP25(1)/186/37/4; *CPR, 1399–1401*, 459; Borthwick Institute, Arch. Reg. 5A, fos. 334–5; *CCR, 1405–9*, 72–3.

John Leek to that of January 1404, Simon Leek to that of October 1404 and the appointment of William Leek as escheator of the two counties on 12 November 1403.[44] Their administrative efforts did not go unrewarded for Rempston successfully channelled royal patronage in their direction. On 20 November 1399, the day after the dissolution of the first parliament of the reign, at which he represented the county, William Leek, as a king's esquire, was awarded an annuity of 10 marks,[45] while a month earlier, on 22 October, his brother, Ralph, one of the county coroners, had been granted the keeping of the royal manors of Mansfield and Linby.[46] In the following year, on 8 July, John Leek, again as a king's esquire, was granted an annuity of 10 marks,[47] and at the end of his 1399–1400 shrievalty, the head of the family, Sir John, had a generous pardon of account of 110 marks.[48] But it was not only the Leeks who benefited from their connection with Rempston's ascendant star. John Gaitford, already an experienced lawyer and local administrator, was Rempston's lieutenant in the office of steward of Sherwood Forest, and was returned with William Leek to the first parliament of the reign. It was an opportunity that he put to good use: during the parliamentary session he gained his reappointment to the remunerative office of county alnager and confirmation of the £20 annuity he had enjoyed since 1392.[49] Shortly after the dissolution he was appointed escheator of Nottinghamshire and Derbyshire for the second time in his career.[50] Also prominent in local administration during the first years of the new reign was Rempston's brother, William, who succeeded Gaitford as escheator (although only for the county of Nottinghamshire) and, like Gaitford, was appointed to the first county bench of the new reign. Up to

---

[44] It probably also explains the election of William's brother, Ralph Leek, as one of the county coroners. On 31 May 1404, Ralph, as coroner of Notts. (the first reference to him in the office), with the Essex knight, Sir William Coggeshall, and others, heard the confession of one John Stanton, who had been involved in the futile rising of Maud de Vere, dowager countess of Oxford: *Select Cases in the King's Bench under Richard II, Henry IV and Henry V*, ed. G. O. Sayles, Selden Society, 88 (1971), 153–4. He was clearly here acting as the agent of Rempston from whose custody Stanton had recently been delivered: *CPR, 1401–5*, 432.

[45] *CPR, 1399–1401*, 118; regranted under the duchy seal: DL42/15, pt. 1, fo. 22ᵛ.

[46] *CFR, 1399–1405*, 8. This grant was not effective for long as the manors were soon afterwards granted to Eleanor (d. 1432), wife of Sir Nicholas Dagworth (d. 1402) of Blickling (Norfolk), a former chamber knight of Richard II, to hold from 1 Oct. 1399: *CPR, 1399–1401*, 116, 393, 479, 537; Blomefield, *An Essay Towards a Topographical History of the County of Norfolk* (London, 1805–10), vi. 384–5.

[47] *CPR, 1399–1401*, 321.

[48] E199/68/32; *CPR, 1399–1401*, 378.

[49] *CFR, 1399–1405*, 38, 45; *CPR, 1399–1401*, 120.

[50] *CFR, 1399–1405*, 3. For his career: Payling, p. 291.

his death in 1404 he was the most active of the county's justices: as a lawyer of the *quorum*, he served on nineteen of the twenty-three days the bench met between January 1400 and September 1402.[51]

Between August 1399 and Sir Thomas Rempston's death in October 1406, five of the nine men elected to represent the county in parliament were closely connected to him (including John Kniveton of Scarrington, a Nottinghamshire MP in 1401, who was his lieutenant when he was constable of Nottingham Castle in 1399).[52] So were all three of the Nottinghamshire men appointed to escheatorship, the first of the sheriffs and several active members of the county bench (including William Jorce of Burton Joyce, who mainperned for him in November and December 1399).[53] Never again during the Lancastrian period were the connections of one man to have such a dominance over the administration of the shire.

Nevertheless, despite the prominence of Rempston's affinity, the new king did not neglect to broaden the basis of his support in the county. In view of the open-handed generosity that he displayed in the first years of his reign, it was inevitable that this should be so, especially given the traditional association between the county's gentry and the duchy of Lancaster. Three leading Nottinghamshire men, all duchy tenants, Sir Thomas Hercy of Grove, Sir Hugh Husy of Flintham, and Richard Stanhope of Rampton had, according to the duchy register, been amongst those who came to Bolingbroke, '*en nostre compaignye apres nostre darrain arrivaille en Engleterre et a nostre parlement a Londres*'.[54] These men had the right to expect some recognition for their services. Husy, who had been retained for life by Gaunt at a fee of £20 per annum in March 1395,[55] was confirmed in this annuity,[56] received £12 for the wages of himself and the men he had brought to Henry in 1399,

---

[51] E372/248, Item Not[d].

[52] For Kniveton's career: Payling, p. 292.

[53] *CFR, 1399–1405*, 24, 32. William Jorce of Burton Joyce was one of the 7 men-at-arms who garrisoned Nottingham Castle under John Kniveton between 20 July and 9 Nov. 1399: E101/42/27. On 23 Feb. he was granted for life as a king's esquire 12*d*. p.d. at the exchequer: *CPR, 1399–1401*, 207. He made his will on 9 July 1403, '*proponens in partes extraneas transmigrare*' (perhaps in Rempston's company) ordering that his debts to Rempston be repaid. It was proved on the following 11 Oct.: Borthwick Institute, Prob. Reg. 3, fo. 98.

[54] DL42/15, pt. 1, fo. 70[v].

[55] 'Indentures of Retinue with John of Gaunt, Duke of Lancaster, Enrolled in Chancery, 1367–1399', ed. N. B. Lewis, in *Camden Miscellany* 22, Camden Society, 4th series, vol. i (1964), 105. This annuity was confirmed by Richard II on 26 Apr. 1399: *CPR, 1396–9*, 548.

[56] He had confirmation on 19 Sept. 1401: DL42/15, pt. 1, fo. 91[v].

was summoned to the great council of 1403[57] and later married as his second wife, Joan, the widow of Henry's councillor and steward of Tutbury, John Curson of Kedleston (Derbyshire).[58] Hercy was similarly rewarded with an annuity of 20 marks charged on the honor of Pontefract[59] and a payment of £40 in wages of war. Neither of these men, however, played a very prominent role in local administration during the reign: Husy's service in the parliament of October 1407 and Hercy's on the county bench from 1404 to 1407 were the extent of their contribution.

The same could not be said of Richard Stanhope. At the time of the Lancastrian revolution of 1399 he was in his early twenties and had but recently inherited a substantial estate in the north of the county; his early support for Bolingbroke was an act of political opportunism that paid dividends. His connection with Lancaster may date to before 1399 for he was already married to the sister of the Lancastrian knight, Sir Ralph Staveley, who had been steward of Bolingbroke's household as earl of Derby,[60] and this family connection may explain why he came to Bolingbroke soon after his landing. His reward was immediate. He was one of the forty-six esquires elevated to the Order of the Bath on the eve of the new king's coronation[61] and, on the following 18 March, as a king's knight, he was granted a royal annuity of 40 marks.[62] A further grant of royal favour followed on 11 May 1402, when he was awarded the wardship and marriage of John, son and heir of Sir Thomas Boyvile of Stockerston (Leicestershire) and Little Packington (Warwickshire).[63] In the following year he fought for Henry IV alongside many other midland knights at the battle of Shrewsbury and, on 17 August 1405, he was granted, 'in recompense for the great loss' he sustained there, the wardship and marriage of the eleven-year-old son and heir of Sir Nicholas Goushill of Barlborough (Derbyshire) who had met his death

---

[57] *PPC*, ii. 88.

[58] This marriage had taken place by 11 Aug. 1411: *Descriptive Catalogue of Derbyshire Charters*, no. 1505. His first wife had died in 1409: *TE*, i. 352.

[59] DL28/27/6 (annuities chargeable on north parts of the duchy c.1415).

[60] For Staveley: Roskell, *The Knights of the Shire for the County Palatine of Lancaster, 1377–1460*, Chetham Society, NS 96 (1937), 107–11. The marriage probably took place before 1399 for it had produced a daughter of marriageable age by Feb. 1403: *Calendar of Papal Letters*, v. 529.

[61] *Chronicles of London*, ed. C. L. Kingsford (Oxford, 1905), 48.

[62] *CPR, 1399–1401*, 240. His brother, Stephen, also entered the royal service: ibid. 52.

[63] Ibid., *1401–5*, 92. This grant, as far as it related to the keeping of the lands, was revoked in Mar. 1405 because of the seisin of Boyvile's feoffees: ibid. 499–500; C44/22/13.

in the battle.[64] While sheriff in 1404–5 he saw further military action against the Scrope rebels in the north and against Glyndwr in Wales, for which he was rewarded a payment of £40.[65] But it was not only on the battlefield that he earned these considerable marks of royal favour. He was very active in local government; in addition to serving as sheriff in 1404–5, he was a county justice from 1404 to 1407 and represented the county in four successive parliaments between September 1402 and March 1406. His early career is a useful illustration not only of the military use to which Henry put his considerable affinity but also of the prominence that an ambitious member of this retinue might enjoy in county politics. In the second half of the reign, however, Stanhope began to take advantage of his privileged position. His persistent involvement in local disorder, for which he was finally brought to book in the next reign, made him less useful to the crown, and he held no county office between his removal from the bench in February 1407 and his restoration a decade later.[66]

But if Stanhope was, in the first part of the reign, the most active and, with the exception of Rempston, the best rewarded of the royal retinue in the county, he was only one of the four county knights who were honoured with the title of 'king's knight' during the reign. Sir John Clifton of Clifton had attended Bolingbroke at the St Inglevert jousts in the spring of 1390[67] and on the Prussian expedition later in the same year.[68] This service was recognized after the usurpation with the grant, on 5 February 1400, of an annuity of 40 marks for life or until the king 'shall otherwise provide for his estate'.[69] There followed his summons to the great council of 1401,[70] his election with Stanhope to represent the

---

[64] *CPR, 1405–8*, 53. This grant was a very valuable one. The Goushill lands, the manor of Barlborough, and a moiety of the neighbouring mill of Killamarsh in the north-east corner of Derbys. (near Stanhope's brother-in-law's manor of Staveley), were extended at as much as 30 marks p.a. in Sir Nicholas Goushill's inquisition *post mortem* of Oct. 1405: C137/52/7.

[65] *CPR, 1405–8*, 84, 102; J. H. Wylie, *History of England under Henry the Fourth* (London, 1884–98), ii. 228.

[66] Below, pp. 189, 191–3, 194–5.

[67] He may be the '*jœune et frisque*' Sir John Clifton referred to by Froissart as distinguishing himself in the lists: J. Froissart, *Œuvres*, ed. Kervyn de Lettenhove, 25 vols. in 26 (Brussels, 1867–77), xiv. 134. For the earlier connections of the Clifton family with the house of Lancaster: *John of Gaunt's Register, 1371–5*, ed. S. Armitage Smith, Camden Society, 3rd Series, 20–21 (1911), i, no. 405; ii, nos. 863, 1719. Sir John was also connected with Thomas (d. 1397), duke of Gloucester, with whom he contracted to serve in Ireland in May 1392 and from whom he was in receipt of an annuity of £20 p.a.: E101/74/1/43; *Cal. Inq. Misc., 1392–9*, no. 359.

[68] *Expeditions to Prussia*, 131. For his capture by the Polish king: above, p. 121 n. 33.

[69] *CPR, 1399–1401*, 226, 438–9; C81/606/2386.   [70] *PPC*, i. 162.

county in the parliament of September 1402, and, very shortly afterwards, his appointment as sheriff. It was during his shrievalty that a
promising career was cut short: he met his death at the battle of
Shrewsbury at the head of the *posse comitatus*. The king had little reason
to begrudge his investment in Clifton's loyalty. It is less easy to see why
the new king should have granted an annuity to Clifton's south Nottinghamshire neighbour, Sir John Burton of Burton Joyce. Unlike Clifton,
Stanhope and the other king's knight, Sir John Annesley (d. *c.*1410) of
Annesley, he was not from one of the leading county families (although
his father had represented the county four times in parliament), neither
can he be found in the service of Lancaster before the usurpation.
Nevertheless, on 7 November 1400, he was granted £20 per annum
from the issues of Nottinghamshire and Derbyshire. Shortly afterwards
he was elected to represent the county in the parliament of January 1401
and later, in 1407–8, he served a term as sheriff. Little else is known of
him, and his inclusion amongst the royal affinity must remain something
of a mystery, although it may have been due to a connection with
William, Lord Roos, and the Leek family.[71] The fourth and last of the
king's knights from the county, Sir John Annesley, received comfortably
the largest fee of the four; on 12 November 1399 he was granted 100
marks per annum at the exchequer as one of those whom the king had
retained for life, a grant which presumably superseded that of 26 May
1385, when he had been granted a royal annuity of £40.[72] He was an
elderly man who had represented the county in parliament on as many as
nine occasions between January 1377 and September 1388, and was
famous for his victory in a duel with Thomas de Caterton in 1380
over the betrayal of the important Norman fortress of Saint-Sauveur.
Although he followed Gaunt on the *chevauchée* of 1373, he had no
particular connection with Lancaster, and his annuity of 100 marks
must be seen as an honorary grant to an elderly and respected soldier
rather than one made in anticipation of energetic future services,
although he did serve on the Scottish expedition of 1400.[73]

In addition to these king's knights there were a number of king's
esquires paid lesser fees out of the exchequer or the issues of the
county.[74] Some of these esquires, John Gaitford, William Jorce, and

[71] In Nov. 1408 he acted with William, Lord Roos, as a mainpernor for Simon Leek;
CCR, 1405–8, 477.
[72] *CPR, 1399–1401*, 66; ibid., *1381–5*, 571.
[73] For his career: J. G. Bellamy, 'Sir John de Annesley and the Chandos Inheritance',
NMS 10 (1966), 94–105. His service on the 1400 Scottish expedition is his last recorded
activity: below, p. 135 n. 106.   [74] Appendix 6.

John Leek, took an active part in shire government; others, Hugh Annesley, Robert Brut, and Robert Nevill did not. In total these knights and esquires received fees up to as much as £251 11s. 8d. per annum but they do not comprise the full extent of the royal affinity in the county. Others were in receipt of annuities from duchy revenues. As mentioned earlier, Sir Hugh Husy and Sir Thomas Hercy were in receipt of fees of £20 from the honor of Leicester and 20 marks from the honor of Pontefract respectively. Two others who had come to Henry at his landing were also rewarded with annuities. William Wollaton of Watnall Chaworth had £20 from the issues of Belper in Derbyshire[75] and Bartholomew Montgomery of Gotham, probably a scion of that notable Lancastrian family, the Montgomerys of Cubley (Derbyshire), had a lesser annuity of £10 from the honor of Tutbury.[76] Another esquire who had assisted Henry at his landing, John Wastnes of Headon, one of those who had garrisoned Nottingham Castle on his behalf, had 20 marks from the honor of Leicester.[77] But the most important of the duchy annuities was the 40 marks from the Nottingham fee farm of Gunthorpe and Lowdham first granted to Sir Thomas Rempston during the time of Gaunt and confirmed by Henry IV. Only five days after his death in 1406 it was transferred to the wealthiest of the county's knights, Sir Thomas Chaworth of Wiverton, for good service and for life.[78] Although only in his late twenties, he already occupied the important position in local politics that he was to retain for half a century to come; he had been appointed to the county bench in May 1401, served as sheriff in 1403–4 and, with Stanhope, represented the county in the Long Parliament of March 1406 (a parliament that was still in session when, on 5 November, he was granted his duchy annuity). There can be little doubt that his Lancastrian connection preceded this

[75] DL42/15, pt. 1, fo. 20. Wollaton had long been in Bolingbroke's service. In a petition of c.1400, in which he unsuccessfully asked for a life grant of the manor of Ollerton in Sherwood forfeited by Thomas Holland (d. 1400), earl of Kent, he states that he had been in the king's service for 14 years and more without wages or fee: SC8/346 (E1413). He was with Bolingbroke at Calais in May 1390: *Expeditions to Prussia*, 5, 121. On 16 Nov. 1399, as a king's esquire, he was awarded 80 marks from the king's Notts. manors of Mansfield and Linby, 'in recompense for his wages and rewards for the time when he was in the king's company after the king's last advent into England': *CPR, 1399–1401*, 93.

[76] DL42/15, pt. 1, fos. 11ᵛ, 70ᵛ. He received £16 in wages of war for coming to Henry at his landing.

[77] Ibid., pt. 1, fos. 15ᵛ, 99ᵛ. For the seven esquires (John Kniveton, William Fitzherbert, John Wastnes, John Warwyk, William Jorce, Robert German, and Robert Paschall) who garrisoned Nottingham Castle from 20 July 1399 to 9 Nov. 1399: E101/42/27.

[78] DL42/16, pt. 3, fo. 71. On 3 Dec. 1406 he was granted 12 does and 4 bucks from duchy parks in Derbys. for his own park at Alfreton: ibid., fo. 83.

grant, for not only was he very active in local politics before 1406 but he had been summoned to the great council of 1403 with a group of Nottinghamshire and Derbyshire men intimately connected with the new regime and had seen military service in both Scotland and Wales during his shrievalty.[79] He was also a friend of the Leeks of Cotham. His wealth and apparent willingness to take up office (he was sheriff of Lincolnshire in 1408–9) made him the natural choice as the leader of the Nottinghamshire gentry after Rempston's death: the duchy annuity granted to him was a recognition of this reality.

During the first half of the reign those retained by Henry either through the duchy or the royal revenues and those attached to Rempston dominated the administration of the shire to the virtual exclusion of all others. Yet, since these groups included many of the socially significant men of the shire, their dominance cannot be seen as an infringement of county liberties. The pattern of office-holding in the second half of the reign, dating from Rempston's death on October 1406, was somewhat different for three related reasons: first, Rempston's death ensured that the numerous Leek family were no longer so prominent in county politics, although they retained a powerful patron in William, Lord Roos of Belvoir; second, the involvement of many leading county men in a series of disorders in the summer of 1411 resulted in a lack of suitable candidates for office during the last two years of the reign; and, third, partly as a consequence of this dearth, there occurred the rise to prominence of the 'foreigner', William Rigmayden, a younger son of a Lancashire family.

Rempston's death in an accident on the Thames on 31 October 1406[80] had an obvious impact on the personnel of office-holding. Apart from Sir John Leek's service on the bench, no other member of the Leek family held office between his eldest son Simon's election to the

---

[79] *PPC*, ii. 88. On 30 Jan. 1405 he was awarded 100 marks for his good service in Scotland and Wales: E404/20/134.

[80] For the London coroner's inquisition on his death: Nicolas, *Scrope and Grosvenor*, ii. 200 (in Nov. 1428 John Mowbray, duke of Norfolk, narrowly escaped death in a similar accident: *Chronicles of London*, 132–3). According to the *Great Chronicle* Rempston's death came about 'thrugh his own defaute and evil governaunce': *The Great Chronicle of London*, ed. A. H. Thomas and I. D. Thornley (London and Aylesbury, 1938), 86. His last will of 13 May 1403 suggests a ruthless character anxious to avoid a prolonged stay in purgatory; 500 marks was set aside to make financial restitution to those he had wronged, provision was made for the singing of 1,000 memorial masses after his death, and his executors were to take the advice of '*lez pluis seintz hommez*' as to the best use to which the residue of his goods could be put for the salvation of his soul: Borthwick Institute, Arch. Reg. 5A, fos. 334–5.

parliament of October 1404, and Simon's appointment as escheator in November 1413. The election to the Gloucestershire parliament of October 1407 broke the pattern of parliamentary representation that had prevailed since the beginning of the reign in that neither Stanhope nor any follower of Rempston's was returned. The senior of the two men elected, Sir John Zouche of Kirklington, was wealthy and, as the younger brother of William (d. 1415), fourth Lord Zouche of Harringworth, well-connected, but seems to have had no connection with Lancaster. He, like Stanhope and Chaworth, was a young man who was to have a prominent role to play in local politics over the following four decades. His fellow knight of the shire, the Lancastrian retainer Sir Hugh Husy, was taking major office for the first time, despite having been retained by Gaunt as early as 1395.

A more important consequence of Rempston's death, however, was the rise to prominence of William Rigmayden. He was a servant of Lancaster, apparently imported into the county to play a leading part in its administration. His first office was that of escheator, to which he was appointed on 9 November 1406, shortly after Rempston's death; he went on to serve as sheriff in 1408–9, 1412–13, and 1416–17, and as escheator again in 1414–15. He was also active on the county bench between February 1407 and July 1420. Only a professional administrator would have willingly taken on such a burden. His was the sort of career (that of a royal nominee with little land in the county taking shire administration out of the hands of the leading local landholders), that many commons' petitions of the second half of the fourteenth century had sought to outlaw by insisting that the major shire officers be substantial local *vavasours*. Nevertheless, there is no evidence that his role in county affairs was resented by the leading local gentry. On the contrary, they may have been glad of his particularly close royal connection for they elected him to parliament in October 1411 at a time when they were probably especially anxious to have someone to speak on their behalf. Nottinghamshire had been one of those counties singled out by the commons of January 1410 as being particularly lawless and for which they had requested the issue of a commission of *oyer* and *terminer*.[81] In August of the following year their fears about the county's lawless condition were fully justified: a major riot occurred in which a bloody conflict was only averted by the timely arrival of William, Lord Roos. Several leading county men were implicated in this affair: Sir

[81] *RP*, iii. 624.

Richard Stanhope, Sir John Leek, Sir John Zouche, the young Ralph Cromwell, and probably Sir Thomas Chaworth.[82] Their involvement presented the electors of October 1411 with a difficult problem. The choice of potential candidates was greatly reduced since it was unlikely that those involved in the riot, and previously so active in the parliamentary representation of the county, could have been persuaded to go to Westminster to face the king's wrath. Indeed, on 24 October, twelve days after the Nottinghamshire election had been held, the constable of the Tower of London was ordered to receive Stanhope, Leek, Chaworth, and Zouche into his custody. Even if they had been elected it is unlikely that they would have been able to take up their seats when parliament assembled on 3 November. In these circumstances, Rigmayden's return, with a servant of the prince of Wales, Thomas Staunton of Sutton Bonington,[83] is readily understandable.

The reappointment of Rigmayden to the shrievalty in November 1412, as soon as was legal under the statute of 1 Rich. II c. ii,[84] is probably also to be explained in terms of a lack of other suitable and willing candidates uninvolved in the disorders of the previous year, for it was not only Nottingham that was affected; similar disorders took place in Derbyshire, the county to which Nottinghamshire was twinned for shrieval purposes. Two of the leading royal retainers in that county, Sir Roger Leche of Chatsworth and Sir John Cokayn of Ashbourne, both of whom had previously been very active in local politics, were involved in riotous assemblies[85] for which they were arrested with the four Nottinghamshire knights. The riotous behaviour of so many wealthy local knights who were also Lancastrian retainers may explain why another Derbyshire family closely connected with Lancaster, the Montgomerys of Cubley, were so prominent in local affairs during the latter part of Henry IV's reign and in the early part of that of Henry V. Nicholas Montgomery the younger was appointed to succeed his father, Sir Nicholas Montgomery, an ex-constable of Tutbury, as sheriff in

[82] Below, pp. 191–2.
[83] On 7 Jan. 1408 the king granted him 12 oaks from the chase of Needwood: DL42/16, pt. 3, fo. 105. He was appointed master forester of Dartmoor (Devon), by the future Henry V when prince of Wales: *CPR, 1429–36*, 272. Early in Henry V's reign he was granted the wardship and marriages of Lumley (Northants.) and Willoughby of Risley (Derbys.): ibid. *1413–16*, 278, 388–9.
[84] *RP*, iii. 24; *SR*, ii. 4.
[85] Cokayn is said to have collected 200 men and more at Ashborne to resist the malice of Leche because he thought Leche was coming to kill him: KB9/204/2/41; below, p. 191 n. 23. Similar accusations were made against two other leading Lancastrians in the county, Sir John Dabrigecourt and Sir John Blount.

November 1410, and his father served again as sheriff in 1413–14, during the period in which the disorders of the previous reign were being investigated by the energetic new king. Indeed, it is a remarkable fact that of the nine shrieval terms between November 1408, when Rigmayden was first appointed to the office, and November 1417, when Chaworth was appointed to serve his second term in the office, Rigmayden and the Montgomerys served in as many of six of them.

While Rigmayden's career is more readily explained against this background of a lack of suitable local candidates for office, it remains a remarkable one without parallel in the history of Lancastrian Nottinghamshire. He was the younger son of the minor Lancashire landholder, Thomas Rigmayden (d. 1384) of Woodacre in Garstang, and the uncle of another Thomas Rigmayden (d. 1437), an annuitant of Henry IV.[86] William himself was in Bolingbroke's service as early as January 1390[87] and accompanied him on the Prussian expeditions of 1390–1 and July 1392.[88] On Bolingbroke's seizure of the throne, William gained substantially from duchy and royal patronage. On 24 September 1399 he was granted an annuity of 10 marks from the issues of the duchy and had confirmation of an earlier annuity of 10 marks granted to him by Gaunt.[89] By 7 April 1401 he had become constable of Lancaster Castle at a fee of 20 marks,[90] and on that day he had a further grant of the keeping of the Lancashire lands to the value of 45 marks, once of his late wife, Elizabeth, the widow of Richard II's esquire, John Townley of Cliviger, during the minority of the heir, Richard Townley (who came of age in 1408).[91] In the following March he was granted the wardship of his nephew and godson, William Skillicorne of Prees (Lancashire), which he enjoyed to 1406.[92] Hence, despite his landless birth, royal grants ensured that he enjoyed a very respectable income which amounted to 40 marks even after he no longer enjoyed the Townley and Skillicorne

---

[86] When pardoned on 8 May 1398 for treasonable adherence to the Appellants he is referred to as son of Thomas Rigmayden: C67/70, m. 3. For a pedigree of the Rigmayden family: H. Fishwick, *The History of the Parish of Garstang*, Chetham Society, 105 (1879), pt. ii, facing p. 214. For his nephew, Thomas: DL28/27/6; Roskell, *Knights of the Shire*, 208 n. 28.

[87] *CPR, 1388–92*, 177. [88] *Expeditions to Prussia*, 135, 268.

[89] DL42/16, pt. 1, fo. 25. [90] DL42/15, pt. 1, fo. 88.

[91] Ibid.; *Abstracts of Inquisitions Post Mortem, 1297–1637*, ed. W. Langton, Chetham Society, 95 (1875), 157–8. John Townley died on 8 Sept. 1399 seised of the Lancashire manors of Towneley and Cliviger. Elizabeth died on 27 Mar. 1401 seised of the Townley manor of Hapton: ibid. 160.

[92] 'Calendar of Patent Rolls of the County Palatine of Lancaster', *DKR* 40 (1879), 531; *Abstracts*, ed. Langton, 91.

wardships. How he came into Nottinghamshire politics remains a mystery. He was certainly connected with the county by July 1403 when he took out a pardon as an esquire of the county. The fact that his second wife, Elizabeth Townley, to whom he was only briefly married, died in March 1401 opens up the possibility that he came into the county by marriage, but if he had a third wife, and she was a Nottinghamshire heiress or widow, she can only have been a very minor one. He did have some lands in the shire, in and around Blyth,[93] but these, whether acquired by purchase or in the right of his third wife, were far from sufficient to entitle him to the prominent place he took in local administration.

In March 1407, while holding his first office in the county, that of escheator, the king appointed him steward of the archiepiscopal lordship of Southwell, while the temporalities remained in royal hands.[94] It was a grant that might have given some independent basis to his office-holding in the county but, since the temporalities were restored to Bowet in December 1407, his tenure of office was brief. The fact that his prominence in local politics depended entirely on the king meant that when royal patronage was withdrawn he disappeared from the county scene as quickly as he had appeared. He was removed from the county bench in July 1420, and his last commission in the county was in November 1421. Thereafter, although he was one of those involved in riots against the prior of Blyth in 1428,[95] he appears to have been no longer principally resident at Blyth, having moved instead to the town of Leicester. In a plea of debt in the common bench in Hilary 1425 he is styled as 'of Leicester, gentleman',[96] and in the tax returns of 1436 he is assessed in Leicestershire at £32 per annum[97] (an income which must largely have been made up of his Lancaster fees and annuities confirmed in 1423).[98] The last reference to him in central government sources comes

[93] When empanelled as a juror in 1414 he was styled as of Serlby in Harworth near Blyth and when in July 1415 he had a protection as a member of the retinue of the Lancs. knight Sir William Harrington he was styled as of Blyth: KB/204/1/52; 'Calendar of the French Rolls', *DKR* 44 (1883), 572. As late as 1438, he appears as a feoffee for one John Carlton of Blyth in 2 deeds concerning 2 acres of arable land in Hodsock and Blyth: NUL, Cl. D711, 712.

[94] *CPR, 1405–13*, 313.

[95] *CCR, 1422–9*, 409; KB27/672, fines rot. (where he appears as 'of Blyth, yeoman'). For the story of these riots: S. J. Payling, 'Law and Arbitration in Nottinghamshire, 1399–1461', in *People, Politics and Community in the Later Middle Ages* (Gloucester, 1987), 149.

[96] CP40/656, rot. 152.

[97] E179/192/59.

[98] DL42/18, pt. 2, fo. 25. At this date his annuities consisted of 20 marks from the vill of Lancaster and 10 marks from the duchy.

in May 1439 when he had a pardon of all fines incurred before the English coronation of Henry VI.[99] There are two possible explanations for his sudden disappearance from Nottinghamshire politics: either he no longer wished to hold office on grounds of age (he had been of age in 1385[100] and is designated as '*senex*' in a list of duchy annuitants of *c*.1415)[101] or else he had come into county politics as a servant of Henry IV's queen, Joan of Navarre, who had in June 1403 been granted the town of Mansfield and other royal estates in Nottinghamshire.[102] The second explanation is attractive since his appearance in the county tallies chronologically with this grant and his disappearance quite closely with her disgrace (she was deprived of her dower in September 1419), but there is no firm evidence to associate the two. What is clear is that his career as a professional administrator in the service of the crown has few parallels in the history of Lancastrian England.

There is nothing either particularly sinister or surprising about the very close connections that existed between the crown and local officers in both Nottinghamshire and Derbyshire during the reign of Henry IV. In Derbyshire nearly all the leading gentry were in receipt of duchy of Lancaster annuities, the total annual value of which was an astonishing £812 13s. 4d. in 1412,[103] and it is natural that these annuitants should dominate the administration and parliamentary representation of the shire; in Nottinghamshire duchy influence was less extensive but the county gentry were still in receipt of duchy annuities worth £123 6s. 8d., together with annuities assigned on royal revenues worth a further £251 11s. 8d. per annum.[104] The dominance of these annuitants over local office entailed neither the exclusion of a recognizable body of men wealthy enough to consider a role in shire government as their birthright, nor the promotion of men, with the exception of Rigmayden, disqualified

[99] E159/213, brevia directa baronibus, Easter 15 HVI, rot. 14^d.

[100] *Abstracts*, ed. Langton, 76.

[101] DL28/27/6. And yet he was not too old in 1424 to fight at the battle of Vernueil: *Letters and Papers Illustrative of the Wars of the English in France during the Reign of Henry VI*, ed. J. Stevenson, Rolls Series (1861–4), II. ii. 394.

[102] *CPR, 1401–5*, 234, 271.

[103] E179/91/44 (printed, with minor errors, in *FA*, vi. 412–15) lists 21 duchy annuities, nearly all charged on the honors of Tutbury and High Peak, totalling £832 13s. 4d. I have included the £20 p.a. paid to William Wollaton of Watnall Chaworth out of Belper amongst the Nottinghamshire annuities. The total value of the annuities charged on the duchy honors of Tutbury and High Peak was even greater. In 7–8 H IV annuities worth £939 3s. 5½d. were charged on Tutbury and a further £150 0s. 10d. on High Peak: DL28/27/9.

[104] Appendix 6.

by lack of landed wealth or county status. The explanation for Rig-mayden's role may lie in the local disorder of the last years of the reign. Certain members of his affinity in Nottinghamshire and Derbyshire were so given to fighting each other, that the king was probably reluctant to entrust them with the shrievalty for fear that they would use the still considerable power of that office in furtherance of their feuds. He thus turned to Rigmayden.

If, as seems probable, Henry did not get value for money in terms of the holding of local office in the second half of his reign from his extensive Nottinghamshire and Derbyshire affinity, this does not mean his investment was wasted. Nearly all of the annuities paid to the gentry of these counties were granted in the first years of the reign and were a reward for the very considerable support he had received from these counties of traditional Lancastrian influence on his arrival in England in June 1399. Of the thirty-seven men listed in the duchy register as coming to him at that time, as many as fifteen were from Derbyshire and four were from Nottinghamshire.[105] Many of the Derbyshire contingent were duchy officials and it was they who brought the largest retinues. Sir Walter Blount, constable of Tutbury, was paid £233 6s. 8d. for the men he brought, a sum exceeded only by Robert Waterton of Methley (Yorkshire), steward of Pontefract, who received £285 9s. 8d. Others who were less well rewarded included Sir Thomas Wendesley, steward of High Peak, who received £160; John Curson, steward of Tutbury, £100; Sir John Dabrigecourt, master forester of Duffield Frith, £60 10s. 7d.; and Sir John Cokayn, chief steward of the north parts of the duchy, 100 marks. But Henry was able to draw support from a wider circle than those in duchy employment. Few of the leading Derbyshire families went unrepresented, while from Nottinghamshire came Sir Thomas Hercy, Sir Hugh Husy, Richard Stanhope, Bartholomew Montgomery of Gotham, and William Wollaton.[106] These supporters were worthy

[105] DL42/15, pt. 1, fos. 70–1. Tuck is mistaken in his statement that most of the men who came to Henry were from Yorks. and Lancs.: A. Tuck, *Richard II and the English Nobility* (London, 1973), 214.
[106] Wollaton is not listed in the duchy register but he was certainly with Henry soon after his landing: above, p. 128. This military support was repeated on the inglorious Scottish expedition of August 1400. From Notts. came Sir John Annesley, Sir Hugh Husy, Robert Nevill, William Wollaton, Bartholomew Montgomery, all royal or duchy annuitants by this date, John Knyveton, Thomas Staunton, and the sheriff, Sir John Leek, who headed the county levy of 200: E101/42/35; 43/3. For the general involvement of the royal affinity in this campaign: A. L. Brown, 'The English Campaign in Scotland, 1400', in H. Hearder and H. R. Loyn (eds.), *British Government and Administration* (Cardiff, 1974), 47.

and expectant of reward, and Henry did not disappoint them. He was generous in his grants of duchy and royal annuities.

During the great crisis of the reign in July 1403, when he faced the combined attack of Owain Glyndwr and the Percies, this generosity was repaid in full. It would be going too far to say that it was the gentry of the north midlands, and particularly Derbyshire, who put him on the throne in 1399 but it would scarcely be an exaggeration to say that it was they who kept him there in 1403. It was fortunate for him that on 12 July, when he first heard news that the Percys had risen in revolt, he was at Nottingham (on his way north to Scotland).[107] Although he appears first to have considered returning to the capital to raise troops, he was persuaded by that veteran campaigner, George Dunbar (*c*.1336–*c*.1420), ninth earl of Dunbar and March, to strike quickly, relying on the support of his north midland affinity. Moving the short distance to Derby on 13 July and to Burton-on-Trent on 15 July, he called out the *posse comitatus* from the surrounding shires, and thence, moved without delay to Shrewsbury. The exact composition of his army is unknown but it is clear from the names of those who died in the battle that a very significant part of it came from Nottinghamshire and Derbyshire.[108] From Derbyshire came Sir Hugh Shirley of Shirley, Sir Nicholas Goushill of Barlborough, Sir Walter Blount, Edmund Cokayn of Ashbourne, and Sir Thomas Wendesley,[109] all of whom met their death in the battle, and from Nottinghamshire, Sir John Clifton,[110] the sheriff of the two counties, Sir Robert Goushill of Hoveringham,[111] Nicholas Burdon of Maplebeck,[112] and Sir Richard Stanhope,[113] the first three of

[107] I have relied on Wylie's account of the Shrewsbury campaign in Wylie, *History of England under Henry the Fourth*, i. ch. 25, with the revised itinerary, ibid. iv. 291.

[108] Six of the 9 knights (excluding Edmund, earl of Stafford) listed in the *Annales Henrici Quarti* as being killed on the king's side came from Notts. and Derbys.: *Johannis de Trokelowe, et Henrici de Blandeforde, monachorum S. Albani, necnon quorundam anonymorum, chronica et annales*, ed. H. T. Riley, Rolls Series (1866), 369. The other 3 were annuitants of Henry, prince of Wales, Sir John Massy of Puddington (Chester), Sir Hugh Mortimer of Chelmarsh (Salop), and Sir John Calveley of Leics.

[109] Shirley, Nicholas Goushill, Cokayn (wrongly as Sir John, probably a mistake for Edmund), and Blount are named in the *Annales*. Sir Thomas Wendesley of Wensley, steward of the High Peak, is known from his tomb at Bakewell church to have been killed in the battle: J. C. Cox, *Notes on the Churches of Derbyshire* (Chesterfield, 1875–9), ii. 17–19.   [110] Names in *Annales*.

[111] Named in *Annales* with an account of the unfortunate way in which he met his death: *Trokelowe*, 367–70.

[112] On 12 Aug. 1403 the wardship of Burdon's lands and the marriage of his heir were granted to his widow, Milicent, in consideration of his good service, especially at the battle of Shrewsbury, where he was killed: DL42/15, pt. 2, fo. 8ᵛ.

[113] His participation is known from *CPR, 1405–8*, 53.

whom were killed. No doubt there were many other gentry from these counties whose survival has meant that their names have escaped record. However much the special relationship between Henry IV and these members of the Nottinghamshire gentry was compromised by the disorders later in the reign, it is clear that the investment he made in their loyalty in 1399–1400 was justified by the events of 1403. Moreover, the affinity he built up from his father's Lancastrian affinity in the two counties continued to play an important role in local politics for two decades after his death. It was not until the majority of his grandson, Henry VI, that the traditional ties between the north midland gentry and the crown broke down.

Henry V

There was a much higher degree of continuity in the personnel of major office in Nottinghamshire between the reigns of Henry IV and Henry V than there had been between those of Richard II and Henry IV. Twelve of the 24 major office-holders of Henry V's reign had also served under his father. Three of the new additions came from the lowest social rank of the major office-holders, the lawyers of the *quorum* of the peace: Thomas Hunte of Linby was added to the commission early in 1416, and Nicholas Coningston and John Bowes in February 1422. Other new additions were sons of men who had been servants of Henry IV as both earl of Derby and king: Sir Gervase Clifton, who had been a minor when his father, Sir John Clifton, was killed at the battle of Shrewsbury,[114] was added to the afforced peace commission of February 1422, and Sir Thomas Rempston, the son of Sir Thomas Rempston (d. 1406), represented the county in the parliaments of May 1413 and January 1416. Two other men emerged from prominent county families: Sir Henry Pierpoint, the son and heir-apparent of the elderly and long inactive Sir Edmund Pierpoint, was elected to the parliaments of November 1417 and December 1421; while William Mering, a king's esquire and the son of Alexander Mering, a justice of the peace in 1406–7, represented the county in the parliament of May 1421. There was nothing surprising about the appointment and election of these men, all four of whom served at Agincourt, nor of the continued employment of the Lancastrian

---

[114] He was said to be 14 and more in Oct. 1403: E152/389.

affinity, so active in the previous reign: Sir Thomas Chaworth, Sir Richard Stanhope, William Rigmayden, Sir Hugh Husy, and Sir Thomas Hercy all continued to serve as local officers.

Much more noteworthy was the election of three lesser men to parliament, men who had previously played no part in shire affairs and were to lapse back into obscurity after their election.[115] The first of these returned was Henry Sutton of Averham, who sat in the Leicester parliament of April 1414 with the Yorkshire knight, Sir Robert Plumpton. Their return is probably to be explained in the same terms as that of William Rigmayden and Thomas Staunton in November 1411, for those involved in the riots of August 1411 were not eligible candidates. Indeed, it was during this Leicester parliament that the commission of enquiry into disorders in the county, before which the rioters were indicted, was issued. Sutton thus owed his election to a shortage of willing candidates, while the well-connected and wealthy Plumpton, a retainer of the chancellor, Henry Beaufort, bishop of Winchester, was probably returned in the hope that he would intercede on the county's behalf to prevent an over-zealous enquiry into the disturbed condition of the county or, even worse, a visitation of the king's bench. The elections of William Compton of Hawton, returned with the soldier, Sir Thomas Rempston, to the parliament of March 1416, and Ralph Husy, returned with Sir John Zouche to that of October 1419, are less easily explained, although the latter may have been acting as deputy for his much more important brother, Sir Hugh Husy. This devolvement of representation on lesser men was not unique to Nottinghamshire and may have been due to parliament's diminished importance in the absence abroad of the king and many of the magnates.[116] It is noteworthy in this regard that, after the treaty of Troyes in May 1420, when parliament once more became a forum of debate between crown and commons rather than simply a tax-granting body, the county was represented by leading shire men alone: Sir Thomas Chaworth and Ralph Makerell served in the parliament of December 1420; Chaworth and Sir William Mering in that of May 1421; and Sir Richard Stanhope and Sir Henry Pierpoint in that of December 1421.

It is worth asking if the county was temporarily denuded of office-holders by the war in France. The crown, at least on the eve of the third expedition of the reign, perceived this to be a problem. In the parliament

---

[115] For their careers: Payling, pp. 292–3.

[116] L. Clark and C. Rawcliffe, 'The History of Parliament, 1386–1422: A Progress Report', *Medieval Prosopography* 4 (1983), pt. 2, 19–20.

of May 1421 the commons presented a petition, probably instigated by the crown, requesting that the statute of 1340 concerning the one-year terms of escheators and sheriffs should be suspended because of a shortage of men sufficient to hold these offices, a shortage occasioned both '*par pestilences diverses dedeinz le Roialme, come par les guerres dehors*'. The result was a statute suspending the earlier statute for four years from the following November.[117] There is certainly evidence to suggest that a shortage of suitable officers had been a problem earlier in the reign. The choice of sheriffs in 1415 had to be put back a month to 1 December to allow for the return of those who had accompanied the king on the Agincourt campaign.[118] Without such a deferment it would have been difficult to fill the office. From Nottinghamshire, for example, three county knights, Sir Thomas Chaworth, Sir Thomas Rempston, and Sir Hugh Husy, and three esquires, Thomas Staunton, Robert Brut, and William Mering, are known to have accompanied the king on this campaign.[119] If one adds to these absentees the still greater number of the aristocracy of Derbyshire, who also accompanied the king,[120] the field of potential sheriffs remaining, exclusive of the man in office, Sir Thomas Hercy, was small. As it transpired, Simon Leek, who does not appear to have been at Agincourt, was appointed, but, in other counties, the choice fell on one of the returning soldiery.[121] Later in the reign, however, it is difficult to demonstrate that the French war significantly lessened the availability of suitable men to hold office: although, from the Nottinghamshire gentry, Sir Henry Pierpoint, Gervase Clifton, Robert Strelley, Thomas Staunton, and Hugh Annesley accompanied Richard, Lord Grey of Codnor, on the expedition of 1417,[122] only William Mering, another who served in the 1417 expedition, and Robert Brut are known to have gone to France from the county in 1421,[123] and

---

[117] *RP*, iv. 148; *SR*, ii. 206. [118] *CFR, 1413–22*, 128–9.

[119] 'Calendar of the French Rolls', *DKR* 44 (1883), 561, 564, 568, 575; E404/31/153; 256; 309; 370; N. H. Nicolas, *History of the Battle of Agincourt* (London, 1833), pp. 355, 377, 381, 382, 384. This list may not be exhaustive. Rigmayden took out letters of protection on 23 July 1415, having been appointed escheator on 12 Nov. 1414 (he was not replaced until 14 Dec. 1415), but he does not appear to have served at Agincourt. He was still in England in 18 Oct. 1415 when he conducted an inquisition *post mortem* at Dunham: *Notts. IPM, 1350–1436*, 156.

[120] Wright, pp. 8, 152 n. 59, 60.

[121] e.g. Sir William Talbot in Cornwall: E404/31/334. [122] E101/51/2.

[123] For Mering, who was knighted in 1421: A. Cameron, 'Meering and the Meryng Family', *TTS* 77 (1973), 45; E101/70/705. For Brut: 'Calendar of French Rolls', *DKR* 44 (1883), 635. In 1421 Annesley, by then a knight, mustered and drew wages to go to France but failed to set sail. His lands were seized and he was imprisoned in the Fleet for his dishonesty: E101/71/757; *PPC*, ii. 303.

only Sir Thomas Rempston made a career out of foreign service.[124] Even so the statute of 1421 may have been made with an eye to the forthcoming expedition. Its effect was short term. In Nottinghamshire and Derbyshire it resulted in a six-month extension to the terms of Sir Ralph Shirley as sheriff and William Wilbram as escheator but the crown did not thereafter make use of the suspension.

Minority of Henry VI

During the minority of Henry VI the personnel of major office-holding in the county reached a high level of continuity. Thirteen of the twenty-four men who held major office in this period had done so before 1422. Sir Thomas Chaworth (d. 1459), Sir Richard Stanhope (d. 1436), Sir John Zouche (d. 1445), Sir Henry Pierpoint (d. 1452), Sir William Mering (d. 1449), and Ralph Makerell (d. 1436), major office-holders under Henry IV and Henry V, continued to be prominent, all sitting on the county bench, serving four terms as sheriff between them, and taking 10 out of the county's 20 parliamentary seats between 1422 and 1436. Of the new additions to the ranks of the office-holders, three, Richard Bingham, Richard Wentworth, and William Clerk of Gedling were lawyers appointed to the *quorum* of the peace; four, Sir Robert Markham, Hugh Willoughby, his son, Richard Willoughby, and Norman Babington, a younger brother of Sir William Babington, CJCB, were from the élite of the county families; three, John Cokfeld, Thomas Darcy, and Hugh Hercy, were wealthy members of the second rank of county society; and the remaining one, Thomas Curson of Bulcote, a scion of the Derbyshire Cursons of Kedleston, a less wealthy member of that same rank.

It is possible to see in the appointments of Cokfeld and others to the shrievalty the emerging influence of Ralph, Lord Cromwell, who became treasurer of England in August 1433. Although Cokfeld was a very substantial man in his own right, assessed for taxation at as much as £106 per annum in 1436, and he might have secured his prominent place in local affairs by virtue of this alone, he seems to have been quite clearly associated with Cromwell. His sister, Agnes, was the wife of John Tailboys of Stallingborough, a leading member of Cromwell's Lincoln-

---

[124] Above, pp. 60–1.

shire affinity,[125] and it was to Cokfeld and others that Cromwell surrendered the keeping of the crown's Nottinghamshire manors of Mansfield and Linby on 14 November 1439.[126] It appears significant that this surrender should have occurred only nine days after Cokfeld had been appointed to the shrievalty of Nottinghamshire and Derbyshire for the second time, an appointment which Cromwell, as treasurer, was well-placed to influence. Another who may have owed his pricking as sheriff to Cromwell was an altogether less substantial man, namely, John Hickling of Linby, who served as escheator in 1436–7 and then immediately afterwards as sheriff in 1437–8. Assessed at only £20 per annum in 1436 he held no other county offices, and it is surely more than coincidental that they should have come to him during Cromwell's treasurership. The fact that he farmed the royal manor of Linby from Cromwell in 1433–4[127] certainly suggests that this was so. Darcy too probably owed his appointment to the shrievalty in November 1435 to Cromwell's influence. For him, as for Hickling, all the offices that he held came during the decade when Cromwell was treasurer; first, the shrievalty of Lincolnshire in November 1433, when he was already past 50 years of age and hence somewhat elderly to embark upon a public career, then, two years later, that of Nottinghamshire and Derbyshire, and, finally, a seat on the Holland bench in 1440. A younger son of the baronial house of Darcy of Notton, extinct in the senior male line since 1418,[128] he was definitely a member of Cromwell's affinity by

[125] This marriage had taken place well before Easter 1444 when it had already produced a married granddaughter: Thoroton, ii. 253–4; CP25(1)/186/39/20. For Tailboys: A. Rogers, 'Parliamentary Electors in Lincolnshire in the Fifteenth Century', *Lincolnshire History and Archaeology* 5 (1970), 54–5.

[126] Associated with Cokfeld in this grant were Cromwell's servants, William Heton, Richard Gowsell, parson of Cromwell, and William Stanlowe: *CFR, 1437–45*, 120. This arrangement was probably made by Cromwell to ensure the continued reliability of payment to the exchequer of the farm of these manors, which he regularly took as part of his fee as a royal councillor: B. P. Wolffe, *The Royal Demesne in English History* (London, 1971), 108, 278.

[127] HMC, *Report on the Manuscripts of Lord De L'Isle and Dudley*, i (1925), 216.

[128] He was a younger son of Philip (d. 1399), Lord Darcy. In 1410 the reversion of the Darcy manor of Ordsall in north Notts. was settled on him: CP25(1)/186/37/36; Thoroton, iii. 452. Through his wife Grace he had a claim to the Northants. manor of Earls Barton, which he pursued unsuccessfully, and it is not clear where the rest of his lands, assessed at £80 p.a. in the tax returns of 1436, lay: CP40/722, rot. 325. Despite this high income, he is an obscure figure. As early as May 1407 he had a protection, as 'of Yorkshire, esquire', for staying in the Welsh service of Henry, prince of Wales; in 1412, as 'of Seamer' in Yorks., he had a pardon as a feoffee of his late brother, John (d. 1411), Lord Darcy; in 1434 he was sworn to the peace in Yorks.: *CPR, 1405–8*, 326; *1408–13*, 446; *1429–36*, 378. It appears he spent much of his life in that county, and it is hence difficult to explain his appointment to the shrievalties of Lincs. and Notts. save in terms of his connection with Cromwell.

1440, and there is no reason to doubt that he had been so for some years.[129]

It would have been surprising if Cromwell had not used his influence as treasurer to secure the appointment of his own connections to the shrievalties of those counties in which he had a direct interest, and he was able on occasion to do so in Nottinghamshire and Derbyshire. It is not, however, until later that his influence is seen at work in parliamentary elections.

Majority of Henry VI

During the majority of Henry VI there was a significant change in the personnel of the major office-holders. It is a singular and impressive fact that not a single man elected to represent the county in parliament before February 1445 inclusive was elected thereafter. In part this was due to demographic factors as one generation came to replace another. By the late 1440s men who had previously been prominent in shire representation were either dead or too old to make the journey to parliament: John Bowes, who represented the county in the parliaments of September 1429, May 1432, October 1435, and November 1439, died in 1444;[130] Sir John Zouche, four times a knight of the shire of the county between October 1407 and January 1442, died in 1445; his fellow MP in 1442, Sir William Mering, a shire knight in May 1421 and February 1425, died in 1449; while Sir Thomas Chaworth, seven times one of the county's MPs, was in his late sixties when he represented the county for the last time in February 1445. This followed a similar thinning in the ranks of the active parliamentary representatives during the 1430s with the deaths of Sir Richard Stanhope (d. 1436), Ralph Makerell (d. 1436), and Norman Babington (d. 1434). The consequence

---

[129] In 1434, when Cromwell was treasurer, he was one of those, along with members of Cromwell's Lincs. affinity, to whom the debt-burdened priory of Newstead-upon-Ancholme (Lincs.) was committed. Six years later, in 1440, he was a victim of a failed ambush by Cromwell's enemy, Henry, Lord Grey of Codnor: KB27/741, rex rots. 2, 2^d. Cromwell subsequently used his local influence to force a settlement on Grey on behalf of Darcy and his Derbys. followers, the Stathams: below, p. 198. When Darcy died at Ordsall on 6 Apr. 1442 Cromwell certified his death into the court of king's bench: KB27/723, rex rot. 24^d.

[130] For his career: J. S. Roskell, 'John Bowes of Costock, Speaker in the Parliament of 1435', *TTS* 60 (1956), 18.

was that very few of those elected in February 1445 and before were available for return after that date. Moreover, these deaths were matched by those deaths of the heads of a number of other leading families who had played a less prominent role in local politics: Sir Hugh Willoughby died in 1448, Sir Henry Pierpoint in 1452, and Sir Gervase Clifton in 1453. Their deaths naturally meant that their heirs came to take over their role in county administration: Robert Clifton (d. 1478) was returned to parliament, appointed to the bench, and served a term as sheriff even before the death of his elderly and inactive father, Sir Gervase Clifton (d. 1453); Richard Willoughby (d. 1471), who had been elected to parliament as a young man in July 1435, was first appointed to the bench in July 1448, a few months before his father's death, and served as sheriff in 1449–50; William Chaworth (d. 1467) was sheriff in 1457–8 and appointed to the bench in February 1459 within a fortnight of his father's death; and John Stanhope (d. 1493) was very active in local office from November 1449, when he was first returned to parliament. Demographic factors are also to be seen at work on the *quorum* of the peace. Between August 1430, when Richard Wentworth and Richard Bingham were first appointed, and February 1441, the *quorum* attained a remarkable degree of stability: apart from the two assize justices, it consisted of John Bowes, first appointed in February 1422, and Sir William Babington, first appointed in November 1399 and who resumed an active part in the bench's affairs after his retirement as chief justice of the common pleas in 1436, together with Wentworth and Bingham. Bowes's departure to take up office as recorder of London in July 1440, followed by his death in 1444 and that of Wentworth in 1448, saw the emergence of a new *quorum* consisting of Sir William Babington's son and heir-apparent, William Babington, William Nevill of South Leverton, and Richard Willoughby, together with the old guard of Babington senior and Bingham. The elder Babington's death in October 1454 occasioned the addition of another member of his family, Thomas Babington, to the *quorum*.[131]

Nevertheless, changes in the personnel of office-holding in this period are not to be explained solely in terms of demography: another factor, seen particularly clearly in the case of parliamentary representation, was Cromwell's influence. Although he had held a pre-eminent place in county politics from *c*.1430, and had probably used his influence to secure the appointments of Thomas Darcy, John Hickling, John

---

[131] For the membership of the *quorum*: Payling, pp. 299–303.

Cokfeld, and John Statham to the shrievalty in 1435–6, 1437–8, 1439–40, and 1444–5,[132] it was not until the late 1440s and early 1450s that he mobilized his resources to secure the return of his own men to parliament. It was no coincidence that he should have chosen to do so at this time. The highly charged political circumstances of these years made magnates all the more eager to have their own men in the commons. For Cromwell this need was perhaps particularly acute in the aftermath of the first battle of St Albans, fought on 22 May 1455, which saw him the subject of Warwick's enmity, and his removal from the office of king's chamberlain.[133] It is in this context that the return of Richard Illingworth, a member of his legal council, to represent Nottinghamshire in the parliaments of February 1447, February 1449, November 1450, and, most notably, July 1455, is to be seen.[134] In normal circumstances, and without his powerful patron's support, he would not have been elected.

His was a quite remarkable career: with no prospects of a landed inheritance at birth, by his death in 1476 he held lands in seven counties,[135] the reward of a successful career in the law spanning 40 years. Admitted to Lincoln's Inn in 1435 and governor in 1443–4, 1447–9, and 1457–8, his career culminated in his appointment as chief baron of the exchequer in September 1462.[136] His success contrasts starkly with the obscurity of his origins. His family cannot be identified but there is little doubt that he was a Nottinghamshire man by birth, probably from Kirkby-in-Ashfield in the west of the county.[137] In the 1440s he made a string of landed acquisitions in this area,[138] and it is

[132] Above, pp. 140–1. For the close connection between Cromwell and the Derbys. Stathams: below, p. 195.

[133] R. A. Griffiths, *The Reign of King Henry VI* (London, 1981), 747, 768 n. 172.

[134] Others of Cromwell's followers were elected for neighbouring counties during these years. John Sacheverell of Hopwell, later one of his executors, represented Derbys. in the parliaments of Feb. 1449 and Nov. 1449, and Thomas FitzWilliam of Maplethorpe, his reeve at Burwell in 1446–7, was returned for Lincs. in March 1453: *CPR 1452–61*, 341; HMC, *De L'Isle*, i. 223.

[135] For these lands: Payling, p. 183, n. 3.

[136] J. C. Wedgwood, *History of Parliament, 1439–1509* (HMSO, 1936–8), i. *Biographies*, 491–2.

[137] As early as Trinity term 1431 he appeared personally in the court of king's bench to sue one Richard Martyn of Kirkby, wheelwright, for a personal assault at Kirkby: KB27/681, just. rot. 2. This is the first reference to him.

[138] In February 1444 he acquired from Sir Henry Pierpoint a meadow called 'Akbrygge' and Pierpoint's lands in Hardwick in the parish of Kirkby, while in July 1446 the crown granted him in fee, at the nominal rent of 1d., 200 acres of waste ground bordering these lands: NRO, Portland DD 2P 1/2; CCR, *1447–54*, 129, 443; *1454–61*, 490; CPR, *1441–6*, 428. More important was his purchase of the manor of Kirkby Hardwick from Sir John

probably no coincidence that it is during this decade that he is first found in Cromwell's service. In November 1446 he acted as an arbiter with Cromwell's councillor, William Stanlowe, in a Kentish dispute,[139] and it seems probable that at this date or later he too was a member of Cromwell's council. In 1451–2 he acted as Cromwell's deputy in the office of chief steward of the north parts of the duchy of Lancaster,[140] and was later one of the feoffees for the execution of Cromwell's will.[141]

Despite his Nottinghamshire birth and purchased lands at Kirkby Hardwick, Illingworth could not be said to be a member of that county's aristocracy. He was a man of very different stamp from those usually returned. Although a lawyer, he is not found serving as a feoffee for that county's gentry; he never attested an election return for the shire; nor did he hold any other major office there save for that of MP. Moreover, after Cromwell's death in 1456, and despite his purchase of Cromwell's Nottinghamshire manors of Bunny, Stanton-on-the-Wolds, and Shelford in 1463,[142] he played no further part in shire affairs, moving instead to Surrey, where he had lands at Mitcham,[143] probably in right of his wife

Conyers of Hornby in Yorks. and Margery, one of the co-heiresses of the barony of Darcy. It is not clear when this purchase took place. Margery had livery of her purparty of the Darcy inheritance in May 1433, and the manor was in Illingworth's hands by Apr. 1453: *CCR, 1429–35*, 207–8; NRO, Portland DD 2P 1/4. In 1503 his grandson, another Richard, sold the manor back to the Conyers family: CP25(1)/186/39/18; CP40/965, rot. 148; Thoroton, ii. 294.

[139] *CCR, 1441–7*, 446, 448. For Stanlowe: Rogers, 'Lincolnshire Electors', v. 51–2.

[140] Somerville, p. 425; DL28/5/7, fo. 21 (he spent 72 days in the accounting year on the duchy's business).

[141] *CPR, 1452–61*, 341. He also acted with Cromwell in the purchase of the Fanhope lands: *CAD*, vi, C6071.

[142] For these purchases: CP25(1)/294/74/16; *CCR, 1461–8*, 251–2, 306; *1468–76*, nos. 70, 75. In 1461 his Notts. lands had been supplemented by a royal grant of the forfeited lands of John Brokstowe in Kirkby Woodhouse and elsewhere: *CPR, 1461–7*, 22. In the same year he was granted £40 p.a. for life from the fee farm of Nottingham: ibid., 24.

[143] He held commissions in Notts. in 1448 and 1450 but he was never appointed to the county bench: *CPR, 1446–52*, 139, 319. He first appears as a JP in Surrey in Jan. 1457. The fact that he was twice governor of Lincoln's Inn in the 1440s means that he can only have been an occasional resident at Kirkby Hardwick. In 1446 he is found styled as 'of London, gentleman', and I have only once found him styled as 'of Hardwick' (in Hilary 1455): KB27/741, fines rot.; CP40/776, rot. 164. His son and heir, Ralph, did, however, settle in the county. He acted as escheator of Notts. and Derbys. in 1478–9 and was buried in the church of Stanford-on-Soar in 1498: Thoroton, i. 6. Richard (d. 1476) himself was buried in the church of St Alban in Wood Street, London, although he did remember the county of his birth in his will, leaving 5 marks to the repair of the parish churches of Kirkby-in-Ashfield and Bunny, and a further 40s. to the churches of Stanford-on-Soar and Stanton-on-the-Wolds (to be shared with the Derbys. church of Breadsall). He also made several bequests to religious houses in Notts., including £10 to the priory of

Alice Nynne, the widow of the London alderman, Thomas Chalton (d. 1452).[144]

During the late 1440s and early 1450s it was not only Illingworth's four returns to parliament that were unusual. His fellow MP in February 1447 was the Yorkshire esquire, Nicholas FitzWilliam; in February 1449, the middling Nottinghamshire esquire, John Roos of Laxton; and in both November 1450 and July 1455, another middling Nottinghamshire esquire, John Wastnes of Headon.[145] It would seem that Wastnes too was one of Cromwell's affinity (although, unlike Illingworth, he was also a man of some independent importance in the county as witnessed by his appointment as sheriff ten months after Cromwell's death) and, though definite proof is lacking, it is probable that Roos and FitzWilliam were also in some way associated with Cromwell. It would be difficult to explain their return in any other terms. However these returns should not be seen solely in the light of that lord's influence and his desire to have his own men in parliament at a time of political crisis. That he was so effectively able to exert his influence on the electoral process in favour of men who might not otherwise have been returned was in part due to the demographic crisis amongst the county élite. During these years there were unusually few leading shire men available for return, a similar position to that which had prevailed, for different reasons, at the elections of October 1411 and April 1414.[146] In short, the successful exertion of magnate influence on elections in Nottinghamshire, even for one as powerful as Cromwell, was dependent on other factors. Indeed, one might even go so far as to suggest that Cromwell might not have sought to push his candidates, and in particular the 'outsider', Illingworth, in face of the opposition of the county élite. It is notable that on all four occasions on which Illingworth was returned, the elections were unusually well-attended by the leading men of the shire:[147] in January 1447 the retired CJCB, Sir William Babington, his eldest son, William Babington,

Beauvale: PROB 11/6, fos. 192ᵛ–193; J. Stow, *A Survey of London*, ed. C. L. Kingsford, 2 vols. (Oxford, 1908), i. 296.

[144] She was his second wife. Nothing is known of his first. In his will he made provision for prayers to be said for Chalton's soul: PROB 11/6, fo. 192ᵛ. Chalton was a mercer and London alderman from 1433 until his death, serving terms as mayor in 1433–4 and 1449–50 (during Cade's revolt), and was a very rich man, rich enough to bequeath Alice as much as 1,000 marks in cash in his will of Dec. 1451: S. L. Thrupp, *The Merchant Class of Medieval London, 1300–1500* (Chicago, 1948), 330: Lambeth Palace, Reg. Kemp, fo. 271.

[145] For biographies of FitzWilliam, Roos, and Wastnes: Payling, pp. 293–5.

[146] Above, pp. 130–2, 138.

[147] For attendance at elections: Appendix 7.

Sir Henry Pierpoint, and Robert Clifton;[148] in January 1449 Sir Thomas Chaworth, Sir Thomas Rempston, Sir Henry Pierpoint, and John Cokfeld;[149] in October 1450 Pierpoint, Cokfeld, William Babington, and Robert Strelley;[150] and in June 1455 Richard Willoughby, William Babington, and William Mering.[151] Clearly Cromwell was able to secure the return of his own men with the approval of the shire élite rather than in face of its opposition.

A more general factor in determining elections and appointments in Nottinghamshire between 1437 and 1460 was the household connections of several of the new heads of the leading county families. The majority of Henry VI saw the reconstruction of the royal affinity in the county. Since the first years of the reign of his grandfather, Henry IV, when a significant number of Nottinghamshire gentry had been granted annuities assigned on duchy or royal revenues, this affinity had become gradually depleted. Henry V had confirmed his father's surviving annuitants in their fees[152] but had not sought to extend the affinity. He had no need to do so: his military success was sufficient to guarantee the adherence of the baronage and gentry. The affinity further withered during his son's minority[153] so that when Henry VI took over the reins of government only Sir Thomas Chaworth and the obscure Robert Brut of

[148] C219/15/4/70; also John Roos, John Cokfeld, and John Wastnes.

[149] C219/15/6/71; also William Babington, Henry Pierpoint, William Chaworth, Thomas Nevill of Rolleston, Robert Strelley, and Robert Clifton.

[150] C219/16/1/69; also William Mering, John Roos, and Henry Boson.

[151] C219/16/3/48. This return is rendered slightly irregular by the presence of the Derbys. esquires Robert Eyre and John Statham, the one a servant of Shrewsbury, the other of Cromwell: below, p. 166.

[152] Sir Thomas Chaworth: DL42/16, pt. 1, fo. 34 (23 Jun. 1414); Sir Hugh Husy: ibid., pt. 1, fo. 7; William Rigmayden: DL42/17, pt. 1, fo. 5ᵛ (2 July 1413, conditional on his not being retained with anyone else); William Leek: ibid., pt. 1, fo. 24; Robert Morton: *CPR, 1413–16*, 171 (12 Jun. 1413, same condition as Rigmayden); Robert Brut: ibid., 158 (1 Feb. 1414, condition as for Morton). Sir Richard Stanhope had already exchanged his annuity of 40 marks with Roger Deincourt for the War. manor of Ansty.

[153] The decline of the Lancastrian affinity is clearly reflected in the expenditure of duchy revenues on annuities. T. B. Pugh has calculated that in the early years of Henry IV annuities absorbed nearly £9,000 p.a. of these revenues, and that this had fallen to £5,000 p.a. in the latter part of Henry V's reign: Pugh, 'The Magnates', 107–8. Thereafter there was no excess duchy revenue to be spent on annuities. Henry V tied up £6,000 p.a. from the duchy for the performance of his will, an arrangement which lasted down to 1443, and he endowed his queen, Catherine of Valois (d. 1437), with another £4,000 p.a. From 1437 to 1445 the net revenues of the duchy were assigned to the expenses of the household, while in 1445 £4,000 p.a. was assigned to Margaret of Anjou and other revenue enfeoffed for the building of the king's personal foundations at Eton and Cambridge: B. P. Wolffe, *Henry VI* (London, 1981), 100; G. L. Harriss, 'Marmaduke Lumley and the Exchequer Crisis of 1446–9' in J. G. Rowe (ed.), *Aspects of Late Medieval Government and Society: Essays Presented to J. R. Lander* (Toronto, 1986), 146.

Thorney are known to have still been in receipt of fees.[154] Another
Nottinghamshire man, Thomas Staunton of Sutton Bonington, was one
of the marshals of the king's hall, while another, Sir William Mering, an
old soldier, continued to be styled king's knight.[155] All four, three
directly and Staunton through his father, could trace their royal connections back to the first decade of the century: the royal affinity in the
county had become frozen in time. Nor was this process unique to
Nottinghamshire, the neighbouring counties of Derbyshire, Leicestershire, and Yorkshire were similarly affected, as too, probably, were most
of the other counties of England.[156]

The subsequent extension during the 1440s of the royal affinity in the
counties was the reflection of a general and very substantial increase in
the size of the king's household establishment. The *feoda et robe* sections
of the surviving household account books[157] show that the number of
esquires of the hall and chamber in receipt of royal robes increased from
206 in 1441 to 303 in 1451.[158] During the same period the Nottinghamshire contingent grew from five to eight. In 1441 Thomas Staunton, an
usher of the chamber from 1439, William and Thomas Mering, the sons
of Sir William (d. 1449), William Babington, the son of the retired
CJCB, Sir William Babington (d. 1454), and William Middleton of
Girton were in receipt of household robes.[159] By the end of the decade
they had been joined by Henry Boson of Syerston, John Stanhope of
Rampton, and Robert Clifton of Clifton.[160] The financial year 1451/2
saw the further addition of Robert Strelley of Strelley, although by this
date the Nottinghamshire contingent had been reduced by the death of

---

[154] Sir Thomas Chaworth: DL42/18, pt. 1, fo. 132 (20 Nov. 1439); Robert Brut: *CPR,
1422–9*, 20.

[155] Sir William Mering had been associated with the crown since 1408 when granted all
dead roots in the Yorks. forest of Galtres: *CPR, 1408–13*, 395. He was not, however, in
receipt of a royal annuity and no further grant is recorded for him on the patent rolls until
Mar. 1442 when, while serving as an MP and styled as a king's knight, he had 2 tuns of
wine p.a., 'for good service to Henry IV, Henry V, and the king': ibid., *1441–6*, 56.

[156] Wright, p. 84; Ross, 'The Yorkshire Baronage', 359, 369–70; G. G. Astill, 'The
Medieval Gentry: A Study in Leicestershire Society, 1350–1399', Ph.D. thesis (Birmingham, 1977), 230–1.

[157] These survive for 1441–2, 1443–4, 1446–7, 1447–8, 1448–9, 1450–1, and 1451–
2: E101/409/9; 11; 16; 410/1; 3; 6; 9.

[158] E101/409/9, fos. 36ᵛ–37; 410/9, fos. 42ᵛ–43ᵛ. Cf. R. M. Jeffs, 'The Later
Mediaeval Sheriff and the Royal Household', D.Phil. thesis (Oxford, 1960), 153 n. 1.
Wolffe, *Henry VI*, 98; Griffiths, *Henry VI*, 297.

[159] E101/409/9, fos. 36ᵛ, 37.

[160] E101/410/3, fos. 30ᵛ, 31.

Henry Boson and the exclusion of William Middleton.[161] This policy of adding to the household men who were politically significant in the shires in their own right should have served to bring the county closer to the court. William Babington, John Stanhope, Robert Clifton, and Robert Strelley were all the heirs-apparent or heads of major county families, and of the Nottinghamshire men added to the household, only William Middleton and Thomas Mering (as a younger son) can be said to have been comparatively insignificant in their own right. And yet it is clear that the expansion of the household did not have the effect of creating a strong royal party in the shires. When the test came in 1460 and 1461, the household failed in its trust.[162] The explanation for this failure is no doubt a complex web of individual motivations, overlaid, above all else, by the personal incapacity of Henry VI. An analysis of the careers of the Nottinghamshire contingent may reveal a fuller explanation.

It is first worth asking what part this household body played in the administration of the shire during the 1440s and 1450s, and whether their prominence survived Edward IV's accession. Of the nine esquires in receipt of robes only the two lesser men, William Middleton and Thomas Mering, played no part in county government,[163] while the two men most intimately connected with the household, William Mering and Thomas Staunton, one from the upper reaches of the second rank of county society and the other from the lower reaches of the same rank, played a subsidiary role. Although Staunton was twice sheriff, in 1440–1 and 1448–9, he never sat on the county bench, represented the county in parliament, or held any office after 1461;[164] William Mering was escheator in 1447–8, sat on the county bench from May 1457 to July 1458 and again from 10 July 1461 to his death in 1466. Henry Boson, of a similar social rank to Mering, was similarly inactive, serving as a knight of the shire in November 1449 and as escheator for the three months before his death in 1451. The other four men, however, all from the first rank of local society, were extremely active. In part this was due to their social position, but their high level of activity in the 1440s and 1450s

---

[161] E101/410/9 (1451–2), fos. 42ᵛ–43ᵛ. Middleton had robes only at Whitsun. According to his own testimony, William Ayscogh, bishop of Salisbury and the king's confessor, had earlier extorted 20 marks from him as the price of not having him excluded from the royal household: *Select Cases in Chancery, 1364–1471*, ed. W. Paley Baildon, Selden Society, 10 (1896), pp. 136–7.

[162] Jeffs, 'The Later Mediaeval Sheriff', 169–71.

[163] For their careers: Payling, pp. 295–6.

[164] It is just possible that he was the Notts. JP of 1479–82 but this is more likely to have been his younger namesake, Thomas Staunton (d. 1482) of Staunton-in-the-Vale.

may have owed something to their royal household connection: Babington, a household esquire by 1442 and probably before, represented the
county in the parliaments of November 1439 and February 1445, served
as sheriff in 1456 and as a justice of the *quorum* from February 1441 to
July 1461; Robert Clifton, a household esquire by 1447, was a knight of
the shire in the Reading parliament of March 1453, sheriff in 1450–1
and 1459–60, and a justice of the peace from November 1451 to
December 1460; Robert Strelley, who was not in receipt of household
robes until 1452, served as sheriff in 1445–6 and 1451–2, as a JP from
February 1444 to November 1458, and as a knight of the shire in the
Yorkist parliament of October 1460, during which he was reappointed
to the bench; while John Stanhope, a household esquire by 1444 and
amongst the retinue that escorted Margaret of Anjou to England in the
following year,[165] was even more active, serving as a knight of the shire in
November 1449, March 1453, November 1459, and October 1460, as
sheriff from November 1454 to January 1456, and as a justice of the
peace from April 1454 to November 1458.

The first and most obvious point to be made about this impressive list
of offices is that none of these men was seen as a Lancastrian partisan:
both Babington and Stanhope were appointed to the shrievalty when
York was protector,[166] while Stanhope and Strelley represented the
county in the Yorkist parliament of October 1460. Moreover, all four
continued their prominence in local politics into the 1460s and beyond,
although Babington played a lesser role after Edward IV's accession and
Strelley was excluded from office during the 1470s because of his
adherence to the Readeption government.[167] The second point concerns
the use to which the Lancastrian regime put its household servants in
the shires during Henry VI's majority. The prominence of household
sheriffs is well known. The late Dr R. M. Jeffs calculated that between
1437 and 1460 as many as one-fifth of those appointed to the shrievalties
(to which the king had the right of appointment) were household

---

[165] BL, Add. MS 23938, fo. 14ᵛ.

[166] For the shrieval appointments of York's protectorships: Jeffs, 'The Later Mediaeval
Sheriff', 174–7. Very few household men appear to have been appointed although this
view may owe something to Jeffs's omissions: below, p. 151 n. 168.

[167] Clifton was sheriff in 1467–8 and a JP from 1461 until his death in 1478; Stanhope
was sheriff from Nov. 1461 to Nov. 1463, a knight of the shire in June 1467 and Oct. 1472,
and a JP more or less continuously, from 1461 until his death in 1493; Babington was a JP,
again more or less continuously, from 1463 until his death in 1474; and Strelley was
sheriff in 1463–4, and a JP from 1460 to May 1470, Nov. 1470 to July 1471, and June
1486 until his death in 1488. For Strelley and the Readeption: below, p. 155 n. 196.

servants.[168] The percentage for the joint shrievalty of Nottinghamshire
and Derbyshire is even higher, with as many as 9 of the 24 terms being
taken by current household men. This appointments policy is not seen
by Jeffs as a deliberate one (although he makes exceptions for the wake
of Cade's revolt, especially in those counties disturbed by the rebellion,
and the tense last years of the reign) but as forced on the crown by the
reluctance of the leading local gentry to take on an office that was
becoming increasingly burdensome financially.[169] In some counties this
may have been so; the shrievalty of Lincolnshire appears to have been
particularly avoided, so too does that of Cambridgeshire and Huntingdonshire,[170] but the higher percentage of leading families that took up
the office in the joint bailiwick of Nottinghamshire and Derbyshire
throughout the Lancastrian period demonstrates that such reluctance
was not general. Rather, the high percentage of household sheriffs, at
least in that bailiwick, is to be explained in terms of a royal policy of
drawing those men who were natural candidates for the office into
household service and the same argument can be used in the case of
parliamentary representatives. But in both cases it must be conceded
that on occasions the crown appears to have made a particular effort to
ensure the return of household men and the appointment of household

[168] Jeffs, 'The Later Mediaeval Sheriff', 166 n. 1. This must be taken as a rough
estimate as Jeffs's calculations are not free from errors. First, he has reckoned that the king
had the shrieval appointment in 25 bailiwicks, giving a working estimate of 575 yearly
terms of office from the appointments of Nov. 1437 to those of Nov. 1459 inclusive (an
estimate which takes no account of shrieval terms that lasted more or less than a year, but
these were very few). In fact, the king had the appointment in only 24 bailiwicks. Second,
and much more seriously, he has omitted certain household sheriffs from his calculations
while adding others who were not household men when they held the office: ibid., 341–3.
To take the shrievalty of Notts. and Derbys., he cites 5 terms as taken by household men
(1440–1 Thomas Staunton, 1445–6 Robert Strelley, 1447–8 Nicholas Fitzherbert,
1451–2 Robert Strelley, 1458–9 Nicholas Fitzherbert). He has omitted Staunton's
second term in 1448–9 while including Strelley's first term in 1445–6, some years before
he entered household service. Moreover, the *feoda et robe* lists show that Robert Clifton
was a household esquire when he served as sheriff in 1450–1, while both John Stanhope,
the sheriff from Nov. 1454 to Jan. 1456, and his successor, William Babington, sheriff
from Jan. to Nov. 1456, were household esquires down to the failure of the lists in 1452. It
is worth pointing out that Jeffs's identification of household sheriffs after 1452 rests on the
unstated assumption that all those named in the *feoda et robe* list of that year continued as
household esquires down to 1460. It seems unlikely that this was the case for not all those
who failed to survive York's slimming down of the household establishment in Nov. 1454
would have subsequently re-entered it. It should thus be borne in mind that Jeffs's figures
for the number of household sheriffs in the later years of Henry VI refer to men who either
were still or had been household esquires.
[169] Ibid., 56–7, 213.
[170] Ibid., 57–65.

sheriffs. The most notable examples are the elections to the Reading parliament of March 1453 and the Coventry parliament of November 1459, both of which incurred contemporary accusations of royal electoral interference, and the shrieval appointments of November 1458 and November 1459. Bale's Chronicle remarks of the Reading parliament that, 'the comones toke a displeisur be cause they wer restrayned from free eleccion of the knightes of the shir',[171] and the composition and compliant conduct of the commons gives some circumstantial support to this accusation. Nearly half of those returned to represent the shires were household servants, a percentage matched only by the notoriously partisan Coventry parliament.[172] The shrieval appointments of November 1458 and 1459 reveal a similarly high percentage of household servants amongst the appointees: ten out of twenty-three in 1458, and eleven out of twenty-two in 1459.[173] The returns and appointments for Nottinghamshire and Derbyshire reflect these figures: in 1453 two household esquires, Robert Clifton and John Stanhope, were returned from Nottinghamshire and two, Walter Blount and Nicholas Fitzherbert, from Derbyshire;[174] while in November 1458 Fitzherbert was appointed sheriff to be succeeded by Clifton a year later. Although only one of the four men returned to the Coventry parliament was a household esquire (namely Stanhope), Lancastrian influence is equally apparent: Stanhope's partner was John Strelley of Linby, the Nottinghamshire receiver of Jasper, earl of Pembroke, while two servants of the Lancastrian John, earl of Shrewsbury, Robert Barlow and Robert Eyre, were returned for Derbyshire.[175]

These returns and appointments make it quite clear that there was a substantial body of men in the localities closely attached to the house of Lancaster, predominantly through the household, who could be effectively called upon to serve in parliament or the shrievalty as the occasion demanded it. Nevertheless, it is one thing to say that a man was in receipt of household robes; quite another that he was a Lancastrian partisan prepared to lay down his life or his lands in that cause. Indeed,

---

[171] *Six Town Chronicles of England*, ed. R. Flenley (Oxford, 1911), 139–40.

[172] See the useful table in Wolffe, *Henry VI*, 217 n. 7.

[173] Jeffs, 'The Later Mediaeval Sheriff', 341–3. These figures compare with 8 in Nov. 1456 and 5 Nov. 1457.

[174] Thomas Blount, Walter's brother and another household esquire, was returned for the borough of Derby.

[175] For Strelley: Payling, p. 296. For the Derbys. election: Wright, p. 115. Dr Wright has omitted to note that Barlow and Eyre were amongst Shrewsbury's Derbys. feoffees in Mar. 1458: C139/179/58/19.

two of the household contingent from Nottinghamshire and Derbyshire, Walter Blount and Thomas Mering,[176] actively took the side of York. It is worth asking how closely tied was the bulk of the household to the Lancastrian interest. In Nottinghamshire and Derbyshire, only Thomas Staunton was a member of the permanent household establishment. As a marshal of the hall from 1433 to 1439 and usher of the chamber from 1439 to 1460, he did well, although not spectacularly so, from royal patronage: in addition to the offices of master forester of Dartmoor,[177] constable of Dryslwyn castle and keeper of Glyncothi forest,[178] keeper of the crossbows within the Tower of London,[179] receiver of Queen Margaret's honor of Leicester,[180] constable of Castle Donington,[181] steward and constable of Melbourne,[182] and, as late as January 1460, the office of the tronage and pesage in the port of Southampton,[183] he had various grants of fees and wardships to supplement his own moderate landed income.[184] In June 1439 he had a joint grant with the king's surgeon, William Stalworth, of forfeited lands in Hertfordshire worth 20 marks per annum;[185] in April 1442 he joined Robert Twyford in a

---

[176] For Blount: Wedgwood, *Biographies*, 86. Thomas Blount followed his brother into the Yorkist camp.

[177] His father, another Thomas Staunton, who had represented Notts. in the parliament of Nov. 1411, had been appointed to this office by Henry V as prince of Wales. In July 1433 the elder Thomas surrendered this grant to the intent that the younger Thomas should have it. The office had a fee of 10 marks from the duchy of Cornwall: *CPR, 1429–36*, 272. In Dec. 1437 the younger Thomas had a life grant of the office (the earlier grant being only for the lifetime of his father) but, in Nov. 1439, surrendered it to Robert Babthorpe: ibid., *1436–41*, 130, 351.

[178] He was granted these offices for life in Mar. 1439 but neither appointment appears to have been effective: ibid., 245; R. A. Griffiths, *The Principality of Wales in the Later Middle Ages: The Structure and Personnel of Government, i. South Wales, 1277–1536*, Board of Celtic Studies (Cardiff, 1972), 264, 398 n.

[179] He was granted this office for life in Aug. 1439, and appears to have enjoyed it down to 1460, although from Oct. 1440 to 1449 he held it jointly with Robert Waleys: *CPR, 1436–41*, 298, 474–5: *1452–61*, 17. The office was worth 12*d.* p.d.

[180] He was appointed by Queen Margaret on 30 Jan. 1449 to hold the office during pleasure. He was still in office in 1458–9: Somerville, p. 566. His wages were 100*s.* p.a.: DL29/212/3263.

[181] He was granted the office by Henry V's feoffees at a fee of £10 p.a. and had this grant confirmed on 6 Mar. 1444: DL37/11, m. 4ᵈ. On 24 Oct. 1444 his son John was associated with him in the office: Somerville, p. 573. Both were superseded by William, Lord Hastings, in July 1461.

[182] He was appointed to these offices for life in 1437 and his son John was associated with him in the stewardship in 1444. They were superseded by Richard Hastings, brother of William, Lord Hastings, in July 1461: ibid., 557, 558.

[183] *CPR, 1452–61*, 580, 581.

[184] His father, Thomas Staunton the elder, had been assessed in Notts. in 1412 at £10 p.a.: below, p. 223.

[185] *CPR, 1452–61*, 580, 581.

grant of £18 per annum from the issues of the manor of Bolsover;[186] and, in November 1446, he had the wardship and marriage of Alice, daughter and heir of John Saltby of Grantham.[187] These grants and offices were sufficient to give Staunton a worthwhile stake in the continuance of Lancastrian rule, and his disappearance from politics after 1461 suggests that he retained his loyalty to Lancaster. His Nottinghamshire colleagues in the household, however, had no such incentive to remain loyal. Their benefits from Henry VI's patronage beyond the household robes they received at Whitsun and Christmas and the standard pardons of account as sheriffs, were minimal. Staunton's brother-in-law, William Mering did best: in October 1442 he was appointed parker of the Nottinghamshire park of Clipstone; in March 1444 he was granted £10 owed to the king by Thomas Nevill of Rolleston; and, in July 1445, he joined his father, the king's knight, Sir William Mering (d. 1449), in a grant of two tuns of wine yearly.[188] His other grants were reversions that never fell in: in February 1442 he was awarded the office of constable and sheriff of Flint on the death of Sir Thomas Rempston (d. 1458);[189] and, in May 1443, the constableship of Lincoln Castle on the death of William Percy of Welton by Lincoln.[190] However, despite these grants, the issue of royal commissions in 1446, 1450, and 1458 to investigate his involvement in local disorders,[191] and his brother Thomas's allegiance to York, probably served to seduce him away from his Lancastrian allegiance. His fellow Nottinghamshire men in the household, the wealthy esquires Robert Strelley, John Stanhope, William Babington, and Robert Clifton, gained next to nothing from the crown in spite of

[186] *CPR, 1441–6*, 63. Twyford was one of the old Lancastrian affinity in Derbys., having been granted the Bolsover revenues as early as 1406: ibid., *1405–8*, 85.

[187] Ibid., *1446–52*, 7. In August 1458 he was associated with the king's chamberlain, Thomas, Lord Stanley, in a grant of the advowson of the parish church of Eccleston (Lancs.): ibid., *1452–61*, 435.

[188] Ibid., *1441–6*, 139, 253, 326.

[189] Ibid., 42. Rempston was succeeded in 1458 by John Doone, which suggests that Mering had fallen out of favour.

[190] Ibid., 197. But in 1447 the reversion of this office was granted to Humphrey Forster. Percy was still alive in Oct. 1460 when the office was granted to Sir Thomas Nevill, a younger son of Richard, earl of Salisbury.

[191] *CPR, 1446–52*, 40–1 (riots in Lincs.); ibid. 319; *1452–61*, 440–1 (to find security of the peace to Thomas Nevill). The Feb. 1450 commission would appear to be connected with an offence of the previous Dec. when Mering and 60 of his followers had broken down the close of Sir John Talbot, Sir Thomas Percy, and John Roos at Darlton in north Notts., and cut down numerous trees: CP40/756, rot. 394; 757, rot. 422. In 1457 he was required to find security of the peace to one Richard Symson: KB27/785, just. rot. 10[d].

their energetic involvement in local government.[192] Stanhope's solitary grant of a tun of wine yearly from the port of Kingston-upon-Hull in 1447[193] stands in marked contrast to his grandfather's considerable gains from the patronage of Henry IV. Babington gained only two insignificant grants, both in 1441, of the keeping of small parcels of Nottinghamshire lands in the hands of the crown,[194] while no grants are recorded to either Clifton or Strelley.[195]

It is not therefore surprising that these men should have so readily abandoned the ineffectual Henry VI.[196] They had nothing to lose from his deposition. Indeed, they made their readiness to come to terms with the Yorkists quite clear in October 1460 when three of them, Babington, Strelley (by then a knight), and Stanhope, stood for election to the Yorkist parliament of that month, an election conducted by the fourth, Clifton.[197] And although none of the four appear to have taken up arms for the house of York in 1461,[198] neither did they rally to Lancaster as their grandfathers had done in 1403. That the Lancastrian cause should

[192] The esquires of the household from the West Riding were similarly poorly rewarded: Arnold, 'West Riding', 119–22.

[193] *CPR, 1446–52*, 30.

[194] *CFR, 1437–45*, 193–4, 292. Because he had waited on the king at Coventry during his shrievalty of 1456, he secured an additional £30 on the standard pardon of account of £80, but he had to wait until Apr. 1459 before this additional sum was granted: E159/235, brevia directa baronibus, Easter 37 H VI, rot. 9ᵈ.

[195] Strelley had *inspeximus* and confirmation in July 1441, a decade before he entered the household, of the charters which gave his ancestors free warren in their demesne lands at Strelley and elsewhere: *CPR, 1436–41*, 563. In Jan. 1453, at the end of his second term as sheriff, he had pardon of account of £100 because he had attended the king in London with the defensible men of Notts. during York's Dartford uprising: E159/230, brevia directa baronibus, Mich. 32 H VI, rot. 16ᵈ.

[196] Strelley was amongst those who, with George, duke of Clarence, and Richard, earl of Warwick, had their lands seized in Apr. 1470: *CPR, 1467–76*, 218. His support for the Readeption may have owed more to his connections with the Nevills (he was, or had been, the Notts. receiver of Warwick's uncle, Edward, Lord Bergavenny: above, p. 100) and Clarence (through his son-in-law, Humphrey Salway formerly marshal of the court and the head of a family closely connected with Clarence: above, p. 82; VCH, *Worcestershire*, iv (1924), 342–3) than any latent loyalty to Lancaster. He had certainly had no problem adapting to the Yorkist regime in the 1460s when extremely active in local government. His lands were restored in 1472 but he played no further part in local politics until Henry VII's accession: SC1/44/54; *CCR, 1467–76*, 372. Stanhope served as sheriff during the Readeption but, although he was replaced by the Yorkist, Sir Henry Pierpoint, on Edward IV's return, his career did not suffer. Babington was removed from the commission of the peace during the Readeption but Clifton was not.

[197] Below, pp. 161–2.

[198] Clifton may have done so for he was knighted at Edward IV's coronation on 27 June 1461 and, in July 1461, his son, Gervase, later a knight of the body to Richard III, was appointed steward of the duchy of Lancaster honor of Tickhill for life: W. A. Shaw, *The Knights of England*, 2 vols. (London, 1906), i. 133; Somerville, p. 528.

have been abandoned in a county of traditional Lancastrian allegiance like Nottinghamshire, gives eloquent testimony to T. B. Pugh's conclusion that the 'invincible political connection' built up by Gaunt and Henry IV 'disintegrated in the nerveless hands of Henry VI'.[199]

[199] Pugh, 'The Magnates', 108.

6

PARLIAMENTARY ELECTIONS AND
THE COUNTY BENCH

THE composition of the county bench and the regulation of county
elections were the subjects of several commons' petitions during the
second half of the fourteenth and first half of the fifteenth centuries.
The commons were concerned to limit the crown's freedom of choice in
its selection of justices of the peace and to gain statutory protection for
free communal election of the parliamentary knights of the shire. In the
fourteenth century they had waged a successful campaign to limit
shrieval terms to one year and confine the crown to the selection
of substantial local *vavasours*.[1] Their early fifteenth-century petitions
concerning justices of the peace and knights of the shire are to be
seen in the context of this long-term policy of seeking to confine the
administration and representation of the shire not only to that sector of
society from which they themselves were drawn but also to landholders
resident in the counties in or for which they were to act. There seems
little reason to doubt Dr Saul's contention that this reflected a desire on
the commons' part to exclude from office lesser men who owed their
prominence to the patronage of a magnate (and were hence, in the view
of the commons, liable to partiality in the execution of their office) and,
more importantly, a growing identity of gentry with the shire in which
they resided. He has argued that in 1300 it was commonplace to find
men holding local office in any number of counties where they happened to
hold lands but by 1400 each county had assumed an identity of its own
with the major offices of the shire monopolized by the leading resident
county gentry.[2] In the previous chapter an élite of leading gentry was
shown to have dominated office-holding in Lancastrian Nottinghamshire.[3] This chapter will extend the discussion by examining county
elections and the county bench against the background of the commons-
inspired legislation of the early fifteenth century.

[1] N. E. Saul, *Knights and Esquires: The Gloucestershire Gentry in the Fourteenth Century*
(Oxford, 1981), 108–11.
[2] Ibid., 161–3.   [3] Above, pp. 111–14; Appendix 5.

Parliamentary Elections

Although elections had been held in English counties since at least 1194,[4] it was not until 1406 that the first statute relating to their conduct was promulgated. Before the statute of that year custom demanded that elections be held in the county court, the sheriff, as the returning officer, making his return by endorsing the names of those elected on the writ of parliamentary summons.[5] It was to impose some statutory check on the validity of these shrieval returns that the commons of the Long Parliament of 1406 petitioned, successfully requesting that from henceforward the return should be made in the form of an indenture drawn up between the sheriff, on the one hand, and the named electors, who were to append their seals to the same, on the other.[6] The statute enacted as a result of this petition was the first of a series concerning parliamentary elections enacted during the early fifteenth century: in 1410 a statutory fine of £100 was introduced for sheriffs who failed to observe the provisions of the 1406 statute; in 1413 a residence qualification was laid down for electors and elected; and, most importantly, in the famous statute of 1429–30, the franchise was defined as freeholders worth 40s. per annum or more and elections were formally subjected to the majority rule.[7]

It is from the indentures to which the 1406 statute gave rise that much of our knowledge of fifteenth-century elections is derived. For Nottinghamshire these survive for 31 of the 37 parliaments that met between October 1407 and October 1460.[8] Generally they name only the more important of the county electors followed by a statement that others unnamed had also participated in the election. Only rarely do they give what appears to be an exhaustive list of those present.[9] The Nottinghamshire indenture of October 1449 lists 223 names, that of October

---

[4] R. F. Hunnisett, *The Medieval Coroner* (Cambridge, 1961), i, 151.

[5] M. M. Taylor, 'Parliamentary Elections in Cambridgeshire, 1332–8', *BIHR* 18 (1940–1), 21–6. For early returns: *Parliamentary Writs and Writs of Military Summons*, ed. F. Palgrave (London, 1827–34), II. ii. 58 ff. The content of this paragraph and much of what follows is treated in detail in my article, 'The Widening Franchise: Parliamentary Elections in Lancastrian Nottinghamshire', in D. Williams (ed.), *England in the Fifteenth Century* (Woodbridge, 1987), 167–85.

[6] *RP*, iii. 601.

[7] *SR*, ii. 156, 162, 170, 243–4; *RP*, iii. 641; iv. 8, 350.

[8] For these indentures: Appendix 7.

[9] For a general discussion of election indentures: J. S. Roskell, *The Commons in the Parliament of 1422* (Manchester, 1954), 7–13.

1460, 266, and that of May 1467, as many as 362.[10] There can be little doubt that the listing of such a large number of attestors in an indenture indicates that the election it witnesses was contested: the form of the return of October 1460 makes it clear that there were four candidates for the two parliamentary seats, and a case in the exchequer of pleas shows that there were three candidates in May 1467. By returning so many attestors to the validity of his return, the sheriff gave himself additional security should one of the disappointed candidates choose to challenge his conduct of the election, as Sir Henry Pierpoint (d. 1499) did in 1467.[11]

As a corollary to this observation, the majority of indentures, which simply list a couple of dozen or so of the more prominent electors, suggest that the elections they attested went uncontested. Indeed, some of these short indentures explicitly state that the elections they witnessed were made '*ex unanimi assensu*',[12] and that of December 1441 goes so far as to state that the ten named electors had simply consented to the election: '*in pleno comitatu predicto et electioni predicto concensientes*'.[13] In other words, most elections were a matter of those assembled in the county court giving their assent to the only candidates: this would explain the lack of any recognizable electoral body (reflected in the rapid turnover of attestors from election to election and the high percentage who attested only one election) and perhaps also the infrequent attendance of the leading shire gentry at the elections.[14] If what was transacted in the county court at election time was a simple witnessing of the electoral return into chancery, it is not surprising that the shire élite should generally have absented themselves. It was rare for more than two or three of the leading shire gentry to act as attestors in any one election, and for six out of the thirty-one documented Nottinghamshire elections none attested. Four of these occurred during Henry V's reign when representation itself intermittently fell into the hands of lesser men,[15] and, on the fifth occasion, the election of August 1427, the

---

[10] C219/15/7/66; 16/6/30; 17/1/83.

[11] E13/153, pleas before the barons, Trinity 7 E IV, rots. 15–16.

[12] Roskell is mistaken in dismissing this phrase as a formal echo of the phraseology of the writs for the writs make no mention of unanimous assent: Roskell, *The Commons*, 8.

[13] C219/15/2/65.

[14] Appendix 7. The printed indentures for Lancs. and Lincs. exhibit the same characteristics: Roskell, *The Knights of the Shire for the County Palatine of Lancaster, 1377–1460*, Chetham Society NS 96 (1937), 21–3, 206–27; A. Rogers, 'The Lincolnshire County Court in the Fifteenth Century', *Lincolnshire History and Archaeology* 1 (1966), 69–76.

[15] Above, p. 138.

sheriff, Sir Thomas Gresley of Drakelowe in Derbyshire, neglected to summon the suitors of the county court to the election.[16] Occasionally, however, the elections could be exceptionally well attended: on 27 September 1423 Sir John Zouche, Sir Nicholas Strelley, his son, Sir Robert, Sir Edmund Pierpoint, Sir Gervase Clifton, Simon Leek, and Robert Markham gathered at Nottingham to attest the return of Sir Thomas Chaworth and Sir Henry Pierpoint; while, nearly twenty-six years later, on 13 January 1449, the two knights of the shire of 1423, Sir Thomas Chaworth and Sir Henry Pierpoint, their sons William Chaworth and Henry Pierpoint, Sir Thomas Rempston, Thomas Nevill of Rolleston, William Babington, Robert Strelley, and Robert Clifton came together at the same place to attest the return of two lesser men, Richard Illingworth and John Roos.[17] There is no apparent reason why these two elections should have been so well attended for neither appears to have been contested, but the fact that such large gatherings of the leading gentry at the county court were rare suggests that the meetings of this court did not form a focus and meeting place for the leading gentry (even a contest was not guaranteed to bring out any more than a few of the greater men of the shire)[18] nor, judging from the rapid turnover of attestors, for the wider gentry and freeholder community of the shire.

The rarity of election contests explains why it was not until the parliament of 1429–30 that any statement of the majority rule was made and the franchise defined. But even after the statute enacted in that parliament, contests remained infrequent: it is probable that the shire aristocracies sought to avoid them because of the expense entailed in turning out a substantial proportion of the enfranchised voters[19] and, more importantly, the factional ill-feeling to which contests so often gave rise. Elections may have been informally pre-arranged before the meeting of the county court. Such pre-arrangement was common in Elizabethan England and Sir L. B. Namier has suggested that in the

---

[16] C219/13/5/75; Roskell, *The Commons*, 15–16.

[17] C219/13/2/67; 15/6/71.

[18] The probable contest of October 1449 was attested by only Sir Henry Pierpoint and John Stanhope, who was himself returned, amongst the leading men of the shire: C219/15/7/66. The contests of October 1460 and May 1467 were better attended by the leading men but several were absent: C219/16/6/30; 17/1/83. This reluctance to attend contests may have been due to a general desire to avoid being drawn into the disputes they often entailed.

[19] In the second half of the 18th c. the chief objection to contests was their expense, and it may be legitimate to project this back into the 15th c.: L. B. Namier and J. Brooke, *The House of Commons, 1754–1790*, 3 vols. (London, 1964), i. 4.

eighteenth century candidates were often agreed, 'at the Assizes or local races'.[20] The need to avoid contests was probably even greater in the fifteenth century for such contests frequently gave expression to factional feuding. It was not uncommon for one of the contesting parties to bring a large band of armed followers to the county court to prevent a lawful election and force the returning officer to make a fraudulent return, as happened, for instance, at the Suffolk election of February 1453.[21] In such circumstances it was natural that, in counties free from faction, uncontested elections should have prevailed. In the absence of private correspondence, how such elections were arranged must remain a matter for speculation. It is possible that the sheriff, as the official responsible for the conduct of the election, would take it upon himself to canvass the opinion of the leading men of the shire, so arriving at a generally acceptable nomination. Whatever the truth of this, it is clear that the mass of the forty-shilling freeholders were only rarely called upon to exercise their vote in the county court. Little evidence survives about how contests were conducted: probably they were first adjudicated by the acclamation of the assembled electorate, either by hands or voices, and that it was only when it was not immediately apparent which of the candidates had the greater support that a formal vote was taken. Such polls would hence have been even rarer than contests, and it is not therefore surprising that no fifteenth-century county poll list has yet been discovered. However, there is strong reason to believe that, although not so designated, the unique Nottinghamshire indenture of October 1460 is the transcript of such a list.[22]

Its uniqueness lies, first, in the fact that the attestors are not listed in order of rank, as they are in all previous indentures, and, second, in the considerable duplication of names. There are 414 entries representing only 266 different attestors. Aside from these peculiarities the form of the return is normal: it is an indenture drawn up between the sheriff, Robert Clifton, on the one part, and the attestors on the other, witnessing the election of Sir Robert Strelley and John Stanhope to represent the county in parliament with full and sufficient power to bind the

[20] J. E. Neale, *The Elizabethan House of Commons* (London, 1949), 69–70; L. B. Namier, *The Structure of Politics at the Accession of George III*, 2nd edn. (London, 1957), 65.

[21] R. Virgoe, 'Three Suffolk Parliamentary Elections of the Mid-Fifteenth Century', *BIHR* 39 (1966), 188–91, 194–6. For further examples of the violent disruption of elections: C. H. Williams, 'A Norfolk Parliamentary Election, 1461', *EHR* 40 (1925), 79–86; Virgoe, 'The Cambridgeshire Election of 1439', *BIHR* 46 (1973), 95–101; Carpenter, 'The Beauchamp Affinity', *EHR* 95 (1980), 528–9.

[22] C219/16/6/30.

community to whatever may be done there. No indication is given that some of the attestors had voted for others than those eventually returned, and yet this appears to have been precisely what happened. It would seem that the sheriff's clerk, when drawing up the indenture for return into chancery, had simply copied a poll list drawn up at the election. The attestors can be divided into four distinct sections, the names in each of which are in approximate order of rank but are strung together without any indication that they were intended to be separate: first come fifty-seven names headed by the esquire, Richard Sutton of Averham; second, 161 names, headed by recently knighted Sir Robert Strelley; third, forty-five names, headed by the lawyer, William Babington; and, finally, 151 names headed by John Stanhope. It is this last section which so strongly indicates that the names of the attestors were drawn from the record of a poll. As many as 139 of the 150 names that follow that of Stanhope are common to the second section headed by Strelley. Since work on borough elections and later county elections has shown that, in a contest, each elector was able to register two votes[23] there can be little doubt that these 139 names represent the electors who voted for the two successful candidates, Strelley and Stanhope. If this is the case then the first and third sections, which contain no names common to the second and fourth, must represent the electors who voted for the two un-successful candidates, Sutton and Babington. In short, there were, in modern parlance, two separate 'tickets': the one enjoying support that was both numerous and well co-ordinated, with 93 per cent of those voting for Stanhope also supporting Strelley; the other, although favoured by some wealthy men, enjoying support less numerous and much less well co-ordinated, with only 16 per cent of Sutton's electors also voting for Babington.

Some clue to why the election ended as it did can be found in the names of the listed attestors. An examination of the income and geographical distribution of those attestors who can be identified (see Table 6.1)[24] reveals that the election was decided by the large number of small freeholders that came down from the wapentake of Bassetlaw, the largest and most northerly of the Nottinghamshire wapentakes and the very region in which Stanhope's considerable estates were concentrated, to

---

[23] A. Rogers, 'Parliamentary Elections in Grimsby in the Fifteenth Century', *BIHR* 42 (1969), 212–20; D. Hirst, *The Representative of the People? Voters and Voting in England under the Early Stuarts* (Cambridge, 1975), 20.

[24] Of the 262 attestors, excluding the 4 candidates, 125 can be identified by place, largely from the 1451 tax returns, but also from the plea rolls of both benches and inquisition *post mortem* jury lists.

TABLE 6.1. *Distribution of attestors, October 1460*

Wapentake	Candidate			
	Strelley	Stanhope	Sutton	Babington
Bassetlaw:				
South Clay	21	22	3	1
North Clay	17	17	3	2
Hatfield	8	7	4	1
Broxtow	6	11	5	15
Thurgarton	3	4	6	7
Newark	2	2	7	3
Bingham	0	1	4	2
Rushcliffe	1	1	0	3

support Stanhope and Strelley. Of the fifty-seven attestors who voted for both men and whose place of residence can be identified, no fewer than forty-five came from this wapentake,[25] and it is clear that many of these were Stanhope's neighbours and perhaps his tenants. It is particularly significant that seven of them appear amongst a group of men to whom he is alleged to have illegally given livery of cloth in January 1450. Moreover, there is a significant overlap between the electors of October 1460 and those of October 1449, the first occasion on which he was returned in what appears to have been a contested election. Many small freeholders from the north of the county, such as Robert Norrys of Clayworth, John Acton of Dunham, and others are to be found as attestors in only these two returns.[26] Furthermore, an examination of the geographical distribution of the attestors of October 1449 again shows that a very high proportion came from the north of the county: of the 109 electors who can be identified by place, sixty-two came from Bassetlaw, with as many as thirty-five of these from the South Clay division of that wapentake, in which lay the bulk of Stanhope's estates. It is significant

[25] These figures and those below modify those given in Payling, 'The Widening Franchise', 183, by the addition of places of residence from the interesting suit of Michaelmas term 1451, in which Sir John Talbot (d. 1460), later earl of Shrewsbury, accused Stanhope of having at Rampton on 20 Jan. 1450 illegally given livery of cloth of 24 local tradesmen against the statute of 1 Hen. IV, c. 7: CP40/763, rot. 483^d; 769, rot. 138.

[26] The attestors of October 1449 also include 7 of those to whom Stanhope allegedly gave livery 3 months later. John Reyner of East Drayton, yeoman, is the only one of these to appear as an attestor in 1460.

that these northern freeholders are not to be found at elections in which Stanhope was not returned. In the election of June 1455, which saw the return of Richard Illingworth and John Wastnes, only four of the twenty-seven attestors who can be identified by place came from Bassetlaw. Clearly Stanhope wielded a considerable amount of electoral influence, the mobilization of which was liable to ensure that he would prevail in a contest, as he did in October 1449, October 1460, and May 1467. His prosecution in Michaelmas 1451 for illegally distributing livery of cloth suggests that such distribution was the means by which he ensured that this mobilization could be affected. Conversely, his fellow successful candidate in October 1460, Sir Robert Strelley, whose estates were concentrated just to the north-west of Nottingham in the southern part of Broxtow wapentake,[27] was unable or unwilling to organize support amongst his own neighbours. Only six of the fifty-three electors who voted for both him and Stanhope and can be identified by place came from this wapentake. In other words, it was the support of Stanhope's neighbours for Strelley that resulted in Strelley's return, and it must therefore have been Stanhope who engineered it. The fact that they were first cousins may explain why he was prepared to do so.[28]

What of the most important of the defeated candidates, William Babington? There can be no doubt that those supporting him were of a generally higher social status than those supporting his opponents. A rough guide to the respective social status of each body of electors can be gained by comparing the indenture with the taxation returns of 1451. Only 22 per cent of Strelley's 160 electors appear in the taxation returns; only 25 per cent of Stanhope's 150; only 29 per cent of Sutton's fifty-six; but as much as 50 per cent of Babington's forty-four.[29] A comparison between the individual attestors supports the impression given by these statistics. Babington counted amongst his leading supporters: Richard Willoughby of Wollaton; Richard Bingham, the son of Willoughby's step-father, Richard Bingham, JKB; and two active local JPs, Thomas Nevill of Darlton and Thomas Curson of Bulcote. These men were of a higher rank than the leading supporters of Stanhope and Strelley: William Middleton of Girton; Stanhope's uncle, Thomas Stanhope of Haughton; and George Clay of Finningley.[30] Nevertheless,

---

[27] Above, p. 20.
[28] Strelley's mother, Agnes (d. 1421), was Stanhope's aunt: above, p. 83.
[29] E179/159/84.
[30] For Middleton: Payling, p. 296. For Thomas Stanhope: above pp. 70–1. George

the quality of Babington's voters was not matched by their quantity, and they were overwhelmed by the small freeholders Stanhope brought down from the north of the county.

The chief importance of this election lies in its demonstration of the potential importance of the small freeholder in the election process. Too much, however, should not be made of this. Not only were these freeholders only rarely called upon to exercise their electoral function, but when they were so called they must often have simply followed the lead of their immediate leading gentry neighbours, as the freeholders of Bassetlaw followed Stanhope in October 1449 and October 1460. Sir L. B. Namier remarked of the elections of the mid-eighteenth century that, even though the electorate was comparatively numerous, such was the dependence of the small freeholders on the greater men of the shire that they could seldom exercise a free choice in the event of an electoral contest.[31] What was true of the eighteenth century was probably even more true of the fifteenth. On the other hand, the small freeholders still had to be mobilized by the competing candidates: both Babington and Strelley failed to bring out their neighbours and tenants in the Nottinghamshire election of October 1460, effectively allowing the less wealthy Stanhope to determine the election's result.

Before leaving the subject of parliamentary elections something should be said on the question of non-resident electoral attestors. The statute of May 1413 had insisted that electors and elected should be resident in the county for which they were to act on the date of the writ of parliamentary summons.[32] There seems little reason to doubt that this was generally observed during the Lancastrian period with respect to parliamentary representatives even before this statute was enacted: the three Yorkshiremen who represented Nottinghamshire in parliament all had substantial estates in the county[33] while the one Nottinghamshire man, Sir Thomas Chaworth, who was returned for another county, representing Derbyshire in the parliament of May 1413, had extensive landholdings in that county with a residence there at Alfreton.[34] But it

Clay of Finningley, whose father George Clay (d. 1458) was assessed at £16 p.a. in 1451, was a descendant of Edmund Clay, chief justice of the common bench and then the king's bench in Ireland 1385–8: F. Elvington Ball, *The Judges in Ireland, 1221–1921*, 2 vols. (London, 1926), i. 157–8, 166.

[31] Namier, *The Structure*, 65.   [32] *SR*, ii. 170.
[33] Sir Robert Plumpton, his son, Sir William Plumpton, and Nicholas FitzWilliam: Payling, pp. 292–4.
[34] Sir Thomas Chaworth (d. 1347) made his will at Alfreton: *TE*, i. 47–9. Another Nottinghamshire MP, the lawyer John Bowes, was returned for London to the parliament of 1442 while recorder there: below, p. 176.

was Dr J. S. Roskell's opinion that the rule regarding residence of electors was probably not observed.[35] The Nottinghamshire evidence suggests that contraventions of this rule were few: of the 635 men who attested elections there between 1407 and 1460 only seven can be said not to have been permanently resident in the shire.[36] One of these was a serving sheriff, Sir Thomas Gresley of Drakelow, who headed the list of attestors to the Nottinghamshire election of October 1419, and a further three, Sir Robert Plumpton (an attestor in April 1412), Sir John Gra (an attestor in February 1426), and Sir John Byron (an attestor in January 1449 where he is wrongly named Thomas) held significant estates in the county.[37] The attestation of the other three, however, is less easy to justify. John Whichecote of Witchcott in Staton Lacy (Shropshire) and Harpswell (Lincolnshire) occurs sixth on the list of 223 attestors of October 1449. Like the two men returned, John Stanhope and Henry Boson, he was a household esquire, but more important in this context is his close connection with John (d. 1460), earl of Shrewsbury.[38] The election of June 1455 presents a similar aspect: amongst the 61 attestors witnessing the return of Richard Illingworth and John Wastnes were two Derbyshire men, Robert Eyre of Padley and John Statham of Horsley, the first a servant of Shrewsbury, and the second of Cromwell.[39] The attendance of these three men at Nottinghamshire elections, together with the return of Cromwell's servant, Richard Illingworth, to the parliaments of February 1447, February 1449, November 1450, and

[35] Roskell, *The Commons*, 15.

[36] I have excluded the substantial midland landholder, Sir Ralph Shirley, who attested 6 Notts. elections between Oct. 1411 and Mar. 1432 for he was resident at Ratcliffe-on-Soar before being disseised of that manor by Humphrey, earl of Stafford, in Michaelmas 1433: E. P. Shirley, *Stemmata Shirleiana* (London, 1873), 43, 388; above, p. 9.

[37] For Plumpton: above, p. 138. For Gra: above, p. 8. Sir John Byron of Clayton (Lancs.) held the Notts. manor of Over Colwick, where his grandson, another Sir John, settled in the reign of Edward IV: Thoroton, iii. 5; J. C. Wedgwood, *History of Parliament, 1439–1509* (HMSO, 1936–8), i. *Biographies*, 147.

[38] For his relationship with Shrewsbury: KB27/789, rot. 50; CCR, *1441–7*, 309; CPR, *1452–61*, 497, 502. For his household service: E101/409/6 (1446–7); 410/9 (1451–2). For his Salop lands: *FA*, iv. 268. He served as escheator in Salop in 1450–1 and as sheriff of Lincs. in 1465–6. He held his Lincs. estates in the right of his wife, Elizabeth, one of the daughters and coheiresses of John Tirwhit (d. 1430): C139/53/14.

[39] This was probably Robert Eyre (d. 1497), a feoffee of John, earl of Shrewsbury's Derby. manors in Mar. 1458 and later steward of George (d. 1538), earl of Shrewsbury, rather than his father, Robert Eyre (d. 1460): C139/179/58/19; R. Meredith, 'The Eyres of Hassop, 1470–1640', *Derbyshire Archaeological Journal* 84 (1964), 1–2. It seems that Shrewsbury engineered the younger Robert's return to the Coventry parliament of Nov. 1459: Wright, p. 115. For Statham's connections with Cromwell: below, p. 195. For Cromwell's particular interest in securing the return of his own men to this parliament: above, p. 144.

July 1455, show that magnate influence was a potential factor in the county's elections: yet, as shown in the previous chapter, this influence was not only rarely exerted but was dependent for its effectiveness on the co-operation of a substantial number of the leading men of the shire.[40]

The County Bench

During the fourteenth century the commons had attempted to win the right to nominate the local justices of the peace, or at least to secure the submission of the list of appointees to parliamentary scrutiny.[41] By the early fifteenth century, however, they had accepted the crown's right of appointment[42] and had turned their attention, as they had already with other local offices, to placing some statutory limitation on the crown's freedom of choice in its selection of appointees. In the parliament of November 1414 they gained the crown's assent to a petition that JPs should be chosen, '*des pluis suffisantz persones . . . demurantz deins mesmes les Countees*', excepting from this residence qualification only the justices of assize and the chief stewards of the duchy of Lancaster,[43] while a further statute, enacted in response to a commons petition of 1439–40, laid down that those appointed to the local benches were to have a minimum annual landed income of £20, the same qualification as had been laid down for sheriffs and escheators in 1368 and 1371.[44]

The crown issued new commissions of the peace frequently but irregularly. In 1426 a council ordinance determined that new commissions should be issued each year,[45] but this was not adhered to. There was no regularity about the issue of the forty-three commissions enrolled for Nottinghamshire during the Lancastrian period (some commissions were not enrolled but there is no evidence that these were any more than very few in number): for example, no commission was issued for the county between February 1407 and March 1413, and yet as many as thirteen commissions were issued between April 1454 and

[40] Above, pp. 146–7.
[41] Saul, *Gloucestershire*, 129–31.
[42] *Proceedings Before the Justices of the Peace in the Fourteenth and Fifteenth Centuries*, ed. B. H. Putnam (London, 1938), p. lxxvii.
[43] In enacting the statute the crown added the lords to this exemption: *RP*, iv. 51; *SR*. ii. 187.
[44] *RP*, v. 28; *SR*, ii. 309–10; above, p. 110.   [45] *PPC*, iii. 220.

December 1460. Nor was it the general practice, at least after the county commissions of July 1424, for new commissions to be issued at the same date for the country as a whole. Between November 1399 and July 1424 seven of the thirteen Nottinghamshire commissions enrolled were part of general revisions of the county commissions, but thereafter such general revisions fell out of fashion. It is clear that most new commissions were issued in response to a situation in a particular county or area; most often, one suspects, because of the need to appoint new justices to replace those who had died since the issue of the last commission. Very rarely can directly political motives be discerned, and, when they were in operation, they affected the lords commissioned rather than the local gentry who discharged the work of the commission. Occasionally an afforced commission may have been issued in response to some real or anticipated breakdown of order or to deal with the extra business arising from such a breakdown. The Nottinghamshire commission of February 1406 is a clear example: to the thirteen justices commissioned in November 1404 were added Robert Waterton of Methley (Yorkshire), one of the most trusted of Henry IV's servants, three professional lawyers from neighbouring counties, William Lodington, John Foljambe, and Thomas Tickhill,[46] and one further member of the local gentry, Alexander Mering. All five of these new additions were removed from the next commission of February 1407, and, since the same period saw a similar expansion and contraction of the East Riding commission, there seems little reason to doubt that the afforcing of the Nottinghamshire commission was intended to deal with the aftermath of Scrope's rebellion.

Composition of the Commission of the Peace

The personnel of the county commissions can be conveniently divided into five only partially overlapping categories: the first consisting of those whose appointment to the commission was simply honorific, who had no direct interest in county affairs and who could not be expected to

---

[46] For Lodington: Somerville, pp. 450, 453. For Tickhill: ibid., 453. John Foljambe of Derbys. was crier in the court of the marshalsea of the household in 1399 and foreign apposer of estreats in the exchequer 1406–7: *CPR, 1399–1401*, 80; *1405–8*, 213, 226. For Waterton: H. Armstrong Hall, 'Some Notes on the Personal and Family History of Robert Waterton, of Methley and Waterton', *The Publications of the Thoresby Society* 15 (1905–9), 81–102.

take an active part in the sessions, being simultaneously commissioned in several counties; the second, magnates with a landed stake in the county who may have been expected to sit but, in practice, rarely did; the third, the justices of assize, appointed from the central court justices and the serjeants-at-law, who were included *ex officio* on the commissions for all the counties of their circuit; the fourth, the local gentry, predominantly drawn from the leading county families and who, with very few exceptions, owed their appointment to their landed wealth; and fifth, men of legal training, also drawn from the local gentry, but who owed their appointment principally to their knowledge of the law rather than to their landed wealth. There was some overlap between the last two categories since a few of the lawyers of the *quorum* were very substantial men who could have commanded a place on the bench with or without their legal training, but it remains true that, for the most part, the *quorum* was composed of lesser men entitled to a place on the bench by their legal training alone. The ninety-two men commissioned in Nottinghamshire between 1399 and 1460 can be divided between these categories as follows: eleven, including the chief stewards of the north parts of the duchy of Lancaster, are to be accounted honorific members of the commission; a further seventeen were magnates with some landed interest in the county (some with a much greater interest than others); nine were justices of assize for the circuit of which the county was part; seventeen were local lawyers of the *quorum*; and another thirty-one were local gentry not of the *quorum* (in addition there were three non-resident lawyers, appointed to the exceptional commission of February 1406; one Yorkshire esquire, Robert Waterton of Methley; and three Derbyshire knights, Sir Hugh and Ralph Shirley, and Sir John Cokayn).[47]

With the exception of the chief stewards of the duchy of Lancaster, who since 1417 had appeared on the commissions for those counties in which the duchy held lands, honorific appointments to the county bench were not a regular or significant feature of the commission before the minority of Henry VI. This changed briefly and dramatically with the exceptional general commissions of July 1424,[48] which, in Nottinghamshire, saw the addition to the commission of Henry Chichele, archbishop of Canterbury, John Langdon, bishop of Rochester, Humphrey, duke of Gloucester, Humphrey, earl of Stafford, Sir Walter Hungerford, steward of the royal household, and William, Lord Clinton, all members

---

[47] The Notts. commissions of the peace and their members are tabulated in Payling, pp. 299–303.

[48] *Proceedings*, ed. Putnam, pp. xxvii, lxxxi–lxxxii.

of the royal council. While the number of magnates added in Notting-hamshire was exceptional, occasioning an increase in the number of commissioned justices from twelve to twenty-two, other counties were also affected: for example, the West Riding commission increased from twelve to nineteen, and that for Berkshire from eleven to fifteen.[49] Whatever the underlying cause of these additions (the royal councillors may have seen themselves as symbolically taking on greater responsibility for law and order in a time of royal minority), it seems that they were soon regretted. In July 1428 the council agreed that lords, '*tam de consilio quam alii*', should not sit on the county benches save in such emergencies as riot and forcible entry,[50] and many of the new magnate appointees were subsequently removed from the commissions. This suggests that their appointment may, in the first place, have been due to some real or anticipated breakdown in order; an emergency that had passed by 1428.

After the removal of Chichele and Langdon from the Nottinghamshire commission in July 1429, no ecclesiastic appears on the Nottingham-shire bench until John Kemp, archbishop of York, was appointed in April 1439. His addition to the commission was more than simply honorific for the archbishopric was one of the greatest landholders in the county, and thereafter Kemp, or his successor at York, William Bothe, appear on every county commission. Appointments that were merely honorific do not recur in Nottinghamshire until May 1454, during Richard, duke of York's first protectorate, when York and Richard, earl of Warwick, were added to the commission, and York with either Warwick or Richard, earl of Salisbury, continues to appear down to 1460, except on the commission of November 1459 issued during the Coventry parliament. There is no evidence that any of these men actually sat; their appointment, save in the case of the archbishops of York, being a reflection of national rather than local politics.

Of much greater significance was the appointment of those lay lords with a landed interest in the county. The heads of the four magnate families with a significant landed stake in the county, Cromwell, Grey of Codnor, Roos, and Talbot, were more or less automatically appointed to the bench unless disqualified by youth or, in the case of Henry (d. 1444), Lord Grey of Codnor, from 1439, personal disgrace,[51] but other lords with a less significant landed interest in the county also appear. Their appointment was a combination of national and local considerations for they often found their way on to the commission when highly placed at court. Henry (d. 1425), Lord FitzHugh of Ravensworth in north York-shire, whose Nottinghamshire lands were worth only some £20 per annum,[52] was appointed to the Nottinghamshire bench in February 1422, when chamberlain to Henry V, as part of the general afforcing of the county commissions. Later, in July 1424, John (d. 1455), Lord Scrope of Masham, was added to the commission with Chichele and other royal councillors. He held only one manor in the county,[53] but he had married a daughter of Sir Thomas Chaworth and was a member of the minority council. He continued to appear down to May 1436 when he disappeared from both the Nottinghamshire bench and the royal council. Another first appointed to the Nottinghamshire commission in July 1424 was Humphrey, earl of Stafford. His appointment at this date was honorific, a reflection of his position as a royal councillor, and he was removed with other honorific nominees in 1429. His reappearance on the Nottinghamshire bench in May 1436 and his continuous ap-pointment until his death in 1460 was the result of his acquisition from Sir Ralph Shirley in 1433 of the Nottinghamshire manors of Ratcliffe-on-Soar and Colston Basset.[54] The appointment of Queen Margaret's chamberlain, John, Viscount Beaumont, to the same bench from November 1458 until his death in July 1460 is to be seen in the context of both the favour in which he was held at court and his wardship of the Grey of Codnor lands.[55]

Every Nottinghamshire commission, except for those issued between November 1417 and July 1420 inclusive, had at least one, and often as many as four, lay magnates with a greater or lesser landed interest in the county. But it is clear that these men sat infrequently: in the 82 sittings for which the names of the attending justices are known, there are only two instances of a lay magnate attending.[56] On 12 January 1458 John, earl of Shrewsbury, sat at East Retford to hear indictments against Humphrey Bourchier and others for their forcible entry into three Nottinghamshire manors once of Ralph, Lord Cromwell. It was a matter of personal concern to the powerful Shrewsbury for he was one

[52] Appendix 1.

[53] *Notts. IPM, 1350–1436*, 163–4.

[54] In 1438 he also inherited the Notts. manor of Kneesall from his mother, Anne de Bohun: Thoroton, iii. 135.

[55] *CPR, 1446–52*, 519. In addition the Notts. manor of Stoke Bardolph was part of his son William's maternal inheritance: Thoroton, iii. 10.

[56] The names of the attending justices at 78 of these sittings are listed in Payling, pp. 304–9. The names of the justices sitting at a further 4 sessions can be found in KB9/222/1/44, 247/7, and 285/50.

of Cromwell's feoffees in the entered lands.[57] Indeed, it was probably
only such personal interest that could have moved a man of Shrewsbury's
prominence to sit on the county bench. In general, lay magnates had no
time for the mundane routine work that employed most of the local
justices' time.[58] Even a lesser magnate like Henry, Lord Grey of
Codnor, is rarely to be found amongst the active justices. Grey's only
recorded sitting in Nottinghamshire was at East Retford on 8 April 1434
when he sat with the deliberate intention of invalidating an indictment
drawn up against members of his affinity.[59] Nor did the justices of assize,
two of whom would be on the commission at any one time, often appear
at the sessions of the peace. Unlike the lay magnates, they were entitled
to payment for their attendance, and hence their names appear amongst
the payments recorded on the pipe roll. Only three such entries,
however, are recorded amongst the Nottinghamshire payments: Sir
John Cokayn, JCB, was paid for sitting on 2 March 1418,[60] and William
Ayscogh, JCB, and John Portington, JCB, were paid for each sitting on
one day between 1 October 1442 and 22 April 1444.[61] In addition,
Cokayn and James Strangways sat together at Nottingham on 27
February 1415,[62] and Cokayn alone on 4 March 1420.[63] Since the assize
justices would generally only sit when the taking of the county assizes
corresponded with a meeting of the bench, as happened, for example, in
February 1415,[64] their sittings must perforce have been rare; the more
so after the quarter sessions' dates were changed by the statute of
1414.[65]

The appointment of magnates and assize justices who would take
little or no active part in the sessions meant that it was the local gentry

---

[57] Above, p. 99.   [58] Wright, p. 95.   [59] Below, p. 189.
[60] E370/160/3/22ᵈ; E372/265, Notᵈ.
[61] E372/289, Item Not.   [62] KB9/207/2/38.
[63] Just. 3/195, rot. 41. He was not paid for sitting on this day and hence it is possible that
it was not an ordinary sitting of the bench at which indictments were heard but rather the
simple taking of a mainprise before a local justice.
[64] The assizes had been taken on 26 Feb. and the two justices of assize sat as JPs the
following day: Just. 1/1524, rot. 12; KB9/207/2/38; below, pp. 189–90 n. 17.
[65] The assize justices came to Nottingham twice a year, in late Feb. around the Feast of
St Matthias the Apostle and in late July around the Feast of St James the Apostle. Before
the statute of 1414 (2 Hen. V, st. 1, c. 4) the second quarter session of the year, held in the
second week in Lent under the earlier statute of 1362 (36 Edw. III, st. 1, c. 12),
corresponded with the Feb. coming of the assize justices whenever Easter fell in late Mar.
or early Apr., but, after 1414, when the second quarter session was moved to the final week
after the close of Easter, no such correspondence occurred. For the dates of the Notts.
assizes: Just. 1/1514, rots. 72–86 (27 Feb. 1400 to 27 July 1411); 1524, rots. 8–14 (25 July
1412 to 27 July 1422); 1537, rots. 2, 12–18 (1 Mar. 1423 to 25 July 1429). No further
assize rolls survive for the period.

who bore the burden of service. The number of gentry commissioned varied from commission to commission with a tendency to increase as the Lancastrian period progressed.[66] The commission of November 1399 consisted of three local magnates, two justices of assize, and seven local gentry, three of the latter and the assize justices forming the *quorum*. By the 1440s the number of commissioned gentry had increased: the commission of March 1449, for example, consisted of four magnates, the two assize justices and eleven local gentry. In May 1457 as many as thirteen local gentry were commissioned, six of whom were appointed to the *quorum*. Nevertheless, even allowing for this increase, in any one commission there would be a number of wealthy county gentry omitted (although over a lengthy period all the leading families would be represented). After the death of Sir John Markham, JCB, in 1409, no Markham appears on the bench until his grandson, Sir Robert Markham (d. 1495), was appointed in February 1462, while the wealthy and well-connected Thomas Nevill of Rolleston had been at the head of his family for over thirty years before he was belatedly appointed to the local bench in June 1454. Since neither Sir Robert Markham (d. 1446) nor Thomas Nevill of Rolleston were very active in local government, neither serving in parliament although both acted once as sheriff, their omission may have been a matter of their own personal choice. But one wonders if the same was true of Sir John Zouche of Kirklington, who represented the county five times in parliament and was a regular member of *ad hoc* commissions of local government. He appeared only briefly on the bench from 1427 and 1431 and is not named on any peace commission enrolled on the patent roll.[67] Other wealthy men found longer but only intermittent employment on the bench: Sir Nicholas Strelley (d. 1430) served from 1407 to 1416 and then from 1420 to 1423, and Sir Gervase Clifton from 1422 to 1423 and later from 1436 until his death in 1453. It is impossible to determine what lay behind such omissions, although for others the reasons are clear. Sir Thomas Rempston (d. 1458) did not appear on the commission until 1449 because of his lengthy service in France; Sir Richard Stanhope was excluded from 1407 to 1417 because of his extensive involvement in local disorders; and Sir Henry Pierpoint (d. 1452) was not reappointed

---

[66] For a discussion of the increasing size of the commissions throughout the 15th c.: Wright, pp. 95–6.
[67] He was paid for 6 days between 30 Sept. 1427 and 5 Oct. 1431: E372/275, rot. 36^d; 277, rot. 29. He is the only man known to have sat as a JP who is not to be found on any of the patent roll commissions.

after 1429 because of his dispute with Cromwell over the Heriz inheritance.[68] It seems that, with few exceptions, the head of a leading family was excluded from the bench only if he had no wish to serve or if he was disqualified by minority, absence from the county, or some other cause. It is certainly true that the thirteen families which formed the county élite provided most of the JPs not appointed to the *quorum*: sixteen of the thirty-one non-*quorum* gentry JPs came from these families, twelve of which provided at least one JP during the Lancastrian period (the exception was the Cressys of Hodsock, who died out as early as 1408 after providing JPs in the fourteenth century).

All of the non-*quorum* local gentry appointed to the commission could be expected to play an active role in the sessions. Indeed, it was very rare for a commissioned gentry JP not to sit on at least a few occasions during the period of his commission, although this is not to say that the burden of labour was evenly divided, even amongst the non-*quorum* gentry members of the commission. Some were much more active than others. For example, between September 1440 and April 1442, Sir Thomas Chaworth attended on twelve of the eighteen days on which the justices met, while his fellow knight, Sir Hugh Willoughby, attended only twice.[69] Such examples could be multiplied. These varying levels of activity are partly to be explained by the fact that certain justices, in particular those from the north of the county, confined their activity to the vicinity of their estates. The most easily illustrated example is that of Sir Gervase Clifton of Hodsock. Briefly commissioned as a JP in 1422–3, it was not until 1436, when he moved from Clifton near Nottingham to Hodsock in the far north of the county, that he commanded a regular place on the commission. Of the thirteen days between July 1437 and July 1448 for which the place of his sitting is known, as many as nine were at East Retford, two at Blyth, one at Wellow, and only one at Nottingham in the south of the county. The records of payments suggest that he attended nearly all the northern meetings, where he was most frequently to be found sitting with only his neighbour, Richard Wentworth of Everton, a lawyer of the *quorum*. It is probably significant that his reappointment to the bench in 1436 coincided not only with his move to Hodsock, but also with the death of Sir Richard Stanhope of Rampton, for more than thirty years the dominant landholder in the north of the county. It seems likely that, from his restoration to the bench in November 1417, it was Stanhope who had been the principal

[68] Payling, 'Inheritance and Local Politics in the Later Middle Ages', *NMS* 30 (1986), 78–9.   [69] E372/287, Item Not^d; 289, Item Not.; E199/91/36A/26.

justice of the northern meetings. The record of payments, with Stanhope being paid for between one-quarter and one-third of the days on
which the justices met, certainly supports this hypothesis.[70]

Nevertheless, although the local gentry appointed to the commission
did not ignore their responsibilities as JPs, the bulk of the work fell on
those men of legal training appointed to the *quorum*.[71] Between 1400
and 1461 the total number of days for which individual members of the
quorum are recorded as having been paid represented a little over half
the total number of days for which the county JPs were paid (619 out of
1,118).[72] The number of *quorate* on which this burden fell varied from
commission to commission, increasing as a greater number of local
gentry were commissioned. In November 1399 the *quorum* consisted of
the two assize justices, automatically appointed to the *quorum* of all the
county commissions within their circuit, and three local gentry, Sir John
Markham, CJB, William Babington, and William Rempston. Markham's
position as a justice of the common pleas meant that the burden of work
effectively fell on Babington and Rempston. By the end of Henry IV's
reign the situation was even less satisfactory: from Markham's death in
December 1409 until Thomas Hunte of Linby's appointment to the
commission in about February 1416,[73] Babington was the only working
member of the *quorum* and, as such, was bound to attend every meeting
of the JPs. Such a situation was not only unfair to him, particularly after
his appointment as king's attorney in the court of common pleas in
January 1414, but was hardly conducive to the effective functioning of
the commission. The increasing size of the *quorum* as the Lancastrian
period progressed may have been designed to spread the burden of
labour more evenly amongst those appointed. Throughout the 1430s it
consisted of four local gentry (in addition to the two assize justices):
Richard Bingham, John Bowes, Richard Wentworth, and William
Babington, by then a knight and chief justice of the common pleas. As

[70] All payments to the JPs are tabulated in Payling, pp. 310–14.

[71] The names of those justices commissioned to the *quorum* are enrolled on the
chancery patent rolls (C66) and the exchequer originalia rolls (E371). They are listed in
Payling, pp. 299–303.   [72] See the table in Payling, p. 223.

[73] Hunte (d. 1428) does not appear on the enrolled commissions until Nov. 1416, and
yet he sat as a JP as early as 28 Feb. 1416: E370/160/3/22^d. From his appointment in
*c.*1416 until John Bowes became an active member of the *quorum* in 1424, Hunte assumed
Babington's heavy workload. Between Aug. 1418 and July 1424 he sat on 39 of the 41 days
on which the justices met (compared with Babington's 6 and Bowes's 2). Earlier in his
career he had been clerk of the pleas in the exchequer, an office he held from 1395 to
1419: *Officers of the Exchequer*, comp. J. C. Sainty, List and Index Society, Special Series,
18 (1983), 95. In 1418 he was seneschal of the royal court at Mansfield: BL, Add. Ch.
57735.

chief justice, Babington played no very active role on the commission until after his retirement from that post in February 1436, but a clear division of labour existed between the other three. Wentworth, resident at Everton in the far north of the county, was responsible for attending the northern meetings of the justices, while Bingham and Bowes attended the Nottingham and Newark meetings either singly or, more often, together. From Babington's retirement until Bowes departure from the county to take up the recordership of London in July 1440,[74] there were, for the first time, four active *quorum* justices, and this figure was maintained until the mid-1440s with the addition of Babington's son and heir apparent, another William, to take over the absent Bowes's workload. The promotion of Bingham to a seat on the king's bench in 1445, and the deaths of Bowes in 1444 and Wentworth in 1448, occasioned a re-ordering of the *quorum*: William Nevill of South Leverton, a lawyer from the north of the county, was appointed to take over the northern meetings from Wentworth, while Richard Willoughby, the son and heir apparent of the wealthy Sir Hugh Willoughby, was added to share the work of the two Babingtons in the south of the county. No further change occurred on the *quorum* until Sir William Babington's death in 1454, after a continuous service of more than fifty years on the county bench, resulted in the addition of his younger son, Thomas, later recorder of the borough of Nottingham,[75] thereby maintaining a working *quorum* of four. This was increased to five in December 1455 with the addition of Thomas Nevill of Darlton, the son and heir-apparent of William Nevill of South Leverton; there were now, for the first time, two *quorum* justices based in the north of the county. By the Yorkist commission of December 1460, however, the *quorum* had been reduced to only three local gentry, including Bingham: William Nevill had not been reappointed to the commission after July 1458, Richard Willoughby was disqualified by his service as sheriff, and William Babington, although commissioned, was not named on the *quorum*. This reduction proved temporary and does not disguise the general trend: namely that, as the number of local gentry commissioned increased, so too did the number appointed to the *quorum*. It was a trend only in its infancy during the Lancastrian period.[76]

[74] For Bowes's career: Roskell, 'John Bowes of Costock', *TTS* 60 (1956), 8–19.

[75] He is first to be found acting in this office in Dec. 1463: *Records of the Borough of Nottingham, 1155–1702*, ed. W. H. Stevenson (London etc., 1882–1900), ii. 425.

[76] For the substantial increase in the size of the commission, and the *quorum* within it, during the 16th c.: M. L. Zell, 'Early Tudor JPs at Work', *Archaeologia Cantiana* 93 (1977), 125–43.

The personnel of the *quorum* was varied: on the one hand there were the successful career lawyers who rose to a place on the bench of the central courts (Lancastrian Nottinghamshire provides the examples of Sir John Markham, Sir William Babington, and Richard Bingham), and on the other, lawyers, sometimes from relatively minor local families, whose appointment to the county *quorum* marked the limit of their professional achievement.[77] And yet, for the most part, even the lesser men appointed to the *quorum* were not without some social significance in their own right. Some were younger sons of major county families, a legal training being an effective way of compensating for a want of expectations. William Rempston, active on the bench up to his death in *c.*1404, was a younger brother of Henry IV's intimate, Sir Thomas Rempston; William Nevill of South Leverton, who served on the *quorum* from 1444 to 1458, a younger brother of the wealthy Thomas Nevill of Rolleston; and Thomas Babington, a JP of the *quorum* from 1454 to 1461, a younger son of Chief Justice Babington. Others were wealthy men in their own right. Richard Willoughby and William Babington jun., who served together on the *quorum* from the 1440s right up to 1471, are obvious examples. Another is Richard Wentworth, who, from 1430 to his death in *c.*1448, was the *quorum* justice for the north of the county. He was a younger son of the south Yorkshire esquire, John Wentworth (d. *c.*1415) of North Elmsall, by Agnes, a sister and coheir of Sir William Dronsfeld (d. 1406) of West Bretton.[78] His mother settled on him her extensive Dronsfeld properties in south Yorkshire, namely the manors of West Bretton, Bulcliffe, and Cumberworth,[79] and Richard was able to add to these lands by marriage. His wife, Cecily, whom he married in the late 1440s, was one of the daughters and coheirs of the wealthy Nottingham merchant, John Tannesley (d. *c.*1418), and it was she who brought him the north Nottinghamshire manor of Everton.[80] As a result, he was assessed at as much as £65 per annum in the tax assessments of 1436.

[77] I have excluded from the discussion that follows not only the 3 non-resident lawyers appointed to the exceptional commission of Feb. 1406 but also Nicholas Coningston and Robert Staunton, both of whom were appointed to only one Notts. commission, and neither of whom is recorded as having sat. They were more concerned with affairs in neighbouring counties.

[78] J. Hunter, *South Yorkshire: The History and Topography of the Deanery of Doncaster* (London, 1828–31), ii. 453.

[79] Ibid., 243–5.

[80] In his will of 1414 Tannesley bequested Cecily 100 marks for her marriage and settled the remainder of one-third of his Nottingham properties on her and the heirs of her body after the death of his wife, Alice (d. 1439): Borthwick Institute, Arch. Reg. 18,

It is sometimes said that the lawyers of the *quorum* were exempt from the £20 per annum property qualification laid down by the statute of 18 Hen. VI, c. 11;[81] this is not the whole truth of the matter. The crown reserved the right to appoint lawyers with less than £20 per annum from land only if there was an insufficient number of lawyers, '*de bon governaunce*', who fulfilled the qualification.[82] It is clear that most of those appointed were worth more than £20 per annum: in addition to the wealthy lawyers mentioned above, John Bowes of Costock, a JP of the *quorum* from 1422 until his death in 1444, was assessed at £26 per annum in 1436; William Nevill of South Leverton at £20 per annum in 1451;[83] and William Saundby of Saundby, the northern justice of the *quorum* from 1404 to 1407, at £20 per annum in 1412. It may be, however, that some of those incomes assigned to lawyers in the tax returns were derived in part from fees rather than lands. Bowes, for example, was in receipt of 10 marks per annum from Henry, Lord Grey of Codnor, in 1436[84] and this, together with other fees, may account for his relatively high assessment since his landed resources were meagre.[85] Moreover, other lawyers of the *quorum* were certainly worth less than £20 per annum. William Clerk of Gedling, who served briefly on the *quorum* in 1429–30,[86] was assessed at as little as £5 per annum in 1436, while Richard Bingham, the future justice of the king's bench, was assessed at only £12 per annum in the same year. It is quite clear that some members of the *quorum* were, or at least started their careers as, men of slender landed resources. On the other hand, neither were they men of no traceable origins: their landed poverty was often the result, as in the cases of William Nevill, Thomas Babington, and Richard Bingham, of the misfortune of having been born younger sons or scions of younger branches of established families. In short, the lawyers of the *quorum* were, in terms of social rank, the most substantial men of legal training in the county. There were below them in the social scale many other local lawyers, such as those who served as clerks of the peace, as

---

fo. 368. Richard had married Cecily by Christmas 1429: *Yorkshire Deeds*, ed. W. Brown *et al.* (1905–55), vi, no. 507. For the manor of Everton: CP25(1)/186/39/13; NRO, DD MG 1/16; 1/18; 1/20.

[81] Wright, p. 94.
[82] *RP*, v. 28.
[83] He was assessed at only £15 p.a. in 1436.
[84] E163/7/31, pt. 1.
[85] For his landed inheritance: Roskell, 'John Bowes of Costock', 10–11.
[86] He was later, between 1435 and 1446, deputy to the clerk of the king's works at the royal hunting lodge at Clipstone (Notts.): *The History of the King's Works: The Middle Ages*, ed. H. M. Colvin (HMSO, 1963), ii. 921. He then served as one of the county coroners from *c.*1445 to *c.*1457: *CPR, 1446–52*, 48; KB9/290/10.

receivers of common law writs for the county sheriff, as attorneys for local knights in the common law courts, and as pleaders in the county court.[87]

The most interesting of the careers of the Nottinghamshire lawyers of the *quorum* is, with the exception of that of Chief Justice Babington, that of Richard Bingham. Although he was a descendant of the knightly family of Bingham, which died out in the main line towards the end of the fourteenth century, his own prospects at birth were very poor. His father, John Bingham, who represented the borough of Nottingham in the parliaments of March 1416 and December 1420, was the younger brother of Ralph Bingham, the head of a junior branch of the Binghams of Bingham that had become established at neighbouring Car Colston at about the same time as the senior line failed.[88] These Binghams of Car Colston were a good deal less wealthy than their fourteenth-century ancestors had been, and played only a subordinate, if active, role in local affairs: Ralph long held the office of county coroner, serving from *c.*1418 to *c.*1437, and John joined him in that office during the 1420s.[89] Nevertheless, from these relatively humble origins, with little or no landed inheritance to look forward to,[90] Richard's highly successful legal career enabled him to die a very wealthy man. The first reference to him comes in the Easter term of 1424 when he acted as a mainpernor in the court of king's bench for a Nottinghamshire husbandman.[91] Six years later in August 1430 he was appointed to the *quorum* of the county bench and in 1431–2 served a term as escheator. But it was not until over a decade later that real advance in the legal profession came his way: in February 1443 he was one of those ordered to take up the estate and degree of a serjeant-at-law, and two years later, in May 1445, he was promoted to a puisne justiceship of the king's bench.[92] Advance of another sort was soon to follow: after the death of Sir Hugh Willoughby

[87] For local attorneys in the central courts: J. H. Baker, 'The English Legal Profession, 1450–1550', in *The Legal Profession and the Common Law* (London etc., 1986), 84–8. For county court pleaders in the early 14th c.: R. C. Palmer, 'County Year Book Reports: The Professional Lawyer in the Medieval County Court', *EHR* 91 (1976), 776–801.

[88] Thoroton, i. 240. John was dead by Michaelmas 1434 when Richard was acting as his executor: CP40/695, rot. 149.

[89] *CCR, 1413–19*, 420, 473; *1435–41*, 89, 93; Just. 3/203, rot. 36; *CCR, 1422–9*, 441. Ralph was assessed at £13 p.a. in 1436.

[90] Richard's mother, Margaret, daughter and coheiress of Richard Wilford of Wilford, was a very minor heiress, who brought him lands at Wilford on her death sometime after 13 Dec. 1442: NUL, Cl. D 903.

[91] KB27/652, rex rot. 13[d]; *CCR, 1422–9*, 315. For a more detailed treatment of his career: Payling, pp. 229–31.

[92] *CCR, 1441–7*, 87; *CPR, 1441–6*, 343.

in November 1448, he married as his second wife[93] Hugh's very wealthy widow, the substantial heiress, Margaret Freville.[94] As a consequence of this marriage and his judicial rank, which he retained down to 1471, Richard was, during the last thirty years of his life, a man of substantial wealth, although those estates he held in his own right remained relatively meagre.[95]

His career is a striking example of the benefits of a legal career culminating in judicial appointment. Most of his fellow lawyers of the *quorum* did not aspire to such heights: they were amateurs whose appointment to the *quorum* marked the culmination of their legal careers. It was necessary that this should be so for, since the bulk of the work of the county bench fell to members of the *quorum*, it was important that the *quorum* should be principally composed of men permanently resident in their counties and not of men whose legal practices kept them in London during the law terms. As a council ordinance of 1426 put it, since no session of the peace could be held without the presence of a member of the *quorum*, 'it semeth expedient that suche be ordeyned to be in the quorum as can and wol truely and duely laboure the said office on every behalf as the case requireth'.[96]

The Pattern of the Quarter Sessions

Evidence concerning the date and place of the sessions of the peace is to be drawn from a variety of disparate sources: indictments sent into king's bench under writs of *certiorari* and *terminari*, and subsequently enrolled on the plea roll of that court (KB9 and KB27);[97] the terminal dates recorded on the pipe roll between which the JPs were paid (E372);

[93] His first wife was Elena, the widow of William Wastnes (d. 1420) of Headon in north Notts.: CP25(1)/292/68/153.
[94] This marriage had taken place before Trinity term 1450 but not before 20 Feb. 1450: CP40/758, rot. 96[d]; 775, rot. 430. Richard had earlier acted as a feoffee for the Willoughbys: *CPR, 1429–36*, 462.
[95] He died in May 1476. For his colourless will: NUL, Mi. 5/168/53. He purchased only two manors, both in his native Notts., that of Besthorpe Hall in Caunton in 1433 and that of Watnall Chaworth in 1440: Thoroton, iii. 140; CP25(1)/186/39/16; E326/5404; *CCR, 1441–7*, 29. The family he established through his issue by his first wife failed in the male line in the first half of the 16th c.: BL, Add. MS 6667, p. 590.
[96] *PPC*, iii. 220.
[97] The partial survival of the indictment files means that some enrolments have no corresponding indictments: on the other hand, some returned indictments have no enrolments, presumably because the defendants never appeared to answer.

the few surviving estreats of the fines and amercements made before the JPs;[98] the very occasional references in the gaol delivery rolls to specific meetings of the JPs (Just. 3); and, in one instance, the lengthy record enrolled on the plea roll of king's bench of a case before the JPs which was adjourned from session to session.[99] From these sources the dates of 140 sittings of the county JPs can be discovered, and the places of 73 (see Table 6.2).

TABLE 6.2. *Month, place, and day of the week of known meetings of the county justices*

Month		Place		Day of week	
January	26 (2)	Nottingham	31	Monday	41
February	5	East Retford	19	Tuesday	13
March	9	Newark	15	Wednesday	22
April	21 (1)	Southwell	3	Thursday	33
May	7 (2)	Wellow	3	Friday	8
June	3	Blyth	2	Saturday	23
July	24				
August	7				
September	17 (1)				
October	20				
November	1				
December	0				
TOTAL	140		73		140

Note: The figures in brackets indicate the number of these meetings held before the statute of 2 Hen. V, st. 1, c. 4.

An analysis of the meetings of the county justices shows that the statute of 2 Hen. V, st. 1, c. 4[100] made in the Leicester parliament of April 1414 was neither slavishly adhered to nor totally disregarded. This statute, which superseded an earlier and similar one of 1362,[101] had laid down that sessions be held four times a year: in the weeks following Michaelmas, Quasimodo, the Translation of St Thomas the Martyr,

[98] E370/160/3/22ᵈ (1 Aug. 1415 to 2 Apr. 1418); E137/36/1/1–2 (6 Oct. 1438 to 9 July 1439); E137/215/16 (Michaelmas 1447 to 11 July 1448: the first 3 entries are illegible); E101/122/18 (6 Oct. 1455 to 12 July 1456).
[99] KB27/656, rex rot. 20.
[100] *SR*, ii. 176–7; *RP*, iv. 20–1.   [101] *SR*, i. 374; *RP*, ii. 271.

and Epiphany, 'and more often if Need be'. The figure above indicates that most meetings of the county justices were held at or near these dates but that it was not uncommon for the justices to meet outside the quarter sessions,[102] including three occasions in June, the month of the hay harvest, and seven in August.[103]

A clearer idea of the pattern of the sessions is given by those years for which a complete list of the meetings of the county bench survives: for example, 1438–9.[104] The Michaelmas session was held in the first week after the Feast of St Michael: on Monday 6 October five justices, headed by Sir Thomas Chaworth and the recently retired CJCB, Sir William Babington, sat at Nottingham; on the following day, three of these justices, Chaworth, John Bowes, and Thomas Curson, travelled east to sit at Newark; and three days later, on Friday 10 October, the Michaelmas session was completed when two justices from the north of the county, Sir Gervase Clifton of Hodsock and Richard Wentworth of Everton, sat at Blyth. No further meetings of the bench took place until the following Epiphany session: the first meeting was held at Nottingham on Monday 12 January before an impressive array of six justices, again headed by Chaworth and Babington, but there then followed a delay of a fortnight before three of these six justices, Chaworth, Bowes, and Curson, sat at Newark on Wednesday 28 January. On the following day, Chaworth moved north to Wellow, where he sat with Clifton, Wentworth, and Bowes, to close the session. The next meeting of the bench was the first of the Easter session at Nottingham on Monday after Quasimodo, 13 April, before five of the six justices that had convened there three months earlier, together with Sir Hugh Willoughby. Two days later, on Wednesday 15 April, two of these justices, Bowes and Curson, sat at Newark and, on the following Saturday, Curson sat with the northern justices, Clifton and Wentworth, at East Retford. Finally came the summer session: six justices, headed by Chaworth, Babington, and Willoughby, sat at Nottingham on Monday after the Translation of St Thomas the Martyr, 13 July; four of the six, Chaworth, Bowes, Cokfeld, and Curson, moved on to Newark to sit there on the following Wednesday; while on Thursday, Clifton, Wentworth, and Cokfeld brought the session to a close at East Retford.

---

[102] For the same conclusion for East Anglia: P. C. Maddern, 'Violence, Crime and Public Disorder in East Anglia, 1422–1442', D.Phil. thesis (Oxford, 1984), 119.

[103] In 1343 the commons had petitioned that no sessions should be held in Aug. and the season of the hay harvest: *RP*, ii. 141.

[104] E137/36/1/1–2.

While the pattern of sessions was not always as regular as this (especially in the years immediately following the statute of 1414),[105] it is clear that the basic pattern of meetings of the bench was based on the quarter sessions even though the justices sometimes met outside them. Sittings were held three times within each session; first, at Nottingham, generally on the Monday following the relevant feast day, then at Newark (or, less frequently, Southwell), and finally at East Retford (or occasionally Blyth or Wellow) to deal with business in the north of the county. Each session was usually completed within a week but sometimes stretched over a longer period. A very similar system prevailed in Lindsey during the late fourteenth century and in Norfolk and Suffolk during the sixteenth century, although in other counties each quarter session was held in a different town rather than adjourned from place to place within each session.[106]

How many, on average, of the commissioned justices attended any particular sitting of the county bench? The two methods of approach to the available evidence give a similar answer. The simplest and most obvious method is to calculate the average attendance of the seventy-nine sittings for which the names of all the sitting justices are known. This gives an average of 3.23 justices per sitting, the minimum number being two and the maximum seven (see Table 6.3).

TABLE 6.3. *Number of JPs present at each recorded sitting*

No. present	No. of times
2	31
3	22
4	14
5	4
6	5
7	3

[105] The pattern of meetings in 1415–18 was most irregular, very few sittings being held in the statutory periods and no identifiable quarter sessions on the later pattern: E370/160/3/22^d.

[106] *Records of Some Sessions of the Peace in Lincolnshire, 1381–1396*, ed. E. G. Kimball, i. Lincoln Record Society, 49 (1955 for 1953), pp. xxxiii, lxvi; A. Hassell Smith, *County and Court: Government and Politics in Norfolk, 1558–1603* (Oxford, 1974), 88–9. D. MacCullough, *Suffolk and the Tudors: Politics and Religion in an English County, 1500–1600* (Oxford, 1986), 22–3.

An alternative and more comprehensive method, making use of the payments recorded on the pipe roll, is to divide the total number of days for which the justices were paid by the total number of days for which their clerk was paid.[107] This gives an overall average for the period 1400 to 1461 of 3.13, although it was an average that had a tendency to fluctuate significantly over time, reaching a peak of 5.12 between October 1442 and April 1444, and a trough of 2.00 between January and August 1452.[108] Nor was the average attendance the same for the three main meeting places of the bench. Sittings held at Nottingham were the best attended, with an average attendance as high as 4.13, and those at East Retford the worst, with an average of 2.50. There can be no doubt that it was the Nottingham sittings, with which the quarter sessions opened, that were the most important; all eight of the recorded sittings at which six or more of the county justices were present being held there. By contrast, there were rarely more than two justices at the northern sittings, usually held at East Retford.

This study of the workings of the county's parliamentary elections and sessions of the peace demonstrates two things. First, neither the meetings of the justices of the peace, even when held at Nottingham, nor the elections held in the county court,[109] served as regular communal meetings for the leading shire gentry. While both occasions could be well attended, as were most notably the elections of September 1423 and January 1449, and less notably the peace sessions of 6 October 1455, 12 July 1456, and 10 October 1457,[110] much more frequently only one or two of the leading gentry were present. Second, during the Lancastrian period, the commons secured the completion of the statutory embodiment of their view of the nature of local administration and representation, and these statutes were generally observed: local administration, justice, and representation were now firmly in the hands of

---

[107] This method rests on the assumption that the clerk attended all the meetings of the county justices. Putnam believed that the clerk only sat at quarter sessions (*Proceedings*, ed. Putnam, p. xcvi) but the Notts. evidence suggests that the justices very rarely met in his absence. All the meetings recorded in the estreats of fines listed above were held in his presence. The only Notts. meeting from which he is known to have been absent was held on either 7 Oct. 1445 or 12 Jan. 1446: E101/581/7/7; E372/292, Item Not.

[108] See the table in Payling, p. 314.

[109] All these elections were held at Nottingham except that of 20 Oct. 1449, which was held at Newark: C219/15/7/66.

[110] All were attended by 7 JPs: KB9/280/47; E101/122/18; KB9/285/50.

the leading resident county gentry.[111] It was they who transacted the business of the county bench with the assistance of the most prominent county lawyers, and it was they who dominated the county's elections, although often absent in person, and consequently the representation of the county in parliament. As Dr Saul has observed, during the fourteenth century the leading gentry had, in terms of office-holding, become increasingly identified with their county of residence. No longer did they hold office in a number of counties in which they held lands: their local administrative activities were increasingly circumscribed by the boundaries of the county or bailiwick in which they resided. Of the twenty-seven Nottinghamshire men who held the joint shrievalty of Nottinghamshire and Derbyshire during the Lancastrian period, only four either held office in, or represented, another county. Two of these exceptions are readily explained: Thomas Staunton owed his election for Leicestershire to the parliament of February 1447 to his household service;[112] while Thomas Darcy was appointed to the Lincolnshire shrievalty in 1433–4 and the Holland bench in 1440 through the patronage of Ralph, Lord Cromwell.[113] Only the two wealthiest Nottinghamshire men, Sir Thomas Chaworth and Sir Hugh Willoughby, held office outside the county by virtue of their extensive estates alone: Chaworth, early in his lengthy career, represented Derbyshire in the parliament of May 1413 (later serving as a JP in that county from 1444 to 1458) and served as sheriff in Lincolnshire in 1408–9 and 1418–19; while Willoughby served as the Lincolnshire sheriff in 1438–9. It is significant that Chaworth, Willoughby, and Darcy all held the shrievalty of Lincolnshire, an office it was notoriously difficult to fill.[114] It is in this identity of the leading gentry with the administration of the shire of their residence that the clearest sense of the county as a community is seen.

---

[111] The unusual career of the interloper William Rigmayden was the product of exceptional circumstances: above, pp. 130–4.

[112] Above, pp. 153–4.

[113] Above, p. 141.

[114] Above, p. 151.

7

ARISTOCRATIC CRIME AND THE
REGULATION OF LOCAL CONFLICT

LATE-MEDIEVAL aristocratic disorder is no longer seen solely in
terms of the crown's inability to restrain the excesses of a lawless
aristocracy. Recent work has demonstrated a sophisticated appreciation
of the natural limitations of the judicial power of the crown and of the
role of extra-legal methods of dispute settlement in the regulation of
aristocratic conflict.[1] This is not, however, to deny that the disputes of
the leading men of the shires posed a genuine threat to public order. Not
only did these men have the resources to bring large groups of armed
men into the field to defeat or intimidate opponents but also the
responsibility delegated to them by the crown for the administration of
local justice provided them with the opportunity to abuse royal judicial
power in the furtherance of their own interests.[2] Moreover, the local
failings of the judicial system were overlaid by the inadequacies of the
central courts, which could neither resolve by verdict the civil suits that
came before them nor serve as a realistic deterrent to criminal activity.[3]
Inevitably this combination of ineffective central courts and the aristocratic domination of the judicial system at the local level resulted in the
politicization of justice with the result that shifts in the balance of power

[1] E. Powell, 'Arbitration and the Law in England in the Late Middle Ages', *TRHS* 33
(1983), 49–67; id., 'Settlement of Disputes by Arbitration in Fifteenth-Century England',
Law and History Review 2 (1984), 21–43.
[2] For particularly flagrant examples: P. C. Maddern, 'Violence, Crime and Public
Disorder in East Anglia, 1422–1442', D.Phil. thesis (Oxford, 1984), 210–39; Powell,
'Proceedings before the Justices of the Peace at Shrewsbury in 1414: A Supplement to the
Shrewsbury Peace Roll', *EHR* 99 (1984), 535–50.
[3] For the very low verdict rate in personal actions and the ineffectiveness of mesne
process: M. Blatcher, *The Court of King's Bench, 1450–1550* (London, 1978), 59, 63–89;
The Reports of Sir John Spelman, ed. J. H. Baker, 2 vols., Selden Society, 93, 94 (1976–7),
ii. 89–92; C. Rawcliffe, *The Staffords, Earls of Stafford and Duke of Buckingham, 1394–1521*
(Cambridge, 1978), 164–5, 173–4; Maddern, 'Violence, Crime and Public Disorder',
141–6; Powell, 'Arbitration and the Law', 51. Only 5 of 387 Nottinghamshire cases on the
plea side of the court of king's bench involving gentry or magnates as plaintiffs or
defendants reached verdict between 1399 and 1461: KB27/554–799. For the procedural
difficulties that hampered real actions during the period: D. W. Sutherland, *The Assize of
Novel Disseisin* (Oxford, 1973), 183–99.

at both central and local level had a profound effect on the results of disputes in the localities.[4] All this is familiar territory, and long ago led Sir W. S. Holdsworth to write of the period that the law was no longer a shield for the weak and oppressed—rather it was a sword for the unscrupulous.[5]

As far as this interpretation goes it is a correct one: the judicial machinery of the crown was quite incapable of imposing good order on an aristocracy frequently disposed to violence, and was periodically exploited as a weapon of faction. And yet to conclude from this that fifteenth-century society was one of unrestrained lawlessness and depravity is, according to the most recent interpretation of late-medieval violence, to misunderstand both the nature of that society and the place of royal justice within it. As Dr M. T. Clanchy has pointed out, good order in the medieval period ultimately depended not 'on law courts of any sort but on people's attitudes to their neighbours'.[6] Disorder was to be most effectively restrained not primarily through a punitive system of justice, which the crown lacked the resources to maintain at any acceptable level of impartiality, and which was hence a potentially fearsome weapon in the hands of those powerful and ruthless enough to exploit it, but through the reconciliation of those whose disputes threatened public order. In these circumstances the problem of maintaining public order was, from the crown's point of view, as much political as judicial.[7] Emphasis had to be laid on the restoration of social peace through reconciliation rather than through the punishment of those parties for past crimes against the king's peace.

Since aristocratic crime rarely lacked a coherent motive, being frequently the product of local conflict over property rights with the forcible entries and attendant riots this frequently entailed, it was not inappropriate that this should have been so.[8] But it was not the courts of

---

[4] A. Smith, 'Litigation and Politics: Sir John Fastolf's Defence of his English Property', in A. J. Pollard (ed.), *Property and Politics: Essays in Later Medieval English History* (Gloucester, 1984), 59–75; S. J. Payling, 'Inheritance and Local Politics in the Later Middle Ages', *NMS* 30 (1986), 67–96; A. Sinclair, 'The Great Berkeley Law-Suit Revisited, 1417–39', *Southern History* 9 (1987), 34–50.

[5] W. S. Holdsworth, *A History of English Law* (1922–38), 4th edn. (1936), ii. 416.

[6] M. T. Clanchy, 'Law, Government and Society in Medieval England', *History* 59 (1974), 78.

[7] Powell, 'Public Order and Law Enforcement in Shropshire and Staffordshire in the Early Fifteenth Century', D.Phil. thesis (Oxford, 1979), 332.

[8] J. G. Bellamy, *Criminal Law and Society in Late Medieval and Tudor England* (Gloucester, 1984), 69–71; N. E. Saul, *Scenes from Provincial Life* (Oxford, 1986), 91; G. L. Harriss, 'Introduction', in K. B. McFarlane, *England in the Fifteenth Century* (London, 1981), p. xx.

common law alone, even if they had been able to work effectively, that were the best vehicle for bringing about this reconciliation: the common law was an antagonistic process, verdict and judgment leading to complete victory or utter defeat for the litigant and leaving no room for that compromise wherein lay the best opportunity for lasting peace.[9] Instead, the modern stress, most cogently argued in the works of Dr E. Powell, is on extra-judicial arbitration as the most efficient means of dispute settlement. Although such extra-judicial solutions have been seen as an alternative to common law, their popularity depending on the paralysis and partiality of the royal courts, Powell has argued that an informal machinery of dispute settlement existed alongside the royal courts and was complementary to them rather than a testimony to their failure. He cites the prominence of common law justices as arbiters and the part played by justices of assize in encouraging arbitration in some of the civil suits that came before them, the collusive litigation often employed to confirm the terms of an award, and the use of legal action as a lever to prompt a reluctant opponent to submit to arbitration.[10] The aim of this chapter is to examine the involvement of the leading families of Lancastrian Nottinghamshire in local disorder against the background of this recent reinterpretation of late-medieval justice, examining the respective roles of the formal judicial machinery of the crown and informal methods of dispute settlement in restraining or forestalling violent conflict.[11]

Judicial records leave no doubt that the leading men of the shire, although not infrequently involved in illegal activities, were in general only occasionally involved in outright violence. Perhaps the most common forms taken by this illegality were intimidation, extortion, and other like interference in the due processes of royal justice, for which their tenure of local office gave them ample opportunity. In 1414, for example, Sir John Zouche was indicted for threatening a member of a coroner's jury who had opposed his will, and extorting forty shillings and a horse worth the same from him by way of recompense;[12] in 1440, juries sitting before

---

[9] *Civil Pleas of the Wiltshire Eyre, 1249*, ed. M. T. Clanchy, Wiltshire Record Society, 26 (1971), 11.

[10] Powell, 'Arbitration and the Law', 56–60, 62–3; id., 'Settlement of Disputes', 23, 38–41.

[11] This chapter is in part a revised and updated version of my article 'Law and Arbitration in Nottinghamshire, 1399–1461', which appeared in J. Rosenthal and C. Richmond (eds.), *People, Politics and Community in the Later Middle Ages* (Gloucester, 1987), 140–60.

[12] KB9/204/2/7.

the justices of the peace in Rutland and Kesteven accused Sir Hugh Willoughby of having several men falsely appealed of felony and extorting £29 13s. 4d. from them while he was serving as sheriff of Lincolnshire in the previous year;[13] and, again in 1440, a Nottinghamshire jury indicted Henry, Lord Grey of Codnor, for exploiting his position as a JP in the county to invalidate a felony indictment laid against members of his affinity.[14] More striking is the systematic intimidation practised by Sir Richard Stanhope in the north of the county during the latter part of the reign of Henry IV. Three petitions were presented against him in the Leicester parliament of April 1414. His neighbours, the king's tenants of Darlton and Ragnall, claimed that they dare not sue him '*pur doute de lour vies*', while one Oliver Billing of Whimpton Moor in Ragnall and his wife, Agnes Sewell, claimed that '*il est taunt doubtez deinz le dit Countee del commune pœple q'ils n'osent rienz dire ne faire encountre sa volunte et sa entent pur doute de estre batuz ou tuez ou de perdre lour biens*'.[15] Such overstated complaints were the common coin of such petitions, but in this case they are given some independent support by what is known of Stanhope's activities from other sources and his removal from the county bench in February 1407. As a result of these petitions he was committed to Kenilworth Castle since, in the view of the king and the lords in parliament, as '*un de les plus puissant et riotous persons du dit Countee*', the truth of the complaints laid against him could not be adequately investigated while he remained at large.[16]

With the great men of the county able to exercise such a malign influence over the functioning of royal justice at the local level, it is unlikely that the recorded crimes of this sector of society represent anything approaching the total extent of their criminal activity. The jurors serving before the justices of the peace, being predominantly drawn from the yeomanry and the lower reaches of gentry society, must often have been reluctant to indict their social superiors;[17] a fact that

[13] KB9/232/2/88; 235/49; 244/35; KB27/733, rex rot. 29.

[14] KB27/742, rex rot. 40^d.

[15] *RP*, iv. 29, 30.

[16] SC8/97/4081 (PRO 31/7/114 is a copy of this now only partially legible original; it is unclear why it escaped enrolment on the parliament roll). His imprisonment was brief for he was free by 23 June 1414 when he appeared in the court of king's bench at Shrewsbury to plead a pardon to indictments laid against him before the commissioners of enquiry: KB27/613, rex rot. 9^d.

[17] Saul, *Gloucestershire*, 170–1; J. B. Post, 'Some Limitations of the Medieval Peace Rolls', *Journal of the Society of Archivists* 4 (1970–3), 635. Jury lists for Notts. sessions of the peace are to be found in: KB9/188/21; 199/45,46; 207/2/38; 219/21,23; 230B/181,239; 231/1/25, 35,38; 251/40; 256/39; 278/59; 289/78. The only one of these juries

renders unrewarding any quantitative approach to the problem of the extent to which the leading shire gentry were involved in local disorder. Indeed, so selective was the reporting of crime, and those descriptions of individual offences that came to the attention of the courts so *ex parte*, that the approach must be qualitative and contextual. Individual aristocratic offences must be seen in the context of the manner in which they came into the royal courts, whether through private petitions to king, parliament, or the chancellor; indictments made before the justices of the peace and later called into the court of king's bench by writs of *certiorari* or *terminari*; civil pleas in the courts of common pleas and king's bench; or indictments laid before royal commissions of *oyer* and *terminer* or enquiry. Once the court of king's bench had become stationary at Westminster, no longer acting as a court of first instance in its visitations of particular counties, the latter were the most potent means by which the crown could intervene in local affairs and the most likely to reveal the offences of the shire aristocracies; both because the commissioners were often drawn from the ranks of the royal justices, the higher nobility, and the king's personal servants, rather than from the local aristocracy, and because the juries of presentment, particularly the grand juries, were of a higher social status than those sitting at sessions of the peace.[18] Such commissions were issued for Nottinghamshire twice during the Lancastrian period: in 1414 and 1440. The former illustrates the commission at its most impartial, as an effective, if limited, method of regulating local conflict; the latter, at its most partial, employed as a weapon of faction just as the more limited special *oyer* and *terminer* commissions (issued to investigate specific trespasses at the plaint of the injured party) had been before they more or less fell out of use in the early fifteenth century.[19] Together they amply illustrate the problems that faced the crown when it attempted to intervene in local affairs.

The enquiry commission of May 1414, issued during the course of the Leicester parliament in which the petitions against Stanhope were

to contain a member of the shire élite (Sir Edmund Pierpoint) was that which sat in the exceptional peace session of 27 Feb. 1415 held before the justices of assize in the wake of a commission of enquiry. It indicted the Lancs. knight, Sir John Byron, for abducting his mother, Joan, from Over Colwick 6 days before: KB9/188/21; KB27/619, rex rots. 3, 22[d].

[18] Powell, 'Public Order', 19–23; J. B. Avrutick, 'Commissions of Oyer and Terminer in Fifteenth-Century England', M.Phil. thesis (London, 1967), *passim*.

[19] R. W. Kaeuper, 'Law and Order in Fourteenth-Century England: The Evidence of Special Commissions of Oyer and Terminer', *Speculum* 54 (1979), 734–84.

presented, was part of a much wider campaign to restore peace to the localities, headed by the king's bench perambulation of Leicestershire, Staffordshire, and Shropshire.[20] The last years of Henry IV's reign had been characterized by a series of disturbances in the midlands and elsewhere and Henry V was determined to put an end to this disorder before embarking on his French conquests. The king's government had been aware for several years that Nottinghamshire was amongst those counties in which the level of disorder had become unacceptable. During the parliament of January 1410 it was one of ten counties for which the commons had requested a commission of *oyer* and *terminer*,[21] and this request was partially and belatedly granted on 26 October 1411 when William Hankeford and Robert Hill, JCBs, were commissioned to enquire into all riots, maintenances, and other offences in Nottinghamshire, Yorkshire, and Derbyshire. The fact that they were ordered to send their inquisitions before the king and council suggests some connection between the disturbances which provoked this commission and the statute of riots enacted in the parliament of the following month.[22] There can at least be no doubt that it was the major riot that had taken place in Nottinghamshire in the previous August that resulted in that county's inclusion within the commissioners' terms of reference, and the commitment of four of the leading knights of the county, Sir Thomas Chaworth, Sir Richard Stanhope, Sir John Zouche, and Sir John Leek, all of whom had been involved in the riot, to the Tower of London on 24 October, two days before the issue of the commission, was probably to facilitate the commissioners' task.[23] But whatever the results of this enquiry, it was not until Trinity term 1414, when the proceedings before the commissioners of enquiry of that year were returned, that any evidence of the county's recent disturbed state reached king's bench. It is probable that the petitions against Stanhope were the immediate pretext for the issue of this commission on 14 May

---

[20] Powell, 'The Restoration of Law and Order', in G. L. Harriss (ed.), *Henry V: The Practice of Kingship* (Oxford, 1985), 53–74.

[21] *RP*, iii. 624. During this parliament a commission was issued for the arrest of Henry Pierpoint, his offence is unknown: *CPR, 1408–13*, 222.

[22] Statute 13 Hen. IV, c. 7; *CPR, 1408–13*, 374; Bellamy, *Criminal Law*, 61–2.

[23] *CCR, 1409–13*, 243. Two Derbys. knights, Sir Roger Leche and Sir John Cokayn, who had been involved in riots in that county, were committed to the Tower at the same time: ibid.; above, p. 131. All six were released on 30 Nov. after examination in chancery: *CCR, 1409–13*, 244, 261. Chaworth took the precaution of suing out a pardon for all riots, insurrections, and felonies on the following 14 Dec.: C81/653/7066.

1414,[24] but it is clearly to be seen against the wider background of disorder in the county dating back to 1410, for which Stanhope, although prominent in it, was not solely responsible. The indictments laid before the commissioners appear to present a balanced picture of recent disorders, assigning the élite of the shire their full share of blame.

Not surprisingly it was the grand jury, sitting at Nottingham on 2 June, less than three weeks after the issue of the commission, that made the bulk of the important presentments, and amongst these the most significant was that relating to the riot of August 1411, a riot occasioned by the dispute between the esquire, Alexander Mering, and the franklin, John Tuxford, over the ownership of a third of the manor of Markham Clinton.[25] In so far as a failed arbitrament led to lawless recriminations, this dispute bears a striking resemblance to the dispute between Sir Edmund Ferrers of Chartley and Hugh Erdeswick, which precipitated the king's bench visitation of Staffordshire.[26] According to the grand jury, a loveday held on 19 August at Dunham to reconcile the competing claims of Mering and Tuxford, and involving six of the leading men of the shire as arbiters, floundered on Mering's refusal to come to terms. In response, Tuxford, through the maintenance of Stanhope, who, along with Sir Thomas Chaworth and Henry Pierpoint, had acted as an arbiter for him at the loveday, and Stanhope's brother-in-law, Ralph Cromwell, forcibly expelled Mering from the disputed lands two days later. Mering, in turn, on 24 August, with the equally powerful maintenance of Sir John Zouche and Sir John Leek, both of whom, along with Hugh Willoughby, had earlier acted as his arbiters, raised 500 men at nearby Muskham to make a forcible re-entry, the same number being raised by Tuxford to defend his possession. A potentially dangerous conflict was averted by the timely arrival of William, Lord Roos.[27] The grand jury saw Stanhope and Zouche as the main culprits in this affair, indicting both as '*communis manutentor et sustentator querelii ad grave nocumentum totius communitatis Nottynghamii*', and for other offences

---

[24] It was enrolled under 22 May on the patent roll, but was dated at Leicester on 14 May: *CPR, 1413–16*, 222; KB9/204/2/2.

[25] For these grand jury presentments: KB9/204/2/6–7.

[26] Powell, 'Public Order', 293–5.

[27] This grand jury account of the riot is the most circumstantial, although some of the lesser juries also made presentments concerning it. The Bingham jury made no mention of powerful maintainers; the Newark town jury indicted only Tuxford; while the jury of Bassetlaw, in which wapentake the riot took place, mentioned Stanhope and Zouche as maintainers, adding that Roos came to arrest Tuxford: KB9/204/2/10, 22, 26.

unconnected with the riot: Stanhope for various trespasses against
Agnes Sewall, one of those who had petitioned against him in the
Leicester parliament, and Zouche for the intimidation of a juror and for
preventing a royal bailiff from executing a royal writ in the archbishop of
York's lordship of Southwell (of which Zouche was steward). Another of
the maintainers of 1411, the young Ralph Cromwell, was indicted for a
more serious offence: he was said to have feloniously delivered a felon
under the custody of one of the county coroners from the church of
Woodborough. Other presentments were laid against the leading men
of the shire by the lesser juries: the Nottingham town jury made a series
of indictments against Robert Pierpoint, a younger son of Sir Edmund
Pierpont, for various thefts, assaults, and extortions[28] (accusations
amplified by the grand jury); the Bingham jury accused Henry Bowet,
archbishop of York, of extorting money for the probate of wills;[29] and
most significantly of all, the Bassetlaw jury indicted Stanhope, the
dominant landholder in that wapentake, for the assault and false
imprisonment of a royal esquire, Robert Morton of Bawtry.[30]

The crown itself must take much of the credit for producing these
even-handed and extensive indictments. During the Leicester parliament, which ended just two days before the commissioners held their
first session, Stanhope had been committed to prison to answer the
petitions laid against him,[31] an essential preliminary to an objective
enquiry, while the crown had acted wisely in its choice of commissioners.
Henry V chose to avoid the appointment of any local magnates or gentry,
instead relying on royal lawyers and men personally connected with
himself. The commission was headed by his chamberlain, Henry
(d. 1425), Lord Fitzhugh of Ravensworth, and the comptroller of the
royal household, the Norfolk knight, Sir John Rothenale. The other two
commissioners were lawyer, John Hals, a king's serjeant and later a
justice of common pleas and king's bench, and John Barton the younger,
who had represented Buckinghamshire in the parliament in which the
commission was issued.[32] In these circumstances it is not surprising that
the presenting juries should have co-operated, especially since the
imprisoned Stanhope, Sir Thomas Chaworth, Sir Edmund Pierpoint,

[28] KB9/204/2/20.
[29] KB9/204/2/10.
[30] KB9/204/2/26.
[31] Above, p. 189.
[32] For Barton: A. E. Goodman, 'The Parliamentary Representation of Bedfordshire
and Buckinghamshire, 1377–1422', B.Litt. thesis (Oxford, 1964), 348–9.

and Sir John Zouche were excluded from the grand jury and their respective wapentake juries.[33]

Indeed, this commission shows royal intervention in local affairs at its most effective, at least as far as the eliciting of indictments was concerned. But how successfully did it fulfil its purpose? If this was the exemplary punishment of the indicted, it certainly did not succeed. The issue of the comprehensive general pardon of December 1414, available *de cursu* from chancery, on the payment of 16*s*. 4*d*. and a few other incidental payments, effectively allowed nearly all those who had been indicted during the wider campaign against lawlessness, of which the Nottinghamshire enquiry was but a small part, to escape conviction and punishment.[34] This has led Dr Powell to conclude that this campaign was never intended to punish crime but was rather an exercise in political management not primarily designed to secure convictions but to resolve, or at least defuse, existing disputes within the county aristocracies before the king departed for France.[35] This view tallies well with the Nottinghamshire evidence where the aim of the enquiry appears to have been to deter the leading gentry from further maintenance of the dispute between Mering and Tuxford, which was not yet concluded, and to serve as a warning to Stanhope that the new king would not tolerate his oppressive activities. There is nothing to indicate, as there is for Shropshire and Staffordshire,[36] that the king took large securities of the peace from those indicted in Nottinghamshire, but the success of the enquiry is to be measured by the fact that the dispute between Mering and Tuxford was brought to a peaceful conclusion two years later[37] and that Stanhope appears to have discontinued his worst excesses. His

[33] Chaworth himself had only recently been released from the Tower of London when the commissioners came to the county. His arrest had been ordered on 8 Jan. 1414, not in connection with recent disorders in the county but for suspected complicity in Oldcastle's revolt: *CPR, 1413–16*, 148. He was released on the following 12 May: *CPR, 1413–19*, 116, 121; J. H. Wylie and W. T. Waugh, *The Reign of Henry V*, 3 vols. (Cambridge, 1914–29), i. 271, 274 n. 7. Pierpoint and Zouche were named on the grand jury panel but their names were subsequently crossed out. In their absence the jury was headed by Sir Nicholas Strelley, Sir William Nevill, Sir Hugh Husy, Sir Robert Barry, and the young Gervase Clifton: KB9/204/2/9.

[34] For this pardon: Powell, 'The King's Bench in Shropshire and Staffordshire in 1414', in *Law, Litigants and the Legal Profession*, eds. E. W. Ives and A. H. Manchester (London and New Jersey, 1983), 100. All the leading Notts. men indicted came into king's bench to plead pardons taken out under either this general pardon or the earlier one of Apr. 1413: above, p. 189 n. 16; KB27/614, rex rots. 9, 12; 615, rex rots. 21, 41; 616, rex rots. 17^d, 28^d.

[35] Powell, 'The King's Bench', 101–3.

[36] Powell, 'The Restoration of Law and Order', 70–1.

[37] Powell, 'Arbitration and the Law', 58; Payling, 'Law and Arbitration', 148.

restoration to the county bench in November 1417 marks the completion of his rehabilitation.

The lack of partisanship demonstrated in the presentments made before this commission of 1414 was not matched in 1440, when a commission was issued in very different circumstances. Although it was in the form of an apparently general commission of *oyer* and *terminer* with a mandate to enquire into all offences, it was issued not directly on royal initiative in the face of mounting evidence of a crisis of order, but in response to a single private petition to the king in council by the Derbyshire esquire, John Statham of Morley, and on the payment of a mark into the hanaper. He complained of attacks on his family, servants, and property by Henry, Lord Grey of Codnor, and requested a commission of *oyer* and *terminer* on the grounds that Grey had been guilty of offences against not only him but also many others in the county.[38] It is remarkable how quickly the crown acted on this petition: only four days elapsed between the last attack complained of and the issue of the commission.[39] This suggests that the commission had a powerful sponsor: subsequent events, as well as what is known of Statham, indicate that this was so. Statham was one of the principal members of Cromwell's Derbyshire affinity.[40] Cromwell's appointment to the commission of *oyer* and *terminer*, together with that of the two leading Nottinghamshire knights connected with him, Sir Thomas Chaworth and Sir William Babington, the retired CJCB, and a long-time rival of Grey's in Derbyshire, Sir Richard Vernon,[41] implies that this commission, mandated to enquire into offences in both Derbyshire and Nottinghamshire, was never going to be impartial despite the presence of three justices of the common pleas amongst the commissioners. Its intention from the outset was the destruction of Grey as a force in local politics.

Since the original indictments no longer survive, the presentments made before these commissioners have to be reconstructed from the plea and controlment rolls of the king's bench, and these make it clear

[38] C81/1545/79 (I am extremely grateful to Dr G. L. Harriss for this reference). For the Stathams as the perpetrators rather than the victims of violence: D. Crook, 'Derbyshire and the English Rising of 1381', *Historical Research* 60 (1987), 9–23.

[39] This commission was enrolled under 10 July on the patent roll but the endorsement of Statham's petition shows that it was issued on the following day: *CPR, 1436–41*, 450; C81/1545/79. The last attack complained of had occurred on 7 July.

[40] HMC, *Report on the Manuscripts of Lord De L'Isle and Dudley*, i. 216, 230; *CPR, 1452–61*, 200, 341. This connection with Cromwell explains the grant of the keeping of the royal castle of Horsley to Statham and his son, another John, in December 1439: *CFR, 1437–45*, 115.

[41] Wright, pp. 66, 114.

that the commission concerned itself exclusively with the alleged crimes of Grey and his followers, a total of 165 of whom, mostly yeomen, husbandmen, and labourers from his manors of Codnor and Denby, were indicted for various felonies and trespasses.[42] If these indictments are to be taken at their face value, Grey himself was guilty of a great number of offences, including incitement to murder and abusing his position as a justice of the peace in both counties. But most significant are the indictments concerning what appears to have been a campaign against Cromwell's followers. Lengthy presentments were made concerning the attacks on Statham and his manor of Morley, which had taken place on 6 and 7 July 1440, while other presentments related to the attempted ambush of Thomas Darcy, one of Cromwell's affinity in Nottinghamshire and Lincolnshire, and the vandalism on the property of James and Thomas Stanhope, the stepsons of Cromwell's sister.[43] Most revealing of all is a presentment made by a Derbyshire jury concerning a raid on Cromwell's park at West Hallam, which had taken place on 19 August, more than a month after the commission had been issued and a few weeks before the commissioners sat. The raiders, identified as followers of Grey, had killed a buck, torn out its internal organs and deposited them at the gates of the park, '*in despectu*' of Cromwell.[44] It is tempting to think, in view of the obvious partiality of these presentments, that they reflect only one side of a dispute, and that similar offences committed by Cromwell and his supporters against Grey went unreported.[45] This is the more likely since the sheriff who empanelled the indicting juries was Cromwell's neighbour, John Cokfeld of Nuthall, a man who had benefited from Cromwell's patronage in the past and whose sister and heir-apparent was married to one of Cromwell's leading Lincolnshire retainers, John Tailboys of Stallingborough.[46] Moreover, while the composition of these juries is unknown, two releases of attaint and *decies tantum* from known followers of Grey to one

[42] For a complete list of all those indicted, including those who appeared and made fine before the commissioners: KB29/75, rots. 24–7. For the presentments made against them: KB27/724, rex rots. 8, 9, 30; 725, rex rots. 4, 5, 25^d, 27; 727, rex rots. 3^d, 17; 728, rex rots. 2^d, 23^d, 34; 729, rex rot. 1^d; 731, rex rot. 5; 741, rex rots. 1, 2; 742, rex rots. 39, 40; 749, rex rot. 3. In view of the petition presented in the parliament of Nov. 1439 to Feb. 1440 against a criminal gang led by the Derbys. gentleman, Peter Venables of Aston, which is said to have behaved like 'Robynhode and his meyne', it is striking that the presenting jurors made no mention of its activities: *RP*, v. 16–17.

[43] KB27/741, rex rots. 1, 2; 742, rex rot. 39. For Darcy: above, p. 141.

[44] KB27/741, rex rot. 1.

[45] In Hilary 1441 Grey sued Statham for trespass: KB27/719, just. rot. 71.

[46] Above, pp. 140–1.

Nottinghamshire and one Derbyshire jury enrolled on the close roll give an indication of the composition of the petty juries which tried the private bills presented before the commissioners, and both strongly suggest that the juries were rigged. The Derbyshire jury was headed by none other than Statham himself and two of his sons, and the Nottinghamshire jury by Darcy, a servant of his named Richard Burgh, who had complained before the commissioners that Grey had falsely imprisoned him, and John Stanhope, a kinsman of Cromwell, whose uncles' lands had been vandalized by Grey's servants.[47]

Nor are the empanelling of such juries and the presentments made the only indications of partiality. There is also the testimony of Grey himself. Statham's petition had provoked the crown into taking strong measures against him. On 16 July, five days after the issue of the commission, he was ordered under pain of £1,000 to surrender himself to the Tower, and, although he was released a month later, it was only on condition that he moved no more than three miles from London.[48] He was thus absent from Derbyshire when the commissioners took the presentments against him and his servants, and was probably still in London in the following March, when he petitioned the king for a general pardon. This was granted when Cromwell's old adversary, Humphrey, duke of Gloucester, interceded on Grey's behalf, but only on condition that he find security of the peace in 1,000 marks. Soon afterwards he presented a further petition complaining about Cromwell's role as one of the commissioners, claiming that Cromwell was his 'mortal enemye . . . and noon egal Juge' and asking that he be ordered to attend no further sessions.[49] His request was granted but the damage had been done.[50] His position in local politics was fatally undermined. Many of his supporters had been outlawed, and, while he was able to free himself from the presentments made against him by pleading his pardon in king's bench in Trinity 1442,[51] his outlawed supporters had to wait until the general pardon of 1446 before they could inlaw themselves.

---

[47] *CCR, 1441–7*, 30, 37–8.   [48] Ibid., *1435–41*, 384, 388.

[49] E28/67, 7 and 16 Mar. (again I am grateful to Dr G. L. Harriss for this important reference); *CPR, 1436–41*, 507; *CCR, 1435–41*, 471.

[50] Sessions were held at Nottingham on 7 Sept. and 3 Oct. 1440, 27 Apr. and 2 Oct. 1441; at Newark on 15 Oct. and 5 Dec. 1440; at Derby on 5 Sept. 1440; at Whitwell on 21 Oct. 1440 and 8 Dec. 1441; and at Chesterfield on 25 Apr. 1441: E372/288, Item Not.; KB27/728, rex rot. 34; 731, rex rot. 5. In the absence of original indictments it is difficult to discover which commissioners sat, but Cromwell is known to have done so on 5 and 7 Sept. 1440, both of which sessions were presided over by Humphrey, earl of Stafford, and on 8 Dec. 1440: KB27/724, rex rot. 8, 9, 30.

[51] KB27/725, rex rots. 4, 5.

Not content with bringing the formal judicial machinery of the crown against Grey, Cromwell, ever watchful for opportunities to augment his already very substantial wealth, also used his powerful position in local politics to harness the procedure of arbitration to impose a crippling burden of compensation on his rival. On 28 August 1441 Grey had made a feoffment of his valuable manors of Hoo in Kent and Toton in Nottinghamshire, together with the smaller manor of Stoke in Derbyshire, to a group of Cromwell's nominees. The condition attached to this feoffment was that Grey and his servants should stand to the judgment of Maud (d. 1446), countess of Cambridge, William Alnwick, bishop of Lincoln, and three of the *oyer* and *terminer* commissioners, John (d. 1460), Viscount Beaumont, Sir Thomas Chaworth, and Sir William Babington, in all matters hanging between them, on the one part, and Cromwell, Darcy, and Statham, on the other. Less than a fortnight later, on 9 September 1441, these arbiters returned their award: Grey was to find security of the peace in chancery or before the Nottinghamshire justices of the peace in the sum of £800, a rather superfluous stipulation in view of the large security of the peace he had already had to find as a condition of his pardon.[52] Because he failed to find this additional security, the manors, which represented about a quarter of his landed income, remained in the hands of Cromwell's nominees not only up to Grey's death in July 1444 but also throughout the minority of his son and heir. It was not until 1455 that Cromwell gave instructions that they should be restored.[53] Moreover, the accounts of Cromwell's executors suggest that the loss of these manors was not the full price exacted in vengeance from the unfortunate Grey: they record that, at his death in 1444, he owed Cromwell £1,600 on a broken obligation, and £157 1s. 4d. of a further total payment of 2,000 marks he had undertaken to make.[54] Even assuming the issues of the confiscated manors were counted towards the payment of this latter sum of 2,000 marks, this amounted to a crippling burden of debt for one of the lesser baronage. He had indeed paid a heavy price for daring to challenge Cromwell's local authority.

In this case it could be argued that Cromwell had acted to the benefit not only of himself but also of local society in bringing down a magnate whose lawless activities, attested in sources beyond the indictments laid before the commissioners,[55] had disturbed the local peace. Nevertheless, it

---

[52] C139/116/35/14, 15, 17.
[53] Magdalen College, Cromwell Papers, Misc. 356(2).
[54] Ibid., Misc. 355, 357; 127/34.   [55] Below, p. 206.

is doubtful whether the commission of *oyer* and *terminer* used so overtly as a weapon of faction as it was in Nottinghamshire and Derbyshire in 1440 and 1441 made any real contribution to the regulation of local conflict, serving instead to exacerbate rather than heal local divisions.[56] But even at their best and most impartial *oyer* and *terminer* commissions were a limited method of controlling local disorder. They were occasional expedients, dependent on local co-operation and a strong government to enforce that co-operation. At most they could deter those in conflict from resorting to further violence and force them to compromise their differences through extra-judicial settlements. This was the delayed effect of the king's bench visitation of Shropshire in 1414[57] and the more direct effect of the commission of *oyer* and *terminer* which sat in Derbyshire in April 1434. This commission, headed by John, duke of Bedford, had been precipitated by a murderous feud between the Nottinghamshire knight, Sir Henry Pierpoint, and the Derbyshire esquire, Thomas Foljambe of Walton, which had culminated in the maiming of Sir Henry and the murder of his brother-in-law, Henry Longford, and another of his companions, William Bradshaw, in the parish church of Chesterfield in the previous January.[58] After present-ments had been made against both the Pierpoints and the Foljambes by juries sitting before the commissioners, process begun against those indicted,[59] and appeals lodged against the Foljambes and their sup-porters on the plea side of the king's bench by Sir Henry and Bradshaw's widow,[60] the two principals agreed to compromise. On 13 July 1435 they entered into mutual recognizances in £1,000 to abide by the award of six arbiters: Sir Henry chose his neighbour, Sir Gervase Clifton, William Hondeford, and the Yorkshire lawyer, John Portington, later JCB; and Foljambe chose Sir Thomas Gresley of Drakelow, John Statham of Morley, and the Nottinghamshire lawyer, Richard Bingham, later JKB.

[56] Kaeuper, 'Oyer and Terminer', 781–4.
[57] Powell, 'Settlement of Disputes', 32.
[58] For an account of this dispute and the proceedings of the commission: Wright, pp. 128–33.
[59] Sir Henry Pierpoint and his son Henry appeared in king's bench in Trinity term 1434 and pleaded self-defence to the assaults against Thomas Foljambe and his servants for which they had been indicted. No jury came to try this plea and the Pierpoints were allowed to make fine in Hilary 1438, Sir Henry paying £4 and his son half a mark: KB27/693, rex rot. 6; 707, fines rot. Thomas Foljambe was put to greater inconvenience for the greater crimes. He suffered a period of imprisonment in the Marshalsea (from 13 Oct. 1434 until an unknown date) before being acquitted before the Derbys. justices of assize on 24 July 1437: KB27/694, rex rot. 2; 695, rex rot. 20.
[60] KB27/695, just. rots. 53, 55.

These arbiters were unable to reach a conclusion by the following Michaelmas, but an award was returned by the umpire, John Kemp archbishop of York, in the following Hilary, after which date no more is heard of the appeal in king's bench against Foljambe.[61]

This apparent connection between the royal investigation of crime through commissions of *oyer* and *terminer* and the conclusion of disputes by arbitration raises the wider question of the role of arbitration in the maintenance of a social peace that the crown was unable to impose from above. It is clear that, although arbitration could be fostered by direct royal intervention in local affairs, such intervention was not a necessary preliminary to the extra-judicial resolution of aristocratic conflict. A later dispute involving the unfortunate Pierpoints presents a similar aspect to their feud with the Foljambes in that it illustrates the use of arbitration in the aftermath of a major crime, but it did not involve the crown's direct intervention. During the early 1450s the Pierpoints were in dispute with the Plumptons of Plumpton in Yorkshire and Kinoulton in Nottinghamshire over land in Mansfield Woodhouse. According to a writ sued in king's bench by Henry Pierpoint, Sir William Plumpton had raided his property there on 20 June 1453. The characteristic delays of the common law process meant that the case did not come before a jury until the Nottinghamshire assize session of 25 February 1457. It progressed no further: Plumpton successfully claimed that the jury had been arrayed *in favorem et denominationem* of Pierpoint and a new jury had to be summoned.[62] Before this new jury could sit, the dispute, for a reason now impossible to determine, took a murderous turn. On 21 July 1457 a double murder occurred: at Papplewick in Sherwood Forest Henry Pierpoint met his death at the hands of John Grene, Plumpton's steward and brother-in-law;[63] and Grene himself was then murdered at Pannal near Wetherby by Henry's brother, John Pierpoint of Radmanthwaite (the fact that Pannal lies as many as sixty-five miles north of Papplewick makes it improbable but not impossible that both murders took place on the same day).[64] The indictment of Grene and his

---

[61] *CCR, 1429–35*, 365; *1435–41*, 32–4, 53; KB27/697, just. rot. 80[d].

[62] KB27/771, just. rot. 54[d]; 773, just. rot. 51.

[63] KB9/290/10 (inquisition at Rolleston before William Clerk and John Thornhagh, the Notts. coroners).

[64] KB9/289/20 (indictment before Sir William Plumpton, John Thwaytes, and John Stafford, West Riding JPs, sitting at Selby on 4 Oct. 1457). A further indictment laid before the same JPs at Wetherby on 17 Nov. 1457 presents a different picture of events, placing Grene's murder at Kirkby Overblow, a few miles to the south of Pannal, and

accomplices before the Nottinghamshire coroners and that of John Pierpoint and others before the West Riding justices of the peace, headed by Plumpton himself, initiated crown pleas against those involved in these murders,[65] and these pleas were soon supplemented by private appeals lodged in king's bench by Pierpoint's widow, Thomasia, and John Grene's nephew and heir, Richard Grene.[66] It was not, however, the cumbersome process of common law that brought the dispute to a close. While this process was pursuing its laborious course, the two parties, on 10 February 1459, submitted to the arbitration of six arbiters: Sir John Melton, the murdered Pierpoint's brother-in-law, John Stanhope, and Richard Illingworth, on behalf of the Pierpoints; the Derbyshire knight, Sir William Vernon, William Babington, and the Leicestershire lawyer, Richard Neel, later JKB and JCB, on behalf of the Plumptons; with the powerful John, Viscount Beaumont, as umpire. This arbitration apparently failed, but the dispute was finally brought to a close when the Nottinghamshire judge, Richard Bingham, returned a successful award on 28 May 1462. In its terms it said no more than that both parties were to abandon the appeals they had pending.[67]

If arbitration was to be found operating only in such cases as this and the dispute between Pierpoint and Foljambe, its purpose being principally to fix compensation for past acts of violence by one party against another and bring to an end the legal actions to which this violence had given rise, then the obvious popularity of the process in the fifteenth century must be seen simply as an indictment of the royal

---

indicting Henry Pierpoint as one of the accessories: KB9/289/19. The indictment of a man already murdered was clearly an attempt by the jurors at Plumpton's instigation to shift the blame on to the Pierpoints as the first to resort to murder.

[65] KB27/798, rex rot. 11 (for process to outlawry in Michaelmas term 1460 on the coroner's inquest called into king's bench by a writ of *certiorari* dated 22 June 1458: KB9/290/11); KB27/798, rex rot. 1[d] (for appearance of John Pierpoint and others in the same term to answer indictments laid before West Riding JPs called into king's bench by a writ of *certiorari* dated 20 Jan. 1458: KB/9/289/18); KB27/808, rex rot. 6[d] (for pardon, dated 1 May 1458, pleaded by John Pierpoint in Easter term 1463 and verdicts of not guilty against others indicted with him returned on 15 Mar. 1464).

[66] KB27/790, just. rot. 17[d], 70 (for Thomasia's personal appearance in king's bench in Michaelmas term 1458 to prosecute her appeal); 791, just. rot. 67 (for the continual failure of the sheriff to return writs of *capiat* issued against those appealed); 804, fines rot. (for termination of Grene's appeal).

[67] *Plumpton Correspondence*, ed. T. Stapleton, Camden Society, os 4 (1839), p. 3 n. *a.*; Leeds District Archives, Chambers MS 3 (Plumpton Coucher Book), no. 552. In Easter term 1462, on the last day of which the award was returned, both Thomasia Pierpoint and Richard Grene paid fines of half a mark for failure to prosecute their appeals: KB27/804, fines rot.

system òf justice, which was failing to deter or punish such acts and was capable only of exerting some pressure on the disputants to compromise.[68] Nevertheless, there is strong evidence to suggest that arbitration is to be seen in a much more positive role than this; as a means of forestalling conflict and avoiding violence by reaching compromise solutions to disputes, which, by the nature of landed society, generally involved title to property, before they degenerated into violence and recrimination. It must be emphasized here that disputes which degenerated into lurid acts of violence, like those between Pierpoint and Foljambe and Pierpoint and Plumpton, were exceptional. Murder was rare; when disputes did flare into violence it took the form of seizure and vandalism of property rather than vicious assaults on persons.[69] Indeed, several recent studies of individual disputes have indicated that even comparatively minor acts of violence were a last rather than a first resort for the disputants.[70]

The traditional explanation for the failure of the courts to resolve civil cases and punish criminal acts rests on three implicit assumptions: that the only alternative to litigation in the settlement of disputes was violence; that the late-medieval landholder was naturally predisposed to conflict with his neighbours; and that local society itself imposed no restraint on the violent prosecution of feuds. Recent work has undermined all three of these assumptions. It is now clear that arbitration acted simultaneously as an adjunct and an alternative to litigation. For the disputant it had significant advantages over the common law: at its best it could quickly and cheaply produce a compromise acceptable to both parties, circumventing the inflexible verdicts of the common law, and ensuring that this compromise fitted into the social and political context in which it was made, namely that of the local landed community.[71] The fact that such compromises were most frequently to be found within the confines of this community emphasizes the self-regulating properties of local society. As Dr Wright has pointed out, the infrastructure of kinsmen and neighbours that composed a community provided an alternative and probably older system of justice to that imposed by the crown.[72] It was common for a preamble to a returned award to state that the award had come about '*par mediacion de lour amys dambe partiez*' and '*pro perpetua amicitia et amicabili affinitate*' between

---

[68] Bellamy, *Criminal Law*, 82–3.
[69] Ibid., 69–70; Saul, *Gloucestershire*, 174.
[70] Smith, 'Litigation and Politics', 71; Sinclair, 'The Great Berkeley Law-Suit', 47.
[71] Powell, 'Arbitration and the Law', 55–6; Wright, p. 122; D. Hay, 'The Criminal Prosecution in England and its Historians', *Modern Law Review* 47 (1984), 21.
[72] Wright, p. 119.

them.[73] A Nottinghamshire example of this mode of dispute settlement at work comes from early in the minority of Henry VI. In 1425 two of the shire élite, the near neighbours Sir Nicholas Strelley and Hugh Willoughby, were in dispute over the ownership of a ditch lying between their estates at Bilborough and Sutton Passeys: '*ad instanciam amicorum*', they agreed to abide by the award of five of their neighbours, Sir William Babington, CJCB, Sir Thomas Chaworth, Sir Henry Pierpoint, Sir Gervase Clifton, and John Cokfeld of Nuthall, and a successful settlement was returned.[74]

Two converging forces were working to bring such disputes to an end: on the one hand, neighbours in dispute could look to their mutual friends for its peaceful resolution; while, on the other, their mutual friends themselves had a vested interest in bringing the dispute to a close and were well placed to exert pressure for a compromise. With this in mind it is not surprising that the two most violent feuds involving the élite of Lancastrian Nottinghamshire concerned families from outside the county: the Derbyshire Foljambes and the Yorkshire Plumptons. Here the internal restraints of a close-knit local society, whether centred on the county or some smaller unit, were not operative, although it is significant that in both cases, after the disputes had degenerated into acts of violence, cross-county arbitrations, drawing arbiters from Nottinghamshire and surrounding counties, were arranged.

The advantages of arbitration as a method of dispute settlement are nowhere more clearly seen than in those disputes over landed property, often arising within rather than between families, so characteristic of late-medieval England. In the resolution of such disputes the arbiter enjoyed a striking advantage over the common-law judge for he, unbound by the rules of common law, was free to make a division of the disputed estates or fix financial compensation for the loser. For example, in the dispute of the late 1440s between Sir Thomas Rempston and his mother, Margaret, over the ownership of the valuable manor of Bingham, the arbiters, although awarding the manor to Sir Thomas, were able to compensate his mother by providing that he should pay her £10 per annum.[75] Furthermore, the greater flexibility of the arbitration

---

[73] Powell, 'Settlement of Disputes', 27, 35; NUL, Cl. D 674.

[74] NUL, Mi. D 1104.

[75] The arbiters were Sir Thomas Chaworth, Richard Willoughby, Thomas, prior of Beauvale, and William Gull, rector of St Peter's, Nottingham: C1/21/9c; above, p. 60 n. 210. See also the division of the disputed third of the manor of Markham Clinton between Mering and Tuxford: Payling, 'Law and Arbitration', 147–8.

process allowed for the settlement of disputes for which there was no existing remedy at common law. Nottinghamshire provides the excellent example of the dispute over the division of the valuable Cressy of Hodsock inheritance. On the death of Hugh Cressy on 27 September 1408, Sir John Markham and Ralph Makerell, the husbands of Hugh's sisters and coheiresses, were unable, after diverse '*tractatus et colloquium*', to agree on the division of his extensive estates.[76] This deadlock, for which there was no remedy at common law, was broken by the intervention of the kinsfolk of the Cressy family and several prominent gentry drawn principally from the wapentake of Bassetlaw in which Hodsock lay. Eight arbiters are named in the returned award, dated at East Retford on 18 April 1409: Sir Henry Vavasour of Hazlewood in south Yorkshire, Hugh's first cousin and the husband of his divorced wife Margaret Skipwith;[77] Sir Richard Stanhope, the leading landholder in the Bassetlaw wapentake, more notable for his contribution to disorder than his efforts in curbing it; Sir John Leek and his eldest son Simon, the only two arbiters from south of the Trent and whose participation is probably to be explained by their connection with Sir John Markham;[78] Sir Thomas Hercy of Grove near East Retford; his neighbour George Monboucher of Gamston; Edmund FitzWilliam of Wadworth in south Yorkshire, whose son, another Edmund, had married a daughter of Hugh's sister, Katherine, now the wife of Ralph Makerell, by her first husband, Sir John Clifton;[79] and William Saundby of Saundby, a lawyer formerly of the Nottinghamshire *quorum*. But, if the words of the award are to be taken literally, these were not the only men involved in bringing about a settlement. The agreement between the disputants was said to have been brought about both '*per mediacionem cognatorum aliancium et amicorum*' of the parties, namely the eight arbiters, and '*per consilium aliorum plurimorum de consanguinitate et affinitate*' of the parties. The witness list suggests the identity of these others: in addition to naming the arbiters, it lists thirteen further names, first two of the young heads of leading families from the south of the county, Thomas Rempston and Robert Strelley, followed by eleven Bassetlaw landholders from the middling ranks of the county gentry. The award these twenty-one men returned not only shows arbitration as an effective means of terminating

---

[76] NUL, Cl. D 674. [77] Above, p. 25 n. 31.
[78] On 24 Dec. 1409, soon after the award was returned and only a week before his death, Sir John Markham named Sir John and Simon Leek amongst his feoffees in those Cressy manors that had been awarded to him: C137/78/30.
[79] Hunter, *South Yorkshire*, i. 251.

a major property dispute (in this instance, the terms of the award were simple, the division was to be accomplished by the drawing of lots, each party drawing one of two bills naming estates of equal value) but also very clearly demonstrates the operation of kinship and ties of locality in bringing disputants together.[80] Nearly the entire gentry community of Bassetlaw were involved in making the award.

A more complex and revealing illustration of the self-regulatory properties of gentry society is to be found in the dispute between two minor gentry from the wapentake of Broxtow, David Preston and John Brokstowe, which came to a head in 1440. Like so many late-medieval land disputes it involved an entail: the elderly and impoverished Brokstowe was determined to disinherit his daughter and sole heiress, Preston's wife, Joan, of the manor of Broxtowe Hall and other lands he held in fee tail. The early part of the dispute is described in a document drawn up by Sir Hugh Willoughby in reply to a bill sued against him by Brokstowe.[81] The story it tells shows how far the leading county gentry were prepared to go in bringing potentially disruptive disagreements to an end. According to Willoughby's testimony, Brokstowe's determination to sell the lands had been undiminished by the ruling of John Cokfeld of Nuthall and the lawyer, Thomas Hunte of Linby, that the lands should pass according to the entail. Despite this award, Brokstowe asked Willoughby, the wealthiest landholder in the area of the disputed lands, to purchase the remainder of the lands from him in fee. There can be no doubt that Willoughby was genuinely concerned to prevent the dispute escalating into violence. He had already advanced Brokstowe 20 marks in a vain attempt to remove the need for the sale of the lands, and, in January 1438, he had intervened to resolve a disagreement between Preston and Brokstowe over the terms on which Preston held the manor of Broxtowe Hall on lease.[82] He now neatly side-stepped the difficulties inherent in Brokstowe's embarrassing offer. With the help of the wealthy Derbyshire knight Sir Thomas Gresley (d. 1445), he persuaded Brokstowe to agree to the making of a fine by which the remainder of the estate would be settled first on Brokstowe's issue (thus allowing the entail to run its course) and then on Willoughby's children by Margaret Freville. In return Willoughby paid the impecunious Brokstowe a further £20 since, in his words, he 'perceyved well the distresse and the grete necessite that the saide John stode inne'. Not content with this and

---

[80] For a particularly good example of this process: Bennett, 'A County Community: Social Cohesion amongst the Cheshire Gentry, 1400–1425', *Northern History* 8 (1973), pp. 25–8.   [81] NUL, Mi. L 2a.   [82] NUL, Mi. D 203.

still determined to disinherit his daughter, Brokstowe failed to levy the
fine and instead leased the manor of Broxtowe Hall to Sir Thomas
Chaworth as a preliminary to an outright sale. This ploy failed when
Willoughby warned Chaworth of the lease's illegal purpose.

Until this point, Willoughby's energetic mediation had prevented the
dispute dissolving into violence, but it now took an unwelcome turn.
Brokstowe looked from Chaworth to Henry, Lord Grey of Codnor.
Grey's involvement ensured that the peace would not be maintained. He
was a disaffected element in local politics, already in dispute with
Cromwell, and he had no hesitation in maintaining Brokstowe. Between
4 November 1439 and 11 March 1440 his servants aided Brokstowe in
the systematic plunder of the manor of Broxtowe Hall, which Preston
had held on lease since 1429.[83] Their attacks on the manor were the
subject not only of petitions by Preston to the chancellor, claiming that
his tribulations were the result of Grey's 'grete maintenaunce and
lordship',[84] but also of indictments laid before the commissioners of *oyer*
and *terminer* at Nottingham 7 September 1440.[85] They formed part of
that catalogue of offences which this commission attributed to Grey and
by which Cromwell brought about the destruction of Grey's influence.
At a more mundane level they led to Brokstowe's outlawry for felony,[86]
but left Preston struggling to overcome the consequences of Brokstowe's
conveyance of Broxtowe Hall and other lands to Grey. After some
further vicissitudes, Preston was ultimately able to establish his wife's
title.[87] Not only is this dispute a classic example of the evils of maintenance so often complained of by the commons in parliament,[88] but it
also demonstrates that, whatever the advantages of arbitration over the

---

[83] NUL, Mi. D 202 (for the original lease of 28 Jan. 1429). Willoughby's award of Jan.
1438 and later litigation concerning the lease suggest that it may in part have been
responsible for the dispute: CP40/720, rots. 330, 433; KB27/718, just. rots. 81, 108,
108[d].
[84] C1/9/432; NUL, Mi. L 1c (for the quotation). See also Preston's unsuccessful
appeal of 1442 against those who raided his property: KB27/725, just. rot. 88; 727, just.
rot. 31; 728, rex rot. 37; 738, fines rot., rex rot. 9[d].
[85] KB27/728, rex rot. 34; 741, rex rot. 2; 742, rex rot. 40[d].
[86] E153/1436/4 (inquisition at Nottingham on 30 Oct. 1441 concerning Brokstowe's
lands and goods). He secured a pardon on 24 May 1443: KB27/728, rex rot. 34.
[87] Brokstowe had conveyed Broxtowe Hall to Grey on 9 Mar. 1440: NUL, Mi. D 204,
1659. On 13 Apr. 1442 Grey enfeoffed another Derbys. esquire, Henry Bradburne, who
in turn enfeoffed another Derbys. esquire, John Statham of Horsley: *Notts. IPM, 1437–*
85, 21; NUL, Mi. D 199. It is not clear who was in actual possession of the lands at this
time but Preston finally established his right through a writ of *formedon* in the descender
sued in Easter term 1459: NUL, Mi. D 207; CP40/793, rot. 334.
[88] e.g. *RP*, iii. 21, 42; 1 Rich. II, c. 9; Saul, *Gloucestershire*, 90–1.

common law as a method of dispute settlement, the consensus on which it depended was both fragile and limited. The pacific effect of the disposition of the majority to the non-violent settlement of disputes could be undone by the disaffection of a single powerful element within local society. The readiness of the latter to maintain the disputes of lesser men led to the breakdown of consensus and the promotion of violence.

Nevertheless, it should not be assumed that the intervention of barons like Grey in the disputes of their neighbours was always baneful in effect. The modern reinterpretation of aristocratic violence has rendered unfashionable an emphasis on the evils of baronial maintenance. The emphasis has shifted instead to the role the baronage undoubtedly played in the peaceful resolution of local disputes. Drs J. B. Post and C. Rawcliffe have shown that baronial councils exercised an equitable jurisdiction similar in type if not in scale to the burgeoning jurisdiction of the court of chancery,[89] and it seems clear that the personal and political ties of magnates with the local gentry gave them a particular interest in settling disputes within their own areas of influence, especially within their own affinities. As Dr Wright has pointed out, the affinity provided a ready-made umpire in its lord, while lords themselves saw the maintenance of peace within their own affinities as one of the obligations of lordship.[90] Even a magnate of such poor reputation as George, duke of Clarence, was active in this role.[91] The best Nottinghamshire evidence for the magnate as arbiter comes from the second half of the Lancastrian period, when Cromwell exercised a significant degree of influence within the county. In this context, he is to be seen in a very different light from that of the ruthless manipulator revealed in his dealings with Henry, Lord Grey of Codnor. Although he was not above exploiting the process of arbitration to his own advantage, as he did in his dispute with Grey, there can be no doubt that he generally took his responsibilities as an arbiter very seriously. In the late 1440s or early

---

[89] J. B. Post, 'Courts, Councils and Arbitrators in the Ladbroke Manor Dispute, 1382–1400', in R. F. Hunnisett and J. B. Post (eds.), *Medieval Legal Records Edited in Memory of C. F. A. Meekings* (London, 1978), 292–7; id., 'Equitable Resorts Before 1450', in E. W. Ives and A. H. Manchester (eds.), *Law, Litigants and the Legal Profession* (London and New Jersey, 1983), 70–8; C. Rawcliffe, 'The Great Lord as Peacekeeper: Arbitration by English Noblemen and their Councils in the Later Middle Ages', in J. A. Guy and H. G. Beale (eds.), *Law and Social Change in British History* (London and New Jersey, 1984), 34–54.

[90] Wright, p. 125; Bellamy, *Criminal Law*, 78–9.

[91] M. A. Hicks, 'Restraint, Mediation and Private Justice: George, Duke of Clarence, as "Good Lord"', *Journal of Legal History* 4 (1983), 56–71.

1450s he wrote to two members of his Norfolk affinity, who were at odds, urging them to do no more to further their quarrel until they had discussed the matter with him, ending his letter with a warning, 'ye faile not herof, as I may do anything for you herafter'.[92] Nor can there be any doubt about his effectiveness in this role. This is very clearly illustrated in a long and complex award he returned which brought to an end a potentially very damaging dispute within one of the greatest Nottinghamshire families, the Willoughbys of Wollaton. It is an award that repays detailed examination for not only does it illustrate the positive connection that existed between the law and arbitration in the use of collusive litigation to confirm the terms of an award, but it also suggests that one reason for the popularity of arbitration in the later medieval period was the failure of the law governing the descent of real property to adapt to the increasing sophistication of family settlements made possible by the feoffment-to-use.

The dispute had its origins in the over-generous provision made by the wealthy Sir Hugh Willoughby for his children by his second wife. Such provisions made at the expense of the common-law heir were a frequent cause of strife in fifteenth-century England. When Sir Hugh drew up his will in September 1443 he was at the head of a very large family;[93] by his first wife he had two surviving sons, the eldest being Richard, while by his second wife, the wealthy heiress Margaret Freville, he had as many as five sons and six daughters, nine of whom remained unmarried. In these circumstances it is understandable that he should have wished to make some provision for these younger children. What was controversial was the extent to which this provision was to the disadvantage of Richard, his common-law heir. Margaret was to enjoy a life interest in virtually his whole estate, the issues of which were to be used to provide the considerable sum of 200 marks for each of the children who remained unmarried at his death. Even worse for Richard was the permanent alienation of two manors and a valuable parcel of land at the heart of the Willoughby inheritance. These were settled on Margaret with remainders over to her issue by Hugh and her own right heirs. Richard was to inherit nothing until after her death, and even then his expectations were to be much reduced. He had every reason to feel deeply aggrieved at the settlement, especially since Margaret was little

    [92] *Paston Letters and Papers of the Fifteenth Century*, ed. N. Davis (Oxford, 1971), ii, no. 515.
    [93] For this will: NUL, Mi. F 6, no. 14. It is imperfectly calendared in *TE*, ii. 130–4, with the codicil concerning the settlement of the Willoughby lands omitted.

older than himself and had valuable lands in her own right from which she might have been expected to make at least some provision for her many children by Hugh.[94]

In this situation, it is not surprising that Hugh should have anticipated that his eldest son would not acquiesce in the settlement, and that given freedom of action he would attempt to overturn it at law. Hence Hugh added a clause to his will that Richard should find security to Margaret within a year of his father's death that he would not in any way hinder the performance of the will. If he would not do this, the whole of the Willoughby inheritance was to go to Margaret and her heirs by Hugh. As death approached, Hugh took a firmer measure to secure obedience to his wishes. On New Year's Day 1448 he obliged Richard to swear an oath at Cromwell's new manor house at South Wingfield before Cromwell himself, three leading local knights, Sir Thomas Chaworth, Sir Richard Vernon, and Sir Thomas Blount, and two spiritual representatives, the abbot of Welbeck and the provincial of the Dominican friars, that he would both allow Margaret undisturbed possession of the manor of Wollaton and allow Hugh's feoffees to dispose of the other lands according to the terms of the will.[95]

Hugh died in the following November, and Richard, immediately disregarding his oath, began a subtle campaign to win his father's lands. By labouring the jurors in the inquisitions taken on his father's death he sought to have it returned that all the Willoughby lands were held in fee tail. This was true for the bulk of them but not for the manor of Sutton Passeys, the lands in Wollaton, and the sub-manor of Willoughby, which had been permanently alienated from him in his father's will. To circumvent this difficulty he prevailed upon the Nottinghamshire jurors to fraudulently return that these lands had been settled by deed jointly on Hugh and his first wife, namely Richard's mother, and their issue.[96] As a result of the returned inquisitions, Richard was able to sue out the king's hands all his father's lands save those to be assigned in dower.[97] In addition, he brought an assize of novel disseisin against Margaret for the Leicestershire manors of Cossington and Hambleton and sued her in king's bench for taking away 200 marks worth of his goods and chattels from Wollaton.[98] Clearly the situation was now even more fraught with

[94] Above, p. 35.   [95] NUL, Mi. D 1624.
[96] C139/135/37. There is no record of any such settlement in the cartulary relating to the Willoughby lands in Sutton Passeys and Wollaton: NUL, Mi. D c 3. Moreover, the jurors were shown no deeds in evidence: C139/135/37.
[97] *CFR, 1445–52*, 119, 131.
[98] NUL, Mi. D 3284/2; KB27/752, rex rot. 63; 753, rex rot. 33[d].

difficulty than it had been at Hugh's death, and it was at this point that Richard and Margaret agreed to arbitration, whether of their own volition or at Cromwell's insistence is unknown. On 11 September 1449 they entered into mutual bonds in the large sum of 1,000 marks to be bound by Cromwell's award, whereupon Cromwell, who was plainly prepared to disregard the oath Richard had previously taken before him, called to his assistance the formidable legal expertise of Sir John Fortescue, CJKB, and John Portington, JCB, one of the assize justices for the midland circuit before whom Richard's assize of novel disseisin was pending. They returned their award in London on 15 November, a year to the day after Hugh's death.[99]

Inevitably the main part of the award was concerned with the division of the estates. Under its terms Richard was to have immediate possession of a considerable part of the Willoughby lands, including the valuable manor of Wollaton. The price he had to pay was the permanent loss of the two outlying Lincolnshire manors at Dunsby and Wigtoft, which were settled on Margaret and her heirs, but this was greatly preferable to losing the estates alienated under the terms of his father's will. Indeed, the most unfortunate provision of Hugh's will was that those lands permanently alienated from the common-law heir lay at the heart of the Willoughby inheritance, a provision to some extent forced on him by the fact that these were the only lands he held in fee simple. The arbiters noted the undesirability of this provision in their award when they stated that Richard was to have the main Nottinghamshire lands of the inheritance, either in possession or reversion, 'for his great ease and quiet and to that end that no other person but he shall have interest in the said towns of Wollaton, Sutton and Willoughby'. For her part, Margaret too had little reason for complaint. She could not reasonably expect to hold on to all she had gained under the terms of her late husband's will, and yet from the award she gained much more than her common-land dower entitlement, and also at the same time secured the permanent alienation of the two Lincolnshire manors to her and her heirs. Together with the considerable estates she held in her own right, principally the Warwickshire manor of Middleton, this made her a very rich widow.

Having settled the estates in a satisfactory manner it remained to the arbiters to ensure that the settlement would withstand any subsequent challenge at law, particularly urgent was the need to insure Margaret's

[99] Both halves of their indented award survive: NUL, Mi. 4662, 4763.

heirs against a challenge by Richard or his heirs for the two Lincolnshire manors, both of which had been entailed to the main Willoughby line in the fourteenth century. To solve this problem the arbiters chose to break the entails on all the Willoughby lands. The award provides that Richard and Margaret should jointly enter the inheritance and suffer a common recovery with single voucher. The two clerks who thus recovered the lands were then to settle them according to the terms of the award by deeds enrolled in common pleas. It is an interesting sidelight on this award that early in the following century the common recovery was to become much used for the breaking of entails to effect just the sort of settlement envisaged by Sir Hugh. The recovery prescribed in this award is a very early example of this collusive form of action.[100]

Taken as a whole, the return award was a masterly document, obviously drawn up by lawyers, and perhaps by Fortescue himself. Every possible cause of future dissension was dealt with, even down to provision for the keeping of the crops harvested at Wollaton in the previous year and the payment of any fines later to be incurred for any unlicensed alienations made by Sir Hugh. Most elaborately of all, further complex collusive litigation was to be undertaken in common pleas at Margaret's expense to secure the title of her son, Baldwin, to the small manor of Car Colston. This potentially highly divisive inheritance dispute was thus brought peacefully to a conclusion. Cromwell himself must take much of the credit, for although he probably had very little to do with the actual drafting of the award, except perhaps as it related to the actual division of the inheritance, which was not made on common-law principles, it seems likely that it was his authority in the county that resulted in the dispute being settled by arbitration rather than forcible disseisins.

With respect to the particular role of arbitration in fifteenth-century society, it is significant that a dispute of this nature, resulting as it did from the provisions of a will breaking earlier entails, would have been most uncommon before the late fourteenth century, when feoffments-to-use first became commonplace, and rarer still from the early sixteenth century, when it was well established that entails could be broken by common recovery. However, in between these times, with the aristocracy increasingly employing the use to devise land by will, and with a large proportion of aristocratic land bound by earlier entails, such disputes were very frequent. Furthermore, they had potentially serious

---

[100] 'The Reports of Sir John Spelman', ii. 204–5.

consequences for public order since they often occurred within the
leading magnate and county families. The story of the dispute between
Ralph, second earl of Westmorland, and his uncle (of the half-blood),
Richard, earl of Salisbury, is too well known to need repetition here, but
it is worth mentioning that Ralph's chagrin at his disinheritance was
exacerbated by the fact that some of the lands settled on his uncle had
earlier been entailed to him.[101] A similar, if less dramatic example, is the
dispute within the Talbot family after the first earl had attempted the
partial disinheritance of his common-law heir.[102] Although this dispute
was eventually peacefully settled, it is interesting to reflect on the very
serious repercussions it would probably have had if John, Lord Lisle,
the main beneficiary of the resettlement of the Talbot estates, had not
died with the first earl at the battle of Castillon in 1453. A closer parallel
with the Willoughby dispute is to be found in the feud that arose within
the wealthy Warwickshire family of Mountford in the 1450s. Sir
William Mountford attempted to disinherit his son by his first wife in
favour of his son by his second. Such an arrangement was bound to
cause trouble but the more so because the lands concerned were
entailed to the main Mountford line.[103] On William's death, an attempt
at arbitration between the two rival heirs failed because of the competitive
maintenance of the earl of Warwick and the duke of Buckingham:
maintenance which was doubly dangerous because it not only threatened
public order in Warwickshire but also reflected and deepened the
national divisions which eventually contributed to the fall of Lancaster.
In this context, Cromwell's achievement in peacefully bringing to an end
the dispute within the equally important family of Willoughby is the
more impressive. These reflections suggest that the apparent increase in
the use of arbitration in the fifteenth century may owe something to the
inability of the common law to resolve disputes arising from unusual

[101] K. B. McFarlane, *The Nobility of Later Medieval England* (Oxford, 1973), 67–8.

[102] For an interesting discussion of this dispute, which lasted from 1453 to 1466: A. J.
Pollard, 'The Family of Talbot, Lords Talbot and Earls of Shrewsbury in the Fifteenth
Century', Ph.D. thesis (Bristol, 1968), 51–62.

[103] R. A. Griffiths, 'The Hazards of Civil War: The Mountford Family and the "Wars
of the Roses"', *Midland History* 5 (1979–80), 1–19; M. C. Carpenter, 'Law, Justice and
Landowners in Late Medieval England', *Law and History Review* 1 (1983), 219–25. It is
not true to say, as Griffiths has done, that Sir William's action 'was quite legal in common
law'. A parliamentary petition, probably of 1461–2, claims that the main Mountford
manors of Coleshill and Ilmingdon had been entailed to the main line, 'as by severall gyftes
by fynes and dedes therof made redy to be shewyd more openly appereth': Birmingham
Public Library, A 590, printed by Griffiths, 'The Hazards of Civil War', 14–15. This was
certainly true for Coleshill, entailed by fine in 1371: 'Warwickshire Feet of Fines, 1345–
1509', *Publications of the Dugdale Society*, 18 (1943), no. 2188.

post mortem family settlements made through feoffments-to-use, and that, hence, it paralleled the developing equitable jurisdiction of the chancellor.[104] If this was the case Dr Saul's dictum that, by the later medieval period, 'society's ability to control the descent of land had outrun its ability to resolve the disputes to which it gave rise'[105] needs revision: equity and arbitration filled the gap left by the common law's failure to adapt.[106]

The Nottinghamshire evidence leaves no doubt either of the importance of arbitration as a means of dispute settlement or of its connection with the formal machinery of the law, a connection demonstrated not only by the use of collusive litigation to confirm the terms of an award but also in litigation employed as an inducement to compromise. Richard Willoughby sued his step-mother for trespass in king's bench and brought an assize of novel disseisin against her before submitting to Cromwell's arbitration. Similarly, in a later dispute, in which Richard himself acted as an arbiter, Sir Robert Clifton had brought the same assize against Sir Robert Strelley for lands in Lenton and Radford before submitting to arbitration, the arbiters awarding him the lands and Strelley a payment of 4 marks.[107] Moreover, the courts of common law gave support to arbitration by accepting the plea of an award as a bar to further legal proceedings,[108] and hence indirectly encouraged those with suits pending before them to seek extra-judicial solutions.

Nevertheless, despite the obvious merits of arbitration as an informal method of settlement working in conjunction with the law, it would be unwise to overlook its flaws. The first and most obvious of these was the lack of any machinery to enforce an award which either of the disputants was not prepared to honour. The only common-law remedy available to encourage observance was the action of debt on the recognizances that generally preceded any submission to arbitration, and hence the only effect of such failed arbitraments was to create a further bone of contention between the parties.[109] Second was the potential use of the

---

[104] For the early history of the chancellor's equitable jurisdiction: M. E. Avery, 'The History of the Equitable Jurisdiction of Chancery before 1460', *BIHR* 42 (1969), 129–44; Post, 'Equitable Resorts' and J. A. Guy, 'The Development of Equitable Jurisdictions', in *Law, Litigants and the Legal Profession*, 68–86.

[105] Saul, *Gloucestershire*, 204.

[106] This gap was later partially closed by common-law reforms associated with the statute of uses of 1536: E. W. Ives, 'The Common Lawyers in Pre-Reformation England', *TRHS*, 5th series, 18 (1968), 172. See more generally: J. G. Bellamy, *Bastard Feudalism and the Law* (London, 1989), 133–9.

[107] *CAD*, vi. 114; C146/4665.

[108] Powell, 'Arbitration and the Law', 56, 63.   [109] Ibid. 63–4.

arbitration process as another of the weapons with which the locally powerful could attack their less powerful neighbours. The award imposed by Cromwell on Grey in 1441 serves as an example, and Dr Wright has cited a suit of 1410 from the plea side of king's bench in which several retainers of William, son of Sir Richard Vernon (d. 1401) of Haddon, were said 'to ride with him to market towns and elsewhere to maintain him in his pleas under colour of negotiating and of holding love-days in the said pleas'.[110] Third, and most important, was the possibility that the arbiters themselves might be drawn into a dispute. Nottinghamshire provides the notable example of the conflict between Alexander Mering and John Tuxford, in which a failed loveday provoked a major riot due to the competitive maintenance of three of those who had, five days before, acted as arbiters. It was not, however, in these flaws, potentially significant though they were, that the greatest weakness of the arbitration process lay, but rather in its complete dependence on either the willingness of the disputants themselves to come to a settlement or, where no such willingness existed, the effectiveness of the social pressure that could be exerted on the disputants by a local community or lord anxious to maintain peace. If the parties remained intractable then the only hope of restraint lay in the imperfect checks of the law. In short, arbitration depended for its efficiency, as did any other informal and non-coercive means of dispute settlement, on a desire at the local level for the maintenance of social peace. Since a complete breakdown of order served only the interests of the singularly ruthless or the common criminal, this desire was generally in evidence. For much of the Lancastrian period in Nottinghamshire, for example, it is clear that the local community was generally prepared to make efforts to restrain those disputes that arose within it, and, for most of the period, the notable exception being the later years of the reign of Henry IV, the index of aristocratic disorder in the county was low. But if this desire for peace should break down, as it did most spectacularly in Devon in the 1450s, when the dispute between Thomas Courtenay (d. 1458), earl of Devon, and William (d. 1461), Lord Bonville, exploded into violence,[111] good order had to be imposed from above by the active exertion of royal authority. However sophisticated the processes of extra-judicial dispute

---

[110] Wright, pp. 123–4.

[111] M. Cherry, 'The Struggle for Power in Mid-Fifteenth Century Devonshire', in R. A. Griffiths (ed.), *Patronage, the Crown and the Provinces in Later Medieval England* (Gloucester, 1981), 123–44; R. L. Storey, *The End of the House of Lancaster* (London, 1966), 84–92, 165–75.

settlement became, it could not compensate for a king who was incapable of making that exertion. In this sense, the maintenance of order in the later medieval period depended on the crown. This is not to deny either the advantages of arbitration as a means of dispute settlement or the part that local communities and magnates played through it in regulating disorder, but it is to recognize the limitations of a system that depended for its effect on goodwill rather than coercion.

CONCLUSION

THIS study has emphasized the political independence and influence of a small élite of early fifteenth-century Nottinghamshire gentry families distinguished from their gentry neighbours by wealth and a continuing tradition of knighthood. It was an élite of varied and varying composition, ranging from ancient and conservative families, like the Strelleys and the Pierpoints, who had added little to their estates since their emergence to prominence in the thirteenth century, to families much more recently established amongst the leading gentry, such as the Willoughbys and Markhams, who owed their advancement to the profits of the law. This variety, a reflection of the fluctuating composition of the élite, was produced by the frequent failure of families in the main male line and the consequent transfer of property from one family to another. These transfers ensured that the élite remained permeable, allowing those families who had profited greatly from the law or royal service to supplement through inheritance those lands that their profits had enabled them to acquire on the sluggish land market. But this permeability was not the only consequence of these transfers: the cumulative effect of marriages contracted between failed families and families already established amongst the élite was to concentrate landed wealth in the hands of fewer families. It was for this reason, combined with the new avenues for rapid social advancement, most notably the law, which opened up during the later medieval period, that the gentry élite of early fifteenth-century Nottinghamshire was much more clearly defined than it had been a century earlier.

While the development and composition of this élite is readily delineated, it is much more difficult to evaluate the degree of corporate identity that existed between its members. They certainly did not form an inward-looking clique. Their lands in other counties provided them with the motivation and the means to extend the range of their social connections beyond the county boundaries, and the degree to which they successfully did this meant that as a group the élite of the county families was neither closely interrelated nor interdependent. For them, kinship overlapped with county but was not subsumed within it. It is difficult to discern any precise or coherent sense of community in their marriages (save perhaps where heiresses were involved) and conveyances beyond that inevitable degree of interaction guaranteed by neighbour-hood. Nor did the quarter sessions of the county bench or the monthly meetings of the county court, both generally ill-attended, serve as regular forums at which they gathered. From such evidence it is difficult to maintain the idea of a coherent county community, at least as far as the natural leaders of that community are concerned.

Nevertheless, before abandoning an idea which has served seventeenth-century historians so well,[1] it is worth sounding a note of caution for there is no doubt that the degree of interaction between these leading shire families is underestimated by both the incompleteness and the nature of the surviving sources. What we do not know may be more important that what we do. No evidence survives of their informal gatherings beyond the formalized lists of witnesses to deeds: there are no attendance lists for baptisms, marriages, or funerals, or records of other less solemn occasions that might have been expected to bring the leading men of the shire together. Further, without some sense of a community of shared interest among the most prominent gentry of a shire, it is difficult to explain the commons' petitions of the late fourteenth and early fifteenth centuries, which sought successfully to confine the administration and representation of the shire to the greater gentry resident within that shire. These petitions reflect what Dr Saul has seen as the increasing identification of the gentry with the county of their residence.[2] A tantalizing glimpse of the strength of this identification is provided by the revealing and oft-quoted comment of the Norfolk lawyer John Jenny on that county's 1455 election: '[it is] a evill precedent for the shire that a straunge man shulde be chosyn . . . for yf the jentilmen of the shire will suffre sech inconvenyens, in good feithe, the shire shall noght be called of seche wurship as it hathe been'.[3] A similar

---

[1] This service seems to be coming to an end. Dr C. Holmes has recently called into question the degree to which localism and county should be stressed at the expense of constitutional and religious factors operating at a national level: C. Holmes, 'The County Community in Stuart Historiography', *Journal of British Studies* 19 (1979–80), 54–73. It might, however, be argued that the local and the national were not mutually exclusive and that it was the tension between them, with political and religious allegiances competing with, and ultimately overriding, local loyalties, that exacerbated the mid-17th.-c. crisis.

[2] N. E. Saul, *Knights and Esquires; The Gloucestershire Gentry in the Fourteenth Century* (Oxford, 1981), 259.

[3] *Paston Letters and Papers of the Fifteenth Century*, ed. N. Davis (1971–6), ii. 120–1.

sentiment in a different context is to be found in an early fifteenth-century cartulary's description of a dispute between the executors of a Devon esquire and the Somerset knight, Sir Thomas Fichet, over some lands in Somerset: 'the executors were foreigners from the county of Devon, and doubted whether they could hold possession and sustain the dispute against Sir Thomas, because the tenements were *hors de lour pais et en le pais* of the said Sir Thomas'.[4]

In face of such evidence, it may be appropriate to stress that which indicates a sense of corporate identity within the shire administration. There can be no doubt that, even if the leading men of early fifteenth-century Nottinghamshire did not strongly identify with each other, they did feel corporately responsible for the administration of the county in which they lived. As a body they dominated the major offices of local government, providing the majority of the county's parliamentary knights of the shire, sheriffs, and justices of the peace, and, although they were landholders in several other shires, they rarely played a part in the administration of any other counties. Moreover, two pieces of Nottinghamshire evidence suggest that this sense of identity with shire extended beyond a feeling of joint responsibility for its administration. The decoration of the windows of Kemp's great hall in the archbishop of York's palace at Southwell, with the arms of ten of the eleven surviving families of the Nottinghamshire élite, reflects both the identity of these families with the county and a contemporary awareness of their pre-eminence within the shire community.[5] Secondly, the role they played in arbitrating property disputes, most notably illustrated by the Strelley *v.* Willoughby dispute of 1425,[6] suggests that the bonds which bound local society together were stronger than the low level of mutual dependence in marriages and conveyances would imply. This is not to suggest that the leading shire gentry formed a coherent community which acted with a corporate political will of its own (the divisions occasioned by

[4] E315/60, fo. 27ᵛ, published as *The Hylle Cartulary*, ed. R. W. Dunning, Somerset Record Society, 68 (1968), no. 86. The distinction drawn in this document between Somerset and Dorset implies that the term *pais* is being employed to mean 'county'. In other sources the words *pais* and *counte* are used interchangeably: *RP*, iii. 302; *Calendars of the Proceedings in Chancery in the Reign of Queen Elizabeth*, ed. J. Bailey, 3 vols. (London, 1827–32), i, p. iii.

[5] Above, p. 16. A similar sense of county identity is reflected in the more extensive heraldic decoration of the windows of the church at Nettlestead in Kent, which date from about the same time as those of the palace of Southwell: W. E. Ball, 'The Stained-Glass Windows of Nettlestead Church', *Archaeologia Cantiana* 28 (1909), 157–249, esp. 239–40.

[6] Above, p. 203.

the dispute between Alexander Mering and John Tuxford in 1411 demonstrate that this was not so), but only that the horizontal bonds that drew them together were as potent a factor in local politics as the more frequently emphasized vertical ties between the gentry and their baronial superiors.

There can be little doubt that most of the work done hitherto on the baronial affinity, through its concentration on the exceptionally powerful retinues of Edward Courtenay (d. 1419), earl of Devon, Richard Beauchamp (d. 1439), earl of Warwick, Humphrey Stafford (d. 1460), duke of Buckingham, and William (d. 1483), Lord Hastings has tended to exaggerate the impact of the affinity as a general phenomenon on fifteenth-century shire politics. If the emphasis is shifted from these great magnates at the heads of their powerful affinities to the leading non-baronial landholders as members of well-defined shire establishments, a very different picture of baronial–gentry relations emerges. The leading gentry looked to their landed wealth rather than to a baronial patron for their place in shire politics, and it was this wealth that made them attractive to both crown and baronage as recipients of patronage. In England as a whole, their corporate wealth was not far inferior to that of the baronage and, in some counties, of which Nottinghamshire was one, they were, at the county level, individually and corporately wealthier. In such counties baronial influence, if it was to be exercised at all, had to be exercised through them. Moreover, in these counties their greater independence was reflected in the more direct connection between them and the crown, particularly in counties where the crown was territorially or tenurially strong.

It is a fact not always given its due weight that the crown, particularly in the immediate aftermath of the Lancastrian usurpation of 1399, headed what was incomparably the greatest of all affinities. It was the crown that could afford to pay the greatest rewards to its servants, and hence it was the king's affinity that attracted the wealthiest and most ambitious gentry. The history of Lancastrian Nottinghamshire amply illustrates the political importance of this fact. The gentry of the county, both the leading families and those immediately below them in rank, benefited very greatly from royal patronage in the aftermath of Henry IV's accession. From 1400 the new king was paying nearly £400 per annum in fees from the crown and duchy of Lancaster revenues to the gentry of the county.[7] They repaid this royal generosity by rallying to the

---

[7] Above, p. 134.

Lancastrian cause at the battle of Shrewsbury in July 1403. Thereafter, however, the royal affinity in the county, as in other shires, was allowed to wither; old fees were confirmed but few new ones were granted. An attempt to reconstruct the affinity in the 1440s by drawing some of the leading county gentry into a greatly expanded royal household failed for, although several of the greater gentry of the county drew household robes and in return played an even more than usually active role in county administration, they did not, in marked contrast to their grand-fathers, benefit in any more substantial way from royal patronage. Thus, having no worthwhile vested interest in its continuance, they abandoned the Lancastrian regime to its fate in 1460–1. That the gentry of a county of traditionally Lancastrian sympathy like Nottinghamshire should so readily have abandoned the house of Lancaster is a telling testimony to the ineptness of Henry VI and his government. It also serves to warn against seeing the fall of Lancaster, and late-medieval politics in general, solely in terms of the relationship between the crown and the nobility. The crown's relationship with the leading gentry was of equal importance for, in many counties, it was they who, in the absence of a great lord with his principal residence in the county, formed wealthy, independent, shire establishments and were the principal factor in shire politics.

APPENDIX I

Nottinghamshire Tax Returns of 1412 (E179/159/48)

Resident Landholders

(*a*) Lay magnates:

William, Lord Roos of Belvoir	(£80)	£90
Robert Thornburgh[1]	(£10)	
John Talbot, Lord Furnival		£40
Ralph, Lord Cromwell		£40
Sir William Bourchier[2]	(£40)	£54
Sybil Beauchamp[3]	(£14)	
Joan, Lady Beauchamp		£30
Alice, Lady Deincourt		£30
Richard, Lord Grey of Codnor		£20
Henry, Lord FitzHugh		£20
Michael de la Pole	(£20)	£25
Earl of Suffolk[4]	(£5)	
Sir Geoffrey Scrope of Masham		£20
John Nevill		£10
Constance, Lady Despenser		£5
William, Lord Zouche		£4
TOTAL		£388

[1] John (d. 1393), Lord Roos, had granted his manor of Sutton-on-Trent to Thornburgh for life, a grant later confirmed by William, Lord Roos: *Notts. IPM, 1350–1436*, 129, 155.

[2] He held the manor of Kneesall in the right of his wife, Anne, widow of Edmund (d. 1403), earl of Stafford, and daughter and heiress of Eleanor de Bohun (d. 1399) by Thomas (d. 1397), duke of Gloucester: *CP*, v. 177–8; Thoroton, iii. 135.

[3] Gloucester had died seised of Kneesall and two-thirds of the manor of Arnold, part of the moiety of the de Bohun inheritance he enjoyed in Eleanor's right, the other third of Arnold being held in dower by Eleanor's mother, Joan (d. 1419), countess of Hereford: *Notts. IPM, 1350–1436*, 133–4. On Gloucester's death, Eleanor settled the two-thirds of Arnold, along with the reversion of Joan's third, on Sybil Beauchamp, one of her servants and later one of her executors, for Sybil's life: *CPR, 1399–1401*, 366; *Testamenta Vetusta*, ed. N. H. Nicolas, 2 vols. (1826), i. 149.

[4] These two entries both appear to relate to Michael de la Pole, earl of Suffolk, who, on 18 Sept. 1415, died seised jointly with his wife Katherine (d. 1419) of the Notts. manor of Grassthorpe, and their eldest son and heir, Michael de la Pole, who was killed at the battle of Agincourt on 25 Oct. 1415: *Notts. IPM, 1350–1436*, 156, 165–6; *CP*, xii, pt. 1, 422–3.

(*b*) Lands temporarily out of magnate hands:

Queen Joan (Bardolf)[5]	£35
John Niandser (Scrope of Bolton)[6]	£80
TOTAL	£115
TOTAL FOR MAGNATE LANDS	£503

(*c*) Greater knights:

The class of 'greater knights' is composed of those families assessed at £100 p.a. or more in 1412, 1436, or 1451, excluding the Cokfelds, assessed at £106 p.a. in 1436 (and £80 in 1451), as their wealth was temporarily inflated by the life interest of John Cokfeld's wife, Margaret, in the manors of Gamston and Haughton, which she enjoyed by the grant of her first husband, Ralph Monboucher (d. 1416: *Notts. IPM, 1350–1436*, 157–8), and with the addition of the Leeks of Cotham and the Cressys of Hodsock, who both failed in the main male line before 1436 but were certainly each worth in excess of £100 p.a. In total, this class comprises 13 families, of which only the Babingtons, much of whose wealth was acquired later in the century, and the Cressys of Hodsock, who failed in the male line in 1408, are not represented in the tax returns of 1412.

Sir Thomas Chaworth	£92
Hugh Willoughby	£80
Gervase Clifton	£60
Margaret, widow of Sir Thomas Rempston	£60
Milicent, widow of Sir John Markham	£30
Sir John Zouche	£25

[5] On the attainder of Thomas, Lord Bardolf, in Dec. 1406, the Notts. manor of Stoke Bardolph with Shelford came into the hands of the crown and was granted, with the rest of the Bardolf inheritance, to Queen Joan: *CPR, 1405–8*, 46; *RP*, iii. 606–7. In 1409 the reversion was granted to Bardolf's daughters and coheiresses, Anne and Joan, and their husbands, Sir William Clifford and Sir William Phelip: *Calendar of Inquisitions Miscellaneous, 1399–1422*, nn. 382, 385; *CPR, 1408–13*, 95–6; *Notts. IPM, 1350–1436*, 3. In 1453 the manor came to William, son of John (d. 1460), Viscount Beaumont, by Elizabeth, daughter of Joan by Sir William Phelip: *Notts. IPM, 1437–85*, 38–9; *CP*, xi. 543.

[6] Margaret, one of the three daughters and coheiresses of Robert (d. 1372), third Lord Tybotot of Langar, and widow of Roger (d. 1403), second Lord Scrope of Bolton, married, as her second husband, John Niandser of Niandser in Westmorland, a member of her late husband's household and a man already indicted for felonious killing: *Plea Rolls of the County Palatine of Lancaster*, Chetham Society, NS 87 (1928), 67–9; *CPR, 1413–16*, 251; *RP*, iv. 164; *CP*, xi. 542. In her right he held the very valuable Tybotot manor of Langar until Aug. 1414 when he was forced to abjure the realm after murdering Queen Joan's chancellor, John Tibbay, clerk, a former servant of Scrope who had opposed his marriage to Margaret: ibid.; J. Stow, *Annales or A General Chronicle of England* (1631), 345–6. On Margaret's death in 1431 the manor came to her grandson, Henry (d. 1459), fourth Lord Scrope of Bolton, who married a granddaughter of Sir Thomas Chaworth: *CP*, xi. 543.

Sir Richard Stanhope	£60
Sir Nicholas Strelley	£40
Sir Edmund Pierpoint	£80
Sir John Leek of Cotham	£60
Sir William Nevill of Rolleston	£20
TOTAL	£607

(*d*) Lesser knights and distrainees:

The class of 'lesser knights and distrainees' is composed of all other resident families who: *a*. provided a knight during the Lancastrian period; *b*. were assessed at £40 p.a. or more in 1412, 1436 or 1451; or *c*. were distrained for knighthood in 1410–11, 1430, 1439, or 1458. In total, there were 28 such families, including the wealthy Nottingham merchant family of Samon (they are listed in Appendix 5, except for the Samons and the Leeks of Langford and Sandiacre, who appear to have made their principal residences in Derbyshire from the 1420s): 21 of these are represented in the tax returns of 1412.

Ralph Makerell	£40
Thomas Staunton	£20
Alice Staunton	£33
Alexander Mering	£22
Sir Robert Barry	£20
Sir Hugh Husy	£20
William Sibthorpe	£20
Henry Sutton	£20
William Saundby	£20
William Wastnes	£20
Hugh Cressy	£30
William Leek of Screveton	£40
Thomas Annesley, sen.	£20
Thomas Annesley of Burton Joyce	£20
Margaret, widow of Sir John Annesley	£5
John Samon of Nottingham	£30
Thomas Boson	£20
Thomas Bekering	£20
Thomas Staunton of Sutton Bonington	£10
Sir John Burton	£20
Sir Thomas Hercy	£40
Emma, widow of John Grey	£28
John Leek	£15
Sir Robert Cokfeld	£20
Thomas Basset	40m
Margaret Basset	20m
TOTAL	£593

(*e*) Royal annuities and farms:

Queen Joan (various fee farms)[7]	£61
Geoffrey Lowther (Edwinstowe)[8]	£13
John Ferrour of Blyth (fee farm of Nottingham)[9]	£13
Robert Morton (Arnold farm)[10]	£10
Roger Deincourt (issues of the county)[11]	40m
John Kirkeby, clerk (issues of the shrievalty)[12]	£20
Sir John Burton (issues of the shrievalty)[13]	£20
TOTAL	£170 13*s.* 4*d.*

(*f*) Lesser county gentry:

The class of 'lesser county gentry' is composed of all other identifiable resident assessees of 1412.

William Compton	£20
Roger Pierpoint	£20
William Eland	£20
Thomas Kelham	£20
Peter Assheton	£20
John Bevercotes	£20
William Wollaton	£10
Richard Clydrowe	£10
Thomas Hunte	£8
Hugh Thorpe	£20
Richard Wakefeld	20m
William Cressy	£10
William Skevington	£10
John Kniveton	£14
Ralph Monboucher	£20
Elizabeth, widow of George Monboucher	£16
Richard Leek	£20
Richard Strelley	£10
Lucia Warde	£10
John Lake of Newark	20m
Nicholas Stapleford	£10

---

[7] *CPR, 1401–5*, 234–5, 268–9, 271.

[8] Ibid. *1405–8*, 45; *CCR, 1409–13*, 177.

[9] *CPR, 1374–7*, 84; *1377–81*, 126, 586; *1399–1401*, 86.

[10] Ibid. *1391–6*, 708; *1399–1401*, 39–40; *1405–8*, 115. His appearance in these tax returns show that Morton, who suffered forfeiture for his involvement in Scrope's rebellion of 1405, had been restored to his annuity from the farm of Arnold before 12 June 1414, when it was officially regranted to him: ibid. *1413–16*, 230.

[11] Ibid. *1399–1401*, 240; *1405–8*, 277.

[12] Ibid. *1396–9*, 70; *1399–1401*, 246.

[13] Ibid. 370.

Ralph Adderley	10m
Peter Ker, clerk	£12
Bartholomew Montgomery	£20
TOTAL	£353 6s. 8d.

Non-Resident Landholders (Excluding Magnates)

(g) Lands held by royal grant:

Sir Thomas Beaufort (Freville lands)[14]	£30
Eleanor, widow of Sir Nicholas Dagworth (Mansfield and Linby)[15]	£40

(h) Widows:

Joan, widow of Sir John Paveley	£66
Beatrice, widow of Sir Hugh Shirley	£60
Elizabeth, widow of Sir John Scrope	£40
Hawisia, widow of Sir Andrew Luttrell	£25
Elizabeth, widow of Sir Ralph Newmarche	£20
Agnes, widow of Walter Devereux	£13
Joan, widow of Sir Richard Byron	£20
Elizabeth, widow of Sir William Elmham	£10

(i) Non-resident knights:

Sir John FitzWilliam	£42
Sir Roger Swillington	£40
Sir Robert Plumpton	£20
Sir John Etton	£20
Sir John Mountney	£5
Sir John Eynesford	£43
Sir Henry Nevill	£6
Sir Roger Leche	£10
Sir William Thirning, CJCB	£40
Sir William Boteler	£20
Sir Thomas Clinton	£6

(j) Other non-residents:

Robert Waterton	£30
Achilles Bosevylle	£20
Robert Deincourt	£24
John Bushy	£20
John Swillington	£20
Gerard Ursflete	£20
Richard Keymes	£20

[14] *CFR, 1399–1405*, 85; *CPR, 1399–1401*, 393; *1401–5*, 98.
[15] Ibid. *1399–1401*, 116, 479, 537; *1405–8*, 143.

Robert Harbotell	10m
John Bell	£6
Aydayme Sallowe	£20
George Sallowe	10m
Peter Saltby	£5
Humphrey Halughton	£7
John Hastings	10m
Norman Charnels	10m
Felicia Bugge	£10
John Slory	£6
TOTAL FOR NON-RESIDENT LANDHOLDERS	£810 13s. 4d.

Note: I have been unable to identify Thomas Fleming, assessed at £20. The names of two other assessees, together assessed at £14, are illegible.

APPENDIX 2
Tax Assessments at £40 p.a. and Over in 1436 and 1451

1436	Income (£)	1451	Income (£)
Sir Thomas Chaworth	320	Sir Thomas Chaworth	199
Sir Hugh Willoughby	200	Margaret Rempston	120
Sir Gervase Clifton	193	Robert Strelley	100 10s.
Sir William Babington	160	Sir Gervase Clifton	100
Sir John Zouche	120	William Babington	100
Thomas Nevill of Rolleston	120	John Cokfeld	80
Sir Richard Stanhope	107	Thomas Nevill of Rolleston	79 6s. 8d.
John Cokfeld	106	Henry Boson	74
Margaret Rempston	106	Margaret Zouche	60
Sir Robert Strelley	100	Sir Henry Pierpoint	53 6s. 8d.
Sir Giles Daubeney	99	John Stanhope	50 19s.
Thomas Darcy	80	Richard Sutton	47
Margery Makerell	80	William Mering	42
Ralph Leek of Screveton	72	Richard Willoughby	40
Richard Samon	65		
Richard Wentworth	65		
Sir William Mering	61		
Sir Thomas Rempston	60		
William Sibthorpe	48		
Isabella Halughton	46		
Thomas Okere	44		
Henry Boson	40		
Thomas Curson	40		
John Leek	40		
Hugh Hercy	40		

Note: In 1436 Sir Robert Markham was assessed at £120 p.a. in London. In 1451 Sir William Babington was assessed at £40 p.a. in the town of Nottingham: E179/238/78/6. It is not clear why Thomas Okere, the head of a family from Okeover in Staffs. and Snelston in Derbys., should have been assessed in Nottinghamshire in 1436.

APPENDIX 3
Knightly Families Resident in Nottinghamshire in the Second Quarter of the Fourteenth Century with the Dates of their Failure in the Male Line[1]

Annesley of Annesley	1437
Aslockton of Aslockton	ante 1414[2]
Barry of Teversal	*c.*1473[3]
Barry of Tollerton	1545[4]
Bekering of Tuxford	1425
Bevercotes of Bevercotes	late 16th c.[5]
Bingham of Bingham	*c.*1390
Brett of Wiverton	*c.*1385
Brut of Thorney	post 1442[6]
Burdon of Maplebeck	1403
Burton of Burton Joyce	post 1454[7]
Chaworth	1483
Clifton of Clifton	1869[8]
Cokfeld of Nuthall	1453
Compton of Hawton	1461[9]
Cressy of Hodsock	1408
Cromwell of Lambley	1456
Crophill of Sutton Bonington	1383[10]
Everingham of Laxton	1388[11]
Furneux of Carlton in Lindrick	1349[12]

---

[1] The date at which the senior male line failed. I have used the same rules as outlined in K. B. McFarlane, *The Nobility of Later Medieval England* (1973), 172–3.

[2] Edmund Cranmer (the great-grandfather of Thomas Cranmer (d. 1556), archbishop of Canterbury), who married Isabella, the daughter and heiress of William Aslockton, had succeeded to the Aslockton estates by June 1414: Thoroton, i. 263; KB9/204/2/10.

[3] E179/159/84; Thoroton, ii. 306.

[4] S. P. Potter, *A History of Tollerton* (Nottingham, 1929), 66.

[5] Thoroton, iii. 357.

[6] This family appears to have failed between 1442 and 1451: E404/59/105; E179/159/84.

[7] The last reference to this family is June 1454: *Notts. IPM, 1437–85*, 38.

[8] K. S. S. Train, *Twenty Nottinghamshire Families* (Nottingham, 1969), 14.

[9] *Notts. IPM, 1437–85*, 64.

[10] Ibid. *1350–1436*, 92.

[11] *CP*, v. 190–1.

[12] *CIPM*, ix, no. 176.

Goushill of Hoveringham	1403[13]
Grey of Langford	1383[14]
Hercy of Grove	1570
Heriz of Gonalston	1329
Husy of Flintham	late 16th c.[15]
Jorce of Burton Joyce	1403[16]
Leek of West Leake	ante 1434
Lisures of Fledborough	c.1364[17]
Longviliers of Tuxford	1369
Loudham of Lowdham	1390
Mering of Meering	1635[18]
Mounteny of Stoke-by-Newark	temp. RII[19]
Nevill of Rolleston	1571
Pierpoint of Holme Pierrepont	1773[20]
Rempston of Rempstone	1458
St Andrew of Gotham	1626[21]
Saundby of Saundby	1418[22]
Staunton of Staunton-in-the-Vale	1689[23]
Strelley of Strelley	c.1503
Sutton of Averham	1723[24]
Thorpe of Thorpe-by-Newark	early 16th c.[25]
Vaux of Cotham	ante 1351
Vilers of Kinoulton	temp. E III[26]
Whatton of Whatton	post 1408[27]
Willoughby of Willoughby-on-the-Wolds	1596[28]

[13] *Notts. IPM, 1350–1436,* 143; Thoroton, iii. 62–3.

[14] Ibid. 96–7.

[15] Thoroton, i. 253.

[16] Ibid. iii. 19, 21; Borthwick Institute, Prob. Reg. 3, fo. 98.

[17] W. F. Carter and R. F. Wilkinson, 'The Fledborough Family of Lisures', *TTS* 44 (1940), 29.

[18] A. Cameron, 'Meering and the Meryng Family', *TTS* 77 (1973), 51.

[19] Thoroton, i. 348–9; J. Hunter, *South Yorkshire* (London, 1828–31), ii. 393.

[20] *CP*, vii. 309.

[21] Baker, *The History and Antiquities of the County of Northampton* (1822–41), i. 161.

[22] Borthwick Institute, Arch. Reg. 18, fo. 369ᵛ.

[23] G. W. Staunton and F. M. Stenton, *The Family of Staunton of Staunton* (Newark, 1911), 60.

[24] *CP*, vii. 628–9.

[25] *CFR, 1485–1509,* 371; Thoroton, i. 351–2.

[26] Thoroton, i. 153; *PC*, p. xxviii n.

[27] Thoroton, i. 268.

[28] 'The Family of Willoughby', *TTS* 6 (1902), supplement, 46–7.

APPENDIX 4
Genealogical Tables

Those who headed these families during the Lancastrian period are printed in bold type.

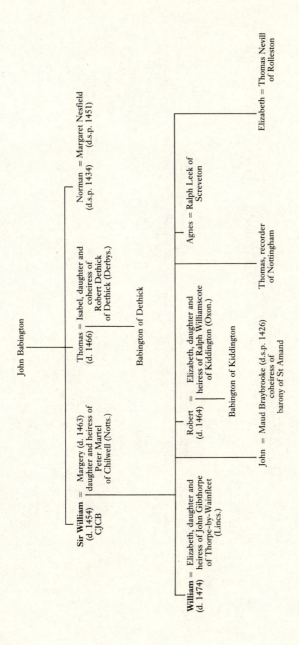

4.1. Babington of Chilwell

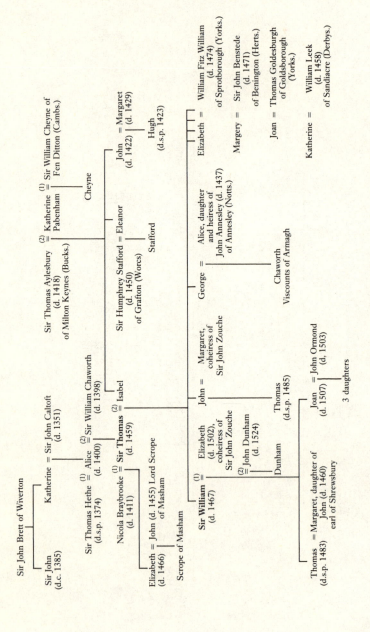

4.2. Chaworth of Wiverton

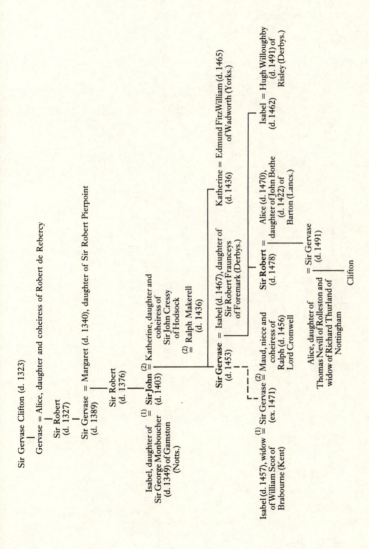

Sir Gervase Clifton (d. 1323)
|
Gervase = Alice, daughter and coheiress of Robert de Rebercy
|
Sir Robert
(d. 1327)
|
Sir Gervase = Margaret (d. 1340), daughter of Sir Robert Pierpoint
(d. 1389)
|
Sir Robert
(d. 1376)
|
Isabel, daughter of ⁽¹⁾ = Sir John ⁼⁽²⁾ Katherine, daughter and
Sir George Monboucher   (d. 1403)   coheiress of
(d. 1349) of Gamston   Sir John Cressy
(Notts.)   of Hodsock
                                        ⁽²⁾ = Ralph Makerell
                                              (d. 1436)

Sir Gervase = Isabel (d. 1467), daughter of   Katherine = Edmund FitzWilliam (d. 1465)
(d. 1453)   Sir Robert Fraunceys   (d. 1436)   of Wadworth (Yorks.)
             of Foremark (Derbys.)

Isabel (d. 1457), widow ⁽¹⁾ = Sir Gervase ⁼⁽²⁾ Maud, niece and   Sir Robert = Alice (d. 1470),   Isabel = Hugh Willoughby
of William Scot of   (ex. 1471)   coheiress of   (d. 1478)   daughter of John Bothe   (d. 1462)   (d. 1491) of
Brabourne (Kent)   Ralph (d. 1456)   (d. 1422) of   Risley (Derbys.)
                                           Lord Cromwell   Barton (Lancs.)

Alice, daughter of   = Sir Gervase
Thomas Nevill of Rolleston and   (d. 1491)
widow of Richard Thurland of |
Nottingham   Clifton

4·3. Clifton of Clifton

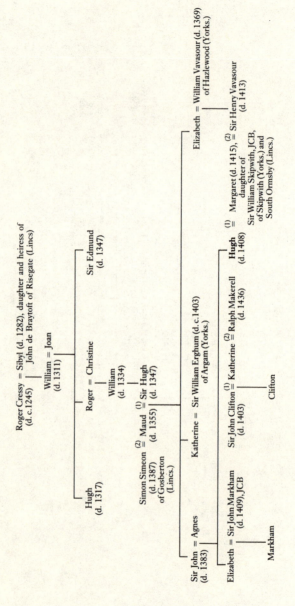

4.4. Cressy of Hodstock

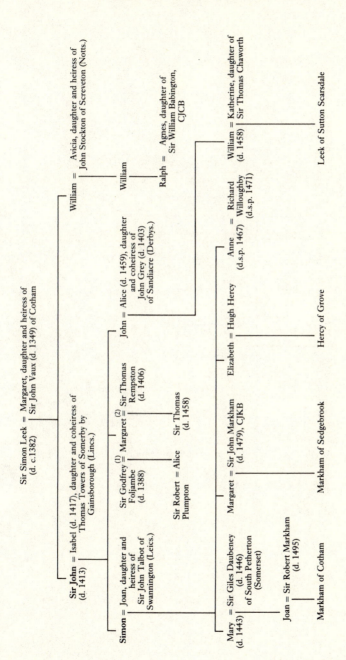

4.5. Leek of Cotham

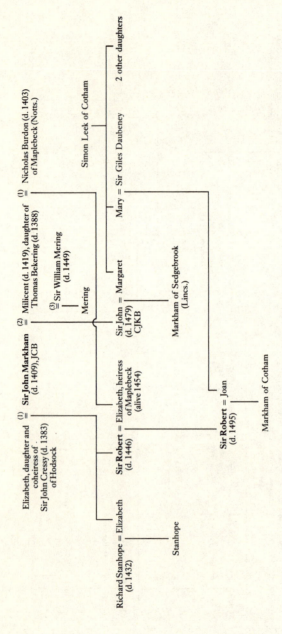

4.6. Markham of East Markham

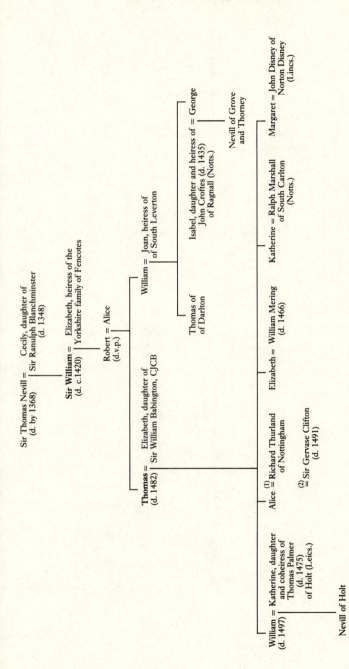

4.7. Nevill of Rolleston

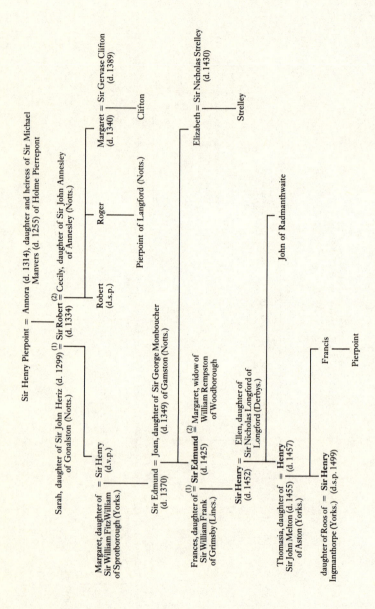

4.8. Pierpoint of Holme Pierrepont

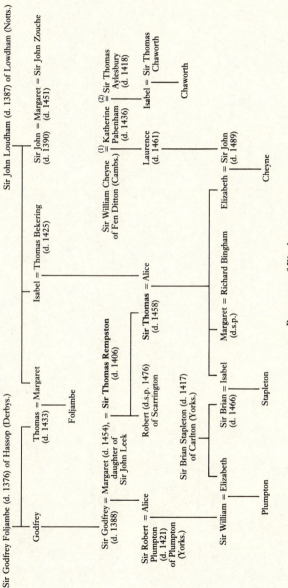

4.9. Rempston of Bingham

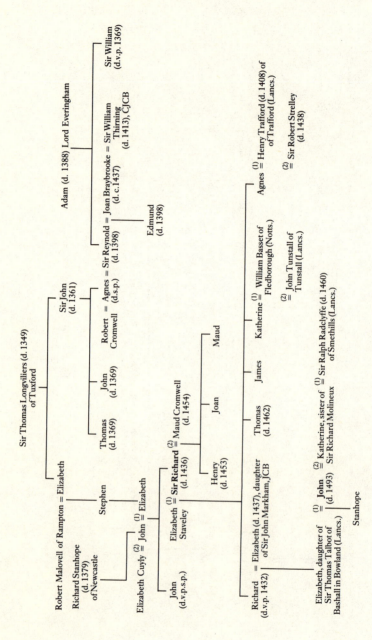

4.10. Stanhope of Rampton

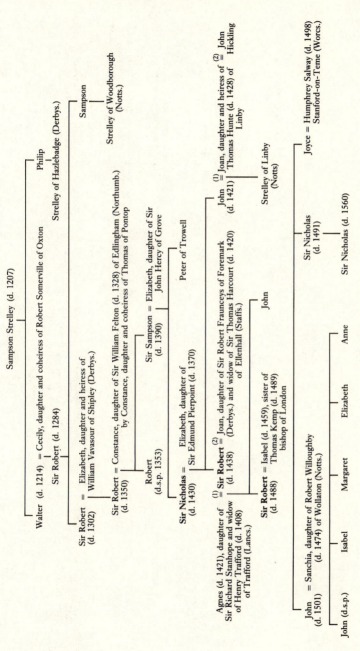

4·11. Strelley of Strelley

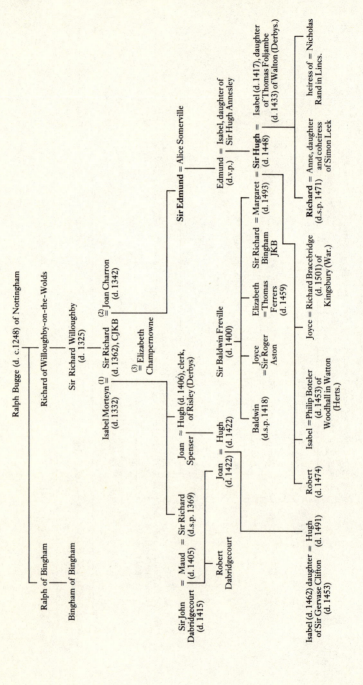

4.12. Willoughby of Wollaton

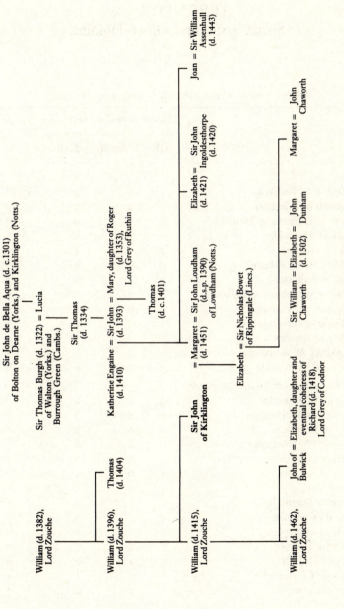

Sir John de Bella Aqua (d. c.1301)
of Bolton on Dearne (Yorks.) and Kirklington (Notts.)

Sir Thomas Burgh (d. 1322) = Lucia
of Walton (Yorks.) and
Burrough Green (Cambs.)

Sir Thomas
(d. 1334)

Katherine Engaine = Sir John = Mary, daughter of Roger
(d.1410)   (d. 1393)   (d. 1353),
                               Lord Grey of Ruthin

Thomas
(d. c.1401)

= Margaret = Sir John Loudham   Elizabeth = Sir John   Joan = Sir William
(d. 1451)   (d.s.p. 1390)   (d. 1421) Ingoldesthorpe   Assenhull
            of Lowdham (Notts.)   (d. 1420)   (d. 1443)

Elizabeth = Sir Nicholas Bowet
            of Rippingale (Lincs.)

Sir William = Elizabeth = John   Margaret = John
Chaworth   (d. 1502)   Dunham   Chaworth

William (d. 1382),
Lord Zouche

William (d.1396),   Thomas
Lord Zouche   (d. 1404)

William (d.1415),   **Sir John
Lord Zouche   of Kirklington**

William (d.1462),   John of = Elizabeth, daughter and
Lord Zouche   Bulwick   eventual coheiress of
                               Richard (d. 1418),
                               Lord Grey of Codnor

4.13. Zouche of Kirklington

APPENDIX 5
Social Status and Office-Holding

(Nottinghamshire offices only, held between 1399 and 1461)

	No. of times in office			JP
	MP	Sheriff	Escheator	
County élite				
Babington of Chilwell	5	3	2	+
Chaworth of Wiverton	7	4	0	+
Clifton of Clifton and Hodsock	3	3	0	+
Cressy of Hodsock	0	1	0	−
Leek of Cotham	2	2	1	+
Markham of Markham	0	1	0	+
Nevill of Rolleston	0	1	0	+
Pierpoint of Holme Pierrepont	4	0	0	+
Rempston of Bingham	2	0	1	+
Stanhope of Rampton	13	2	0	+
Strelley of Strelley	1	2	0	+
Willoughby of Wollaton	2	3	1	+
Zouche of Kirklington	5	1	0	+
Lesser knightage and greater squirearchy				
Annesley of Annesley	0	0	0	−
Annesley of Ruddington	0	0	0	−
Barry of Tollerton	0	0	0	−
Basset of Fledborough	0	0	0	−
Bekering of Laxton	0	0	0	−
Boson of Syerston	1	0	1	−
Brut of Thorney	0	0	0	−
Burton of Burton Joyce	1	1	0	−
Cokfeld of Nuthall	0	2	2	+
Cressy of Oldcoates	0	0	1	−
Curson of Bulcote	0	0	0	+
Darcy of Ordsall	0	1	0	−
Gaitford of Gateford	1	0	2	+
Hercy of Grove	1	1	0	+

Husy of Flintham	3	0	0	—
Leek of Screveton	1	0	1	—
Makerell of Hodsock	3	3	2	+
Mering of Meering	3	2	1	+
St Andrew of Gotham	0	0	0	—
Saundby of Saundby	0	0	0	+
Sibthorpe of Sibthorpe	0	0	0	—
Staunton of Staunton	0	0	0	—
Staunton of Sutton Bonington	1	2	0	—
Sutton of Averham	1	0	2	—
Wastnes of Headon	2	2	2	+
Wentworth of Everton	0	0	0	+
Lesser squirearchy				
Assheton of Ordsall	0	0	0	—
Barbour of Newstead	0	0	0	—
Barry of Teversal	0	0	0	—
Becard of Willoughby-by-Norwell	0	0	0	—
Bevercotes of Bevercotes	0	0	0	—
Bowes of Costock	4	0	1	+
Clay of Finningley	0	0	0	—
Compton of Hawton	1	0	0	—
Doyle	0	0	0	—
Eland of Algarthorpe	0	0	0	—
Hickling of Linby	0	1	2	—
Kellom of Kelham	0	0	0	—
Marshall of South Muskham	0	0	0	—
Monboucher of Gamston	0	0	0	—
Nevill of South Leverton	0	0	4	+
Pierpoint of Langford	0	0	0	—
Roos of Laxton	1	0	1	—
Strelley of Linby	1	0	0	—
Thorp of Thorpe-by-Newark	0	0	0	—

Note: These families have been classed as the 'county élite' or the 'lesser knightage and greater squirearchy' under the same rules as applied in Appendix 1. The class of 'lesser squirearchy' is composed of all those families assessed at £20 p.a. or more in 1412, 1436 or 1451 (excluding the Nottingham merchant families of Alastre, Rasyn, and Tannesley). Younger sons and brothers have been counted with the main branches of their families, but junior branches established beyond one generation have been counted separately.

APPENDIX 6
The King's Affinity in Nottinghamshire

TABLE A.6.1. *Fees of king's knights and esquires*

Date	Annuitant	Sum	Source	Reference
3 Nov. 1399	John Gaitford	£20	Issues of Notts.	*CPR, 1399–1401*, 120
12 Nov. 1399	Sir John Annesley	100m	Exchequer	ibid. 66
15 Dec. 1399	Robert Brut	£10	Issues of Lincs.	ibid. 142
5 Feb. 1400	Sir John Clifton	40m	Issues of Notts.	ibid. 226, 438–9
8 Feb. 1400	Hugh Annesley	£20	Issues of Notts.	ibid. 193
19 Feb. 1400	Robert Nevill	£10	Exchequer	ibid. 206
23 Feb. 1400	William Jorce	12*d*. p.d.	Exchequer	ibid. 207
18 Mar. 1400	Sir Richard Stanhope	40m	Issues of Notts.	ibid. 240
8 Jul. 1400	John Leek	10m	Issues of lands of William Hamsterley	ibid. 321
7 Nov. 1400	Sir John Burton	£20	Issues of Notts./Derbys.	ibid. 370
22 Nov. 1400	Robert Morton	40m	Exchequer	ibid. *1401–5*, 18
TOTAL		£251 11*s*. 8*d*.		

Two Nottinghamshire men with the lesser rank of king's servant were also in receipt of fees: Nicholas Warde of Normanton-on-Soar, keeper of the royal park of Bestwood (Notts.), had £10 p.a. from the issues of the county from 26 Oct. 1400 (*CPR, 1399–1401*, 6, 35); and Roger Doket of Nottingham had 20m p.a. from the issues of Nottinghamshire and Derbyshire from 16 Mar. 1400 (ibid. 279). I have excluded from consideration those king's servants, all minor men, in receipt of 6*d*. p.a. from the issues of the county: e.g. John Lord, Richard Clapham (ibid. 85, 98).

TABLE A.6.2. *Fees charged on the duchy of Lancaster*

Date	Annuitant	Sum	Source	Reference
26 Mar. 1395	Sir Hugh Husy	£20	Honor of Leicester and then the lordship of Higham Ferrers	*CPR, 1396–9*, 548; DL42/15, pt. 1, fo. 91^v
temp. Gaunt	William Rigmayden	10m	Issues of Lancaster	DL42/15, pt. 1, fo. 88
26 Sep. 1399		10m	Vill of Lancaster	DL42/16, pt. 1, fo. 25
23 Nov. 1399	William Leek	10m	Fee of Lancaster in Notts. and Leics.	*CPR, 1399–1401*, 118
2 Dec. 1399	William Wollaton	£20	Belper in Derbys.	DL42/15, pt. 1, fo. 20
11 Jun. 1400	John Wastnes	20m	Honor of Leicester and then lordship of Higham Ferrers	DL42/15, pt. 1, 15^v, 99^v
21 Jun. 1400	Bartholomew Montgomery	£10	Honor of Tutbury	DL42/15, pt. 1, fo. 11
temp. Gaunt	Sir Thomas Rempston	} 40m	Fee farm of Gunthorpe and Lowdham	DL42/16, pt. 3, fo. 71
5 Nov. 1406	Sir Thomas Chaworth			
?	Sir Thomas Hercy	20m	Honor of Pontefract	DL28/27/6.
TOTAL		£123 6s. 8d.		

APPENDIX 7
Nottinghamshire Elections 1407–1460

TABLE A.7.1. *Number of attestors present at elections*

Date of Election	A	B	C	D	E
17 Oct. 1407	12	3	—	—	33.3
12 Oct. 1411	32	1	3	90.6	21.9
24 Apr. 1413	56	0	13	73.2	46.4
23 Apr. 1414	8	0	2	37.5	12.5
5 Nov. 1414	29	2	1	44.8	24.1
24 Feb. 1416	20	0	6	15.0	10.0
1 Nov. 1417	15 (18)	1	4	46.7	20.0
2 Oct. 1419	16	1	3	25.0	25.0
25 Nov. 1420	11 (13)	2	1	45.5	0.0
14 Apr. 1421	10 (13)	0	3	30.0	10.0
24 Nov. 1421	12	3	3	25.0	16.7
26 Oct. 1422	11 (18)	4	5	0.0	0.0
27 Sept. 1423	26	7	6	50.0	30.8
25 Apr. 1425	29	4	7	31.0	10.3
10 Feb. 1426	18	4	10	22.2	5.6
25 Aug. 1427	12	0	0	58.3	58.3
19 Sept. 1429	34	1	0	55.9	41.2
11 Dec. 1430	8 (17)	2	3	25.0	0.0
24 Mar. 1432	13 (22)	4	1	7.7	0.0
22 Jun. 1433	12 (19)	3	6	8.3	0.0
12 Sept. 1435	12 (24)	0	1	25.0	8.3
10 Dec. 1436	19	1	3	36.8	10.5
25 Dec. 1441	10 (17)	3	4	30.0	10.0
16 Jan. 1447	25 (38)	5	3	40.0	20.0
13 Jan. 1449	15	9	5	40.0	20.0
20 Oct. 1449	223	2	2	95.1	52.5
19 Oct. 1450	16	3	5	18.8	0.0
5 Mar. 1453	22	3	6	22.7	9.1
30 Jun. 1455	61	2	4	45.9	31.2
5 Nov. 1459	29	1	6	37.5	6.3
6 Oct. 1460	226	4	12	62.8	36.1

A. Total number of county attestors. The figures in brackets represent the total number of attestors including those burgesses appended to the list of county attestors as witnesses to the borough return before Nottingham became a 'shire incorporate' in 1447. Only 16 of the 29 named attestors of November 1459 are legible.
B. Number of heads or heirs-apparent of families of the county élite present as attestors.
C. Number of county attestors who sealed the indenture immediately preceding.
D. Percentage of county attestors who had never previously acted as attestors in any surviving indenture.
E. Percentage of county attestors for whom this was their only recorded attestation.

Table A.7.1. may usefully be compared with the similar table in J. S. Roskell, *The Knights of the Shire for the County Palatine of Lancaster, 1377–1460*, Chetham Society, NS 96 (1937), 227. No Notts. returns survive for the parliaments of Jan. 1410, Feb. 1413, Nov. 1415, Oct. 1416, Nov. 1439, and Feb. 1445.

TABLE A.7.2. *Number of elections attested by all those who witnessed Nottinghamshire elections between October 1407 and October 1460 (including elections attested after that date by these same attestors)*

Elections attested (no.)	Attestors (no.)	% of total no. of attestors
10+	4*	0.6
5–9	28	4.4
4	28	4.4
3	67	10.6
2	164	25.9
1	344	54.2
	635	

* John Cokfeld of Nuthall, 14 elections; Ralph Bingham of Car Colston, a county coroner a.1418 to p. 1437, 14; Thomas Curson of Bulcote 11; Peter Strelley of Trowell, a county coroner a.1414 to p. 1426, 10.

TABLE A.7.3. *Number of elections attested by heads of families of the county élite, 1407–1460*

Sir Thomas Chaworth	7	(between Apr. 1425 and Jan. 1449)
Sir Hugh Willoughby	7	(Oct. 1411 to Jun. 1433)
Sir Gervase Clifton	7	(Nov. 1414 to Mar. 1432)
William Babington	7	(Dec. 1441 to Oct. 1460)
Sir Edmund Pierpoint	5	(Nov. 1414 to Sept. 1423)
Sir Henry Pierpoint	4	(Feb. 1426 to Oct. 1450)
Henry Pierpoint	4	(Dec. 1430 to Oct. 1449)
Richard Willoughby	4	(Dec. 1436 to Oct. 1460)
Sir Robert Markham	4	(Nov. 1420 to Feb. 1426)
Sir Nicholas Strelley	3	(Oct. 1407 to Sept. 1423)
Sir Robert Strelley (d. 1438)	3	(Oct. 1422 to Jun. 1433)
Sir Robert Strelley (d. 1488)	3	(Jan. 1449 to Oct. 1460)
Sir William Babington, CJCB	3	(Oct. 1407 to Mar. 1453)
Robert Clifton	3	(Dec. 1441 to Jan. 1449)
Sir Richard Stanhope	2	(Nov. 1420 to Mar. 1432)
John Stanhope	2	(Oct. 1449 to Oct. 1460)
Thomas Nevill of Rolleston	2	(Jan. 1449 to Mar. 1453)
Sir John Leek	1	(Oct. 1407)
Simon Leek	1	(Sept. 1423)
Sir John Zouche	1	(Sept. 1423)
Sir Thomas Rempston	1	(Jan. 1449)
William Chaworth	1	(Jan. 1449)

SELECT BIBLIOGRAPHY

1. Manuscript Sources
Public Record Office, Chancery Lane, London

C1	Early Chancery Proceedings.
C67	Patent Rolls (Supplementary).
C137–9	Chancery, Inquisitions Post Mortem, Henry IV to Henry VI.
C146–8	Chancery, Ancient Deeds.
C219	Writs and Returns of Members to Parliament.
C242	Chancery Files, Tower and Rolls Chapel Series, Certificates of Election of Coroners and Verderers.
CP25(1)	Feet of Fines.
CP40	Court of Common Pleas, *De Banco* Rolls.
DL42	Duchy of Lancaster, Miscellaneous Books.
E13	Exchequer of Pleas, Plea Rolls.
E101	King's Remembrancer, Various Accounts.
E152	King's Remembrancer, Enrolment of Inquisitions.
E179	King's Remembrancer, Subsidy Rolls.
E198	King's Remembrancer, Documents Relating to Serjeanties, Knights' Fees, etc.
E199	King's Remembrancer, Sheriffs' Accounts.
E210–11	King's Remembrancer, Ancient Deeds.
E370	Lord Treasurer's Remembrancer and Pipe Office, Miscellaneous Rolls.
E371	Lord Treasurer's Remembrancer, Originalia Rolls.
E372	Pipe Office, Pipe Rolls.
E404	Exchequer of Receipt, Writs and Warrants for Issues.
KB9	Ancient Indictments.
KB27	*Coram Rege* Rolls.
KB29	Controlment Rolls.
PROB	Prerogative Court of Canterbury.
SC6	Special Collections, Ministers' and Receivers' Accounts.
SC8	Special Collections, Ancient Petitions.

Nottinghamshire Record Office, Nottingham

FitzHerbert of Tissington Hall.
Foljambe of Osberton.
Franklin.
Kindersley.

Newark Magnus Charity.
Noble.
Portland.

Nottinghamshire University Library

Clifton of Clifton (Cl.).
Middleton (Mi.).
Newcastle of Clumber (Ne.).
Mellish.

British Library

MS Loan 29/60 (a cartulary of the Pierpoint family drawn up in 1482–3).
Additional Charters.
Additional Manuscripts.

Leicestershire Record Office, Leicester

Ferrers of Staunton Hall (26D53).
Ferrers Cartulary (15D72).
Peake (Nevill of Holt).

Borthwick Institute, St Anthony's Hall, York

Archbishops' Registers.
Probate Registers.

Magdalen College, Oxford

Cromwell Papers.

Sheffield Central Library

Charters of the Cromwell Family.

2. Printed Sources

Abstracts of the Inquisitiones Post Mortem Relating to Nottinghamshire, 1242–1546, 5 vols., Thoroton Society Record Series, 3, 4, 6, 12, 17 (1898–1956).
Calendar of Charter Rolls, 1226–1516, 6 vols. (HMSO, 1916–27).
Calendar of Close Rolls, 1272–1485, 45 vols. (HMSO, 1892–1954).
Calendar of Fine Rolls, 1272–1509, 22 vols. (HMSO, 1911–62).
'Calendar of French Rolls, 1 Hen. IV to 49 Hen. VI', *Deputy Keeper's Reports*, 44 (1883), 48 (1887).
Calendar of Inquisitions Miscellaneous, 1219–1422, 7 vols. (HMSO, 1916–68).
Calendar of Inquisitions Post Mortem, Hen. III to 6 Hen. IV, 18 vols. (HMSO, 1904–88).
Calendar of Inquisitions Post Mortem, Henry VII, 3 vols. (HMSO, 1898–1956).
Calendar of Patent Rolls, 1232–1509, 52 vols. (HMSO, 1891–1916).

Catalogue des Rolles Gascons, Normans et Francois, ed. T. Carte, 2 vols. (Paris and London, 1743).

Derbyshire Feet of Fines, 1323–1546, ed. H. J. H. Garratt, Derbyshire Record Society, 11 (1985).

Descriptive Catalogue of Ancient Deeds in the Public Record Office, 6 vols. (HMSO, 1890–1915).

Descriptive Catalogue of Derbyshire Charters, ed. I. H. Jeayes (London, 1906).

Expeditions to Prussia and the Holy Land Made by Henry, Earl of Derby, ed. L. Toulmin Smith, Camden Society, NS 52 (1894).

Historical Manuscripts Commission:
  Report on the Manuscripts of the Duke of Rutland at Belvoir Castle, 4 vols. (1888–1905).
  Report on Manuscripts in Various Collections, 8 vols. (1901–13).
  Report on the Manuscripts of Lord Middleton (1911).
  Report on the Manuscripts of Lord De L'Isle and Dudley, 6 vols. (1925–66).
  Report on the Manuscripts of Reginald Rawdon Hastings, 4 vols. (1928–47).

'Indentures of Retinue with John of Gaunt, Duke of Lancaster, Enrolled in Chancery, 1367–1399', ed. N. B. Lewis, in *Camden Miscellany* 22, Camden Society, 4th Series, vol. i (1964).

Inquisitions and Assessments Relating to Feudal Aids, 1284–1431, 6 vols. (HMSO, 1899–1920).

Johannis de Trokelowe, et Henrici de Blandeforde, monachorum S. Albani, necnon quorundam anonymorum, chronica et annales, ed. H. T. Riley, Rolls Series (1866).

John of Gaunt's Register, 1371–5, ed. S. Armitage-Smith, 2 vols., Camden Society, 3rd Series, 20–21 (1911).

John of Gaunt's Register, 1379–83, ed. E. C. Lodge and R. Somerville, 2 vols., Camden Society, 3rd Series, 61–62 (1937).

Leicestershire Medieval Village Notes, ed. G. F. Farnham, 6 vols. (Leicester, 1929–33).

Letters and Papers Illustrative of the Wars of the English in France, ed. J. Stevenson, Rolls Series, 2 vols. in 3 parts (1861–4).

Lists and Indexes (PRO):
  Sheriffs for England and Wales, 9 (1898).
  Early Chancery Proceedings, 12 (1901), 16 (1903).
  Supplementary Series:
  Warrants for Issues, 1399–1485, 9 (1964).

List and Index Society:
  Escheators for England and Wales, 72 (1971).

Parliamentary Writs and Writs of Military Summons, ed. F. Palgrave, 2 vols. in 4, Record Commission (London, 1827–34).

Paston Letters, ed. J. Gairdner, 6 vols. (London, 1904).

Paston Letters and Papers of the Fifteenth Century, ed. N. Davis, 2 vols. (Oxford, 1971).

'Pedigrees Contained in the Visitations of Derbyshire, 1569 and 1611', in *The Genealogist*, NS, 7–8 (1890–1).

Plumpton Correspondence, ed. T. Stapleton, Camden Society, OS 4 (1839).

Proceedings and Ordinances of the Privy Council of England, 1386–1542, ed. N. H. Nicolas, 7 vols., Record Commission (1834–7).

Proceedings Before the Justices of the Peace in the Fourteenth and Fifteenth Centuries, ed. B. H. Putnam, Ames Foundation (London, 1938).

Records of the Borough of Nottingham, 1155–1702, ed. W. H. Stevenson, 5 vols. (London etc., 1882–1900).

Register of Bishop Philip Repingdon, 1405–19, ed. M. Archer, 3 vols., Lincoln Record Society, 57, 58, 74 (1963–82).

Return of the Name of Every Member of the Lower House of the Parliament of England, Scotland and Ireland, 1213–1874, Parliamentary Papers, 1878, vol. lxii, pts. i–iii, 3 vols. (London, 1878), pt. i, 1213–1702.

Rotuli Parliamentorum, 1278–1503, 6 vols. (n.p., n.d.).

Rufford Charters, ed. C. J. Holdsworth, 4 vols., Thoroton Society Record Series, 29, 30, 32, 34 (1972–81).

Select Cases in the Court of King's Bench, 1272–1422, ed. G. O. Sayles, 7 vols., Selden Society, 55, 57, 58, 74, 76, 82, 88 (1936–71).

Shaw, W. A., *The Knights of England*, 2 vols. (London, 1906).

Statutes of the Realm, 1101–1713, ed. A. Luders and others, 11 vols., Record Commission (1810–28).

Testamenta Eboracensia, ed. J. Raine, J. Raine jun., and J. W. Clay, 6 vols., Surtees Society, 4, 30, 45, 53, 79, 106 (1836–1902).

'The Visitation of Lincolnshire, 1562–4', in *The Genealogist*, ed. G. W. Marshall, 3–5 (1879–81).

The Visitations of the County of Nottingham in the Years 1569 and 1614, ed. G. W. Marshall, Publications of the Harleian Society, 4 (1871).

Yorkshire Deeds, ed. W. Brown and others, 10 vols., Yorkshire Archaeological Society Record Series, 39, 50, 63, 65, 69, 76, 83, 102, 111, 190 (1909–55).

3. Secondary Works

BAKER, G., *The History and Antiquities of the County of Northampton*, 2 vols. (London, 1822–41).

BARBER, M., 'John Norbury (*c*.1350–1414): An Esquire of Henry IV', *English Historical Review* 68 (1953).

BEAN, J. M. W., *From Lord to Patron: Lordship in Late Medieval England* (Manchester, 1989).

BELLAMY, J. G., 'Sir John de Annesley and the Chandos Inheritance', *Nottingham Medieval Studies* 10 (1966).

—— *Crime and Public Order in England in the Later Middle Ages* (London, 1973).

—— *Criminal Law and Society in Late Medieval and Tudor England* (Gloucester, 1984).

—— *Bastard Feudalism and the Law* (London, 1989).

BENNETT, M. J., 'A County Community: Social Cohesion amongst the Cheshire Gentry, 1400–1425', *Northern History* 8 (1973).

—— *Community, Class and Careerism: Cheshire and Lancashire Society in the Age of Sir Gawain and the Green Knight* (Cambridge, 1983).

BLATCHER, M., *The Court of King's Bench 1450–1550* (London, 1978).

BLOMEFIELD, F., *An Essay Towards a Topographical History of the County of Norfolk*, 11 vols. (London, 1805–10).

BRIDGES, J., *The History and Antiquities of Northamptonshire*, 2 vols. (London, 1791).

BROWN, C., *Lives of Nottinghamshire Worthies* (Nottingham, 1881).

CAMERON, A., 'Sir Henry Willoughby of Wollaton', *Transactions of the Thoroton Society* 74 (1970).

—— 'A Nottinghamshire Quarrel in the Reign of Henry VII', *Bulletin of the Institute of Historical Research* 45 (1972).

—— 'Meering and the Meryng Family', *Transactions of the Thoroton Society* 77 (1973).

—— 'Some Social Consequences of the Dissolution of the Monasteries in Nottinghamshire', ibid., 79 (1975).

CARPENTER, M. C., 'The Beauchamp Affinity: A Study of Bastard Feudalism at Work', *English Historical Review* 95 (1980).

—— 'Law, Justice and Landowners in Late Medieval England', *Law and History Review* 1 (1983).

—— 'The Fifteenth Century English Gentry and their Estates', in M. C. E. Jones (ed.), *Gentry and Lesser Nobility of Late Medieval Europe* (Gloucester, 1986).

CHAWORTH MUSTERS, L., 'Some Account of the Family called in Latin Cadurcis, in French Chaources, and in English Chaworth', *Transactions of the Thoroton Society* 7 (1903).

CHERRY, M., 'The Courtenay Earls of Devon: The Formation and Disintegration of a Late Medieval Aristocratic Affinity', *Southern History* 1 (1979).

—— 'The Struggle for Power in Mid-Fifteenth-Century Devonshire', in R. A. Griffiths (ed.), *Patronage, the Crown and the Provinces in Later Medieval England* (Gloucester, 1981).

CLANCHY, M. T., 'Law, Government and Society in Medieval England', *History* 59 (1974).

—— 'Law and Love in the Middle Ages', in J. Bossy (ed.), *Disputes and Settlement: Law and Human Relations in the West* (Cambridge, 1983).

CLARKE, L., and RAWCLIFFE, C., 'The History of Parliament, 1386–1422: A Progress Report', *Medieval Prosopography* 4 (1983).

Complete Peerage of England, Scotland, Ireland and the United Kingdon, ed. G. E.

Cockayne, new edn. by V. Gibbs, H. A. Doubleday, and others, 12 vols. (London, 1910–59).

COOPER, J. P., 'The Social Distribution of Land and Men in England, 1436–1700', *Economic History Review*, 2nd Series, 20 (1967).

—— 'Patterns of Inheritance and Settlement by Great Landowners from the Fifteenth to the Eighteenth Centuries', in J. Goody, J. Thirsk, and E. P. Thompson (eds.), *Family and Inheritance: Rural Society in Western Europe, 1200–1800* (Cambridge, 1976).

CORNWALL, J., 'The Early Tudor Gentry', *Economic History Review*, 2nd Series, 17 (1964–5).

—— *Wealth and Society in Early Sixteenth-Century England* (London, 1988).

COX, J. C., *Notes on the Churches of Derbyshire*, 4 vols. (Chesterfield, 1875–9).

DENHOLM-YOUNG, N. H., 'Feudal Society in the Thirteenth Century: The Knights', in *Collected Papers on Medieval Subjects* (Oxford, 1946).

—— *The County Gentry in the Fourteenth Century* (Oxford, 1969).

Dictionary of National Biography, ed. L. Stephen and S. Lee, new edn. in 22 vols. (London, 1908–9).

DUNHAM, W. H., jun., 'Lord Hastings' Indentured Retainers, 1461–1483', *Transactions of the Connecticut Academy of Arts and Sciences* 39 (1955).

EMERY, A., 'Ralph, Lord Cromwell's Manor at Wingfield (1439–c. 1450): Its Construction, Design and Influence', *Archaeological Journal* 142 (1985).

EVERITT, A., *The Community of Kent and the Great Rebellion, 1640–1660* (Leicester, 1966).

FARNHAM, G. F., *Leicestershire Medieval Pedigrees* (Leicester, 1925).

FARRER, W., *Honors and Knights' Fees*, 3 vols. (London and Manchester, 1923–5).

FELLOWS, G., 'The Family of Willoughby', *Transactions of the Thoroton Society* 6 (1902).

FOSS, E., *A Biographical Dictionary of the Judges of England, 1066–1870* (London, 1870).

GIVEN-WILSON, C., *The Royal Household and the King's Affinity: Service, Politics and Finance in England, 1360–1413* (New Haven and London, 1986).

—— *The English Nobility in the Late Middle Ages: The Fourteenth-Century Political Community* (London, 1987).

GLOVER, S., *The History of the County of Derby*, ed. T. Noble, 2 vols. (Derby, 1829).

GOODER, A., *The Parliamentary Representation of the County of York, 1258–1832*, 2 vols., Yorkshire Archaeological Record Series, 91–96 (1935–8).

GRAY, H. L., 'Incomes from Land in England in 1436', *English Historical Review* 49 (1934).

GRIFFITHS, R. A., 'The Hazards of Civil War: The Mountford Family and the "Wars of the Roses"', *Midland History* 5 (1979–80).

—— *The Reign of King Henry VI: The Exercise of the Royal Authority, 1422–1461* (London, 1981).

G.T.C., 'The Pedigree of the Family of Babington of Dethick and Kingston', *Collectanea Topographica et Genealogica* 8 (1843).

—— 'Inedited Additions to the Pedigree of Babington', *The Topographer and Genealogist*, ed. J. G. Nichols, 1 (1846).

HARDING, A., *The Law Courts of Medieval England* (London, 1973).

HARRISS, G. L., 'Introduction', in K. B. McFarlane, *England in the Fifteenth Century: Collected Essays* (London, 1981).

HASTINGS, M., *The Court of Common Pleas in Fifteenth-Century England* (Ithaca, 1947).

HIRST, D., *The Representative of the People? Voters and Voting in England under the Early Stuarts* (Cambridge, 1975).

History of the King's Works: The Middle Ages, ed. H. M. Colvin, 2 vols. (HMSO, 1963).

HOLDSWORTH, W. S., *A History of English Law*, 12 vols. (London, 1922–38).

HOLMES, C., 'The County Community in Stuart Historiography', *Journal of British Studies* 19 (1979–80).

HOLMES, G. A., *The Estates of the Higher Nobility in Fourteenth-Century England* (Cambridge, 1957).

HOULBROOKE, R. A., *The English Family, 1450–1700* (London and New York, 1984).

HUNTER, J., *South Yorkshire: The History and Topography of the Deanery of Doncaster*, 2 vols. (London, 1828–31).

IVES, E. W., *The Common Lawyers of Pre-Reformation England* (Cambridge, 1983).

KERRY, C., 'Notes to the Pedigree of the Strelleys of Strelley, Oakerthorpe and Hazleback', *Journal of the Derbyshire Archaeological and Natural History Society* 14 (1892).

LAWRANCE, H., and ROUTH, T. E., 'Military Effigies in Nottinghamshire before the Black Death', *Transactions of the Thoroton Society* 28 (1924).

McFARLANE, K. B., 'Parliament and "Bastard Feudalism"', *Transactions of the Royal Historical Society*, 4th Series, 26 (1944).

—— '"Bastard Feudalism"', *Bulletin of the Institute of Historical Research* 20 (1945).

—— 'The Wars of the Roses', *Proceedings of the British Academy* 50 (1964).

—— *The Nobility of Later Medieval England* (Oxford, 1973).

MADDICOTT, J. R., 'The County Community and the Making of Public Opinion in Fourteenth-Century England', *Transactions of the Royal Historical Society*, 5th Series, 28 (1978).

—— 'Parliament and the Constituencies, 1272–1377', in *The English Parliament in the Middle Ages*, ed. R. G. Davies and J. H. Denton (Manchester, 1981).

'Markhams of Markham, Cotham, and afterwards of Becca', *The Herald and Genealogist*, ed. J. G. Nichols, 7 (1873).

MARKHAM, C. R., *Markham Memorials*, 2 vols. (London, 1913).

MARKS, R., 'The Re-Building of Lambley Church, Nottinghamshire, in the Fifteenth Century', *Transactions of the Thoroton Society* 87 (1983).

MASSINGBERD, W. O., 'Lincolnshire Nevill Families', *The Genealogist*, NS 27 (1910).

MOOR, C., *Knights of Edward I*, Publications of the Harleian Society, 5 vols., 80–84 (1929–32).

NEVILL, E. R., 'Nevill of Rolleston, Grove and Thorney', *The Genealogist*, NS 33 (1917).

NICHOLS, F. M., 'On Feudal and Obligatory Knighthood', *Archaeologia* 39 (1863).

NICHOLS, J., *The History and Antiquities of the County of Leicester*, 4 vols. in 8 parts (London, 1795–1815).

NICOLAS, N. H., *The Scrope and Grosvenor Controversy: De controversia in curia militari inter Ricardum le Scrope at Robertum Grosvenor, 1385–90*, 2 vols. (London, 1832).

—— *History of the Battle of Agincourt*, 3rd edn. (London, 1833).

Northumberland County History Committee, *A History of Northumberland*, 15 vols. (Newcastle etc., 1893–1940).

PALMER, R. C., *The County Courts of Medieval England, 1150–1350* (Princeton, 1982).

PALMER, W. M., 'A History of the Parish of Borough Green', *Cambridge Antiquarian Society Publications* 54 (1939).

PAYLING, S. J., 'Inheritance and Local Politics in the Later Middle Ages: The Case of Ralph, Lord Cromwell, and the Heriz Inheritance', *Nottingham Medieval Studies* 30 (1986).

—— 'Law and Arbitration in Nottinghamshire, 1399–1461' in J. Rosenthal and C. Richmond (eds.), *People, Politics and Community in the Later Middle Ages* (Gloucester, 1987).

—— 'The Widening Franchise: Parliamentary Elections in Lancastrian Nottinghamshire', in D. Williams (ed.), *England in the Fifteenth Century* (Woodbridge, 1987).

—— 'The Coventry Parliament of 1459: A Privy Seal Writ Concerning the Election of Knights of the Shire', *Historical Research* 60 (1987).

PEVSNER, N., *Nottinghamshire*, The Buildings of England, 2nd edn. (Harmondsworth, 1979).

—— *Leicestershire and Rutland*, The Buildings of England, 2nd edn. (1984).

Place-Names of Nottinghamshire, ed. J. E. B. Glover, A. Mawer, and F. M. Stenton, English Place-Name Society, 17 (1940).

POLLARD, A. J., 'The Richmondshire Community of Gentry during the Wars of the Roses', in C. D. Ross (ed.), *Patronage, Pedigree and Power in Late Medieval England* (Gloucester, 1979).

POST, J. B., 'Equitable Resorts Before 1450', E. W. Ives and A. H. Manchester (eds.), *Law, Litigants and the Legal Profession* (London and New Jersey, 1983).

POWELL, E., 'Arbitration and the Law in England in the Late Middle Ages', *Transactions of the Royal Historical Society*, 5th Series, 33 (1983).

—— 'The King's Bench in Shropshire and Staffordshire in 1414', in E. W. Ives and A. H. Manchester (eds.), *Law, Litigants and the Legal Profession* (London and New Jersey, 1983).

—— 'Settlement of Disputes by Arbitration in Fifteenth-Century England', *Law and History Review* 2 (1984).

—— 'The Restoration of Law and Order', in G. L. Harriss (ed.), *Henry V: The Practice of Kingship* (Oxford, 1985).

PUGH, R. B., 'The King's Government in the Middle Ages', in Victoria County History, *Wiltshire*, v (1957).

PUGH, T. B. and Ross, C. D., 'The English Baronage and the Income Tax of 1436', *BIHR* 26 (1953).

PUGH, T. B., 'The Magnates, Knights and Gentry', in S. B. Chrimes, C. D. Ross, and R. A. Griffiths (eds.), *Fifteenth-Century England, 1399–1509* (Manchester, 1972).

RAWCLIFFE, C., *The Staffords, Earls of Stafford and Dukes of Buckingham, 1394–1521* (Cambridge, 1978).

—— 'The Great Lord as Peacekeeper: Arbitration by English Noblemen and their Councils in the Later Middle Ages', in J. A. Guy and H. G. Beale (eds.), *Law and Social Change in British History* (London and New Jersey, 1984).

RICHARDSON, H. G., 'John of Gaunt and the Parliamentary Representation of Lancashire', *Bulletin of the John Rylands Library* 22 (1938).

—— 'The Commons and Medieval Politics', *Transactions of the Royal Historical Society*, 4th Series, 28 (1946).

RICHMOND, C. F., *John Hopton: A Fifteenth-Century Suffolk Gentleman* (Cambridge, 1981).

—— 'After McFarlane', *History* 68 (1983).

ROGERS, A., 'The Lincolnshire County Court in the Fifteenth Century', *Lincolnshire History and Archaeology* 1 (1966).

—— 'Parliamentary Electors in Lincolnshire in the Fifteenth Century', *Lincolnshire History and Archaeology* 3 (1968), 4 (1969), 5 (1970), 6 (1971).

—— 'Parliamentary Elections in Grimsby in the Fifteenth Century', *Bulletin of the Institute of Historical Research* 42 (1969).

ROSENTHAL, J. T., 'Feuds and Private Peace-Making: A Fifteenth-Century Example', *Nottingham Medieval Studies* 14 (1970).

ROSKELL, J. S., *The Knights of the Shire for the County Palatine of Lancaster, 1377–1460*, Chetham Society, NS 96 (1937).

—— *The Commons in the Parliament of 1422* (Manchester, 1954).

—— 'John Bowes of Costock, Speaker in the Parliament of 1435', *Transactions of the Thoroton Society* 60 (1956).

—— 'The Parliamentary Representation of Lincolnshire during the Reigns of Richard II, Henry IV and Henry V', *Nottingham Medieval Studies* 3 (1959).

ROSKELL, J. S., *Parliament and Politics in Late Medieval England*, 3 vols. (London, 1981–3).

ROWNEY, I. D., 'Arbitration in Gentry Disputes of the Later Middle Ages', *History* 67 (1982).

—— 'The Hastings Affinity in Staffordshire and the Honour of Tutbury', *Bulletin of the Institute of Historical Research* 57 (1984).

—— 'Resources and Retaining in Yorkist England: Lord Hastings and the Honour of Tutbury', in A. J. Pollard (ed.), *Property and Politics: Essays in Later Medieval English History* (Gloucester, 1984).

SANDERS, I. J., *English Baronies: A Study of their Origin and Descent, 1086–1327* (Oxford, 1960).

SAUL, N. E., *Knights and Esquires: The Gloucestershire Gentry in the Fourteenth Century* (Oxford, 1981).

—— *Scenes from Provincial Life: Knightly Families in Sussex, 1280–1400* (Oxford, 1986).

SCHOFIELD, R. S., 'The Geographical Distribution of Wealth in England, 1334–1649', *Economic History Review*, 2nd Series, 18 (1965).

SHIRLEY, E. P., *Stemmata Shirleiana, or the Annals of the Shirley Family*, 2nd edn. (London, 1873).

SMITH, A., 'Litigation and Politics: Sir John Fastolf's Defence of his English Property', in A. J. Pollard (ed.), *Property and Politics: Essays in Later Medieval English History* (Gloucester, 1984).

SOMERVILLE, R., *History of the Duchy of Lancaster*, 2 vols. (London, 1953–70).

STOREY, R. L., *The End of the House of Lancaster* (London, 1966).

—— 'Lincolnshire and the Wars of the Roses', *Nottingham Medieval Studies* 14 (1970).

SUTHERLAND, D. W., *The Assize of Novel Disseisin* (Oxford, 1973).

TAWNEY, R. H., 'The Rise of the Gentry, 1558–1640', *Economic History Review* 11 (1941).

THOROTON, R., *The Antiquities of Nottinghamshire*, ed. J. Throsby, 3 vols. (Nottingham, 1790–6).

Victoria County History: *Bedfordshire*, 3 vols. (1904–12), *Buckinghamshire*, 4 vols. (1905–27), *Cambridgeshire*, 4 vols. (1938–59), *Essex*, 8 vols. to date (1903–83), *Huntingdonshire*, 3 vols. (1926–36), *North Riding*, 2 vols. (1914–23), *Nottinghamshire*, 2 vols. (1906–10), *Oxfordshire*, 11 vols. to date (1907–83), *Rutland*, 2 vols. (1908–35).

VIRGOE, R., 'Three Suffolk Parliamentary Elections of the Mid-Fifteenth Century', *Bulletin of the Institute of Historical Research* 39 (1966).

—— 'William Tailboys and Lord Cromwell: Crime and Politics in Lancastrian England', *Bulletin of the John Rylands Library* 55 (1972–3).

—— 'The Cambridgeshire Election of 1439', *Bulletin of the Institute of Historical Research* 46 (1973).

—— 'The Crown, Magnates and Local Government in Fifteenth-Century East Anglia', in J. R. L. Highfield and R. Jeffs (eds.), *The Crown and Local*

Communities in England and France in the Fifteenth Century (Gloucester, 1981).
—— 'The Parliamentary Subsidy of 1450', *Bulletin of the Institute of Historical Research* 55 (1982).
WALKER, J. W., 'The Burghs of Cambridgeshire and Yorkshire and the Watertons of Lincolnshire and Yorkshire', *Yorkshire Archaeological Journal* 30 (1930–1).
WALKER, S. K., 'Lancaster *v.* Dallingridge: A Franchisal Dispute in Fourteenth Century Sussex', *Sussex Archaeological Collections* 121 (1983).
WATNEY, V. J., *The Wallop Family and their Ancestry*, 4 vols. (Oxford, 1928).
WEDGWOOD, J. C., 'Staffordshire Parliamentary History, 1213–1603', *Collections for a History of Staffordshire, William Salt Archaeological Society*, 3rd Series (1917).
—— *History of Parliament, 1439–1509*, 2 vols. (HMSO, 1936–8), i. *Biographies*; ii. *Register.*
WEIR, C., 'The Site of the Cromwells' Mediaeval Manor House at Lambley, Nottinghamshire', *Transactions of the Thoroton Society* 85 (1981).
WOLFFE, B. P., *Henry VI* (London, 1981).
WOOD, A. C., 'Notes on the Early History of the Clifton Family', *Transactions of the Thoroton Society* 37 (1933).
WORMALD, J., 'Bloodfeud, Kindred and Government in Early Modern Scotland', *Past and Present* 87 (May 1980).
WRIGHT, S. M., *The Derbyshire Gentry in the Fifteenth Century* (Chesterfield, 1983).
WYLIE, J. H., *History of England under Henry the Fourth*, 4 vols. (London, 1884–98).

4. Unpublished Theses

ARNOLD, C. E., 'A Political Study of the West Riding of Yorkshire, 1437–1509', Ph.D. thesis (Manchester, 1984).
ASTILL, G. G., 'The Medieval Gentry: A Study in Leicestershire Society, 1350–1399', Ph.D. thesis (Birmingham, 1977).
AYRES, E., 'Parliamentary Representation in Derbyshire and Nottinghamshire in the Fifteenth Century', MA thesis (Nottinghamshire, 1956).
BARBER, M. J., 'Surrey and Sussex at the Opening of the Fifteenth Century, Based on the Land Tax Assessments of 1412', B.Litt. thesis (Oxford, 1949).
BLOOM, M., 'The Careers of Sir Richard II de Willoughby and Sir Richard III de Willoughby, Chief Justice of the King's Bench (1338–1340), and the Rise of the Willoughbys of Nottinghamshire', D.Phil. thesis (Oxford, 1985).
CARPENTER, M. C., 'Political Society in Warwickshire, *c.*1401–72', Ph.D. thesis (Cambridge, 1976).
FLEMING, P. W., 'The Character and Private Concerns of the Gentry of Kent, 1422–1509', Ph.D. thesis (Swansea, 1985).
FRIEDRICHS, R. L., 'The Career and Influence of Ralph, Lord Cromwell, 1393–1456', Ph.D. thesis (Columbia, 1974).

JEFFS, R. M., 'The Later Mediaeval Sheriff and the Royal Household', D.Phil. thesis (Oxford, 1960).

LEONARD, H., 'Knights and Knighthood in Tudor England', Ph.D. thesis (London, 1970).

MADDERN, P. C., 'Violence, Crime and Public Disorder in East Anglia, 1422–1442', D.Phil. thesis (Oxford, 1984).

NIGOTA, J. A., 'John Kempe: A Political Prelate of the Fifteenth Century', Ph.D. thesis (Emory, 1973).

POLLARD, A. J., 'The Family of Talbot, Lords Talbot and Earls of Shrewsbury in the Fifteenth Century', Ph.D. thesis (Bristol, 1968).

POWELL, E., 'Public Order and Law Enforcement in Shropshire and Staffordshire in the Early Fifteenth Century', D.Phil. thesis (Oxford, 1979).

ROGERS, A., 'The Royal Household of Henry IV', Ph.D. thesis (Nottingham, 1966).

ROSS, C. D., 'The Yorkshire Baronage, 1399–1435', D.Phil. thesis (Oxford, 1950).

ROWNEY, I. D., 'The Staffordshire Political Community, 1440–1500', Ph.D. thesis (Keele, 1981).

WALKER, S. K., 'John of Gaunt and his Retainers, 1361–1399', D.Phil. thesis (Oxford, 1986).

INDEX